Grace & GUMPTION

Stories *of* Fort Worth Women

Katie Sherrod, *editor*

TCU Press

Fort Worth, Texas

Library of Congress Cataloging-in-Publication Data

Grace & gumption : stories of Fort Worth women / Katie
Sherrod, editor.
p. cm.
Includes index.
ISBN-13: 978-0-87565-352-5 (cloth : alk. paper)
ISBN-10: 0-87565-352-9
1. Women--Texas--Fort Worth--Biography. I. Sherrod,
Katie.

HQ1439.F67G73 2007
920.7209764'5315--dc22
[B]
2007011511

TCU Press
P. O. Box 298300
Fort Worth, TX 76129
817–257–7822
http://www.prs.tcu.edu
To order books: 1–800–826–8911

Cover photo of Tad Lucas,
Courtesy the National Cowgirl Museum and Hall of Fame.

Book design by Barbara Mathews Whitehead

Contents

Foreword

HE FORT WORTH STAR-TELEGRAM ran a front-page story in February 2007, worrying about whether Fort Worth is losing its distinctiveness. Under the onslaught of development and upscale restaurants, would Cowtown lose its special charm? The answer, according to readers, is a resounding no. The uniqueness of Fort Worth begins with its geographic location within the Grand Prairie and Cross Timbers, situated near the eastern edge of the Great Plains. The specific character of the city, too, is found in the story of the people who came to live on the bluffs overlooking the river that the Spanish named *La Santisima Trinidad*. Among these people are the women whose stories are written here: the brave easterners who accompanied their families or their slave masters to the fringes of anything resembling what they knew; the women who came with the railroads; and the generations born thereafter.

Fort Worth has been blessed with its share of gutsy women. Courage and commitment to high ideals motivated the women who brought about the cultural institutions of the city, from the sisters of Our Lady of Victory to the wealthy philanthropists who gave their funds to causes large and small. No less brave were the women who pushed—and broke—the traditionally male boundaries of business, journalism, and medicine.

And yet, while the story of women in Fort Worth is unique, it is also quintessentially American. The women of Fort Worth have never lived in a vacuum. They were American or they became American, and many of them were keenly aware of the actions of their cousins and sisters in the eastern United States. Their actions mirrored those of women all over the continent, and learning about them can teach us a great deal about the United States as a whole.

First, of course, were the Native American women, members of the various Plains tribes who enjoyed the good water and fertile soils of the Trinity watershed. With their men and families, they were forced out of their homes on the bluffs by the blue-coated soldiers of the U.S.

Army. Like Native Americans all over the southern and western parts of the United States, they reluctantly made their way to the Indian Territory and tried to accommodate themselves to life on the reservations. Other American women, white and black, were always part of the push westward from the East Coast. From the first days of European settlement, women left their established homes and headed to places where comforts were fewer and dangers were greater. Some women dreaded these moves and the separation from loved ones that they entailed, while others faced their options with a great sense of adventure and welcomed the challenges of making a home in a new and more promising place. The women who came to Tarrant County in the 1840s and 1850s joined a stream of Americans seeking their fortunes in the West, following the promises of Manifest Destiny. Too, women have always accompanied their soldier husbands, and those who came to Fort Worth as wives of U.S. Army officers resembled their cohorts elsewhere in the West in the middle of the nineteenth century. The life of Catherine Arnold, for example, surely resembled that of Elizabeth Custer, who went with her famous husband to Wyoming and received the news of his death after the Battle of Little Big Horn.

While the majority of women in Fort Worth since the 1850s have been white and Protestant, they have never been the only residents. At the western terminus of the Old South, in 1860 Tarrant County had 850 slaves, who represented about fifteen percent of the total population. As the ethnic diversity of the United States increased enormously between the Civil War and World War I, Fort Worth's population reflected these changes. The Jewish community resulted from increased immigration from Eastern Europe, which peaked in the first years of the twentieth century. Political upheavals below the Rio Grande around 1910 spurred Mexican immigration. Why stay in Russia and risk facing the tsar and his pogroms or stay in Mexico and fear the competing armies of civil war? Life in America offered greater safety, and many women elected to try their chances in unfamiliar surroundings, including Fort Worth.

Until 1920, most Americans lived on farms. Their numbers diminished quickly, and so the women of early Fort Worth were part of the urbanization that continues today. While farm women toiled in relative isolation, women living in cities enjoyed opportunities for social life and activities in concert with others. As Fort Worth grew, so did women's prospects for meaningful endeavors outside the home. The pursuits that Fort Worth women chose were, for the most part, like those of their counterparts in other regions of the United States.

Grace & Gumption is about women and public life in Fort Worth, about what women did in the open spotlight. These are remarkable women who often forced their ways into masculine preserves to make a difference in the life of the city. For each of the notable women in these pages, there are thousands of others who never did anything to get their names in the newspapers. They were wives, mothers, daughters, and domestic workers whose days were filled with tasks that were hidden in the homes. In their own way, they are equally as significant as the women depicted here, but they are much less obvious and hence difficult to research. Their stories will have to wait for another volume.

Women have always worked. Before the industrial revolution of the late eighteenth and early nineteenth centuries, most white American women labored alongside their husbands in agricultural pursuits. (Slave women performed a wide variety of tasks, receiving pay very occasionally.) As white men began going away each day to earn wages, their wives remained in the home. Influential female writers like Catharine Beecher began to tout the value of women's work in the home, praising motherhood and wifely virtues, promoting what historians have labeled the "cult of domesticity." At the same time, female reformers in the temperance and abolition movements started claiming a uniquely feminine space, arguing that women's unique characteristics as mothers gave them particular talents for "social housekeeping." It became acceptable for a woman to leave her home to do good works. After the Civil War, women responded sharply to industrialization and its accompanying problems, and they began agitating for social change in almost every arena imaginable.

In Fort Worth, black and white women poured their energies into reform movements. The strands of the various reform movements braided together and were often indistinguishable from one another, but all had the purpose of improving the world and particularly the reformers' hometowns. By the 1880s, for example, Woman's Christian Temperance Union members were making known their objections to strong drink across the entire nation. In Fort Worth, as elsewhere, leaders of the WCTU also engaged in other reform movements typical of the late-nineteenth century, confident of the rightness of their causes and the needs of the world. With like-minded peers, the women of the United States and of Fort Worth created sex-segregated clubs of every conceivable purpose in the late-nineteenth and early-twentieth centuries. They improved themselves with study clubs to examine works of literature. Other groups set about creating civic enhancements for the good of the community, such as libraries, kindergartens, and parks. Still others (often with overlapping memberships) worked to enhance high culture by creating showcases for art and music, in museums and musical venues. Through the creation of a variety of institutions, the children of Fort Worth benefited from women's commitment, time, and financial generosity. Some of the women's targets, such as jails, brought these privileged reformers into areas that had previously been off-limits to respectable matrons. The wealthiest women of Fort Worth, with their great fortunes from cattle, oil, and business, assisted charitable, educational, and cultural causes in their city as they poured their families' resources into hospitals, museums, scholarships, and a variety of other beneficiaries. The multitude of women's groups networked with one another, forming federations at the local, state, and national levels. Through their club work and sustained reform efforts, the women of Fort Worth and elsewhere made their presence felt across their communities throughout the first half of the twentieth century.

At the same time that some women worked vigorously without pay for their good causes, others had occupations that earned wages apart from those of their families. Increasingly over the past 150 years, women have entered the paid workforce. Teaching school became a more acceptable occupation for women throughout the nineteenth century. The sisters at Our Lady of Victory were a part of that national trend, faithfully holding classes and bringing with them cultural ideals from the eastern United States. Across Fort Worth, across the United States, women populated the classrooms, spending their time and talents teaching the nation's children. Gifted women—black, white, and Hispanic—enriched Fort Worth children as art and writing teachers.

Many teachers also used their own talents as artists and writers, sometimes paid and sometimes not. Other women writers found their voices working for newspapers. Women gifted in the performing arts, too, could be seen in amateur venues or as professionals in theaters such as Casa Mañana.

For many decades women earned money by extending typically feminine roles through activities such as keeping boardinghouses. In Fort Worth and elsewhere, women professionalized traditional female roles, becoming restaurateurs and hairdressers. With low start-up costs, these types of businesses were well suited for ambitious entrepreneurs, eager to build their livings from modest beginnings. Ninia Baird, for example, became one of the wealthiest women in Texas by baking bread. New technologies made possible other fields of work, such as the telephone operator and the stenographer or secretary. Fort Worth was likely one of the few cities in the United States where a woman could earn her living as a rodeo rider.

While relatively few women entered the professions before the last quarter of the twentieth century, several fields had a handful of unusually purposeful women. Professional schools grudg-

ingly opened their doors to females, and, by 1922, there were enough white women working in Fort Worth that they created the organization called Business & Professional Women. They became physicians, attorneys, and architects, laboring in areas generally reserved for men until the 1970s and 1980s.

In addition to economic clout, women gradually gained access to the power of formal politics. The movement for women's suffrage was as lively in Texas as anywhere. In 1918, Texas women received the right to vote in presidential primaries, and Texas was one of only two southern states to ratify the Nineteenth Amendment granting women the vote in federal elections. American women had been involved in politics for decades, as they worked diligently to influence powerful men to enact reforms meaningful to them. Gradually, women entered into the actual realm of electoral politics. Most of them played support roles but increasingly became candidates for public office themselves. Beginning in the 1950s, Fort Worth women served in office, first at the local and then at the state levels, and finally in the U.S. Congress.

Traditional gender roles shifted further as the social protests of the 1960s spurred the women's movement. Title VII of the Civil Rights Act of 1964 made illegal discrimination against employees on the basis of race or sex. As the women's movement gained momentum, legal barriers to women's participation in public life fell at an unprecedented rate. Today Fort Worth women may be found in almost every public arena.

Someone attempting to write a book such as this in 2107 will have a nearly impossible task, as more than 300,000 females live in Fort Worth, and a very large percentage of them work and serve in public. Today almost half of the students in law school and medical school are female. We would do well, however, to remember that there was a time, not very long ago, when a woman outside the home was brave and not always well received. The women profiled here do in fact personify grace and gumption, and we who benefit from their legacy should remember them and be grateful.

Rebecca Sharpless
Texas Christian University
Fort Worth

Preface

THIS BOOK HAS BEEN A LABOR OF LOVE by women for women.

Women's stories often get lost because so much of women's history resides in private places. These are diaries, family scrapbooks, family letters, or papers stored in boxes in families' attics. Women often are hard to find, and once found, can be hard to track over time as they change their names when they get married. And sometimes they marry more than once, which increases the challenge.

But the loss of women's history is a loss to an entire community, for with it we lose the totality of experiences that shaped that community. We wanted the daughters and sons of Fort Worth to know the stories of the women on whose shoulders they stand. We wanted them to be able to draw strength and inspiration from their foremothers.

The idea for this book was born several years ago, when Judy Alter heard a presentation on women that Joyce Williams and I made at a conference on Fort Worth history held on the Texas Christian University campus. I mentioned then my hope that eventually a book about women in Fort Worth would be published. Judy was intrigued, because she too had been thinking about the hidden history of women in Fort Worth.

In the spring of 2006 she and I met over lunch with Ruth Karbach to talk about which women should be included in such a book. Our initial list covered pages. How to choose? After all, for a large city, one of Fort Worth's charms is that it is really a small town. We knew we would inevitably leave out some important woman and offend those who loved her.

So our first decision was to limit the book to women who are deceased. Then we tried to come up with categories. This was harder than one might expect, because you cannot pigeonhole women. Women always have been multitaskers, and many were relevant to more than one chapter because their talents and contributions reached in many directions.

Once contributing authors were selected, this sorting challenge continued. Meetings often concluded with us bargaining with one another over who "got" which multitalented woman.

The next challenge was space. We could not possibly have room for all the significant women. After all, our goal was to produce a book that would be accessible to as many people as possible. An encyclopedic book would not only be too long for most people to tackle, it would be too expensive. The writers made many hard decisions as they wrestled their material to a reasonable size.

The contributors to this volume were volunteers. All were busy with careers, other writing projects, and various family responsibilities, yet each gave willingly of her time and talent. In the process, we have become a small and close-knit community.

We make no claims to having produced the definitive work on women in Fort Worth. Our goal has been to gather as many women's stories as possible out of the attics and into a public place, to provide snapshots of women's contributions that others may one day enlarge.

We give thanks to Cissy Stewart Lale and Mary Rogers who inspired and advised us. A portion of the profits of this book will go to the Women's Center of Tarrant County. We believe the women in this book exemplify the kinds of contributions the Women's Center is leading women toward today.

Kathie Sherrod
Fort Worth

Chapter 1

FRONTIER WOMEN

by Joyce M. Williams

*J*ANE WOODY FARMER, THE FIRST white woman to live in what would become Fort Worth, must have been pleased and relieved to see Major Ripley Arnold and his dragoons arrive in June 1849 to establish a military post at the confluence of the Clear and West Forks of the Trinity River. Jane, her husband George Preston "Press," and their infant daughter Sue had been living on the bluff above the Trinity River for a few months. They had come to this place, often described as wild and beautiful, to make their home. There was an abundance of land for the taking and plenty of game for food. Today, it is hard to imagine this area as it was then: a prairie with waist-high grass, forests along the river, herds of deer and antelope, wild turkey, prairie chickens, hogs, and even bears and panthers. This is the setting the Farmer family chose to make their home.

Jane and Press were married in Tennessee in 1844. They came through Arkansas and then on to Texas in 1847, settling in East Texas. Promoters with booklets and fliers aggressively

Jane Woody Farmer, circa 1880. *Courtesy Fort Worth Star-Telegram Photograph Collection, Special Collections, University of Texas at Arlington Libraries.*

touted the appeal of Texas, urging settlers to come to this land of abundant wildlife, suitable for all types of crops, and with space for everyone. The land provided building materials; everything else that was needed had to be brought. One guidebook recommended "farming tools, a wagon, comfortable clothing, a good rifle, and a strong dog. Seeds. Bedding and tents for shelter. Two pots for boiling, one pot hook, one tin water can, tinderbox and matches, three pounds candles, one tin hand basin, two tin pint cups, two square tin baking pans, one wooden bowl, three tin plates, knives, forks, and spoons and a small washtub. A large strong wagon with two oxen. Spades, plows, hoes, shovels, axes, and carpenter's tools and a supply of rope."

The settlers would load up the wagon, hitch up the team, walk the cow or two that they wanted to bring, and strike out. On a good day the Farmers might make eight or ten miles. The trip took a long time at this pace, a month or more just from Arkansas. They, like most immigrants, would have walked most of the way. They planned to farm, and Press planned to trade with the Indians who passed through as well as with other settlers scattered around the area.

When they arrived on the bluff above the Trinity the Farmers cut timber and built a log cabin, but while they were away one day Indians burned the cabin. The day Jane watched the troops approach, her family was living in a tent. Fearing further Indian problems, Press had excavated a dugout under the tent in which they could hide.

Plans to build a military fort in North Central Texas to provide protection for settlers had been underway for many years. During the Republic of Texas period, from 1836 to 1845, set-tlement was encouraged for all of Texas and especially North Texas. With Texas' acceptance into the United States in 1845 and particularly following the Mexican War of 1846–1848, a new effort was made to encourage settlement. A line of military forts running south to north along what was the boundary between settlement and Indian Territory was established. Fort Worth was the northernmost in that line of forts.

Farmer family history says that Major Arnold chose the site on the bluff where the family was living for the building of the fort. The Farmers moved a little farther south, and Press agreed to serve as the fort's first sutler—a civilian store-keeper authorized to operate a general store on or near a military camp, post, or fort. He would be responsible for providing supplies for the men and forage for the animals. The dragoons numbered about thirty-five mounted infantrymen with horses and wagons. They set about building the twenty buildings that would surround a parade ground at the current site of the Tarrant County Courthouse.

The Farmers built another log cabin south of the fort. The soldiers built a sutler's store that occupied the southwest corner of the fort. Press served as sutler for several months and continued to have a trading business when others took over the store. Over the next few years the Farmers owned land near the fort, then sold it and moved about ten miles to the southeast where they and their descendants farmed for many years.

A few months later Catherine Arnold and her children—ten-year-old Florida, seven-year-old Katherine "Kate," and infant Sophia "Sophie"—moved to Fort Worth. Blue-eyed, brown-haired Catherine "Kate" Bryant had eloped with six-foot-tall redheaded West Pointer Ripley Arnold against her family's wishes on her fourteenth birthday in 1839. They were married at Pass Christian, Mississippi, near her hometown of Bay St. Louis. Her family soon accepted the marriage.

Arnold followed her soldier husband to posts in Florida, Louisiana, and Indiana. They spent time in Washington, D.C., before coming to Texas. The Arnolds lived in San Antonio and at Fort Graham before coming to Fort Worth, which was certainly the most desolate and remote place they had been. Kate Arnold moved her family into the commanding officer's two-room log house with a connecting passage or dogtrot. There was an attached kitchen and stone fireplaces in each room. The floors were dirt, and the rooms were sided with sawed clapboards. Green wood was used for construction. As it aged and warped, cracks and leaks appeared. Eventually wooden floors were installed, and the windows were covered with waxed paper, muslin, or shutters.

Kate Arnold was described as "a beauty with a queenly carriage and a well-educated mind." She was a gracious hostess, entertaining travelers, traders, visiting military men, junior officers, and community people. In a letter to his wife Lieutenant Samuel Starr wrote, "I have not seen as good a table, as Mrs. Arnold spreads, since I have been in Texas. Mrs. A. is quite a firm little lady, with four children." Four or five servants, at least two of whom had come to the fort with the major, helped her with her household. She was friendly and well liked by the dragoons, serving as a nurse and confidante to them. Arnold, her husband, and her two older children took advantage of the opportunity to study languages, drawing, music, and dance with Adolphus Gouhenaught and his sister, who had settled in the area. Legend has it that Arnold had her piano brought up river to Jefferson and ox-carted to the fort. She placed it in the commissary so all could enjoy it.

By the end of 1849 Tarrant County had been established, an area of about fifty by fifty miles square, with Fort Worth near the center. A census conducted in 1850 indicated that there were about 600 white people and 65 slaves in the new county. Kate Arnold had been joined by Eliza Starr, wife of Lieutenant Starr, and their daughters, Kate and Anne. There were now four women settlers in the area immediately around the fort: Jane Farmer, Lucinda Terrell, Nancy Robinson, and Louisa Brinson. Terrell's husband was a trapper and trader. Louisa Brinson was the daughter of the Johnson family who had a large plantation about twelve miles southeast of the fort as well as land around the fort. Nancy Robinson's family partnered with the Johnsons.

In 1850 Kate and Ripley Arnold had another child, Willis. Before the end of the year both Willis and his sister Sophie were dead from cholera. Willis and Sophie were buried about a mile east of the fort on a plot given to the Arnolds by their friends and teachers, the Gouhenaughts. The children were the first occupants of what would become the city's first cemetery, now Pioneers Rest.

Three other women were living and working at the fort. They were laundresses. Laundresses were a regular part of the frontier military; they were paid by the soldiers, and their numbers were set by military regulations—one for every fifteen men but not to exceed four per company. One ration of food per day was provided. Pay was fifty cents per month for each soldier, more for officers. Single officers paid $2, married officers $4; families paid additional charges. Regulations required that the laundresses' pay be deducted from the soldiers' pay. At Fort Worth three small huts were built on the west side of the fort where the laundresses lived and worked. The floors were dirt, and the roofs were leaky. Big kettles in the front of the huts held the washing. The soldiers at Fort Worth wore sky blue wool trousers and matching waist-length blue jackets. Each year the men were issued two white cotton shirts, two flannel shirts, a pair of long flannel drawers, and two pairs of wool stockings. Summer white cotton uniforms were available, but the soldiers at Fort Worth never received those. Ordinarily each soldier's laundry was washed three times a week in the summer and two times a week during the winter. Laundry was an all-day task six days a week. After sorting and removing stains, clothes were soaked in warm soapy water, often for a day or two. Clothes were scrubbed against a washboard, and then rung out again and again, until the clothes were clean. They were then rinsed and rung again and moved to a boiling pot. Boiling removed the last remnants of soap and killed lice. Finally the clothes were rinsed again and hung out to dry.

Laundresses dressed, as did most frontier women, in plain cotton or wool dresses with cotton underwear, high-topped shoes, and long cotton stockings. While working they wore their hair pulled back and covered with a bonnet.

These washerwomen often have been depicted as shady ladies. Laundresses were generally not refined ladies; some were rough, outspoken, coarse, uneducated, and argumentative. They occasionally caused trouble, smoked,

drank, and even got into fights. But most were good, honest, industrious, kindhearted women who were a good influence on the soldiers. Who were these women at Fort Worth? They left no diaries or letters. Did they come from the scattered settlers in this area, or had they followed the dragoons from San Antonio to Fort Graham to Fort Worth? Could they have been wives of some of the men at the fort? Records only show they were here; they give no names or history for these women who provided much-needed labor and a small feminine presence at this outpost in the West.

By the end of 1850 Jane Farmer had welcomed her extended family to the area around Fort Worth. Her father, Sam Woody, came, as did Press' father, mother, two brothers, and their families. They all settled about ten miles west of the fort.

Life on the frontier offered occasional opportunities for get-togethers to help build cabins, to visit, or to have a real celebration. One such celebration occurred at Christmas 1850 when the officers at the fort organized a dance. Local citizens and especially settlers' daughters from all over the area were invited. One of the fort's wagons was dispatched to the countryside to pick up the dance partners. Many of the young women had no shoes. The officers solved that problem by providing some of the military-issue heavy black leather shoes called brogans for the girls. Lieutenant Starr reported in a letter that even without laces for their stiff cowhide shoes the girls were still able to dance with graceless abandon.

Another such occasion was the marriage of Jane Farmer's sister-in-law, Millie, to James Ventioner in July 1851. This wedding at the fort was attended by family, settlers, and soldiers. Though there was no chaplain for the fort, Major Arnold was occasionally able to arrange for visiting ministers to conduct services. The Ventioners lived in a log cabin three miles west of the fort on a large tract of land.

Soldiers or settlers often hosted gatherings, with a steer cooked over an open fire with all "the fixin's," and dancing. There was no fort band so music was provided by individuals, both soldier and civilian. Kate Arnold often acted as hostess for events at the fort commissary.

Kate Arnold provides a brief insight into life at the fort and Jane Farmer's life in a February 1852 letter she wrote to Eliza Starr, who was then at Fort Gates. "I am content to stay—if the children were at school I should be better satisfied. The Post is about like it was with the same people living near with a few additional families. Mrs. Farmer presented her husband with Twin Boys, but they lived but a few days. Three children in one year, that's worse than you."

Starr now had a third daughter, Jo. She replied, "Poor Mrs. Farmer is unfortunate with her babies, but I think she would soon have a house full at the rate of three per year...." She continued, "Who lives in our old house? Does it look the same as of old?"

Press Farmer's sutler's store on the southwest corner of the fort was set up with utensils, trinkets, personal items, edibles, and wine by the bottle or beer by the glass. Soldiers, locals, and Indians were regular customers. Traders made round trips of 400 to 700 miles, south to Houston and east to Shreveport for supplies. Many settlers contracted with the fort to serve as farriers (blacksmiths), wheelwrights, herdsmen, and interpreters. They also provided timber and

did repair and construction work. In 1851, Lieutenant Starr reported that he could buy fresh beef locally, but there were no flourmills. Beans, vinegar, hard soap, and candles were not available. He could get soft soap, small amounts of tallow, poor quality salt, and abundant supplies of black-eyed peas and corn from local farmers. The lives of the fort and the community were intertwined. Jane, Press, and Sue Farmer must have been happy to have the soldiers, a few more women and children, and more settlers moving into the area.

Improvements were made to the fort and the complement of dragoons and infantry varied between 50 and 100 men. Settlement in North Central Texas was booming. The Indian threat, though ever present, was not as serious a problem as had been anticipated. Most of the contact was for trading purposes although there was occasional theft, captive-taking, and death in the outlying areas.

In 1853 Ripley Arnold was transferred back to Fort Graham. Kate Arnold and her children, Florida, Kate, and Nannie, followed him there. Tragedy struck the family once again when Major Arnold was killed in a gunfight with the fort surgeon. Kate Arnold and one of the children witnessed this horrifying event. She and the children returned to her family in Mississippi for a time. Later she returned to Texas and lived until her death on July 2, 1894, with her daughter Nannie Arnold Hanrick in Waco. Throughout the years she fought for and won, lost and won again a pension as the widow of a frontier soldier even though he was not officially killed in the line of duty. Kate Arnold never returned to Fort Worth, but Ripley Arnold's body did. In 1855 the Arnolds' friend Adolphus

Gouhenaught went to Fort Graham, claimed the body and returned it to Fort Worth to be buried alongside the Arnold children, Sophie and Willis. (In 1902 Ripley and Kate's daughter, Kate Arnold Parker, the only surviving member of the family, returned to Fort Worth as the guest of the city for celebrations honoring Mexican War veterans. She happily met again Abe Harris who had served under her father at Fort Worth and had taught her mother and her to ride.)

By the fall of 1853 Fort Worth was abandoned as a military outpost. Settlers moved into the buildings or tore them apart for use in building elsewhere. There were about twenty people living around the fort. Newlywed Florence Peak and her physician husband Carroll M. settled in one of the abandoned officers' homes. When the last few soldiers left in October, Lieutenant Holliday gave a small handmade rocking chair to the Peaks. Florence Peak, alongside her husband, who was the first civilian doctor in what was then referred to as either Fort Town or Fort Worth, took care of the medical needs of the growing community, both white and black. The small rocking chair was shared with local families during illnesses or at the birth of a new baby. Soon there were more stores, a school, and a hotel, all in abandoned fort buildings.

The Peaks built a home, his doctor's office, and opened a drugstore. She hosted a small group of people in her home for Sunday school. This group eventually organized the First Christian Church.

In 1854 Jane and Press Farmer bought 320 acres for a farm and added son Jacob to their family. New settlers arrived that year with much fanfare. Julia Garrett describes some of these arrivals in her book, *Fort Worth: A Frontier*

Triumph. Caroline and Ephraim Daggett came by carriage and buggy with several wagons, slaves, household goods, and tools. More slaves driving a herd of dairy cows, followed by turkeys, geese, ducks, horses, and mules soon appeared. Caroline Nored Adams, a widow with three children, had married Daggett, a widower with one son, before moving to Fort Worth. They built a home and farm a few blocks south of the original fort site.

Elizabeth Terry, a lady described as a beauty with aristocratic bearing, arrived in her carriage with two pretty girls, two young men, her husband, thirty-six slaves, and wagons of farm tools and fine furniture. Elizabeth and Nathaniel Terry and their family settled on land along the river just north and east of the fort site. They built a large plantation home with a long porch and planted corn, wheat, oats, and watermelons. Their string of fine horses was soon the center of races held at their plantation.

Small groups of Indians traded often at the fort and in the town. In a report from Fort Worth in 1849 Major Arnold stated that his troops had lost no horses to the Indians and that "about one hundred Indians of the different wild tribes are now visiting me. They brought down and delivered up some thirty-five horses, which they had taken from the Wichitas, horses stolen within the last year from citizens. Three Wichita chiefs are here and promise everything for the future. All is peace and quiet on this frontier."

In the summer of 1853 a group of Shawnee and Delawares were driven through town on their way to Indian Territory north of the Red River. Little is recorded about the Indian women who passed through Fort Town. One exception is the story of Cynthia Ann Parker, who lived as a

Comanche for many years. Her Comanche name was Preloch. In 1860 she and her infant daughter Prairie Flower (Topsannah) were captured by Texas Rangers in Northwest Texas. Parker and her daughter were turned over to the Isaac Parker family of Tarrant County who said that she was a family member who had been kidnapped as an eight-year-old. Comanche had raided her family compound in 1836 taking several captives, including Cynthia Ann. She was nourished and trained by her Comanche family, married a leader, Peta Nocona; and had three children. When she was returned to the Parker family she was unhappy; her daughter soon died, and in a short time so did Cynthia Ann Parker, some say from a broken heart. Her oldest son, Quanah, became a Comanche leader in war and peace, a statesman, rancher, and frequent visitor to Fort Worth in later years.

As the community grew, leaders felt that it would be advantageous to have Fort Worth become the county seat. The small community of Birdville had been named county seat when Tarrant County was formed in 1849. Fort Worth residents persuaded the legislature to call an election for 1856. Local citizens put forward a great deal of effort to encourage voters to vote for Fort Worth. Women were actively involved in this effort even though they could not vote.

Election Day was a time for gathering, visiting, and partying. Whiskey barrels offering free liquor were set out at the general store and voting sites. Some perhaps over-eager Fort Worthians stole the whiskey barrel from the Birdville site on the eve of the election. Jane Farmer's father, Sam Woody, who had settled in Wise County just to the north, came down with about fourteen of his friends and neighbors to

Cynthia Ann Parker and Topsannah. *Courtesy Fort Worth Museum of Science and History.*

enjoy the day and vote, even though they did not live in Tarrant County. The election was very close: Fort Worth won by thirteen votes. The evening brought a celebration around Fort Worth's square with speeches, more whiskey, and music. Over the next few months fights and even gunfire and death followed between supporters of Fort Worth or Birdville. Needless to say the election was contested. It was not until 1860 that the legislature declared Fort Worth the county seat. That decision might have been helped along by Jane and Press Farmer and other citizens pledging their money to build the courthouse. By 1860, the population of Tarrant County had reached 6,000. Of that number, 850 were slaves. Although building was begun on a stone courthouse, events beyond Tarrant County would stop the work for a time.

Politics played an important part of life in Fort Worth in the 1850s, not just in the matter of the county seat but also in wider matters of state and national interest. The growing turmoil over states rights and slavery was on everyone's mind. Sam Houston was campaigning for governor of the state against Hardin Runnels. The two men met for a debate in July 1859 at the Terry Plantation. A large crowd gathered for the debate followed by a grand barbeque and tournament hosted by Elizabeth and Nathaniel Terry. An exciting game of hoops was held. Hoops was a game in which six pairs of men and women dressed in colorful sashes and dresses dashed on horseback along a quarter-mile track gathering hoops that had been strung along a wire. The team with the most hoops on their poles at the end was the winner. Unfortunately the names of the Fort Worth women and men who were these daring riders were not recorded.

Union supporter Sam Houston won the election. However, in 1861 Texans voted to secede from the Union and become a part of the Confederacy. In Tarrant County, secession won by a margin of only twenty-seven votes. No matter the vote, even most of those who opposed secession supported the South after the war broke out. Evidence is that Jane Farmer and her family supported the South. Tarrant County raised troops; Press Farmer and most of the able-bodied men in the area enlisted. Jane, Sue, and Jacob, like most of the women and children of the area, were left to try to hold on to their farms and survive. These women and children and the few men left in the area not only grew crops for themselves but also tried to increase production and operate mills for supplying the war effort. Supplies were scarce. Some of the wooden floors at the old fort were torn up to make looms for all the women in the area. They spun cloth and made clothes for themselves and for the army.

Wheat and barley were parched to substitute for coffee. Sycamore balls were soaked in oil for light. No shoes were available. Louisa, one of Florence Peak's slaves, recalled keeping cows and a large garden. She said that all of the women and children worked to make cloth.

In 1862 Jane and Press Farmer sold their farm for slaves and Confederate money. The Terrys also sold their plantation, receiving slaves and Confederate money. Elizabeth Terry had purchased 412 acres in her name that her family was able to keep following the war.

In the spring of 1865 an event occurred that brought a few hours of joy and fun to local residents. Fifteen-year-old Medora Robinson married William Turner at Andrews Tavern, the most elegant dining and party place in Fort Worth. Hundreds of guests attended the wedding. A day of feasting was followed by a night of dancing. There were even enough dance partners for the young ladies, since Confederate troops were in town on leave. The party lasted for two days.

During and after the war Indian problems increased. Outlying farms were raided for cattle and supplies, some homes and mills were burned, and captives were taken. The Ku Klux Klan was active, lynchings occurred, and both blacks and whites lost property.

After the war many slave holders offered jobs, land, or supplies to their former slaves. Delsey Johnson was given eighty acres of land, a wagon, a team of mules, and a horse by the Lee family on whose farm she had been a slave. She and her husband, Robert, who had been a slave on the Mosier plantation, built a one-room log cabin and dug a well on their land. They asked other freedmen and women in the area to come join them. By 1872 ten black families led by Delsey and Robert Johnson had established the community of Mosier Valley a few miles northeast of Fort Worth.

At war's end the population of Tarrant County had dwindled to less than 1,000. Times were hard; supplies and money were very scarce. Supporters of the South were not able to hold office, buy land, or borrow money. Gold and barter were the accepted mediums of exchange. But the survivors at Fort Worth were once again eager to build a community; work began again on the courthouse and new settlers arrived.

Men in Fort Worth were shocked and amazed in 1866 when a woman, Dorcas Williams, was appointed postmistress. Birdville also had a postmistress, fifteen-year-old Alice Barkley. The women said that just as they had handled spinning and weaving cloth and knitting socks for the men at war they would handle this assignment. Semi-weekly mail delivery resumed, although it was often delayed. Barkley often hand-delivered the mail.

Many veterans of the war saw Fort Worth as a land of opportunity. One such veteran was Klehber M. Van Zandt who, with wife Minerva, their four children, and her parents, sisters, and brother made Fort Worth their home in early 1866. They had journeyed from Marshall in East Texas through terribly cold weather with children sick with the measles. The 180-mile journey took more than three weeks. Minerva Van Zandt had saved $72, which financed the move. After Van Zandt settled the family in their home, he took off for New York to buy items for the store that he had opened just south of the square. Goods were shipped to Galveston by steamboat and then wagon-freighted to Fort

Worth. The Van Zandt family was soon living in a five-room farmhouse across the Trinity to the west. They were on the Fort Worth-to-Weatherford stage line and Minerva Van Zandt often served as hostess to passengers who had to wait on their eastward journey if the river was too high for crossing. Following his wife's death in 1869, Van Zandt married Minerva's sister Mattie. Mattie and Klehber Van Zandt added six more children to the family in the years to come. The Van Zandt family was instrumental in the building of the railroad, establishing a bank, opening a newspaper, and promoting Fort Worth.

The first house that Minerva and K. M. Van Zandt lived in was rented from Juliette Fowler, who had seen her lawyer husband killed in a gunfight with the local sheriff on the town square. The men were involved in a feud over the county seat issue. Both died in the fight. Her two children died that same year, and she moved to Dallas. In October 1866 Fowler received a letter from her friends the Peaks, who described Fort Worth at that time: "There is nothing of interest here. It is the same old thing. No new buildings being erected, so dull a place." But the coming of new families and the arrival of the cattle drives would soon change that outlook.

In 1867 the first cattle drive passed through Fort Worth on its way to the railheads in Kansas. In 1868 drives with 75,000 head of cattle came through needing supplies for the last leg of the drive through Indian Territory. Fort Worth became Cowtown, supplying the herds and providing for the rest and relaxation of the cowboys. In 1869 the traffic increased to 350,000 head. Each herd had a complement of about ten or twelve men.

Women were rare on the trail, but they did exist. Amanda Burks accompanied her husband on the trail numerous times. Unlike the cowboys who traveled on horseback she traveled in a buggy and with a tent. She was not unhappy if the spring rains kept the herd in Fort Worth for weeks because she said she enjoyed shopping in good stores. Burks continued to drive cattle after her husband's death and became known as the "queen of the trail drivers."

The stone courthouse was completed in 1867. The Farmers had purchased a 240-acre farm about eight miles southeast of the courthouse where they and their family would live and farm for another seventy years or so. Jane and Press Farmer, like most settlers, owed many debts brought about by the war. The story is told that Press went to town one day with the first money they had seen in four years, a $20 gold piece received in payment from a horse trader who had rented pastureland from them. Farmer used it to pay his debt to a Dr. Burts, who had cared for his family during the war without charge. Burts paid a debt to another person, who then paid a debt, and so it went until the end of the day, when Press Farmer received the same gold coin in payment from another citizen. The people around the square that day determined that that single gold piece had paid off ten debts.

Jane Farmer's home provided an early meeting space for what would become First Baptist Church. She and her husband remained eager participants in the activities of the area until their deaths, Press in 1892 and Jane in 1895.

The social event of the year in 1869 was the marriage of Mary Fox to John Peter Smith. Smith had established the first, though short-lived, school in 1854, and he had become one of the leading citizens of Fort Worth. Ida Clark and her two brothers, Addison, and Randolph arrived in town in 1869 to teach at one of the schools. They soon opened their own school, which would become Texas Christian University. The circus came to town, the debilitating restrictions of Reconstruction were lifted, and Cowtown began to boom.

The frontier was moving west and a city was being organized, thanks to many of these frontier women, founding mothers of Fort Worth, the Queen City of the Prairies.

BIBLIOGRAPHIC ESSAY

For this essay I was able to review an oral history interview with Betsy Dearing Browder, part of the extended Farmer family who were some of Fort Worth's first settlers. That interview conducted in 1996 when I worked at the Fort Worth Museum of Science and History provided valuable information on Jane Farmer and her family as did the book *Pioneer Fort Worth, Texas* by Lila Bunch Race (Dallas: Taylor Publishing Company, 1976).

For general information about the Arnold family and early Fort Worth I relied on Richard Selcer's and William Potter's book *The Fort that Became a City* (Fort Worth: Texas Christian University Press, 1995) and *The Fort in Fort Worth* by Clay Perkins (Keller, Texas: Cross-Timbers Heritage Publishing, 2001). Julia Garrett's book *Fort Worth a Frontier Triumph* (Fort Worth: Texas Christian University Press, 1996) and Oliver Knight's *Outpost on the Trinity* (Norman: University of Oklahoma Press, 1953; Fort Worth: TCU Press, 1990) supplied many stories of early settlers. Catherine Bryant Arnold's life was detailed in Richard Selcer's article, "The Widow vs. the Bureaucrats: the Strange Case of Mrs. Captain Ripley Arnold," *Southwestern Historical Quarterly 107,* no. 3 (January 2004), Texas State Historical Association.

In 1997 I also conducted an oral history interview with Vada Johnson, descendant of Delsey Johnson, who told the inspiring story of her great-grandparents and the establishment of the Mosier Valley community. Review of that

interview and various newspaper articles provided information about the Johnson family. The Fort Scott National Historic website at *www.nps.gov/fosc/laundress3.htm* provided wonderful information about laundresses at frontier forts during the same time period as Fort Worth, 1849–1853.

Suzy Pritchett at the Tarrant County Historical Commission and Tom Kellam at the Fort Worth Public Library were very helpful in providing access to early Fort Worth records, recollections, and general local history.

Chapter 2

LADIES OF VICTORY

by Brenda Taylor Matthews

Observers of Fort Worth in the 1880s saw a city just years from the untamed frontier. Although the previous decade created a golden mecca of opportunity with the entrance of the railroad, the Wild West persisted with rumors of panthers prowling the unpaved streets, cattle overflowing the stockyards, and Hell's Half Acre offering baths, whiskey, and prostitutes. Fort Worth's first good fortune, to be located at the confluence of western migration after the Civil War, was compounded in the early 1870s with the arrival of the cattle drives. New technologies also arrived in Fort Worth—telegraph, telephone, gaslights, and mule-drawn streetcars.

This was the city that the virtuous Sisters of Saint Mary of Namur took in hand when they arrived in the summer of 1884 to open St. Ignatius Academy at the St. Stanislaus Church, just blocks from the Acre's bawdy activities. The Sisters quickly outgrew their space and built a new stone structure in 1888. In just twenty more years they again embarked on a building plan for the larger Our Lady of Victory Convent, Academy, and College in 1909. Thus the grand dame of Catholic education in Texas, Our Lady of Victory, entered the vocabulary of Fort Worth, becoming a fixture in the city for more than a half century.

These "Ladies of Victory," Sisters of Saint Mary of Namur, first arrived in Texas in Waco in 1873. The order was founded in 1819 in Namur, Belgium. In 1863, the Sisters were scheduled to work with Jesuits near St. Louis, Missouri, but the Civil War blocked their move to the American Midwest. Because Buffalo, New York, had "enough women religious," Bishop John Timon placed them instead in Lockport, New York. Within a decade, the Sisters felt their work was established in the north, and they were ready to answer a new call. Ten years after their arrival in America, Bishop Claude Marie Dubuis of Galveston, with the urging of Texas rancher and Judge John B. Murphy, invited the Sisters to open their first school in Waco—Sacred Heart Academy. As their pastor, Father J. L. Bussant, told of their work, other North Central Texas towns requested Sisters to open schools beyond Waco. Within four years, the Sisters had founded academies in Corsicana (Our Lady of the Sacred Heart Academy), Denison (St. Xavier Academy), and Sherman (St. Joseph Academy), towns that were on the train line that ran north along the route of the old stagecoach stops.

The Sisters' dedication so impressed church leaders that in 1885 Galveston Bishop Nicholas A. Gallagher and French-born Father Jean Marie Guyot, who was ordained in 1870 in Galveston and became Fort Worth's second Catholic pastor, sought their assistance in this northern frontier city that had incorporated only in 1873. Guyot ministered to fifteen Catholic families in a city of 6,663. Despite their small numbers, parishioners had bought two lots on Throckmorton Street for $300 from E. M. Daggett several years earlier to build St. Stanislaus, the first Catholic church in the city.

This parish, barely linked to the rest of Texas, much less the eastern United States, was what the Sisters of Saint Mary of Namur encountered just ten years after their arrival in Waco. Having received a Texas charter for St. Ignatius on August 20, Sister Anastasia, Superior of St. Xavier's Academy in Denison, 100-plus miles to the north, accompanied two Sisters, Claire and Patricia, to Fort Worth on September 3, 1884. Although she had purchased two small houses weeks earlier, Anastasia found them still occupied. Undaunted, they searched for other accommodations. Fortunately, they found an available house next to the church, the former Thomas Roche home, and moved in. News traveled fast and within two days, a Texas rancher had delivered his two daughters to be educated. Sister Anastasia returned from Denison within a week with the remaining instructors, Sisters Adolphine and Camilla, and a lay teacher, Nellie Kirby.

The Sisters opened St. Ignatius Academy on September 15, 1884, and began instruction with twenty-nine students. The new year brought more than fifty enrollees. Following the pattern of Fort Worth's first Catholic priest, Father Thomas Loughrey, who had taught as many as forty-six students in the church during the last decade, the Sisters initially used a heavy curtain to cordon off classrooms in the sanctuary of St. Stanislaus. The growth of the school and congregation quickly made St. Stanislaus obsolete. Inspired by Father Guyot's memories of his native French churches, the parishioners embarked on building a larger stone church to accommodate Catholics who had arrived with the railroad. On October 14, 1888, church notables laid the first cornerstone for St. Patrick Church, an $80,000 structure just north of the St. Stanislaus' frame structure. That same year, the Sisters joined the parish in expansion, purchasing the necessary land from Sarah G. Jennings and the parish. They contracted with St. Patrick's architect, James J. Kane, to build the stone St. Ignatius Academy immediately adjacent to the new church. Kane, the city's first architect, had arrived amidst the bustle of the railroad-sparked growth in 1876. Kane was already an established expert, having built the Fort Worth City Hall and overseen the Tarrant County Courthouse renovation. He designed St. Patrick Church in the common church style of Gothic Revival, but styled St. Ignatius in the French Second Empire mode.

Although church leaders had work performed on St. Patrick's only when they had funds (finishing it finally in 1892), the Sisters had a long history of constructing schools to outlast their lifetimes. Borrowing St. Ignatius' projected cost of $50,000 from Wiegman's Bank in Amsterdam, they occupied the new stone structure within a year. Constructed of rough hewn, or rusticated, limestone blocks, the three-story building had a mansard roof, dormers, decorative chimneys, and stained glass borders atop the windows. The building's belvedere, or open tower, loomed over the nearby streets. The Sisters' early journal notes even the installation of a hot water heating system to be added to the original plans. Other improvements in the early years included galleries connecting St. Ignatius to the older two houses and the planting of a new yard and garden on Jennings Street. They also converted the old St. Stanislaus into the boys' school. As growth continued, they added an adjoining structure at right angles to the main building in 1905, housing a refectory, dormitory and trunk room for boarders; five large classrooms, a small auditorium for performances, and a basement with a furnace.

The Sisters patterned their instruction methods after the European classic tradition of grammar and composition, language, mathematics, and natural sciences while continually adapting to changing times. At St. Ignatius the curriculum mirrored that with the four Rs—reading, 'riting, 'rithmatic, and religion. The Sisters also incorporated manners, music, and elocution into the elementary grades. In addition to calisthenics, the Sisters provided for exercise with walks outside the grounds, even spending $3,800 on land on Fort Worth's south side for St. Mary's Grove for a playground. Teachers taught

math with an abacus in hand and a larger one on the floor. Recitation and oral testing went on continuously, with Sisters quizzing students regularly in math even while handing out cloaks. Teachers used the more modern Palmer Method of penmanship, giving out certificates for excellent work. In the early years, students had slates, but pencil tablets soon replaced these more antiquated tools. The Sisters maintained strict discipline, using a small wooden Belgium instrument called "the clicker." Its clicking sound forced many a student to silence and perfect posture and signaled the beginning of lessons and tests. Accommodating the older female students meant offering high school classes that graduated young women from 1904 until 1910. The Sisters even gave valedictorians of each class a scholarship to St. Joseph's, their academy in Lockport—the equivalent to one year of college. In addition to the earlier grade offerings, the older girls studied etymology, geography, mythology, and astronomy. Students also enjoyed voice, violin, and piano instruction from several Sisters. Recitals and graduation ceremonies showed off the students' talents to the community. Furthermore, Sisters Philomena, Clement, and Mary Albertine became known as some of the best instructors in Fort Worth, with student performances in public theaters such as Byers Opera House receiving rave reviews in the local papers.

Still the space was not enough to accommodate the Sisters and their students. With ever-growing enrollments, Mother Teresa, SSMN American Superior from 1904 to 1910, authorized St. Ignatius Sister Superior Helena to purchase at least ten acres suitable for a new boarding school in 1907. Although benefactors offered land east of Fort Worth along the Trinity

River, the Sisters feared flooding and wanted city transportation. By September 18, Sister Helena had identified twenty-six acres for the new facility at the end of the trolley line four miles south of the downtown St. Ignatius. Twenty-two acres of the site belonged to the Shaw Dairy, the largest such facility in the state. Founded by Catholic Great Grandmother Shaw, a widow from Indiana, and her brother, on the site of the later Holy Name Parish, the dairy moved to the south side where four Shaw great-grandsons, William, John, Gus, and Albert, oversaw a prosperous concern.

Since the diocese did not have responsibility for the school, the Sisters obtained an $80,000 loan from Holland Land Co., based in New York, to buy the land and build on it. During the next year, nationally recognized Fort Worth architect Marshall Sanguinet designed the building to the Sisters' specifications. Our Lady of Victory Academy and College opened its doors on September 12, 1910. The school was staffed by eight St. Ignatius Sisters, mostly in their twenties and thirties. Nine more Sisters joined them within days to teach forty-one day students and thirty-one boarders, with more coming daily. Constructed at a cost of $135,000, the building's interior still demanded workers' attention, even to the point of the erection of a temporary chapel. In January, Mother Albertine visited from New York and participated in the completed chapel's first benediction on March 5. After being entertained by the students she left for Buffalo, promising to return for the official ceremonies. On July 19, 1911, the new bishop of Dallas, J. P. Lynch, and several priests dedicated the building and praised the Sisters' mission as teachers.

When completed, the five-story, 64,000-square-foot building had class and music rooms, libraries, study halls, dormitories, recreation and dining halls, and a chapel, but the ten months between the school's opening and its dedication sorely tried its occupants. The building was outfitted with up-to-date conveniences, including an Otis elevator at the cost of $3,195; electricity, steam laundry and vapor heat, but installations were incomplete and problems occurred. Although builders planned city water connections, the artesian well was unfinished. With the modern range still undelivered, the first evening's meals came from St. Ignatius. Although wired for electricity, contractors had yet to connect the lights. One evening during that first week, while climbing the stairs to the dormitory (the elevator was not operational until October 10 and continually malfunctioned over the years), the flashlight went out, leaving the Sisters to find their way up the remaining flights in the dark. Finding no water for bathing, young Sister Beatrix braved the darkness in search of the night watchman. With his help, she returned with a bucket of water and a bar of soap the Sisters shared. The Sisters did not have laundry facilities until October 21 and contractors did not light the furnace until the twenty-ninth. They completed the auditorium on October 22. During the first days, therefore, the Sisters prepared the students' dorms and classrooms amidst the construction workers. Several parents delivered their daughters on the eleventh, coming from Mineola, Oklahoma, and Texarkana, San Antonio, and Oak Cliff, Texas. Without lights, the Sisters entertained the families with borrowed kerosene lamps in the front parlor.

Despite the construction delays, the Sisters' teaching mission at Our Lady of Victory

Exterior of Our Lady of Victory, 1930s.
Photos courtesy of the Sisters of Saint Mary Mother House Archives, Fort Worth.

Academy continued the traditions of their predecessors at St. Ignatius. The school was chartered by the state within a year and immediately began conferring diplomas. The SSMN stated their education philosophy in their first published handbook:

The education imparted in this institution is thorough, practical, and refined, aiming at forming noble Christian women who will grace society with their accomplishments and edify it by their virtues.

With girls in grades one through twelve, the Sisters divided the students into three levels: elementary, grades one through four; preparatory, grades five through eight; and academic or secondary, grades nine through twelve. They again based their curriculum on the classics, history, mathematics, and languages, including English, French, German, and Latin. Students also learned the latest information in the sciences from visiting experts and tested their stamina with physical education. "Refining" elements included elocution lessons and embroidery classes. Girls and young women enjoyed cultural activities such as music in the form of voice, piano, and orchestra, as well as art, with renowned performers from as far as New York gracing Our Lady of Victory's auditorium. Although non-Catholics attended the school, only the Catholics received religious education—the others studied ethics.

In addition to a formalized curriculum, the Sisters maintained a strict dress code. The older

Front Foyer and Reception Room beyond, Our Lady of Victory.
Photo courtesy of the Sisters of Saint Mary Mother House Archives, Fort Worth.

girls wore black aprons to class, whereas the little girls, or "minims," wore gingham dresses.
Winter uniforms included black wool skirts
with a black-and-white checked jacket; the
young women wore a black serge suit with a silk
blouse on Sundays. Black served even for summer, with linen replacing the wool skirt and silk
blouse. The elementary grade girls, similarly,
wore wool dresses in the winter and white in
the summer.

The Sisters, furthermore, held high standards for entrants. Diary notations on October
27, 1910, related the rejection of several boarders for lack of references. Another entry in
November mentioned the rejection of a student
despite the mother having stated her husband
had given money to the school. The Sisters
expected students to lead disciplined lives in
which academic excellence, decorous behavior,
and cultural appreciation were standard. The

Chapel, 1956.
Photo courtesy of the Sisters of Saint Mary Mother House Archives, Fort Worth.

first commencement on June 9, 1911, graduated Myrtle Grant, Anna Sawyer, and Mildred Shaugnessy.

For the next decade the Sisters devoted their energies to educating young women under the first Our Lady of Victory Superior, Sister Margaret Mary. Knowing that she was always cheerful after her daily walk where she chatted with the cows, boarders used those moments to ask for special favors that she seldom refused. Our Lady of Victory, much as St. Ignatius had been in its early years, became a cultural center, where world-renowned performers entertained Fort Worth residents. Violinist Maud Powell, opera star Luisa Tetrazzini, and noted Shakespearean Charles E. Griffith performed, and many plays and musicals brought in much-needed funds to pay off the Sisters' debt to the Holland Land Company.

It was also in the first years at Our Lady of Victory that the Chapel, located not by accident

Joan of Arc Statue in Our Lady of Victory Foyer.
Photos courtesy of the Sisters of Saint Mary Mother House Archives, Fort Worth.

Sister Joachim, First Our Lady of Victory Sacristan.

in the heart of the building on the second floor, became the center of the Sisters' life. Within its walls, women made their first commitment to the religious life as postulants, took temporary vows as a novice, and finally, perpetual vows. The smell of incense and flowers accompanied these women as they relinquished their given names, put on the veil and received religious names. Ruling over this special place from 1921 until the sixties as sacristan was Sister Joachim of the Sacred Heart. Born Eva Montpetit in Canada, Sister Joachim joined the Sisters in

1906 in Lockport. Transferred to Fort Worth in 1921 to take over the chapel duties, the grey-eyed and brown haired, five-foot three dynamo maintained the chapel vestments and chalices with perfection. At Christmas, the chapel took on all the beauty of the season under her supervision. Most importantly, many a novice and Sister spent constant hours in prayer and supplication in its "warm blanket."

These early years of Sister Joachim's career also brought new responsibilities to OLV. With the country again at peace after World War I,

Our Lady of Victory emerged in the twenties to discover itself the Mother House of a new province. In early 1921, Mother General Gonzague, visiting Lockport from Namur, sent a letter requesting the presence of all the Sisters in the region at a retreat scheduled for March 29. Since this marked the first visit of a Mother General to the south, her trip caused much excitement. On March 30, she announced the creation of a new Western Province with Our Lady of Victory as its headquarters. This meant that Fort Worth and OLV not only now had the same stature as the Lockport Mother House, but also that young women could now enter the order in Fort Worth. Over the next several months, there was an exchange of Sisters, with 119 departing north for Lockport and the Eastern Province. Despite some losses, the first Provincial Superior, Sister John Berchmans, set out with 129 Sisters to continue their work in the eight academies they had founded between 1876 and 1910.

Within a few months, Sister Rose Ann came from New York to be the first Mistress of Novices at OLV. Originally from Missouri, she had been in charge of the training of novices in Lockport for many years. Although kind, she enforced a strict monastic system, including silence except at the forty-five minute recreation each evening. Sister Claire became the first to enter the novitiate at OLV, having attended St. Joseph's Academy in Sherman. Over the next few months, Sister Marie Vincentia, having made her postulancy in Lockport, transferred to OLV, and Sisters Maria, Evangelista, Benedictine, Regina, Rita, Mary, and Genevieve joined the first group of novices. Their day began at five o'clock, with prayers at 5:30 and meditation

Sister Genevieve, From First Our Lady of Victory Novitiate group.

until 6:30. For the next fifteen minutes, the novices completed their "charge," usually chores such as dusting or cleaning. They attended mass three times a week until 7:15; they then breakfasted in silence except on Thursday, Saturday, Sunday, and feast days. First-year novices spent the rest of the day cleaning dormitories, corridors, private rooms, and stairs, and working in the laundry. Some second-year novices taught, as did most of the postulants.

Among those first novices, Sister Genevieve's personal story stood out. Born Agnes Adele Kirkpatrick in Ennis, Texas, in 1900, her mother was Catholic and her father Protestant. When she was four, her mother died, having elicited a promise from her father to rear her a Catholic. While living with an aunt, she attended Our Lady of the Rosary, the Sisters' school in Ennis, until it closed in 1907. Her father, despite several moves and a second marriage to a Protestant, continued to help Agnes practice her faith. When the family moved to

Mineral Wells, she attended public schools, but in 1916, she transferred to the Academy of Mary Immaculate (AMI), the SSMN boarding school in Wichita Falls, not knowing the same Sisters had administered her earlier Catholic school in Ennis. After graduation, Agnes attended Our Lady of the Lake College in San Antonio, achieving a first-grade teacher's certificate. For the next couple of years she taught in Rowlett and Las Gallinas public schools, continuing summer retreats at Our Lady of Victory. In 1922, she and one of her classmates from AMI, Mary Crockett, decided to become Sisters of Saint Mary of Namur.

When Kirkpatrick sought entrance from Provincial Superior Mother John Berchmans, she admonished ". . . hurry! The Lord doesn't want your old worn-out bones." At twenty-three, she was four to five years older than most novices, who entered immediately after high school. Kirkpatrick's decision, furthermore, drew the attention of the resurgent Ku Klux Klan, who called on her father, telling him what a tragedy it was for his daughter to enter a convent. Her father, always supportive, told them that if at twenty-three she did not know what she wanted to do, she never would. The Klan responded by burning a cross on OLV's lawn. Despite this rather frightening beginning to the now Sister Genevieve's ministry, she spent the next fifty-nine years as a Sister of Saint Mary of Namur. In 1937, she attained her B.A. at Our Lady of the Lake, and received her M.A. in history at Catholic University of America in 1946. The less-than-five-foot-tall sister taught at SSMN high schools until she retired, serving as superior at Saint Maria Goretti Convent and School in Arlington, Texas, from 1969 to 1989.

In her remaining years she tutored adults attempting to receive a high school diploma and visited patients in hospitals and nursing homes, earning United Way of Tarrant County Outstanding Senior Volunteer of the Year honors in 1976. Sister Genevieve died at Our Lady of Victory Center in 1993 at the age of ninety-two, after a long life that she described as "full of joy."

As illustrated by Sister Genevieve's eventual attainment of a bachelor's and master's degree, the Provincial leadership recognized that their Sisters needed higher education to meet the increasing Texas state certification credentials. The Sisters had already been teaching secondary classes at St. Ignatius; now they added college-level courses at OLV, continuing primarily the classic curriculum of the lower grades. Despite the state's chartering, OLV still needed to gain affiliation with a four-year university to assure student entrance into a higher institution. OLV gained its first formal agreement with Catholic University of America in Washington, D.C., in 1914, and then in 1921 with the University of Texas. Although novices began taking college-level courses in 1922, they did not admit lay students until 1929 when the Southern Association of Colleges and Universities granted accreditation. By September 1930, OLV had implemented a regular junior college curriculum, advancing the sciences with chemistry, zoology, biology, botany, and bacteriology classes by 1944. Provincial Mother Albertine served as president and appointed Sister Mary St. Patrick dean. Sister Beatrix, the last senior teacher at St. Ignatius and the first at OLV Academy, became registrar. The Association of Texas Colleges and Universities granted the college membership in 1931, completing the process. The Sisters made a final affiliation in 1935 with St. Joseph's School of Nursing that continued for twenty years until 1956. Furthermore, reflecting the emphasis for female students on household management, the Sisters built a home economics annex in 1947.

Many Sisters contributed to OLV's increasing stature during the thirties and forties. The first dean of OLV College, Sister Mary St. Patrick, born Theresia Maria McConville in 1882 in Sherman, Texas, entered SSMN in Lockport in 1899. She returned to teach in Texas in 1912, transferring to Laneri Boys School in Fort Worth in 1928 and beginning her career at OLV in 1932. Having attained her Ph.D. in history from Catholic University in 1928, Sister Mary St. Patrick wrote a "Primer on Pan Americanism" in 1937 and spent many years researching a manuscript on the history of the Sisters in Fort Worth, finally retiring in 1956. Similarly, Sister Benita, born Margaret Duggan in 1892, joined the Sisters in Lockport in 1908. Orphaned in Ireland at fourteen, Margaret and her twin Catherine (later Sister Francis Regis), came to Waco to live with their aunt, SSMN Sister Agnes, at Sacred Heart Academy. The five-foot-five, always immaculate Sister received an M.A. from Catholic University, becoming Western Provincial Superior in 1937. Because World War II severed communications with the Namur Mother House, she continued in the position for nine years, even becoming a naturalized citizen in 1942.

During these years, OLV continued to adapt to changing accreditation requirements. Letters from Catholic university reviewers in 1941 cited several concerns over their re-affiliation with OLV: the Sisters continued to operate elemen-

tary classes along with the more exclusive academy and advanced college classes, as well as run the Mother House, in the same structure on Hemphill. Moreover, the Sisters commingled the finances, failing to separate out the funds of any one institution.

By the early 1950s, Provincial Superior Mother Theresa Weber heard constant complaints from even the Sisters over the crowded conditions. Sisters maintained quiet discipline, marching the little girls in precise ranks—until the older students commented on their marching out of step or complimented a little girl's "black-eyed beauty." Sister Jane Francis protested to Mother Theresa, "How can I train the first graders to be business-like and industrious if they are always hearing themselves praised? Isn't there some other way for the college girls to go to their class without passing my students while they are in line?" Mother Theresa, therefore, broached the topic of moving the college and novitiate to Dallas with the new bishop of the Diocese of Dallas.

Bishop Thomas K. Gorman, who had come to North Texas from Nevada, had learned quickly that Dallas and Fort Worth had distinctive personalities. Drawn by a growing economy, eastern businessmen had flocked to Dallas in the previous decades, bringing with them not just ambition but also cultural and educational expectations. Fort Worth, on the other hand, prided itself on its history and image as the city "where the West begins." Although acknowledging the Sisters' need for a new facility for college students and especially the need to achieve higher academic credentials, he questioned Mother Theresa's request to move the institution to Dallas. Why not build on OLV's twenty-six acres

Our Lady of Victory 8th Grade Class, 1945.

in Fort Worth? Mother Theresa insisted that the larger Catholic population in Dallas and the Sisters' two high schools and five elementary schools there gave a stronger base than their one high school and four grade schools in Fort Worth.

Her argument persuaded the bishop and the campaign for the new Our Lady of Victory College in Dallas was officially approved on December 22, 1953. The project was led by Eugene Constantin Jr., longtime SSMN friend and benefactor in Wichita Falls, and Ford dealer Edward R. Maher, whose children had attended the Sisters' schools in Dallas. The campaign quickly became a quest not for the small school envisioned by the Sisters but for an institution capable of attracting national attention. Deftly assisted by Mother Theresa, a tiny "mover and shaker," the campaign raised the $2 million goal within six months. By the middle of 1955 the

Above: Mother Theresa Weber, Our Lady
of Victory Provincial during founding of
University of Dallas.
Above right: Sister Martin Joseph, First
University of Dallas Librarian.
Right: Registrar UD, Sister Mary Margaret
O'Connell advising a student.

*Photos courtesy of the Sisters of Saint Mary
Mother House Archives, Fort Worth.*

Sisters had purchased the 1,000-acre site for a newly chartered University of Dallas west of downtown Dallas.

In December, mindful of the project's scope, the Sisters made the difficult and painful decision to turn the burgeoning task over to the diocese. Mother Theresa's tearful visit to Bishop Gorman and her offer of the $2 million fund did not end the Sisters' association with the university, however, as four Sisters, Francis Marie,

Martin, Mary Ellen, and Mary Margaret, took positions there. Sister Mary Margaret, born in 1912 as Mary Elizabeth O'Connell in Crowell, Texas, became registrar. Like many of her fellow religious, Sister Mary Margaret had attended one of the Sisters' schools, the Academy of Mary Immaculate. She entered Our Lady of Victory in 1931, attaining her B.A. at OLV College and then her MA in history at Catholic University. Described as the "keeper of the university seal," students remembered her as prompt, efficient, and decisive. She worked until her death in 1973 from cancer, and the university recognized her by renaming the dormitory where she and her fellow Sisters resided as Mary Margaret O'Connell Hall.

Despite the energy devoted to the university's founding, the Sisters continued their work on Our Lady of Victory's campus in Fort Worth. In 1953, they opened a new building for the elementary grades, with Our Lady of Victory Elementary School immediately adjacent to the south of the venerable old academy building. OLV Academy also reached its height in the fifties with international recognition bringing young women from Mexico as well as France to board with the young women from local communities and distant ranches. As education improved in rural areas and boarding schools fell out of fashion, the school's resident numbers declined. Peak enrollment occurred in 1960 with 430 students, but fell immediately the next year when high school students transferred, at the request of the bishop, to the new Fort Worth Catholic Nolan High School.

With the last students graduating in 1961, OLV underwent many changes. Many Sisters who taught at other Catholic schools in the area resided at OLV, with forty-four living there in newly converted rooms. The decade, however, brought other changes that directly affected the Sisters at OLV. Following Vatican II in 1965, religious life evolved, with the Sisters relaxing their rituals and dress. The number of Sisters of Saint Mary of Namur began to decline in the seventies with more than fifty Sisters leaving religious life and fewer young women entering. As the Sisters in Fort Worth aged, OLV's third floor, the acad-

emy dormitory, became the infirmary. By the mid-eighties, the Sisters, with urging from the fire marshal, admitted that they could no longer afford to sustain the grand old building. After conducting a feasibility study that produced ideas for OLV's use that ranged from diocesan housing to a hotel, the Sisters decided to build a new Our Lady of Victory Center for the remaining active members and retired Sisters. Finally, in August 1987, twenty-six Sisters and seven lay women, many of whom were aging relatives of the Sisters, moved to the new building directly to the west of the old OLV building.

And what of the grand old Our Lady of Victory? For several years a small group of Sisters continued to live in the building with Sister Margaret Miller operating the Sisters' gift shop on the first floor. By early 1990, though, the Sisters had begun to contemplate the inevitability of the wrecking ball. Plans proceeded with the Sisters holding an auction on December 7, 1991, to sell the building's treasures. With help from the Historic Preservation Council for Tarrant County, the Sisters signed a contract with Historic Landmarks, Inc., saving the building from demolition. It was not until 2004, however, that OLV emerged from the shadow of possible destruction, opening as the Victory Arts Center, leasing forty-six loft apartments and artists' studios.

Today, the Sisters of Saint Mary of Namur housed in Our Lady of Victory Center still give their energies to service. During the Academy's history, each student wrote A.M.D.G. across the top of her papers. It was the Sisters' Latin motto, *Ad Majorem Dei Gloriam* (To the Greater Glory of God), that described each woman's devotion to praying, teaching, and toil. Although many are infirm, the active Sisters continue to work with diocesan projects, teaching, center administration, archive preservation, and hospice, hospital, prison, and mission duties. Nevertheless, only Our Lady of Victory Elementary, the last of the schools founded by the Western Province, remains of the Sisters of Saint Mary of Namur's 120-year history on the frontiers of education in Fort Worth and in Texas.

BIBLIOGRAPHIC ESSAY

The sources for "Ladies of Victory" are numerous. The most important primary source is the Sisters of Saint Mary of Namur Western Province Archives located in Fort Worth at the Our Lady of Victory Center. Archivist Sister Martin Joseph has been most helpful in locating materials and giving oral history on the Sisters. Her assistance and encouragement, as well as the support of the Western Province of SSMN, has made this project possible.

Much of the background material comes from several published and unpublished manuscripts and books on the history of the Sisters of Saint Mary of Namur, including Sister Mary Louise Corcoran's book on the first superior in America, *Seal of Simplicity, a Life of Mother Emilie,* and Sister Jacques Huet's booklet, *Nicholas Joseph Minsart, 1769–1837,* on the SSMN's primary supporter in Belgium during the early years. Also useful was William Hoover's *St. Patrick's: The First Hundred Years.*

Sources for Texas and Fort Worth include *The Handbook of Texas Online,* Oliver Knight's *Fort Worth, Outpost on the Trinity;* and Carol Roark's *Fort Worth's Legendary Landmarks.* Materials on Texas education include such standards as Frederick Eby's *The Development of Education in Texas* and Donald Whisenhunt's *The Development of Higher Education in Texas.* Catholic education background came from *Catholic Women's College in America* as well as several articles.

I am indebted to Texas Wesleyan University for granting me a sabbatical during the fall semester of 2005 to begin this project. The staff and librarians at the West Library at Texas Wesleyan University were most helpful in locating materials and interlibrary loans. I also wish to thank my husband and fellow historian, John Matthews, for listening to my "Sister anecdotes."

Chapter 3

"DUCHESSES WITH HEARTS OF LOVE AND BRAINS OF FIRE"

by Ruth Karbach

ON A CHILL FEBRUARY EVENING in 1882, a petite, studious lady stepped wearily from the train onto the Fort Worth station platform. Frances Elizabeth Willard, national president of the Woman's Christian Temperance Union, had arrived at this Texas cattle and cotton railhead to campaign for prohibition. In the flickering gaslight, Fort Worth was a depressing sight after a rainy deluge that had turned the streets into mire and broken windowpanes all over town. The stenches from the stock pens and hide-and-wool yards adjacent to the station were reminiscent of Chicago, near Willard's "Rest Cottage" in Evanston, Illinois. During the carriage ride north to her accommodations, the celebrated temperance speaker and advocate for woman's suffrage traveled past the rough Irish shanty town and the dangerous saloons, gambling dens, and dance halls of Hell's Half Acre. Frances Willard knew that this town where the politicians and police winked at vice and businessmen profited from its attractions sorely needed the WCTU message. She planned to leave behind dedicated recruits—her "duchesses with hearts of love and brains of fire"—to provide moral instruction and benevolent care to the human flotsam of this adolescent city.

The Fort Worth *Daily Democrat* on February 18 reported that Willard's one-hour, captivating lecture at the packed Fourth Street Methodist Church was "rather remarkable for the amount of practical good sense...for curbing and restraining the great evil of intemperant [sic] use of intoxicating drinks" and encouraging temperance for a "better way of life for all." America's top female Chautauqua speaker, Willard routinely evoked such commendations from Victorian males while Susan B. Anthony and her ilk provoked and outraged them. In reality, Frances Willard had selected the popular temperance cause to bind to her main agenda of suffrage for women, resulting in a political force 200,000 strong. With a stroke of strategic genius, she contended that the equalization of the roles of men and women was necessary to protect the sacred institutions of motherhood and home and sanctioned by the Holy Bible. This rhetoric persuaded traditional women that their involvement outside the domestic sphere was morally justified, and males responded positively to this sentimental, feminine appeal to their chivalry.

Nonetheless, Willard's 1882 Fort Worth audience was mainly women. The skeptical editor of the *Democrat* quipped that Willard's temperance lecture was not attended by locals who frequented the Acre, meaning men, because they "didn't need to any way, as the saloons have about decided to run on a cash basis in the future." He suggested that the local option election be postponed, taking a judicious stance between the fiery temperance faction and the moneyed alcohol interests. A large group of women willing to take the temperance pledge and proudly pin the WCTU white ribbon to their bodices met on February 18, 1882, to organize the Fort Worth union. Marie Caroline "Carrie" Diehl Brown was elected president, with Willard's backing no doubt, and vice presidents were selected from each of the seven white Protestant churches in town. Thus, the first exclusively female organization geared to social and political reform in Fort Worth was born.

President Carrie Brown, a native of France, was a dressmaker, who always went by Mrs. C. D. Brown after her marriage to St. Louis clothier Joseph Mortimer Brown. The modiste was admired for her intellectual achievements, linguistic fluency, and artistic sophistication. As early as 1872, her husband visited Fort Worth on business when his brother-in-law, noted railroad builder General Grenville Dodge, convinced him to join in construction of the Texas & Pacific Railway. Four years later, the Brown family moved to Fort Worth permanently where Carrie

Brown successfully operated her own business at their downtown residence. It was a busy household with their two young sons and three live-in female employees: a seamstress, a sales clerk, and a housekeeper. Carrie Brown's Bazaar of Fashion carried an incredible stock of ready-made women's clothes and hats, luxury fabric, patterns, gloves, hosiery, undergarments, capes, artificial flowers, plumes, and cosmetics; the shop also took custom and mail orders.

Actually, Carrie Brown and her supportive spouse were excellent choices for the fledgling temperance union. They represented the ideal domestic family promoted by Willard and her followers. Episcopalians with a strong, temperate home life, the prosperous couple was generous and sympathetic in helping those less fortunate. Because Joseph Brown had been president of the Missouri Odd Fellows for several terms, he and his wife were experienced working within the framework of a national organization. More importantly, Carrie Brown had her own strong identity and the essential skills to advocate in the community and educate less accomplished White Ribboners.

Just one month after its founding, the local union opened the first public library in Fort Worth at the rear of banker William Boaz's new building on Second Street. The ladies gained credibility with their successful book drive and solicitation of financial support from city leaders and churchwomen. One wealthy cattleman offered to match any $100 donation. The *Daily Democrat* featured frequent columns contributed by WCTU corresponding secretary Henrie C. L. Gorman, later the owner and editor of the *Bohemian* magazine and future president of the Texas Woman's Press Association. She described the reading room's main aim as providing "young gentlemen a pleasant place of resort" to keep them out of the gambling dens and whiskey shops abundant in Fort Worth. In fact, saloons outnumbered churches at least three to one; there were five wholesale liquor dealers and one agent for a St. Louis brewer in this city of 12,000. The library moved around town and settled in 1889 over Stert's Gun Shop.

Elated after a Fort Worth rally—termed a "Grand Prohibition Love Fest" in the *Daily Gazette*—on July 1, 1887, drew 25,000 people, temperance forces were stunned when the largest anti-prohibition rally in Texas took place in Fort Worth just twenty-five days later. As reported on the front page of *The New York Times*, the 20,000-plus parade participants included 800 Tarrant county farmers and 1,500 Fort Worth voters. Temperance advocates were further demoralized with the crushing defeat of a state prohibition amendment. Conservative Texas women, fervent about temperance, now fully realized the need for women to have the power of the vote. At the state WCTU convention at Fort Worth in 1888, Texas became the first southern state, and the only southern state for many years, to endorse the vote for women.

The WCTU women's most lasting contribution to the city of Fort Worth was the first children's home, established in the fall of 1887. Eventually, the county would assume responsibility for this institutional facility and operate it as the Tarrant County Children's Home until 1976. Belle Burchill and Delia Collins co-founded the Bootblack Home for the street boys who slept in packing crates, hallways, or the calaboose, if the police got hold of them, and earned their daily bread as shoeshine boys, candy sellers,

Belle Burchill was a co-founder and the first superintendent of the Fort Worth Benevolent Home for Children, later the Tarrant County Children's Home and Aid Society. The home was originally sponsored by the local Woman's Christian Temperance Union. *Courtesy, Fort Worth Public Library, Genealogy, History and Archives.*

and newsboys. In the winter, hordes of northern street kids hitched rides on the railroad south to warmer climes, and many literally landed in Fort Worth. While searching for needy ragamuffins who congregated near the railway depots and Hell's Half Acre, Burchill and Collins rubbed elbows with the denizens of the Acre.

Katherine "Kate" Belle Murray Burchill was a twenty-seven-year-old bride when she arrived in Fort Worth in 1874 with her husband, a railroad car builder and later a stockman. A graduate of Watertown Institute in New York, Burchill already had twelve years experience as a teacher, chiefly in Bloomington, Illinois. Soon Fort Worth civic leaders encouraged her to start a private school in their town of 2,000. By January 1875 the newly created school board asked Burchill to open a free school at the same location. For two years she persevered there despite indignant parents and unruly students. Cleverly, Burchill learned to establish order among her rowdy charges by playing the organ. One mother was horrified by the teaching of "politics," i.e., the Constitution, to girls. During a commencement exercise, Burchill had the United States flag raised for the first time in public since Reconstruction. The ceremony was not shot up as threatened, though some attendees booed. Local women kept insisting that they wanted a southern woman to teach their children, and she felt forced to resign. Her next, more successful school was privately run in her own building.

Burchill sold that property for the new Wesleyan college when she was appointed postmistress in 1881, the second woman to hold the position in the city. Her four-year tenure was disrupted two years later when she was arrested by a U.S. marshal for destroying third-class mail and detaining a love letter to a married man, with the alleged motivation of blackmail. Disgruntled male employees made the allegations in reaction to her managerial style and liberal views, such as appointing women to important positions in the post office. The townspeople backed Burchill, and she was exonerated when the alleged blackmail victim, shady lawman H. P. Shiel, changed his story in a federal hearing. The progressive postmistress instituted free mail delivery and hired the first black mail carrier in 1884.

Burchill, a Republican, had a four-year hiatus before politicking again to be postmaster. With the support of black Texas Republicans under the leadership of Norris Wright Cuney, she facilely outmaneuvered the faction promoting Joseph M. Brown for the position. At the start of her second term as postmaster in 1889, she added a second black postal carrier. She and her fellow temperance union members also instigated a successful letter-writing campaign to relocate the post office so respectable women would not have to walk by saloons to mail parcels and buy stamps.

Burchill's best friend and companion on missions of mercy, Delia Krum Collins, a widow, moved to Fort Worth around 1886 with her adult sons, Warren and Frank.

Delia Krum, from Middleburgh in the Mohawk Valley, was a graduate of the new, innovative State Normal College at Albany in 1847. The course of study, in addition to academic subjects, included the science and art of teaching, surveying, and weekly lectures by advanced students for evaluation by their professors. Students practice taught in the Model School.

Henry W. Collins, an older student at this experimental coeducational college, made an impression on Krum, and they continued their relationship while teaching in Elmira, New York. In 1849, they married and a few years later relocated to Janesville, Wisconsin. There Delia Collins taught French, German, and art. Her husband became a partner in a pharmacy that evolved into a perfumery that produced the nationally popular Tallman's Florida Water.

Through the Ladies' Afternoon Club of Janesville, Delia Collins worked for educational opportunities for women and helped establish the public library and the Young Men's Christian Association. Also she was a founder of the Art League.

A member of the WCTU, Collins was an accomplished gospel speaker in Wisconsin. The union in Janesville had special ties with Frances Willard, whose childhood years were spent in that area.

The Fort Worth WCTU chose Burchill and Collins as the unsalaried superintendent and secretary, respectively, to establish the Bootblack Home. Banker Martin B. Loyd offered a vacant commercial property on Main and Third for six months rent free.

The dormitory for fifty boys was filled with donated cots, covered with handmade blankets and quilts. A matron supervised the boys and had her own bedroom. There was a kitchen where meals were cooked from food donated by hotelmen, butchers, and grocers; and a bakery gave bread and treats daily. The patronesses felt it was important that the program not create total dependency and decided to charge a nickel per meal and the same per night's stay. The bootblack meals were immediately popular—540 meals were served in the second month of operation. The boys' quarters had a bathtub and laundry, a real luxury for street waifs. Each boy had a pigeonhole for his possessions.

By agreement, boys from the home in trouble with the law were taken to policemen's residences to be picked up by the women instead of jailed in the calaboose where they would be exposed to hardened criminals and heavy lice infestation. Because many of the boys did not go to public schools during daytime working hours, the women taught a night school. The WCTU also started a temperance school for the bootblacks, who like many children of the period drank beer and sometimes hard spirits. Much store was set by these efforts to educate the illit-erate boys, because town folks wanted to be the first city in the South to have a "ragged school," a charitable school dedicated to the free education of destitute children.

The WCTU moved the reading room with its 300 books to the Bootblack Home. Ladies and gentlemen were invited to use the library for free, and, while there or out shopping, have a home-cooked lunch in the front room to subsidize the venture.

The Ladies' Benevolent Association operated a centralized charity out of the back room of the building. Applicants would enter through a side door. Able-bodied men were put to the "test of the woodpile"; slackers were soon revealed. The women managers dispensed clothing, groceries, and medicine to the needy.

With the addition of girls to the program, the renamed Industrial Home for Friendless Boys and Girls mushroomed; its quick success created a strain on financial and physical resources. Soon children were being turned away because of lack of space. In 1888 the benefactors approached the Tarrant County Commissioners for help. The officials responded magnificently with purchase of a $6,000 home on Cold Springs Road near the racetrack. According to Burchill family lore, this spacious house had been built by gambler John L. Tierney for his paramour Madame Brown to run a bordello. A reporter from the *Daily Gazette* enthused that "great taste was displayed by the former owner in the selection of elegant wall paper and handsome woodwork." Canadian-born Madame Brown had come up in the world from the second-rate "boardinghouse" on Bluff Street with four prostitutes and ironically provided the perfect building for a children's home.

The trustees and Burchill planned "more active, aggressive work" with their larger facility; they changed the name to the Benevolent Home and incorporated the association on December 28, 1888. A school was built on site, and the city furnished the schoolroom and paid the salary of the teacher hired by the school board.

By 1890 the home was struggling financially, and its population fluctuated for the next ten years from forty-two to seventy children directly in relation to funds available. Cost to support one child monthly averaged $3 during this decade. Clothing was mended by a ladies sewing group at a rate of 150 pieces per week. After the county commissioners began to contribute $100 per month, Burchill petitioned the city unsuccessfully to provide the same amount. Sometimes the city paid pharmacy bills. Cases of typhoid fever, pneumonia, croup, *la grippe,* and measles were treated by a series of volunteer doctors. A child known as "Little Belle" died from a heart condition in 1891, and there were four other deaths from measles in the '90s.

From 1889 through 1893, Burchill served as postmaster while also volunteering as the superintendent of the children's home. Her right arm, Delia Collins, left the Benevolent Home in 1891 to start another worthwhile WCTU institution: the Rescue Home for Fallen Women. Burchill relied heavily on matron Rosanna French, a widow who had supported herself as a dressmaker. In annual reports Burchill praised French's executive ability, and the matron was given raises and the increased staff she requested.

The Rosa McKnight case in 1894 involved the Benevolent Home trustees in a court battle for one of their charges. When eight-year-old Rosa ran from the property to her mother in a waiting carriage, the Benevolent Home filed a writ of habeas corpus to regain the child. The mother countered with charges of cruelty and mismanagement by Burchill and the trustees. The testimony in the Seventeenth District Court was avidly reported word for word in the Fort Worth and Dallas newspapers. Damaging testimony detailed extreme corporal punishment and abuse by French, who had resigned four months earlier after an in-house investigation of her bruising a child with a hairbrush. Tearfully French testified in court about the hairbrush incident and denied all other charges against her. She claimed she was overworked and blamed Burchill for the problems in the children's home. In response, Burchill testified she had no knowledge or participation in the alleged abuses but admitted that she had used a "very small brass chain" around the ankle of another runaway girl to chain her to a bed; by the time of the hearing, that girl had eloped to marry the young man she had been sneaking out to meet.

Judge Harris decided the Rosa McKnight case on the basis of "best interest of the child," a standard not yet written into Texas law. The Benevolent Home was awarded custody of Rosa McKnight because of the mother's past abandonment of the child. The judge outlined duties of the Benevolent Home trustees, including their responsibility to know the "inner workings of the home." Although Burchill was not deemed unfit for her position, the judge did cite her lack of judgment. As a postscript to the Rosa McKnight case, French left town. She was buried in 1919 in Oakwood Cemetery.

Thereafter, the County Commissioners Court required Burchill to make monthly reports. The trustees of the Benevolent Home

The Benevolent Home for Children at 547 Cold Springs Road, just past Pioneers Rest Cemetery, was purchased in 1888 with Tarrant County funds. Its original construction as a bordello made the building ideal for institutional use.
Courtesy, Bill Collins.

worked to formalize the operation of the home, transferred some of the superintendent's duties to the male trustees and board of women managers, and made the acceptance of Jewish as well as Christian children a policy. They continued to admit only white children.

Two years later the Benevolent Home took a new direction. Influenced by the philosophy of the National Children's Home Society, Burchill and the trustees placed twenty percent of the Benevolent Home's children into foster and adoptive families in 1896. Burchill even served briefly as the first state superintendent of the Texas chapter of the Children's Home Society, but she resigned to devote her efforts to the chil-

dren remaining in the Benevolent Home. The Texas Children's Home and Aid Society eventually became the Edna Gladney Home.

Burchill became a charter member of the Texas Equal Rights Association, the first woman's suffrage organization in Texas in October 1893. As reported in the *Dallas Morning News*, Mayor B. B. Paddock welcomed the TERA delegates to Fort Worth at the second convention and proceeded to expound his personal opinion "that the history of the world would show that no good results ever followed the enfranchisement of women." At this convention in June 1894, a split developed with a spirited fight over sponsoring a speaking tour of

Texas cities by Susan B. Anthony. As president of the recently organized Fort Worth Auxiliary, Burchill, along with Dr. Grace Danforth and Elizabeth Fry, proved powerful adversaries to the state president, who believed Texans were not ready for such a controversial feminist. After the president was deposed, Burchill was elected the Texas vice president. The organization soon died in 1896 from lack of funds and divisiveness.

In 1899, the widowed Burchill announced her retirement from the Fort Worth Benevolent Home. For several years, she devoted herself to her daughter's singing career, even moving to New York City with Edna. Around 1908 Burchill returned to Fort Worth and entered the real estate and oil business. When she died on April 23, 1937, Belle M. Burchill was remembered by Edith Guedry [later Deen] as a "little bonneted lady" with "strength of person." Indeed, she was a Victorian woman who brought progress to a dusty cowtown.

Delia Collins, through her work at the Bethel Mission with the homeless and transient—often alcohol, morphine, cocaine, or opium addicts—became increasingly concerned about the plight of prostitutes and unwed women from "good" families thrown onto the streets. After a Tarrant County grand jury published notices to vacate to owners of the "parlor houses" in Hell's Half Acre, Collins, accompanied by three other women crusaders, visited at Mrs. Porter's, offering to set up a rescue home for fallen women. They were received respectfully by Madame Porter, and the "soiled doves" there agreed that such work was badly needed in Fort Worth. The social reformers then visited Lane's, Belmont's, and the Reeves' "parlor houses."

The first hurdles Collins faced were renting a house for unwed mothers and dealing with outraged neighbors. The search for a location started in 1890, but a plan to find a residence on Samuels Avenue near the Benevolent Home came to naught. Finally, in March 1891, the institution was underway when a house was secured at 117 West Ireland, now Cannon Street, several blocks south of the railroad tracks but too near Hell's Half Acre to suit the matrons. Another stumbling block was the taboo against mentioning sex and pregnancy outside of marriage to potential donors and volunteers. In Collins' own words, "some women who will go to balls in decidedly décolleté gowns will blush to the roots of their hair when we begin to tell them of the necessity of the work." Collins immediately left her position at the Benevolent Home for Children to devote herself to the Rescue Home for Fallen Women, the second Fort Worth institution sponsored by the Woman's Christian Temperance Union. A press release from the Texas WCTU lauded Collins as the "Mother of Rescue Work in Texas," and she was selected state superintendent of social purity at the May convention. Fanny L. Armstrong in her column "WCTU Items," carried by the *Dallas Morning News*, wrote that the Rescue Home provided "poor, sinning ones...food, shelter and raiment and...mother's love." According to the 1910 *Census of Benevolent Institutions*, the Collins home was the oldest such institution in Texas; it was likely the first.

"Mother" Collins confronted the difficult task of reforming the hardcore prostitutes and addicts who comprised twenty-five percent of the home's population. The majority of the residents were girls as young as twelve who had been seduced. Funding proved the greatest challenge of all. A monthly publication, *Byways and Hedges* of the Rescue Home and the Bethel Missions in Texas, edited by Laura Penuel, was sent to prospective donors and the three women's auxiliaries of the Woman's Home. Since finances prohibited expansion of the facility and its programs, the president of the home decided on a new strategy.

Collins went before the Senate Committee on State Affairs in 1893 to request $50,000 state funding for the home via a bill sponsored by Senator James Swayne of Fort Worth. In the words of the *Dallas Morning News*, Delia Collins spoke so passionately of the "misery and ruin of young girls" and "the private sorrows of their mothers" that several senators wept; however, when it came to state money, the senators were not sympathetic enough. Undeterred, Collins continued traveling to organize rescue societies across Texas to refer girls for maternity care and to solicit contributions for their support. This talented lady was called on to reorganize "Sheltering Arms," the Dallas effort to match what the Fort Worth temperance group had accomplished. She appointed an "experienced matron and for an assistant a rescued girl who had been with her for two years," according to the *Dallas Morning News*.

By 1894 the Tarrant County Commissioners provided a vacant building in the 1500 block of South Main next to St. Joseph's Infirmary, truly in the suburbs. The name of the organization had been changed to the Texas Woman's Industrial Home to signify that the residents were being trained to "suitable" occupations. There was a sewing department that handled special orders for kitchen aprons and other garments, with the girls' receiving a commission on what they sold. Cooking and housekeeping classes were planned to enable graduates to support themselves. The main aim of the Industrial Home's training was to produce girls who had "well established moral principles and cultivated personal habits." Just as the girls were expected to grow to self-sufficiency, the managers wanted the rescue home to become self-sufficient. They saw the new setting in a country atmosphere as conducive to market gardening, floriculture, and dairy production.

Statistics from the 1894 report revealed the success of the program and the mortality rate. Yearly population totaled 103 including women, children, and infants. Of the infants, twelve were placed for adoption, and three died. Dismissals of girls from the home indicated a success rate of 80 percent with either employment or a family setting placement. The remaining 20 percent left the home on their own initiative or were asked to leave. There were now six auxiliaries around the state, and contributions came in from WCTU groups in eleven cities. Fort Worth's donations topped the list at $450. The Texas Woman's Industrial Home ran on a very tight annual budget of $1,561, all contributions.

The Medical College staff at Fort Worth University volunteered medical services. The City of Fort Worth contributed $10 monthly for drugs, mainly carbolic acid and camphor; doubtless, they wanted to avoid having responsibility for the indigent residents, thereby decreasing the drain on the pauper and charities fund administered by the chief of police. Paupers' burials for the women and infants who died at the home were provided by the city. A bill for June –September 1895 from George L. Gause, undertaker, is a sad memorial for four women and five

Helen Stoddard used persuasive, intelligent arguments dressed as common sense to convince Texas lawmakers to enact laws prohibiting use of addictive substances, establishing alcohol education programs in public schools and raising the age of consent. *Courtesy, The Woman's Collection, Texas Woman's University.*

children, including one called simply "the Child." By 1895 Collins became dedicated to establishing a foundling home to care for the babies rather than forcing girls to give their infants away.

Collins died from influenza near midnight on December 31, 1896. She was sixty-six. Her dying wish was for her funeral services to be conducted at the Woman's Home. To memorialize her, the name of the institution was changed to the Delia Collins Home. It operated for eighteen more years. Hattie Collins, wife of Warren Collins; Ida

V. Jarvis, and Margaret C. Berney served as presidents after Collins' death.

The very capable Helen Marie Gerrells Stoddard, a Fort Worth resident, was the Texas president of the WCTU when Collins was appointed a state superintendent. In 1885 Stoddard, a widow with a school-age son, accepted the position of preceptress of English at Fort Worth University. Stoddard had come to Texas five years earlier to live with her parents on their farm at Indian Gap in Hamilton County. Born on July 27, 1850, at Sheboygan Falls, Wisconsin, Helen Marie Gerrells was educated at Ripon College and Genesee Wesleyan Seminary. With several years experience as a teacher and as the former head of the mathematics department at the Nebraska Conference Seminary, Stoddard was hired at $500 per year and placed in charge of the preparatory school at the Wesleyan University. This salary was one-half that of the male professors.

Stoddard became interested in the WCTU movement and joined the Fort Worth Union after being inspired by hearing Anna Palmer. A national WCTU evangelist, Palmer spoke on February 6, 1887, at the Cumberland Presbyterian Church in Fort Worth as part of the prohibition amendment campaign in the 1887 Texas election.

After serving in several capacities in the local organization, Stoddard was appointed state superintendent of scientific instruction for temperance under Sarah Acheson, the Texas president. In 1891, Acheson, Stoddard, and Fanny Griffin of Alabama made a presentation in Austin to a legislative committee to make scientific temperance instruction mandatory in public schools, but the bill was tabled.

At the state convention that year, Acheson's ill health prevented her from running for the presidency, and Stoddard was elected president with only four years' experience in the WCTU. She realized that her full-time efforts were needed to meet the challenge of reinvigorating and expanding the Texas unions after the defeat of the prohibition amendment and to lobby in Austin for legal solutions to social problems. She resigned her position at Fort Worth University and devoted herself for the next sixteen years to the demands of the WCTU. She considered Fort Worth her home during her presidency and worshipped at St. Paul Methodist Episcopal Church when in town. She traveled extensively across Texas, organizing, teaching parliamentary law and political advocacy skills, and lecturing and giving audiovisual shows against alcohol and drug use.

Within six months of her election to the presidency of the Texas union, she gained the attention of the National WCTU because of her success in organizing new unions and adding impressive numbers to the Texas membership rolls. She played a prominent role in that year's national conference in Boston. Shortly she became a national anti-narcotics speaker for the WCTU and conducted the union's annual parliamentary law session at its Summer Institute held at the Chautauqua in Michigan.

On March 17, 1896, Frances Willard lectured for ninety minutes at Fort Worth City Hall. The *Fort Worth Gazette* described the audience this time as "large and fashionable"; Willard was greeted by her White Ribbon troops waving handkerchiefs. During this Texas trip, Frances Willard met with Helen Stoddard and must have discussed plans to add Mexico

to the ranks of the World Woman's Christian Temperance Union.

Willard appointed Stoddard the WCTU delegate to the General Assembly of Missionaries in Mexico City and notified *The New York Times* of Stoddard's appointment. Through the missionaries, Stoddard arranged for sponsors and translators for a summer tour of twenty Mexican cities to organize temperance unions. Stoddard served as the first delegate from Mexico to the WCTU World Conference in Toronto in 1897. She also attended world conferences in England, France, and Switzerland. Her lecture on local option law at London Hall was so well received that the French and Swiss delegates requested a copy.

In Texas Stoddard's first success in securing reform legislation was the passage of the Scientific Temperance Instruction Law in 1893. With Stoddard at the head, the Texas WCTU achieved, to quote woman's historian Judith N. McArthur, "the most concentrated succession of legislative victories in its history."

Before her election to the state presidency, Stoddard played a key role in the Fort Worth Union. Probably she influenced the Fort Worth group to back an 1891 attempt to raise the age of consent, i.e., age of judgment to consent to sexual relations. With an age of consent of ten years old, Texas was blacklisted by *Arena,* a national social reform magazine. Mary Clardy, a state organizer with ties to the Farmers' Alliance, was chosen by the Fort Worth union to lead the fight in Austin and succeeded in getting the legislature to protect girls up to twelve years. Stoddard described her later attempt to raise the age of consent to eighteen years old as her most difficult campaign. She presented cogent arguments reprinted in Texas newspapers for raising the

Proposed domestic science instruction produced the most furor over the bill prepared by WCTU president Helen Stoddard to establish The College of Industrial Arts for Girls' (now Texas Woman's University.) In this 1912 photo, student Lillian Kiber is analyzing the chemical properties of vinegar. *Courtesy, The Woman's Collection, Texas Woman's University.*

of the sale of tobacco to minors in 1899, regulation of cocaine sales, pure-food laws, anti-gambling statute, and the statute against cash-on-delivery liquor shipments to dry counties. Her strong position against child labor was influential. In April 1907 she appeared before the legislature with Elisabet Ney and other female leaders to speak for a law entitling women to vote in Texas. Susan B. Anthony's *History of Woman Suffrage* contains an article by Stoddard on the Texas suffrage movement.

Helen Stoddard's legislative successes probably had much to do with the selection of Fort Worth as the site of the national WCTU convention in 1901, a first for Texas. During that convention the city commissioners passed a cocaine regulation statute, and the school board patiently listened to objections to the present textbooks. Locals were treated to the sight of a nighttime parade of women singing a song about Carrie Nation, penned by Laura Humphrey Jaccard of Fort Worth. National Woman's Christian Union leaders spoke from Protestant pulpits throughout the city, including one black church.

Stoddard's crowning achievement was the passage of the bill creating the College for Industrials Arts for Girls, known today as Texas Woman's University. The governor appointed her to the location committee with twelve men. For years, the WCTU had battled for a state woman's college with a practical curriculum. A proposal for a tax on Texas bachelors to finance the education of single women was even batted around women's circles. Such an unusual measure became moot when Stoddard successfully mothered the birth of the college with existing state funds. The course of study offered at the

limit. After what she described as a "dirty battle," the worn Stoddard could celebrate the protection of girls to age fifteen in 1895. Social reformers blacklisted Texas for two more decades until the law was finally changed to seventeen years of age.

Stoddard often wrote the bills she sponsored, and she achieved a high level of respect from state legislators and administrative staff. Other bills credited to her include: prohibition

new educational institution included nursing, home economics, and professional child care, all taught scientifically. Stoddard was chosen secretary of the board of regents. Stoddard Hall, a residence for students, was named in her honor.

The physical demands of travel and recurring bouts of malarial fever took their toll, and Stoddard retired in 1907 from the Texas presidency and relocated to southern California. In her new state, Stoddard was not inactive for long. She was the only woman candidate to run in 1912 for the U.S. Congress on the prohibition platform. By 1920 she was president of the Southern California WCTU. She returned to Texas as an elderly woman and lived in Brownwood with her daughter-in-law. On New Year's Eve of 1940, Helen Stoddard died in a Dallas medical care facility and was buried in San Diego, California, by her son.

Ida Mae Van Zandt Jarvis, a thirty-year member of the Woman's Christian Temperance Union, exemplifies how the WCTU changed the lives of Fort Worth women and influenced them to assume leadership roles in the community. Ida Mae Van Zandt was born on May 20, 1844, in Washington, D.C., to Francis and Isaac Van Zandt, minister of the Republic of Texas. An intelligent, spirited child, she was sent to Franklin College in Nashville, Tennessee, and finished her education at Marshall Academy for Girls.

In 1872 Ida V. and husband James Jones Jarvis, an attorney, moved to Fort Worth to join the Van Zandt clan. When the railroad arrived four years later, she described the town as "quite lawless and colorful." Some townsfolk "took scared" and departed Fort Worth, but not the Jarvises. Instead, they invested in real estate, and

Ida Van Zandt Jarvis transformed herself from a traditional southern Victorian lady into a social activist, women's suffrage advocate, and philanthropist after hearing an inspiring speech by Frances Willard, national president of the WCTU. *Courtesy, Disciples of Christ Historical Society, Nashville, Tennessee.*

J. J. Jarvis joined his brother-in-law K. M. Van Zandt in legal practice, then in the banking business.

Ida Jarvis described herself as a traditional Victorian mother and wife until she heard Frances Willard speak. Her own words describe her journey from that pivotal event: "I used to go around looking for open doors of service to enter, now find myself pushing them open."

In the 1880s, as the local superintendent of unfermented wine, Jarvis convinced the Protestant churches not to serve alcoholic wine during communion. Also she was an instructor for scientific temperance in the schools.

The first city organization that Jarvis led as president was Associated Charities, established August 1891. Jennie Scheuber, future director of the Fort Worth Library, and Mary Peters Young Terrell, future president of the Texas Federation of Women's Clubs, were among the group of reformers who believed a significant segment of the poverty-stricken population was not being served. Many men were unemployed because work on the city's first water system had halted, and a hard winter was expected. The county commissioners agreed to provide $5 a month per family for groceries. Sewing machines and washboards and tubs were bought for women with dependent children to help them earn an income. The most amazing accomplishment of these dedicated women was the building of three free houses for families with invalid heads of household. The ladies regularly drove their buggies to the poor farm and helped make the inmates' lives better with everything from medicine to magazines.

After three successful years, the monthly stipends from the county ceased because the commissioners needed money to build an impressive new courthouse; consequently, Associated Charities closed. In a later article by Jarvis in the *Fort Worth Record,* she wrote: "They got their monument all right and their names are on the corner stones, but they all lost their office at the next election." The disappointed women had found their political voice.

A dedicated Campbellite, Jarvis went far beyond being a Sunday school teacher at First Christian Church by organizing the Texas Christian Women's Board of Missions and serving as its first state president. When J. J. Jarvis was elected president of the board of AddRan

College, Ida Jarvis drew up the charter for what later became Texas Christian University. Married to a man who was rather conservative with his fortune, Ida Jarvis would write poems about her latest philanthropic idea during the predawn hours and place them in her husband's shoes for him to find in the morning. As the greatest fan of her poetry, and deeply charmed by her from their first meeting, J. J. Jarvis gave the necessary money. One source estimates that Ida V. and J. J. Jarvis contributed a lifetime total of $1 million to TCU.

The proceeds from her book *Texas Poems* supplied a scholarship fund for students for the ministry at AddRan College. As editor of the mission page for the *Christian Courier,* she joined the Texas Woman's Press Association in its first year and was an active long-term member. Her second decade as a White Ribboner was spent as the Texas superintendent of unfermented wine and superintendent of scientific temperance instruction during the presidency of Helen Stoddard.

Familiar with the YWCA from a visit to Buffalo, New York, Jarvis rushed to be a charter member in 1906 when the very first one in Texas was organized in Fort Worth. She was elected to a vice presidency for life. The organization started with a cafeteria for working girls and soon grew to include a boarding home, an employment bureau for women, and a physical education program. The Travelers' Aid Department was of special interest to Jarvis. Trained travelers' aid workers officed at the railroad stations to help locate approved housing for young girls and assist indigent, stranded families with meals and railway tickets. The aides reported the activities of recruiters who duped naïve girls into prostitution. As the wife of a former state senator, Jarvis had political entrée and was selected by the Woman's Missionary Union to present a petition about the white slave trafficking in the state to the governor.

In 1910 Mr. and Mrs. Jarvis donated 456 acres of land for the establishment of Jarvis Christian College, an educational institution for black students. Ida Jarvis, who attended graduation exercises at the college every year, said that this gift "paid the biggest dividends of any investment I have ever made."

Jarvis was selected as successor to May Hendricks Swayne, long-term president of the Fort Worth Federation of Women's Clubs, but had to resign early in her presidency to care for her ill husband, who died in January 1914. The federation was a powerful enough political force to have their own meeting room at city hall. Often Jarvis, intimidated by no one, was chosen to be a spokesperson to present the federation's positions and petitions to the city and county commissioners. The federation established a baby hospital to provide free medical treatment for children, and Jarvis was a donor and active manager on its board. The Baby Hospital became the Fort Worth Children's Hospital.

The Woman's Cooperative Home was chartered in 1915 to provide housing and care for destitute women with children; churchwomen from each of the Protestant churches were managers of the home. A founding mother of the Cooperative Home, Jarvis was one of two women who represented the churchwomen on the board of trustees. In World War I, wives and families of soldiers training at Camp Bowie flocked to Fort Worth. With the high casualty rates in the war, destitution of these families increased, and the

Home was at maximum capacity. The organization almost folded several times in its first decade of operation for want of funds, but Jarvis and Gertrude Bloodworth, a WCTU evangelist and officer, personally bailed it out and raised additional funds. Today the children's home is known as the All Church Home.

After Texas Christian University moved to Fort Worth in 1910, Jarvis advocated for and funded the home economics program. Jarvis Hall, a girls' dormitory, another of her pet projects, was fully financed by the Jarvises. By 1928 the American Association of University Women pointed out the need for a woman on the board of trustees of TCU. Ida V. Jarvis was unanimously elected and remained a trustee until her death.

During her last years in the WCTU, Jarvis held the important position of the Texas superintendent of the franchise under Leilia Barlow Ammerson of Fort Worth. For five years Ida V. Jarvis worked for suffrage for women, often pointing out that women were "always taxpayers, never voters." When the Nineteenth Amendment was passed, Jarvis looked forward to seeing a woman become president of the United States.

Ida Van Zandt Jarvis was ninety-two years old when she died on March 11, 1937. "All Fort Worth Mourns Death of Mrs. Jarvis" declared the *Fort Worth Press* on page one. Texas Christian University held no classes the afternoon of her funeral.

The tribute that would have delighted the feisty Ida V. Jarvis the most was the closing of city hall for the day. She left Fort Worth in good hands—after all, her son Van Zandt Jarvis was mayor.

BIBLIOGRAPHIC ESSAY

The title "Duchesses with Hearts of Love and Brains of Fire" is a quote from a Frances Willard speech.

About a decade ago, I "discovered" Helen M. Stoddard and Ida V. Jarvis in the 1896 book *Prominent Women of Texas* by Elizabeth Brooks.

Caroline Diehl Brown proved an obscure subject in local history references. However, the Fort Worth newspapers and the *Dallas Morning News* rescued me.

At the Fort Worth Public Library, I waded through the Burchill Collection and read the contents of an interview of Belle Burchill in Anne Lenore Goerte's "Some Phases of the Development of the Fort Worth, Texas School System, 1864–1930." *Citizens at Last, The Woman Suffrage Movement in Texas*, edited by Ruthe Winegarten and Judith N. McArthur, had invaluable history of the Equal Rights Association. When the legal cases involving Burchill came to light, I checked county and federal court records. The mayor and city commissioners' records had benevolent home reports and letters of appeal.

Without the help of Geoffrey P. Williams at New York Normal School Archives, University of Syracuse, I would have been at a loss in my search for Delia Collins' background and would not have known to read *A Successful Experiment in Teacher Education: The Founding and The Early Years of the Albany Normal School*, by Mary Elizabeth Alpern. *We Were There: A History of Rock County Women* helped fill in Collins' Wisconsin years. City of Fort Worth records produced intriguing bits about the Texas Industrial Woman's Home. Bill Collins, the great-great

grandson of Delia Collins, was gracious in sharing family genealogy and memorabilia.

Fortunately I found many biographical sources about Helen M. Stoddard. They include the Stoddard Collection in the Woman's Collection, Texas Woman's University; *To the Noon Rest: the Life, Work and Addresses of Mrs. Helen M. Stoddard*, by Fanny L. Armstrong; *The Texas Women's Hall of Fame* by Sinclair Moreland; *Thumb Nail Sketches of White Ribbon Women* by Clara C. Chapin; *The Standard Encyclopedia of the Alcohol Problem, Vol. VI*; *Women Torch-Bearers* by Elizabeth Putnam Gorden; *Up Rugged and Isolated Paths* by Rhonda Jane Jones; and *Creating the New Woman* by Judith N. McArthur. *The Union Signal*, national WCTU publication, had numerous references to Stoddard's work.

The Jarvis Collection at Texas Christian University had courtship letters of J. J. Jarvis to Ida Van Zandt and miscellaneous documents that led to a review of the minutes and history of All Church Home and YWCA Archives. *Force Without Fanfare: The Autobiography of K. M. Van Zandt*, edited by Sandra L. Myres, and "Reminiscences of Frances Cooke Lipscomb Van Zandt," written about 1905, provided great family history. *Texas Christian University: A Hundred Years of History* by Jerome A. Moore; *These Carried the Torch* by E. B. Bynum; and Colby Hall's books on the history of the Disciples of Christ in Texas and Texas Christian University were consulted about the Jarvis family's relationships with the university and religious organizations. First Christian Church of Fort Worth archives and an unpublished church history were kindly provided to me. The Disciples of Christ Historical Society in Nashville, Tennessee, located articles by or about Ida V. Jarvis in their publications. Papers in the Woman's Collection, Texas Woman's University, had great overviews of Jarvis' life and contributions. The Texas Press Woman's Scrapbook, in the American History Collection, University of Texas at Austin, had information about Jarvis. An interview of Ida V. Jarvis about the pioneer days of Fort Worth was in the Tarrant County WPA Writer's Project.

Because official W.C.T.U. records and the state publication *The White Ribbon,* for this period are not in public archives, I had to work with these primary sources: the "W.C.T.U. Items" column in the *Dallas Morning News,* Fanny Armstrong's article on the W.C.T.U. in World's Fair Edition of the *Bohemian Magazine,* and the W.C.T.U. meetings held in Fort Worth covered by the local papers. I made a worthwhile trip to the Center for American History at the University of Texas at Austin to review the scrapbook compiled by the Austin WCTU.

I turned to Richard F. Selcer and his *Hell's Half Acre* as my authoritative sources on Fort Worth vice and intemperance in the nineteenth century. In a small Texas town's bookshop I found my own copy of *A Story of the Texas White Ribboners* by Mrs. W. M. Baines, c. 1935, which was a helpful source though blemished by inaccuracies. The search continues for the "lost" book of the Texas *White Ribbon* bound for Stoddard by the *Fort Worth Star-Telegram* and the records of the Fort Worth union and the state WCTU records.

Chapter 4

RANCH WOMEN, COWGIRLS, AND WILDCATTERS

by Judy Alter

Fort Worth owes its growth and success to three things: the cattle empire, railroads, and the petroleum industry. Fort Worth women's involvement in the railroads was pretty much limited to feeding the men who struggled to lay the last twenty miles of railroad track in time to meet the 1876 legislative deadline. But the cattle kingdom gave the city one of its most colorful women, and two women in the petroleum industry were well ahead of their time in their achievements in a field usually reserved for men.

Although many wives and daughters of big ranch owners stayed on the ranch, a few established homes in town—and Fort Worth was the town most of North and West Texas looked to for city needs and excitement. The Waggoner family of the Three D is perhaps the best example of ranching families' establishing homes in Fort Worth. And the most colorful of the Waggoner women was Electra Waggoner Wharton, whose beautiful home and lavish lifestyle were the talk

Electra Waggoner Wharton on the occasion of her wedding. *Courtesy of Historic Fort Worth, Inc.*

of the town in the first decade of the twentieth century.

Electra was the most public of the Waggoner women, but they were a family of women who illustrate just how tough ranch women could be—cowboys are not the only ones who make the myths and legends. Most of the Waggoner women ended up living in Fort Worth.

Elizabeth Halsell was a Waggoner woman only because both of her daughters married Waggoners, but she set the family pattern for strength. Her husband, Electius, an innkeeper in Decatur, was moody, intelligent, and opinionated. During the Civil War, he was a loyal Texan, but he opposed secession and did not keep his opinion to himself. One day near the end of the war a group of secessionists caught Electius in the middle of Decatur and put a rope around his neck. At that point, Elizabeth Halsell wrote herself into history. Shotgun in hand, she opened a path through the bullies, and the hanging was off. Nobody wanted to hang Electius badly enough to risk being shot by Elizabeth.

Elizabeth's oldest daughter, Sicily, married a widower named Dan Waggoner, who ranched with his son Tom, better known as W. T. Several years later, W. T. married Sicily's baby sister Ella. Her parents had died, and Ella lived with Dan, Sicily, and W. T.

Ella Halsell Waggoner had been born in a cabin in Wise County and, as a child, she knew poverty, hard work, and Indian attacks. When she died at age 100, she owned a mansion in Fort Worth's Rivercrest neighborhood and the third-largest building in Fort Worth, a twenty-story structure that in its day was a skyscraper. She lived to see the development of airplanes and television, though one doubts she ever had one.

She was remembered by granddaughter Electra as close with a penny. Once she refused to allow the cook to buy the sugar needed to make young Electra's favorite cake. Another time, she thought her newly hired companion put too much cream in her coffee—so Ella ordered the cook to only put a bit of cream in the pitcher.

If Ella was parsimonious, her daughter Electra was extravagant, and the only Waggoner to become a colorful part of Fort Worth's history. Electra grew up on the Waggoner ranch, riding as hard as any cowboy. After time at a finishing school, she fell in love with Max Lingo, who was in the lumber business in Dallas. Apparently her parents did not approve of Lingo, for when he asked Electra to marry him, they convinced her to take a world tour. In Europe, she met and fell in love with A. B. Wharton Jr., a Philadelphia socialite. When she returned from her tour in 1901, the town of Electra in North Central Texas was named in her honor. The town had alternately been called Beaver and Waggoner. Tom Waggoner did not want the town named Waggoner, and citizens were unhappy with Beaver. So they voted to call their small town, which would later have multiple oil derricks, Electra.

Electra and A. B. were married in June 1902 at El Castile, her family's home in Decatur. Their honeymoon was an extended tour of Europe, after which they planned to settle in Philadelphia. The story varies on whether the newlyweds bought property themselves at 1509 Pennsylvania in Fort Worth or whether W. T. Waggoner bought it and built them a "honeymoon cottage" to persuade them not to leave Fort Worth. Probably Wharton bought it from J. S. Zane-Cetti for $25,000. Building plans were

Thistle Hill. *Courtesy of Historic Fort Worth, Inc.*

announced when the couple returned from their honeymoon, and in 1904 they moved into the house with their infant son. Electra called the house "Rubusmont," which means Thistle Hill, because it sat on a hill nicely situated to catch the Texas breezes.

Electra's husband soon became prominent in Fort Worth. He owned the city's first automobile agency, Fort Worth Auto & Livery, which sold Franklins and Wintons and offered rentals and repair service as well as cars for sale. In 1906, there were ninety cars in Fort Worth, and Wharton owned five of them. The speed limit on city streets was seven miles per hour. Wharton

also owned and showed horses, with some success, and had a personal kennel of dogs that he exhibited at field trials.

The years in Thistle Hill established Electra's international reputation for lavish living and glamour. Legend says that she was the first to spend $20,000 on a one-day shopping spree at Neiman-Marcus in Dallas; the next day she returned to spend almost as much for things she had overlooked the previous day. She had fresh flowers delivered to her house daily and ordered the latest clothes from New York and Paris—though she often returned those that did not please her. Supposedly, she refused to try on

The pergola at Thistle Hill. *Courtesy of Historic Fort Worth, Inc.*

a dress that anyone else had tried on—and she never wore the same outfit twice. The closets at Thistle Hill bulged with furs and fine gowns. At one time, she was said to own 350 pairs of shoes.

The Whartons entertained frequently, and the newspapers of the day reported every detail. In 1906, there was a "phantom dance" for Halloween; guests wore pillowcases and sheets, and the only lighting came from candles in pumpkins. The same year there was an old-fashioned candy pull and an "al fresco" party on the verandah, with card games, professional vaudeville performers, and lunch for 200 people. One New Year's the couple invited 160 friends to a party held in the third-floor ballroom, which was decorated with smilax and tinsel. To be invited to a party at Thistle Hill was to be counted among the upper class, and the detailed newspaper accounts of these parties give a clear picture of the way wealthy Fort Worthians entertained themselves in that day.

The Whartons sold Thistle Hill to Winfield Scott in 1911 and built a new home, Zacaweista ("long grasses" in Comanche), on the North Texas ranch property she had recently inherited from her father. They divorced in 1919, and Electra moved to Dallas, marrying twice more before her untimely death in 1925 at the age of forty-three.

Other branches of the Waggoner family had also moved to Fort Worth. Dan and Sicily moved to 1418 El Paso in 1891. Their home was later sold to Lena Pope during the infancy years of her home for needy children. Electra's brother E. Paul and his wife had a house close to Thistle Hill at Pennsylvania and Summit, and eventually Tom and Ella moved to 530 Hill Street (now Summit Avenue). The family seemed clustered

together, but none made the splash that Electra had.

One Waggoner woman seemed to have inherited her aunt's flair for publicity and extravagant living, as well as her name. She was Electra, daughter of E. Paul and Helen Buck Waggoner. She was born in the house at Summit and Pennsylvania and later remembered that her family seemed to move into every house her grandparents sold. Although Electra lived in Fort Worth as a child, she never made the city her home. Instead she lived at her father's portion of the Three D, in a house called Santa Rosa. But this Electra, a noted sculptor, also left her mark in Fort Worth: the heroic-sized bronze statue of Will Rogers on his horse, Soapsuds, which stands in front of the Will Rogers Memorial Coliseum is her work.

One of the most notable of the other ranch women who moved to Fort Worth was Elizabeth Scott, whose husband bought Thistle Hill, began remodeling it, but died before he could move his wife and son into the house. Less flamboyant than the two Electras, Scott set a quiet standard of style. She went to New York annually to buy new gowns, especially one for the Assembly Ball, and she was active in the community, serving on the board for the Fat Stock Show, donating to the Carnegie Library, and holding life memberships in the Women's Club and River Crest Country Club. She often entertained at Thistle Hill, giving formal and elaborate dinners. But she is not remembered in the way that Electra is.

Today, the phone book and the social directory in Fort Worth are dotted with ranching names—Reynolds, Kleberg, and descendants of W. T.'s good friend Burk Burnett. It is impossible to name them all. The house that rancher

Fountain Goodlet Oxsheer built for his family still stands on the southeast corner of Pennsylvania and Henderson Streets. It now houses offices. Oxsheer was noted for having a boom-and-bust life story—he died in debt—and for extravagant daughters who, like the first Electra, shopped extensively in Dallas.

The early ranchers, having started from scratch and built grand fortunes, gave great wealth to their children, some of whom abused the privilege. Today their extravagance is all but forgotten, and women descended from ranch wealth easily blend in with other Fort Worth women. But there is something to remember about those early, extravagant ranch women: they were raised by men of extraordinary energy and strength, men who survived Indian attacks and frontier hardships and ultimately built a fortune from cattle and, later, oil. In the early twentieth century, women who had inherited that strength and energy had few outlets—and perhaps that is why they spent their energy entertaining and maintaining a lavish lifestyle. And perhaps it is why Electra Waggoner Biggs, who could have had a comfortable and easy life as a rancher's wife and an international socialite, built herself a career as a sculptor. Even if she did not live here, Fort Worth can claim her—at least a little bit.

Fort Worth's first ventures into the social scene were closely linked to its ranching heritage. A horse show began in 1907 to accompany what was by then called the National Feeders and Breeders Show. In 1912, a group of women known as The Assembly honored the queen of the horse show, Elizabeth Reynolds, at a gala held in the Westbrook Hotel. The party was such a success that the next year the assembly began

presenting debutantes. The Steeplechase Club was formed in 1913 to honor the queen of the horse show and provide escorts for her court.

The queen was crowned in the Northside Coliseum, where the stock show would begin the next day. Some 5,000 people watched the ceremony, which was the social event of the season. The arena was decorated with banks of roses and chrysanthemums, an electric fountain, and a Japanese pergola that hung from the ceiling and was decorated with vines. The throne sat on a stage that covered half the arena. The queen entered in a carriage drawn by white Arabians and was escorted by a guard of trumpeters and armed retainers. Newspaper accounts of the event begin with descriptions of preparations for the elaborate pageant, complete with a Dance of Nations, and end with a listing of poultry and livestock entered in competition—a perfect example of "Cowtown and Culture," the slogan adopted by the city in the late twentieth century.

At the 1913 show, Mabel Long was the queen and her court consisted of daughters of the most socially prominent families from several Texas cities and towns. The event was called Kirmess, which means annual festival or fair. The Kirmess (or Kermess or Kermes) pageant continued until 1918, when it was dropped for two years because of World War I. The Assembly, which still introduces debutantes at the annual Assembly Ball, discontinued Kirmess because of the stock market crash. In 1932, the Steeplechase began to present its own debutante class, with the Knights of the Steeplechase as their escorts.

In the 1920s and 1930s, women with ranching instincts found another outlet for their energy—rodeos. Women started riding in rodeo events before the turn of the last century, back when rodeos were often little more than ranch competitions on a dusty town street on a Saturday, where cowboys—and some cowgirls—competed to show off their skills. In the early 1900s women began competing in rodeo events in Wild West shows, riding in relay races and doing trick riding. Sometimes they did stunts men would not do because of the danger, such as the Roman ride, in which the cowgirl stood with a foot on each of two horses as they trotted around the arena.

Fort Worth was a good place for rodeo riders. Most competitors followed a circuit of rodeos, from Madison Square Garden to Cheyenne, Wyoming, and points between. Because Fort Worth was a railhead, it was easy for performers to ship their horses from the city to the various events on the circuit. Many later recalled that the train rides were the most fun of all. The girls played penny ante card games, never betting more than a quarter.

Fort Worth was home to two well-known cowgirls, Tad Lucas and Velda Tindall Smith. Tad Lucas was probably the best trick rider rodeo ever produced, an international star. Velda Smith was Lucas' neighbor. Smith always trailed slightly behind her good friend and never seemed to mind.

Tad Lucas was born Barbara Barnes in 1902 on a ranch outside Cody, Nebraska, the youngest of twenty-four children. Her family called her "Tad." She always had brothers and sisters to play with—and their games usually involved horses. Late in her life, Lucas said she could not remember a time when she did not ride. Like most ranch children, she rode bareback, which helped her develop a sense of balance and tim-

ing. She was put to work at an early age—roping, helping with branding, rounding up cattle, and all the chores that go with ranching.

Lucas came to rodeo the way the event started—by riding wild cows and outlaw stock brought to town by ranchers on Saturdays. They would "ear down" the stock (hold them by the ears) until the rider was mounted and then let go. If a rider's performance was good, the hat was passed to raise prize money, though Lucas recalled the money usually was given to the Red Cross. When she was fifteen or sixteen, she exercised horses for a neighbor, and he took her to the fair in Cody as his jockey. She saw there was a $25 prize for girls in the steer riding competition and tried her hand at it, even though she had never ridden a steer before. She won.

In the early 1920s Lucas moved to El Paso to be with a sister and then ended up in Fort Worth. She joined Colonel Frank Hatley's Wild West Show, where she learned to trick ride. In 1923, with that show, she rode a Brahma (she pronounced it Bray-mer) steer in Madison Square Garden, the only woman to ride a Brahma in that setting. She also tried riding saddle broncs. She was good at it, because she had been riding rough stock all her life.

In 1924 she was part of a troupe that went to England for an exhibition. A month before they sailed, Tad married bronc rider Buck Lucas. The England trip was their honeymoon. When the newlyweds returned from England, they headquartered in Fort Worth between seasons and bought a home on Roberts Cut-Off Road in the northwest part of the city. It would be their home the rest of their lives.

Lucas' star was on the rise. She won the trick riding championship in 1925 and for the following six years. That same year, she was the all-around champion in Chicago. At New York's Madison Square Garden, she was all-around champion and trick riding champion for eight years, setting a new record. Because she won three years in a row—1928 to 1930—she was given permanent possession of the Metro-Goldwyn-Mayer Trophy, worth some $10,000. Lucas even won honors in Australia.

Lucas' daughter, Mitzi (now Mitzi Lucas Riley) was born in 1930, when Lucas was at the height of her fame. She rode in the grand entry parades when she was still an infant; at two, she was given her own pony; at five, she was doing some tricks. Rodeo was in the family blood. Mitzi Riley went on to earn fame as a cowgirl in her own right.

Lucas had her share of wrecks. Once a horse bucked her off over his head, and she ended up sitting on the ground. He was still kicking and a hoof hit her between the eyes. Lucas figured that if her head had not already been going back, he would have sliced it off. As it was, the blow gave her two black eyes. Another time in New York her horse rode right into the wall at the end of the arena—she thought later maybe he had never been in a building and did not recognize walls. The impact broke his neck, and he fell over dead—on top of Lucas. The Humane Society insisted on shooting the horse, which made Lucas furious—he was already dead, and the unnecessary shooting got blood all over one of her best outfits.

That blood was a real blow to Lucas, because she loved the fancy clothes the cowgirls wore. No matter what they were doing, cowgirls put on their best finery. When she broke her arm, Lucas learned to make her own clothes so that they would fit over her cast. She practiced on cheap materials, but, for the arena, she and other competitive cowgirls wore fancy materials purchased in New York.

Another horse fell on her in a race in Deadwood, South Dakota. They were riding on a dangerous shale track, which she called as hard as riding on cement. The horse tried to make a turn, broke its leg, and turned over twice, landing on top of Lucas. The stunned horse lay still, but she knew if he started scrambling, she would be hurt. Cowboys pulled him off her and then had to shoot him.

Her worst wreck was at the 1933 World's Fair. Lucas was known for doing tricks that other cowgirls would not dare attempt, and one of them was going under the horse's belly. But at the fair in Chicago, she slipped and was caught in the horse's hooves, unable to free herself for several seconds. She broke her arm so severely that doctors told her she would lose it. Lucas refused amputation, saying she would rather die; then they told her she would never ride again. Within a year, Lucas proved them wrong, riding with her left arm in a heavy cast, which did limit the tricks she could do. She wore that cast for three years and had seven operations. All this resulted in her left arm's being shorter than her right. For the rest of her life she had limited motion in her left arm and hand.

Lucas never competed in trick riding after she broke her arm. She could do many exhibition tricks with one arm, but she was not ready for competition. She retired from rodeo in 1958. Her trick-riding horse was getting old, and she did not want to break in another. The era of trick riding had passed, so she worked one last rodeo in Huntsville and called it quits.

Tad Lucas. *Courtesy of The National Cowgirl Museum and Hall of Fame.*

Velda Tindall Smith. *Courtesy of The National Cowgirl Museum and Hall of Fame.*

Always one step behind Lucas was her next-door neighbor, Velda Tindall Smith. The cowgirl legend was well established when Smith rode into the arena. As a young child, she lived in Longview, in East Texas, where her father was the yardmaster for the Texas & Pacific Railway. The only cowgirls she saw were at the movie theater on Saturdays. Because she was a sickly, inactive child, she was given a gentle old horse so that she could get some exercise. That gentle old horse

would gallop her right into the rodeo arena.

In 1923, Smith saw Ruth Roach and Florence Hughes Randolph ride in Dallas, and she decided competitive riding was her great ambition. She hired a man named Curly Griffith to teach her to ride. By 1924, she was ready for her debut, though she later admitted that she was so scared she fell off two out of three times. She was twelve years old.

From 1925 to 1927 she rode for the Miller 101 Ranch Real Wild West Show, an extravaganza produced out of an Oklahoma ranch. The Miller 101 toured the country in the teens and 1920s, featuring such attractions as Geronimo; Bill Pickett, the black cowboy who in bulldogging events tamed wild steers by biting their upper lips; and Lucille Mulhall, argued by some to be the first famous cowgirl and certainly the first cowgirl to come to fame as a roper. With this troupe, Smith competed in relay races, steer riding, bronc riding, and trick riding.

Smith married a rodeo cowboy, Louis Tindall. When he was diagnosed as a hemophiliac, Tindall had to give up rodeoing. Smith later divorced Tindall and remarried. She continued to rodeo.

She once recalled watching another cowgirl fatally injured because she rode with hobbled stirrups (stirrups tied together under the horse's belly). When she was thrown the cowgirl could not get free of the stirrups, could not grab onto the mane or the saddle horn, and was flung to the ground. The cowgirl died eight days later. It did not stop Smith from competing. The practice of hobbling the stirrups for cowgirls was greatly debated in those days. Some thought it made for a safer ride, but, as Smith saw, it could make for a more dangerous one too.

Velda Tindall Smith. *Courtesy of The National Cowgirl Museum and Hall of Fame.*

Smith and Lucas lived next door to each other on Roberts Cut-Off Road. They were rodeo contestants, wives, mothers, and good friends. Smith's daughter, Garlene Parris, recalled that her mother never was bothered by being beaten by Lucas and said she could not have lost to a better person. The two had an arena between their houses, and they used to run foot relay races, wearing rubber suits, to get themselves in shape and lose weight.

Both women were known for never saying anything bad about others and always being generous, honest, and helpful to newcomers. The "star mentality" had not yet hit. But they rode in an era when women rodeo stars were wined and dined wherever they went, featured in magazines, and treated like celebrities. That era came to an end in the early 1940s. In 1939 the Cowboys Turtles Association (perhaps a play on their slowness to organize) went on strike in Fort Worth at the Fat Stock Show to protest that rodeo's dropping the cowgirl's bronc riding event. In 1941, trick riding went on a contract basis rather than competitive.

But there was still barrel racing. Women could enter that competition without an entry fee (most men refused to ride the barrels, claiming it was too dangerous), and Smith began to barrel race in her forties. She helped found the Texas Barrel Racing Association and, in 1958, as a grandmother aged fifty-four, she won the Dallas State Fair championship. She was president of the Texas Barrel Racing Association for five years.

In her career Smith consistently placed high in trick riding, flat races, and relay races. Garlene Parris recalls that as her mother grew older she owned great championship horses that were not being ridden. Once she sold the horses and then bought them back at a higher price, because she could not bear to get rid of them. She kept them until they died—or she did. Several horses are buried on ranch property in Kennedale, where there is now a church. Parris wonders if the congregation knows they are singing "Amazing Grace" over the graves of horses.

The place of Fort Worth in the cowgirl legend of America's West is today solidified by the presence of the magnificent and fascinating National Cowgirl Museum and Hall of Fame.

The museum pays tribute to cowgirls from all over the West, but it is no coincidence that, after being founded in Hereford, Texas, the institution found its permanent home in Fort Worth.

The rodeo arena was not a place most people expected to see women. Neither was the arena of the petroleum industry. Many oil wells were named after women, and the Santa Rita was named after the saint of the impossible by two Catholic women who had invested in it. The Permian Basin Museum contains the portraits of many Fort Worth men, but it overlooks two women from the city who were pioneers in that business. The earliest was Edna Coverdale Hart, who was born in 1889 near Stark, Kansas. The family moved to Coffeyville where her father was mayor for many years. She began to hone her skills in Kansas while still in high school. She went to work selling subscriptions to the Coffeyville newspaper and at the age of eighteen won a Maxwell automobile for selling the most subscriptions.

The young Edna Coverdale studied piano and seriously prepared for a concert career. At sixteen, she played in a theater pit orchestra for operas and legitimate road shows. But after winning the Maxwell, she married oilman Ralph F. Hart and moved to Brownwood, Texas. Her husband taught her the business, and the couple became known as pioneers in the oil discoveries in Brown County, near the geographic center of Texas. Oil was discovered there in the late 1800s, but commercial development did not come until 1917. In 1926, an oil boom led to the development of 600 wells. The boom, unfortunately, ended with the 1929 crash of the stock market and the Great Depression.

Edna Hart never forgot her musical talent. In Brownwood, she organized a dance orchestra, "Ten of Hearts," which included her son, Ralph, on the drums.

In the 1920s, Hart became the first woman to own and operate a public utility in the United States. She bought the gas utility company in Bangs, Texas, with money borrowed from her father. As the owner, she was known for supervising everything from the laying of lines to the reading of meters. She eventually sold her company to Lone Star Gas.

During the Depression, she and her son moved to Fort Worth. Her husband took a job as a driller in oil fields in Kansas and apparently the couple divorced somewhere along the way, for he does not figure in her biography in later years. In Fort Worth, Hart sold cars—she had acquired a franchise to sell Austin cars—and insurance, but she was always in touch with the oil business. Eventually she began acquiring state and federal leases in New Mexico, and she and her son formed Hart and Hart, a company that bought producing oil wells. She was known for being able to charm anyone into giving or selling a lease. She and her son were pioneers in developing the drilling technique of water flooding, whereby water is injected into a reservoir to push additional oil out of the rock and into the well bores of a producing hole.

Hart also earned a reputation as a philanthropist, giving many generous gifts to Cook Children's Hospital. Her son says that over the years the family has probably given a million dollars to Cook. And throughout her life she never gave up her interest in music. Nor did she abandon her interest in new ideas. Shortly before she died in 1968, at the age of seventy-nine, she fin-

ished a book, *Rebirth of a Nation,* about free enterprise and humanity's spiritual regeneration.

A memorial written when Hart died said, in part, "She never wasted a minute of her life, and she also lived much of it for others."

Fort Worth can boast another female pioneer in the petroleum industry. Jane Elizabeth Dean Travis was the first woman to receive a degree in petroleum engineering from the University of Texas at Austin. Born into an oil family in 1937, she absorbed the industry all her life. Her father and uncle, Paul and David Dean, were independent oil producers who bought leases in East Texas. Their record included about twenty wildcat discoveries and only a few dry holes. Their company, Great Expectations, which was later sold to Pan American in 1964, had the first planned water flood project in Texas.

Elizabeth Dean did all the things that privileged girls in West Fort Worth do. She was a Steeplechase debutante and was honored at the Assembly presentation ball. She was a member of the Junior League and an officer of the Barnaby Club. But she also vigorously pursued a career with Great Expectations and was known for reservoir engineering work, especially in the Farrell Lake Field (near Lake O' the Pines, Texas). She was an active member of the Fort Worth Petroleum Engineers Society and the Fort Worth Geological Society.

Elizabeth Dean married lawyer Robert S. Travis. She died in 1972 at an early age. According to those who knew her professionally, the Fort Worth oil profession lost one of its most astute and charming petroleum engineers.

Lesbia Wood Roberts once described herself as a "Jack of all trades and master of none." In

Lesbia Roberts.
Courtesy Thompson's Harveson and Cole, Inc.

foods, a division of Waples-Platter Co., and spent long hours "haunting the Carnegie Library's art exhibits."

In college, as a practical matter, she got a teacher's certificate, although her major was business. She taught for several years, making friends of her students, but she saw no future in teaching. She became a secretary and accountant to John E. Farrell, an independent oilman. Lesbia Wood had found her niche, and the rest of her professional life revolved around oil and gas. She eventually became an independent consultant, tracing oil and gas titles and setting up oil and gas accounting records for individuals.

In 1993, she co-authored with Jack Tunstill *Oil Legends of Fort Worth,* a book published by the Petroleum Club. The profits—about $75,000—went to Cook Children's Medical Center to help abused children.

Roberts was actively interested in the preservation of Texas history and genealogy, and she published several books and papers on the subject. She received the 1994 Service Award of TCU and the 1995 Texas Historical Preservation Award. Like Elizabeth Dean, Lesbia Roberts was also active in a variety of organizations in Fort Worth—the Tarrant County Horse Foundation, the North Fort Worth Historical Society, TCU, TWU, local, state, and national historical organizations, the Fort Worth Woman's Club, and local social groups.

In the 1950s, she married William Edward Roberts Jr. who survived her at the time of her death in 2007.

Of her career in the Fort Worth oil and gas industry, insurance executive Don Woodard Sr. said, "She walked with the kings of oil in Fort Worth."

truth, she was a teacher, executive secretary, oil and gas accountant, title analyst, genealogist, historical researcher, and, in her own words, "some sort of artist." Probably she mastered all those callings, but she was certainly an outstanding figure in the oil and gas business in Fort Worth.

Born around 1912, she grew up in Fort Worth, the child of a single mother who, during the depression, could not afford the train fare to let her daughter accept any of several prestigious scholarships offered her, including one to Stanford. Roberts stayed in Fort Worth, attended TCU, and became a lifelong supporter of her alma mater. Her interest in art came out early—as a teen, she designed a logo for White Swan

Ranch wives who moved to Fort Worth stayed within the role generally expected of women. They were first and foremost wives and mothers. But women who entered the rodeo arena or the oil fields were stepping into men's worlds. So were women outlaws, but somewhat surprisingly Fort Worth can claim no famous female outlaws in its colorful history. The dance hall girls and ladies of the night in Hell's Half Acre broke the law, but they cannot be called outlaws. Some believe that Etta Place, girl-friend and robbery partner to the Sundance Kid, worked for a madam in Fort Worth—there is even a bed-and-breakfast called Etta's Place—but the truth is, she was in San Antonio. That is where Harry Longabaugh, the Sundance Kid, met her. And though they visited Fort Worth several times, Fort Worth cannot claim to have had any influence, good or bad, on Etta.

A few sources claim that Bonnie Parker, of the infamous Bonnie and Clyde team, was from Fort Worth. Actually, she was born in Rowena and moved with her family to West Dallas at a fairly young age. With Clyde Barrow, she made one confirmed visit to Fort Worth in 1932. The couple stayed in what was probably then called the Thannisch Block at the corner of North Main and Exchange Avenue. Today it is the Stockyards Hotel, and Room 305 is the Bonnie and Clyde Room. Legend is that they chose that corner room so they could keep a lookout on what was happening on the street below. Some sources say they holed up there between jobs, but only the one visit is documented.

So, for better or worse, Fort Worth does not have any women outlaws. But its bold women were vital contributors to the city's cowgirl cul-

ture and petroleum industry philanthropy. Their spirit and vision helped make Fort Worth unique.

BIBLIOGRAPHIC ESSAY

In the late 1980s I spent a few days at Electra Waggoner Biggs' home on the Three D Ranch, studying scrapbooks. For weeks after that, whenever the Waggoner ranch plane came to Fort Worth, it brought me a new scrapbook and carried away the one I had read. They were huge books, probably 11" x 17", and the articles in them were firmly pasted to the pages, in no particular order and often without the masthead or whatever would date them. But they provided a wealth of information. My efforts to write a biography of Mrs. Biggs came to naught, but I had the basic background information, much of which I used in *Thistle Hill: The History and the House* (Fort Worth: TCU Press, 1988). For this essay, I also consulted Roze Porter's *Thistle Hill: The Cattle Baron's Legacy* (Fort Worth: Branch-Smith, 1980), which goes into much more tangential background information than my slim book.

My information on Tad Lucas and Velda Tindall Smith came primarily from *The Cowgirls* by Joyce Gibson Roach (Houston: Cordovan Press, 1977, and Denton: University of North Texas Press, 1990) and Teresa Jordan's *The Cowgirls: Women of the American West, An Oral History* (New York: Anchor Books, 1984). I was also fortunate enough to speak on the phone with Garlene Parris, Velda Smith's daughter, who willingly and proudly talked about her mother and read the text in advance for me.

For information on wildcatters, I consulted *Oil Legends of Fort Worth* (Fort Worth: The Fort Worth Petroleum Club, 1993), produced by the Historical Committee of the Fort Worth Petroleum Club. My understanding is that Lesbia Roberts deserves large credit for that volume. I am indebted to Guy Thompson of Thompson's Harveson and Cole, Inc. and Mary Rogers of the *Fort Worth Star-Telegram* for information about Lesbia Roberts. I knew and much admired and was charmed by Mrs. Roberts but did not realize the wide range of her interests, even outside her professional field.

I also found Oliver Knight's *Fort Worth: Outpost on the Trinity* (Norman: University of Oklahoma Press, 1953; Fort Worth: TCU Press, 1990) helpful.

Chapter 5

THE MODERN WOMAN

by Ruth Karbach

AY SWAYNE, PERFECTLY groomed in her pink cashmere gown, must have looked around her Victorian parlor with her beautiful rosewood piano with some satisfaction before her guests arrived for a Valentine's Day tea, but dissatisfaction was the reason behind her invitation to the matrons of a bustling Fort Worth of 1889. Many of her friends had been educated in southern academies, just as she had been when she traveled by stagecoach from Fort Worth, east to the railhead, and then on to Kentucky. What was considered proper for the ideal pious, pure, and submissive Victorian woman had circumscribed their educations. In the South, women were not afforded the advantages of a university education out of fear they would abandon their traditional role of wife and mother. Women did not have access to club libraries as did men and struggled to educate themselves. There were no public libraries in Texas.

But progressive ideas about education of the modern woman had reached Fort Worth from

May Swayne led the Fort Worth Federation of Women's Clubs to political power without the leverage of the ballot box. *Courtesy,* Fort Worth Star-Telegram *Collection,*
The University of Texas at Arlington.

New York, Boston, and Chicago. May Swayne proposed to form Fort Worth's first literary club for women—the Woman's Wednesday Club—and establish a club library and follow a course of study. In the club's 1889 charter, the members wrote: "the married ladies of Fort Worth . . . have resolved to form a society for the purpose of mutual improvement, and the promotion of friendship, and for the purpose of any domestic problems that may agitate the brain of the modern woman, That [sic] prodigy who is wife, mother, nurse, dressmaker and cook all combined."

The founder and first president of the Woman's Wednesday Club, May Hendricks Swayne had arrived in 1865 in Fort Worth with her parents, Eliza Anne and Harrison George Hendricks, and her four brothers and three sisters. Her father joined John Peter Smith in his law practice and invested in real estate. Her childhood was spent on the family farm in North Fort Worth where the meatpacking houses were later located. May's youth was marred by the deaths of a brother and sister on the same day, and her father's later death. At eighteen, she married John Felix Swayne, Fort Worth's first city secretary.

The thirteen charter members of the Woman's Wednesday Club were wives of prominent, successful men. Emmie Harper Paddock was the wife of B. B. Paddock, founder of the *Daily Democrat* and director of the Fort Worth and Rio Grande Railway. Hattie M. Pendery was married to grocer D. W. C. Pendery, who founded the Mexican Chile Supply Company. Bertha Wadel Samuels and Jacob Samuels were Jewish pioneers, and he was in the dry goods business. The sophisticated Mary J. Hamilton Hoxie, vice

president of the new organization, came to Fort Worth with her husband who had made a fortune in the Chicago packinghouse industry and was doing the same in Fort Worth. John R. Hoxie also was president of the Farmers and Merchants Bank and owner of the 7,000-acre San Gabriel Ranch. Josephine "Josie" Latham Swayne was married to May Swayne's brother-in-law, James W. Swayne, who became a state senator and district judge and was a partner of Governor James Stephen Hogg in the Spindletop oil syndicate. Soon the elite club had its full complement of thirty members, which included three other relatives of May Swayne: her sisters Octavia Bennett, wife of A. L. Bennett who founded Acme Brick; Sallie Huffman, whose husband Walter A. Huffman made a million in real estate; and her sister-in-law, Mary L. Hendricks.

Around this time, Swayne was influenced by Mary Baker Eddy of Boston and became a practicing Christian Scientist. The WWC's motto reflected her belief in the power of spiritual thought: "Look up and not down; Look in and not out; Look forward and not backward. And Lend a helping hand." On November 27, 1889, the new literary club associated with the Society to Encourage Studies at Home, founded in Boston by Anna Eliot Ticknor. The coursework was designed and overseen by university-educated women committed to teaching their sisters across the country via correspondence work. The Fort Worth matrons enthusiastically pursued the systematic study of great English prose writers and poets as prescribed by the Boston teachers. They were required to answer examination questions, write essays, and thoroughly study the language and construction of selected works.

The club's first civic project provided them with an unusual weekly meeting room in the fantastic Texas Spring Palace. This grand Moorish-Oriental architectural wonder, decorated with Texas agricultural products, attracted thousands of visitors to Fort Worth in 1889 and 1890. E. D. Allen wrote in his *Descriptive Story of the Texas Spring Palace at Fort Worth, Texas,* that the WWC library room, unlike other exhibits in the building, was for "the use and comfort of visitors" and was stocked daily with Texas newspapers, magazines, and literature. The club even provided a Texas-born maid to serve guests. Handmade and manufactured furniture, all of Texas origin, was covered by leather trimmed with nut tassels, and rugs of native bear, timber wolf, coyote, and imported Angora goat were spread underfoot. The room's decorations were singularly stunning in shades of deep maroon to salmon pink with gilt and bronze touches and ornamentation using rice, pine cone petals, moss drapery, palm leaves, and Corpus Christi sea shells. The ladies' creative work was destroyed the next year in the tragic conflagration on the night of the closing grand ball attended by 7,000 people. Miraculously, there was only one death though many heroic rescuers were injured. Emmie Paddock, whose husband had spearheaded the building of the edifice to promote the city, served as treasurer of the Woman's Spring Palace Society and was a member of four committees: finance, correspondence, flowers and grains, and art exhibit. Virginia Scott Scheuber, who had rushed to join the WWC, was the secretary of the society and decoration chairman of the much-admired artistic white-and-gold room in the palace. This was Scheuber's first outing from her role as wife and mother, and she thrived in the club environment. Virginia "Jennie" Scott was born on January 6, 1860, near Plaquemine, a Louisiana plantation and steamboat town located on the Mississippi River. French influence was predominant in Iberville Parish since it was settled by early Acadian exiles. Her father, Maurice Scott, a native of France, had married Louisa Imlar Smith, a German widow with three daughters and three sons. As the youngest of seven children and the only child born to the union of her parents, Jennie Scott with her intense blue eyes and beautiful wavy brown hair must have been the darling of the family. The family moved to New Orleans and owned a coffee warehouse. Scott attended school in New Orleans and also was educated by private tutors. When Jennie Scott was thirteen, she moved to Fort Worth with her parents, who ran the Metropolitan Hotel. During her teens Scott was a member of the Fort Worth Music and Literary Society, Fort Worth's first literary circle. That coeducational group was short lived and was succeeded by the El Paso Literary and Music Society, also coeducational, which met in the drawing room of the El Paso Hotel. Scott was the secretary of the new literary society and probably participated in that group's production of the play *The Lady of Lyons.* When her father died in a booming gold town in Colorado, her mother converted the hotel into a boardinghouse. At twenty-one, Virginia Scott married Charles Scheuber, a thirty-nine-year-old Civil War veteran originally from Wurtenberg, Germany, who had a successful wholesale liquor and cigar business. Louisa Scott moved in with her daughter and son-in-law. The Scheuber's only child, Francis "Frank" Ball, was born in the second year of their marriage.

In her early thirties Jennie Scheuber ascended

into a leadership role in women's organizations reflecting her interest in literature, art, and charitable concerns. She was a director for several women in the WWC's literary study program. As vice president of Associated Charities, she delivered groceries and other items to families in need. The charity's president, Ida V. Jarvis, described "how tirelessly she [Scheuber] rode everywhere, with the black horse and phaeton, from morning till night on her errands of mercy." Scheuber's most significant civic contribution was the founding of the Fort Worth Library Association. On April 2, 1892, twenty women met at the Scheubers' large residence on Taylor Street to form the Fort Worth Library Association. Scheuber was elected a vice president. Ten of the organizers were WWC members, and all the officers were members of the literary club. Within three weeks, the all-female library association was chartered and had expanded to be more representative of Fort Worth women and other organizations. The association's charter directed its objectives: to locate a lot and erect a building for a public library and art gallery. The women raised library funds with teas, dances, cakewalks, and dinners. Close friends Ida L. Turner and Jennie Scheuber even solicited donations on a downtown street while perched on a piano box wagon. The association had raised $1,000 toward their goal when the financial panic of 1893 set their effort back for five years. (See "For the Price of a Good Cigar".)

Mary Peters Young Terrell, a charter member of the library association, had entered the WWC in 1892 after the Terrell children had all reached their teen years. Mary Young attended Marshall Masonic Lodge School for Females. Her father, a medical doctor, had helped charter the school and served as a trustee. Her father died of typhoid fever the year before her graduation, and at age eighteen Young became the main breadwinner for the family. For two decades Mary Young was a career woman who held positions as a schoolteacher and bookkeeper for Texas & Pacific Railway in Marshall. Then this petite, proper woman met jovial Joseph Christopher Terrell, a noted Fort Worth attorney and raconteur, and married him in 1887. Terrell's new wife had many of the characteristics of his first wife—they were both well educated, had been schoolteachers, were devout churchwomen, and even had the same first name.

Mary Y. Terrell inherited five children, ages eight through fifteen, living in an elegant eleven-room home in a country setting just south of the Fort Worth city limits. The Terrell children had had an invalid mother for years. Sue Terrell Hawley recalled in a letter how her new stepmother won her heart with her sensitivity about her feelings for her deceased mother and by taking the burdens of the household off her young shoulders. In middle age, this new wife had to learn to cook, sew, and housekeep, and, as Hawley wrote, "with her great brain and energy" soon excelled at the domestic arts. Given her austere past, Mary Terrell adored her fun-loving stepchildren and was devoted to her husband. The Terrells' home soon became a "shelter and refuge" to many, from lonely teachers to orphaned students.

Equipped with superior administrative skills, Terrell moved easily into the presidency of the WWC in 1895. However, she faced the challenges of dwindling participation and higher expectations of the members. The Boston correspondence school had hired a graduate of Vassar

Hailed as the "Mother of Libraries", Mary Y. Terrell was an organizer of the Texas Library Association and the only woman appointed to the first Texas State Library and Historical Commission in 1909. *Courtesy, The Woman's Collection, Texas Woman's University.*

College to head the rhetoric section, and her revised study program required additional study and written exercises. Terrell opted to require members to answer roll call with a literary quotation and present papers from memory, a practice for which she herself was well known. The office of critic was added with the duty of making an oral report of mispronounced words at the end of each meeting.

Attendance at the WWC meetings did improve with more exciting lectures and the imposition of a fine of $1 for three unexcused meeting absences. One of the high points of the year was the December public presentation of selected passages from *Henry IV* by Hannibal W. Williams of New York City. Under Terrell's leadership, WWC membership became a privilege, and she was successful in keeping the club at full capacity.

On March 27, 1895, a special session of the WWC was called upon the death of Jennie Scheuber's husband from pneumonia. Club members expressed their sympathy to "one who had labored so faithfully to make our Club what it is." Twenty-seven businesses in Fort Worth closed the day of Charles Scheuber's funeral to show their respect, and the Knights of Pythias, United Confederate Veterans, Retail Liquor Dealers, Traveler's Protection Association, Sons of Hermann, and Masons were out in force at the funeral rites.

The thirty-five-year-old Scheuber faced a series of life-altering events during the weeks after her husband's death. Four days after the funeral, in a dramatic move by two national brewing companies, Charles Scheuber and Company was placed in receivership. One week after the funeral, City National Bank, where Charles Scheuber had been the vice president, closed its doors due to insolvency. When it was learned the directors had transferred $104,000 to an out-of-state bank just before the Fort Worth bank's failure, the three largest depositors—the Knights of Pythias, the city of Fort Worth, and Tarrant County—filed lawsuits. In August, Jennie Scheuber relocated to Massachusetts so her son could attend an Ivy League prep school while she worked in the W. B. Clarke Book Shop in Boston. Except for a brief, unsuccessful stint as a bookstore owner in Fort Worth, she lived in the East for the next five years. When Frank entered Harvard University,

Scheuber and her sister opened a boardinghouse on Commonwealth Avenue in Boston. She returned to Fort Worth in 1901.

A second literary study club—the Ninety-three ('93) Club—was founded on November 15, 1893, at the home of Julia Aller, a recent arrival in Fort Worth from Illinois. With "Knowledge is Power" as their motto, the twenty '93 Club charter members were clearly striving to be modern women. Initially the club was devoted to the study of American literature. By the turn of the century, international countries and art appreciation were added to the program. The club established a library of recommended books for each year's programs. Social functions were prohibited at regular meetings to promote serious study.

The '93 Club was an innovation in Fort Worth as it included both single and married women among its members. In fact, the charter members were evenly divided into those two categories. In general, '93 Club members were from a younger generation, born after the Civil War. Membership also depended less on kinship and social position than in the other literary club. For example, Emma Cobb was a bookkeeper, and other members' fathers or spouses were salesmen and carpenters. Despite this more democratic attitude, just two blackball votes could exclude an applicant. Several of the charter members were among the wave of northern and midwestern migrants attracted to the "Queen City of the Prairies" in the 1880s and early 1890s by the numerous railroads that came through Fort Worth. Bernice Juanita Hovey, a graduate of the College of Sisters of Bethany in Topeka, Kansas, was the daughter of Smith B. Hovey, credited with bringing the Rock Island line to Fort Worth.

When Hovey married surgeon W. A. Duringer in 1897, club members were her wedding attendants. Ethel Teachout's father was a superintendent of railway mail service, and the family had moved to Fort Worth five years earlier from Michigan. Newton Hance Lassiter, a railroad attorney, was married to club member Elizabeth "Bettie" Davis Lassiter and was a city alderman in the early 1890s. Eva Pennington, born in Iowa, was the daughter of a Canadian who was a railroad livestock agent. One of the few Texas natives in the club, Annie Lane, was an 1888 graduate of Baylor Female College.

The '93 club was set up for frequent rotation of officers, and all members were required to serve on at least one committee. Corresponding secretary Nelly H. Francis explained in a Texas Clubdom column in the *Dallas Morning News*, "The timidity of the members is largely overcome by the law that places them under obligations to accept any office to which they may be called." Anna Shelton, an early '93 Club member and president, developed into the best-known clubwoman in Fort Worth. Anna "Annie" Shelton, the youngest child of Martha Bronaugh and Dr. John Foster Shelton Jr., was born August 20, 1861, at the family homestead north of the city. On the day of her birth, the first Tarrant County Confederate Company marched off to join the Civil War. Her father enlisted with a Texas Cavalry unit as a surgeon and was absent from the household for six years. During the war, 5,000 inhabitants of Tarrant County fled, leaving a population of 1,000. Times were hard, and women such as Martha Shelton had to scratch out an existence for their children and manage business and home affairs. At the end of the Civil War, the family moved into the city so the

When naysayers doubted her plans, Anna Shelton, president of the Woman's Club of Fort Worth from 1923-1939, impatiently responded, "No one has the right to tell me what I cannot do." Shelton accomplished the "impossible" by raising money to purchase public art, managing the failing Fort Worth Symphony, and rescuing The Little Theater. Portrait by Murray Bewley.
Courtesy, The Woman's Club of Fort Worth.

four Shelton children could attend school, and Dr. Shelton opened a pharmaceutical supply company. When Anna Shelton was thirteen, her mother died. One year later, her sister Lizzie Belle married attorney W. S. Pendleton, and her father sent Annie, his youngest child, to her mother's alma mater, Bethel Women's College in Hopkinsville, Kentucky. James B. Shelton joined his father in the drug business until his death in 1888. The eldest son, John M. Shelton, a local cattle dealer, went west to Amarillo and built a Panhandle ranching and banking empire.

After graduation from the girls' academy, Anna Shelton filled the time-honored role of housekeeper and caregiver for a widowed father. However, in 1890 the entire family's life was disrupted by the yellow press. A scandal broke about Shelton's brother-in-law, W. S. Pendleton, who had been elected mayor of Fort Worth. Reporters discovered that Pendleton's New Orleans marriage to Addie Cullen in July was without benefit of a divorce from his legal wife, Shelton's older sister Lizzie. The local and national press avidly pursued the story. Lizzie B. Pendleton was innocently recuperating in Tennessee after the lengthy illness and death of the youngest of her six children by Pendleton when a local reporter contacted her by telegram about her alleged divorce and her husband's new marriage. Men, who had at first snickered when they heard their new mayor had wed a young, pretty woman, were incensed when they read he was a bigamist; and the *Dallas Morning News* reported Pendleton's name figured "extensively" in the oaths of the bootblacks and hack drivers. Prominent citizens who had backed the political career of Pendleton, a former county attorney, held a public meeting to demand his resignation

as mayor after only four months in office. On his law partner's advice, Pendleton remained in New York while Addie Cullen, at her sister's Fort Worth home on Thirteenth Street, demurely evaded reporters. Lizzie was immediately forced to file for divorce because, by law, the family property was under her husband's sole control. She was granted what remained of the real property and awarded custody of their four living children. Later Pendleton took court action against a New York lawyer who had hoodwinked him into paying for a fraudulent Chicago divorce without notice to his wife. Apparently Pendleton had been corresponding with this lawyer for months about the possibility of a divorce on grounds of incompatibility. Three years later, W. S. and Addie Pendleton returned to Texas to live in Amarillo. Lizzie B. Pendleton called herself a widow.

After her father's death in December 1891, Shelton lived with her sister and her beloved nieces and nephews for the next seven years. Having witnessed her sister's financial vulnerability in the Pendleton scandal, Shelton appeared determined to maintain her financial independence. Now in her thirties, she was no longer content to follow a traditional role and fashioned herself into the civic-minded, informed, "new woman." Recognizing that she, as a single woman, had the advantage of sole ownership and control of her property, she mastered real estate law and banking practices and started buying and selling real estate for profit in the late 1890s.

In 1895, she joined the '93 Club and served in five executive board positions in the next seven years including the presidency. As club secretary, Shelton wrote about the founding of the club: "Its aim the banding of women together for purposes of self culture which was taking firm hold in Texas and that its progressive women to be abreast of the times were ready and eager to enlist." Shelton also likened the five-year-old club's history to an infant learning to walk one stage at a time, an apt analogy in her own life. The study of English literature by the club may have stimulated Anna Shelton to accept a position as a tutor of English at Fort Worth University, a coeducational school. When she decided a teaching career was not her life's mission, she left for New York City in August 1902 and then took a steamer to Paris to study French and Spanish literature and language for the next six months.

Anna Shelton's worth was soon recognized in the clubwoman world. She was a charter member of the Fort Worth Federation of Women's Clubs. When elected the delegate from the '93 Club to the first annual meeting of the Texas Federation of Women's Clubs, she requested the indulgence of her fellow club members because of her excited state of mind. The members supported her by voting $6 of club money to defray her expenses as a delegate. With her business acumen, Shelton quickly rose in the ranks of Texas clubwomen.

The formation of the local and state federations of women's clubs had its roots in 1892 when the Woman's Wednesday Club had joined the national General Federation of Women's Clubs. In 1895 the WWC was chosen by the general federation to campaign in Texas to form a state federation. Although the WWC invitations by letter to women's literary clubs across the state produced a lukewarm response, the seed was planted. The Texas Federation of Women's Literary Clubs was

eventually organized at an 1897 conference in Waco with twenty-one charter clubs. Sallie W. Harrison, a delegate for WWC of Fort Worth, took minutes at this historic meeting. Caroline E. Adams, also a delegate from the WWC, presented a paper on the "Literary Advantages of State Federation." Virginia C. Mitchell, a jeweler's wife, represented the '93 Club but arrived late because she and a friend had gone buggy riding and missed the train to Waco. Mary Y. Terrell of Fort Worth was elected first vice president of the fledging federation. From the start, Terrell was instrumental in the state federation's adoption of public libraries as their main work. Terrell's pioneering work on behalf of public libraries earned her the title of "Mother of Libraries" among clubwomen and librarians. Because of her vision more than 200 public libraries in Texas have been founded by clubwomen.

Terrell moved into the presidency of the Texas federation in 1899 and affiliated with the General Federation of Women's Clubs, which subsequently broadened the scope of the organization and saluted its national allegiance by changing the organizational name to the Texas Federation of Women's Clubs. Anna Shelton was elected the state corresponding secretary for two consecutive terms. Shelton's communication skills were invaluable as Terrell organized the federation's proposed plan of work into departments with committees of clubwomen from across the state. Shelton also sent out Terrell's circular letters to federation clubs advising members of legislation needing their influence with male voters. "Thus was a created a great, silent force for the enactment and enforcement of good laws," Terrell wrote in 1903 in the *Dallas Morning News*.

Following formation of the state federation, selected representatives from four Fort Worth women's clubs, representing 150 women, began meeting every two months for discussion and presentation of a program. In December of 1897, for example, the WWC served as the host organization and publicized a presentation by Mrs. Charlie A. Harrison of her essay on Shakespeare's play *Macbeth,* which had received praise from a Harvard professor and was presented at a Boston meeting of the Society to Encourage Studies at Home. The '93 Club and WWC were joined by two recently formed clubs in this local federation: the Monday Book Club and the Derthick Club. In 1896 the Monday Book Club was established as a junior club of the WWC mainly for their members' daughters; among the charter members was Anne Burnett. That same year the Derthick Club was founded with W. M. Derthick's tome, *A Manual of Music, Its History, Biography and Literature,* with chronological charts and analysis of musical works as its study and performance guide. The Derthick Club of Fort Worth was renamed the Euterpean Club a few years later.

The local federation of clubwomen and the library association were vitally linked in their main work, the establishment of a public library. The 1898 officers in the newly revitalized library association were WWC members and included May Swayne, Mary Hoxie, Jennie Scheuber, Emmie Paddock, Mary Y. Fox Smith, and Smith's cousin, Mary Y. Terrell. Strong women board members such as physician and political activist Ellen Lawson Dabbs; philanthropist and state temperance leader Ida Van Zandt Jarvis; Laura J. Clayton, a state officer in the Daughters of the Confederacy; and postmaster Ida Loving Turner

augmented the clout of the women from the "ultra" club, a moniker given the WWC by Elizabeth Dean, society editor of the *Fort Worth Gazette,* because these women were known as the most exclusive and polished of the city's clubwomen. Because the literary clubs had had to move their clubrooms every year or two, their members were enthusiastic about the prospect of meeting chambers in a cultural institution and committed to pay rent to assist the library in its early years.

The first act of the newly revitalized library association was to expand the membership to increase political support and raise funds. In a press release, the corresponding secretary Mary C. S. Jordan wrote, "We are not strictly 'new women' for we have amended our by-laws so as to admit men into the association; also, we are quite willing to share with them the glory of getting a public library for Fort Worth." Membership was $1.

On November 10, 1898, the Fort Worth Federation of Women's Clubs announced its official organization and urged all clubs interested in women's work to join the four pioneering clubs. The logical choice for the president of the newly chartered organization was Mary Y. Terrell, advocate for Texas public libraries and then vice president of the state federation. Each club was represented by at least one officer. *Dallas Morning News* columnist Pauline Periwinkle, a *nom de plume* for Sara Isadore Sutherland Callaway, lauded the Fort Worth clubwomen for their success toward establishment of a public library, citing their lot, donated building stones and a "nest-egg" in excess of $1,200. She concluded, "Fort Worth club women will pursue to success anything they undertake . . . [there is] an esprit de corps between the clubs of Fort Worth."

When Andrew Carnegie's generous gift in response to a letter of appeal from local club-woman Adelphine Keeler was announced, Mayor Paddock issued a proclamation for a cele-bration at city hall, urging citizens to bring "horns, drums, bells, musical instruments and everything that will make a noise." Jennie Scheuber, the woman whose dream had started the Fort Worth library movement, was named director of the library by the association board. (See "Cracking the Glass Ceiling.") In prepara-tion for her new career, Scheuber enrolled in the summer library program at Amherst College fol-lowed by an internship in the public library of Medford, a suburb of Boston. The clubwomen of Fort Worth did more than make reception arrangements for the 1901 opening of the Carnegie Library—they tackled book shelving and other chores. In a letter written September 12, 1901, to Anna J. Hardwicke Pennybaker, heir apparent to the presidency of the TFWC, the usually indefatigable Mary Y. Terrell conceded that the "heavy work in getting our library in shape [has] dimmed my resources."

During the building of the library, the city federation of women's clubs had doubled its membership by adding the Kindergarten Association, the Symposium Club, the New Century Club, and the Current Literature Club. Formed in 1896, the Kindergarten Association had established a free kindergarten in the Ninth Ward, where the poorest residents dwelled. One year later the Symposium Club, now called the Penelope Club, was founded to study "literature, science, art and vital interests of the day." The New Century Club was described in their year-book as a literary study club for "lady teachers"

in Fort Worth schools but, possibly stimulated by the school board's decision in 1900 not to hire any married female teachers, the club soon expanded to admit married and single women outside the teaching profession. A more progres-sive group—the Current Literature Club—was devoted to reviewing and discussing contempo-rary magazine articles, prose and poetry, and essays on political and philosophical subjects.

Elizabeth Dean, in her Fort Worth publica-tion *The Social Scimitar*, with a circulation of 3,000, listed the city federation's objectives in 1900 as: (1) "the introduction of free kinder-garten system into the public schools"; (2) "cleaning up of the streets"; and (3) a "special effort to entertain . . . convention visitors." As Jennie H. Berney entered her second term as the federation president in November 1900, the group entertained women visiting the National Feeders and Breeders Show with Japanese tea-rooms and city drives in the carriages of the most affluent citizens. However, the appeal on November 16 from Clara Barton, president of the American Red Cross, for relief of the victims of the Galveston hurricane put aside all thoughts of social delights. The women's clubs in Fort Worth made and collected 101 quilts, which were shipped eight days later to the Galveston homeless and destitute.

In 1901 Caroline Eaton Adams was installed as the third city federation president. Adams added standing committees for village improve-ment, education, and philanthropy. The federa-tion took a more active, political stance in the community. A parent-teacher educational con-ference was initiated and sponsored by the city federation. A well-attended meeting at the Hotel Worth resulted in a petition from the eight federated clubs to request $2,400 from the city council for a kindergarten department in the public schools. That request was denied. The city aldermen refused to listen to, much less fund, a plan for purchasing and installing city street signs.

Disappointed and frustrated by their cavalier treatment at city hall, women in the city federation voted for a radical change in their organization in 1902. Reformer Laura B. Kelley Wynne, a FWFWC officer, proposed a "Department Club" as the solution to their lack of political power and limited success in implementing social change. A department club was an umbrella organization with departments geared to civic progress through public education, manual training, and social reform. The potential membership numbers in a department club, which theoretically any civic-minded woman or club could join, appealed to the federation women because ten of their twelve clubs (total membership 250), could not grow because they had intentionally placed a ceiling on the number of members accepted at a given time.

Though Wynne advocated throwing open the doors of the Woman's Department Club to all women, white Fort Worth clubwomen did draw the line racially and in other subtler ways. Despite sending out an appeal to include "country sisters" in Tarrant County, only forty-seven women joined the first month of the WDC's operation. Under the bylaws, an applicant had to be endorsed by three current members, and five negative votes could exclude an applicant from membership. These rules may have been responsible for the less-than-enthusiastic response, especially among less affluent women without society connections. Again any woman was eligi-

Sue Brady, school superintendent, journalist and political activist, presided over the innovative Woman's Department Club. Brady went on to a literary writing career in New York City.
Courtesy, Fort Worth Public Library, Genealogy, History and Archives.

ble for membership but only as an associate without voting privileges. The organizers and former federation members obviously were exercising caution about empowering those not on their social level. The mantle of leadership of the

WDC fell on the capable shoulders of Sue Huffman Brady. A woman of firsts, Brady was in the first graduating class of the first Texas teachers college, the first superintendent of the Fort Worth and Decatur public schools, and the first woman superintendent in the state of Texas. Brady had prestige from her presentation of a paper "The Changing Ideals in Southern Womanhood," at the Woman's Congress at the Columbian Exposition in Chicago, and was an editorial staff member of the *Record,* a Fort Worth newspaper. Supporting the president on the executive board were the revered Mary Y. Terrell and the venerable Ida V. Jarvis. Past president of the federation, Caroline E. Adams; the influential Josephine L. Swayne, the astute Anna Shelton, and the articulate Ellen Lawson Dabbs were all active members. Immediately the Domestic Science Department made arrangements to serve hot lunches at the public schools and established a free cooking school. In June 1903, Brady, Swayne, and Terrell made a presentation to the school board about the need for a domestic science program for tenth- and eleventh-grade girls, and the WDC was allotted $600 in start-up funds. In the fall Elizabeth S. Slaght, a graduate of the prestigious Pratt Institute in New York City, was proudly introduced as the new domestic science teacher hired by the Woman's Department Club. Slaght taught domestic science in the public high school, the Masonic Home, and the Fort Worth Kindergarten College. The gratified school board members, who had enjoyed lunches prepared by girls in the domestic science classes, renewed the program the following year. Laura B. Kelley Wynne took charge of the Department of Philanthropy and Civics and set about meeting the needs of the less fortunate. Committed to the cause, she even worked all the summer of 1903, while others deserted sizzling Fort Worth for cooler climes. The results were a day nursery, a boy's brigade and club with seventy enrollees, and a girls' sewing class with fifty students. Wynne's pet project was the Farmer's Library. Originally set up through the Co-operative Magazine Club that swept the country in the early 1900s, the Farmer's Library was in a pleasantly furnished room in the courthouse and staffed by a volunteer librarian. By the end of 1902 more than 15,000 magazines had been circulated to literature-starved farm families "to encourage a desire for information and cultivate the habit of mutual improvement," Wynne wrote in a press release. Farm families could keep the magazines or pass them along to other rural residents. Free summer concerts in City Park—now the Seventh Street part of Trinity Park—sponsored by the Philanthropy and Civics Department were popular with the populace, though Fort Worth ministers objected to the Sunday events. The city even appropriated $150 to help fund the concerts.

Wynne, whose lawyer husband was an aspirant for the governorship, was well traveled in Texas political circles. She secured a commitment from William Jennings Bryan to give a gratis speech to benefit the Woman's Department Club during his 1904 speaking tour on the Chautauqua circuit. On May 26, the meeting chambers at city hall were filled with an enraptured audience who listened to William Jennings Bryan deliver his popular address, "The Value of an Ideal," in his deep, commanding voice. The club had hit a new high with folks riding the rails from as far as four counties away to hear "The Great Commoner," but surely this event raised the eyebrows of conservative, influential clubwomen who felt political affiliation should be avoided.

While her contemporaries were becoming clubwomen and active in progressive causes, Hallie Bewley was regarded as an old-fashioned wife and mother. In truth, the modest Bewley was an accomplished woman. The first painting of her by her artist son Murray (Percy) Bewley showed her intent upon her writing; and, indeed, this thoughtful, intelligent mother was a writer and had had essays published in the *Louisville Courier-Journal*. An accomplished musician and

the mother of an artist, she was a music and art patron.

Born in 1852 near Bowling Green, Kentucky, Harriet Samuel was the daughter of lawyer and trader Riley Samuel and Mary Davidson. As a young girl, she was so proud of her heritage through her maternal line that she insisted on including their surnames in her own and being addressed as Harriet Ballinger Crittendon Davidson Samuel. Friends jokingly called her "Miss ABCD Samuel." She married Robert C. Howard in 1871, and they had one son. Her second marriage was to handsome Murray Percival Bewley who brought her and her son to Texas

Hallie Bewley often quipped, "It is better to be the mother of an artist than to be the artist." Her son Murray Bewley painted this portrait of her. *Courtesy, The Woman's Club of Fort Worth.*

after the Bewley family's steamboat burned on the Ohio River.

Fort Worth and a feed and seed store gave the Bewleys a new start. By 1882 M. P. Bewley became a miller, and the family moved next door to the buhrstone mill in the vicinity of today's Lancaster and Cherry streets. In a decade, Anchor Mills had converted to steel rollers and added feed to their grain production. The family fortunes rose, and a fine $10,000 residence was built on Burnett Street. During this period, Bewley lost her oldest son and had a stillborn child, but her other three children thrived.

When her nest was empty, Hallie Bewley joined the '93 Club in 1903, but did not throw herself wholeheartedly into club work until her husband's unexpected death in 1906. Then Bewley became a proponent and philanthropist of public art and civic beautification. Twice she served as the '93 Club president. During her first term in 1908–1909, a two-year college course on German history, literature, and art commenced. Members were fined for incorrect exam answers. As her art collection grew and she made frequent visits to art galleries in the United States and Europe, Bewley illustrated her art lectures to the club with original works of art and lantern slides. Through district level and state federation positions, Bewley promoted art education and appreciation across the state. Her many gifts of original artworks to Texas libraries and clubs earned her the title of "Mother of Art" among federation women. She was also known as the wit of the federation because of her gentle but keen sense of humor.

When Anna Shelton returned to the states from France, she spent a period of time in San Antonio visiting with clubwomen there. By December 1903, Lillie Arnold Gracey Dunklin, Evira Merrill, and Shelton had met about organizing a club devoted to the study of history, art, and literature, and named their new club for the Sorosis Club in New York City, one of the earliest women's clubs in the country. The name Sorosis was derived from the Latin word *soror*, which means sisters. Shelton seemed to have been working toward a new vision after her contacts in New York City, Paris, and San Antonio. The charter members were quite a mix of pioneer stock and recent arrivals, career women and older matrons, from Arlington to North Fort Worth. They chose the motto: "No man liveth to himself." The first president, Lillie Dunklin, was a child welfare advocate and the wife of District Judge Irby Dunklin. On the cover of the club's earliest yearbooks was printed the saying: "In essentials, unity; in non-essentials, liberty; In all things, charity," which was later adopted by the Texas federation. When Shelton assumed the club's presidency in 1904, the course of study included the history, literature, and art of Russia and Japan. Club members tackled difficult subjects such as the Reform Irish Land Acts and studied government and civics. At the suggestion of Shelton, the club switched to current events for their study program around the end of World War I, and they spent one year on the timely topic of Americanization. A neighborhood music club of men and women on Wheeler Street, now College Avenue, met for instruction by Guy R. Pitner in the summer of 1902. Soon the group was exclusively female, and Maud Peters Ducker, a well-known soprano, suggested the club adopt the name Harmony Club. In 1903 Lucile Manning Lyons came to Fort Worth with her husband John F. Lyons, who was treasurer for

Celebrity photographer George Maillard Kesslere of New York City captured this portrait of Lucile Lyons after she rose to national prominence in music circles. *Courtesy, Fort Worth Public Library, Genealogy, History and Archives.*

Her intelligence, poise, and charisma catapulted Lyons into the presidency of the Harmony Club the next year, a position she held for twenty years. In her 1923 article in The *New York Times*, Lyons recalled how the Harmony Club members made Fort Worth a cultural center of Texas. After the very low attendance at the few classical concerts in Fort Worth and cancellation of an appearance by Mme. Johanna Gadski, the Harmony Club members canvassed the community and realized that a "bargain-priced musical course" was needed. They sought the best artists for three concerts annually and offered season tickets for two for $5.

The first year the club women had to sell individual tickets one by one, but by the second year season tickets sold out the house, and folks from as far as 400 miles away traveled to Fort Worth for concerts. The Harmony Club series featured up-and-coming artists—often scouted out by young reporters such as Clyde Whitlock—and internationally known performers such as Paderewski. Over a ten-year period the club paid artist fees of $300,000 and spent a total of $50,000 for advertising, printing, and physical properties without any profit to the club or individual in the club.

The most legendary concert sponsored by the Harmony Club was the appearance of operatic tenor Enrico Caruso in 1920. Caruso's fee necessitated such a huge audience that the Coliseum in the stockyards was the only facility in town with a large enough capacity. Standing in the Coliseum in the heat of August and looking at the remnants of a recent cattle show, Caruso's manager questioned how the colossal barn could be made into a concert hall. When Lyons detailed the scheme for conversion, he facetiously asked if she was going to shoot the

a cattle commission company and later president of the Livestock Exchange. The elegant twenty-three-year-old Lyons was thrilled to find a musical society in her adopted city, and the club members immediately selected her as parliamentarian. The daughter of Charlie Ella Burton and John Wiggins Manning, a druggist in Albany, Texas, Lyons was sent to Nashville, Tennessee, for her higher education. After obtaining a license for instruction degree from George Peabody College for Teachers, she completed a bachelor of arts degree at the University of Nashville in 1900.

The Harmony Club singers and their director Guy Pitner posed for this 1907 photograph.
Lucile Lyons is seated to Pitner's immediate left.
Courtesy, Fort Worth Star-Telegram *Collection. Special Collections, the University of Texas at Arlington.*

flocks of pigeons circling the interior of the building too; the unintimidated Lyons replied, "When it comes to shooting the birds, I balk." After the clubwomen worked for months on the facility in the midst of an oil boom that drained away laborers and materials, Caruso arrived in town, approved their arrangements, and played to a crowd of 8,000. Ticket receipts totaled $20,000, the largest sum of money for a single performance by Caruso in his entire career.

With memories of her childhood dreams of attending fine concerts and frustrated musical ambition, Lyons had a special feeling for youth

music education and appreciation and led the Harmony Club to sponsor a Junior Harmony Club. Violinist Ruth Poindexter recalled that, as a teen, she was given a free master lesson by Maestro Francis McMillan in Lyons' home, and Lyons arranged for her and other young women to attend concerts by being ushers.

In the early years of the Harmony Club, the Women's Department Club blossomed and suddenly faded. Its end was obscure, but may have simply been a matter of ambitious, idealistic programs without the womanpower and money to make them last. May Swayne stepped into the breach and reorganized the Fort Worth Federation of Women's Club in February 1906, and was elected president of the resuscitated federation. This time federation representatives from the eight member clubs, including the new Woman's Shakespeare Club, tackled a number of social welfare and civic issues. Jumping into the City Beautiful movement, they supported the parks plan designed by George E. Kessler of Kansas City. They appealed to the men at city hall to do their duty and clean up public areas. Instead, the aldermen foisted the management of City Park onto the clubwomen without funding. Trash and weeds were cleared; a playground and tennis and croquets courts were built; lawns were cut regularly when the women could obtain the city horse to pull the mower; the Trinity River banks were planted with flowers to complement the woodland effect; and entrance gates erected —all at the federation's expense. Summer concerts in City Park resumed. Next, the women originated the Park League from which the City Park Board grew. They also took on the cleanup of Pioneers Rest and Oakwood cemeteries.

Speakers and experts from out of state and Texas universities gave lectures at monthly federation meetings, and special multiple-day sessions were packed with clubwomen wanting to be informed about the issues of the day and desiring the practical know-how to solve community problems. Appeals Court Judge Ocie Speer spoke about "The Legal Status of Women in Texas" to a large audience in the sanctuary of First Christian Church.

The federation established an emergency home for women and children in 1907 and placed Salvation Army Captain Minnie Burdick in charge. Statistics from April two years later listed 389 meals served and 129 beds provided at the shelter. The Humane Society, which protected abused children as well as animals, was another social welfare project that the federation supported. Olive Hall Butler, secretary general of the Texas Humane Society, traveled from San Antonio to address school children and adults in the City Hall Auditorium at the behest of the clubwomen. Swayne herself intervened about the care and method of euthanasia for impounded animals.

Clubwomen inspected jail facilities and made recommendations to the authorities. Their reports were published in Fort Worth and Dallas newspapers. The sanitary conditions were appalling, and the mixing of children and the mentally ill with hardened criminals especially concerned the reformers, avid supporters of a separate juvenile justice system. The women's ire was up when they saw that the color line between blacks and whites was not observed in the jail. They demanded that the women working at the rock piles and in cells be separated by race. One inspection team reported in the *Dallas Morning News* that the police and court clerk's office "walls and floors [were] smeared with tobacco expectorations" and pointed out the police officers were disregarding the ordinance against public spitting. County and city officials responded with incremental improvements.

When Swayne retired from the presidential office of the FWFWC in 1910, she felt the most significant accomplishment of her tenure was the successful campaign to force the Northern Texas Traction Company to comply with the state law requiring half-fare for school children. An important new affiliated organization that year was the Fort Worth Council of Jewish Women.

At the time of Swayne's retirement, participation was low; there was some strain with the mayor's office, and some clubs had dropped out, including the Kindergarten Association after an apparent disagreement with the federation's executive officers. Briefly Ida V. Jarvis was president of the city federation; however, she was forced to retire from public life to care for her ailing husband.

A born diplomat, Ella Hall Galbreath was the right woman for the job of rebuilding the federation and taking positive action. She and other federation members visited with leaders of unaffiliated women's clubs and dissatisfied former members. The Kindergarten Association returned to the fold, and again the FWFWC doubled its club memberships in the next four years with the notable additions of the Young Women's Christian Association and the Southern Association of College Women, which merged with the Association of Collegiate Alumnae and was renamed the American Association of University Women in 1921. Individual memberships grew from a handful to around 100 in the next fifteen years.

In the second decade of the twentieth century, the FWFWC became a powerhouse organization, though its members still did not have the power of the ballot. After conciliatory meetings with Mayor William D. Davis and the city commissioners, the federation women were inspired to "become the housekeeper of Fort Worth," Nettie Stiefel, federation secretary, recorded in the minutes. When a new city hall was built, meeting chambers were planned for the women of the FWFWC. Upon assuming office, Mayor

Robert F. Milam sent a letter to the group asking their cooperation in "all matters pertaining to the city." The Young Men's Business League appeared before the group to request their support for a petition to change to a city manager form of government. The Chamber of Commerce expressed its eagerness for the help of the clubwomen in "building up the city." The federation selected candidates to endorse for employment or contract renewal by the city, county, and the schools, including a letter of support for I. M. Terrell, principal of the black high school. They also endorsed candidates for office, particularly the school board.

Child welfare reform was a primary "plan of work" of the FWFWC. They campaigned to build a boys' shelter home—an industrial home for delinquent Texas boys—and had collected $3,500 toward that goal when the state built the reformatory for boys in Gatesville. In 1914 the clubwomen decided to commit their funds to a children's wing at the proposed city-county hospital. President Galbreath was appointed to the Fort Worth Board of Health to plan the hospital. When they realized that there was greater need for a free children's medical facility, the Fort Worth Free Baby Hospital was opened in 1918 with Ida L. Turner at the helm. The hospital operated under the management of a board of federation women. That institution evolved into Fort Worth Children's Hospital, which merged in 1985 with Cook Children's Hospital. (See *In the Interest of the Children*.)

The federation had a humane committee that worked closely with the Humane Society regarding cruelty to children and horses. Child labor law, compulsory school attendance, and industrial education "to prevent persons becoming public charges" were supported by the club-women. They were involved with the Mothers' Congress, later the Parent Teacher Association, via Texas President Elizabeth "Bessie" Wyeth Hutchinson, a member of the WWC, and allied with that group on educational issues. They attended lectures sponsored by this group, including the one in 1913 by a "gentleman from Ohio" who lectured on sex hygiene to city women at the high school auditorium.

The federation women were pleased when, in response to their advocacy, a juvenile court was created and a juvenile officer and his assistant hired in 1910. They remained watchdogs of the conduct of the new juvenile justice system. Apparently the commissioners eliminated the juvenile officer, and the women went to work to reinstate the office. Six months later they succeeded. Galbreath became an advocate for compulsory statewide juvenile courts, and her visit with the governor resulted later in her appointment to the commission as secretary and treasurer to set up the Texas State Training School for Girls. Ida Jarvis attended the Conference on Texas Charities and Corrections and was a delegate appointed by the governor to the national conference.

The censorship of moving picture shows provides an excellent case study of how the federation went about housekeeping in Fort Worth and how they were listened to and even courted. In June 1910, the federation endorsed Mayor Davis' stand against a film of the brutal Johansson-Jeffries boxing match. Later in the year the women approached the city commissioners about eliminating "offensive advertising of picture shows." Elizabeth Montgomery Purinton contacted the mayor of New York in

1911 about the topic and read that city's censorship ordinance at a federation meeting. A committee of three was appointed to draw up a petition to present to the city commissioners, and they expanded the New York example to give the board of censors the power to eliminate offensive posters and make sure that fire, sanitation, and lighting standards were met in theaters. The very next month, Mr. Calloway of the Odeon Theater invited the clubwomen to attend a picture show in his theater after their meeting, and they graciously accepted. During the summer of 1911 the censorship ordinance was passed without a negative vote. The Moving Picture Censor Board consisted of one man and two women appointed by the mayor. Federation president Ella Galbreath was one of the appointees. The month after the ordinance passed the owner of the Healy Theater donated one day's revenue—$1,000—toward one of the federation's main youth projects, and the New Majestic offered receipts minus daily expenses of $350. After an Oklahoma City police matron spoke to the FWFWC, the Odeon Theater manager invited the women to view a moving picture about the white slave traffic. Fort Worth was the last major city in Texas to abandon local movie censorship, although Dallas re-established a motion picture review board late in the twentieth century.

Jennie Scheuber of the civic committee wielded much power and influence in the FWFWC. The federation minutes are filled with her motions and reports often solicited from experts. The letter of Dr. A. J. McLaughlin, chief sanitation expert at the International Joint Commission in Washington, D.C., telling Scheuber and the clubwomen to "stick to their guns" to keep the drinking water from Lake Worth uncontaminated, was read to men's organizations across the city. Scheuber and Hallie Bewley shared an interest in city design and beautification. They collected petitions to preserve historic areas, block unsightly building, and provide more green space. Joined by Lucile Lyons, they campaigned for voluntary cooperation of merchants in the control of the nature and abundance of advertising signs. At one Texas city-planning conference, Bewley advocated for a city center with governmental and public cultural institutions grouped together. She felt that Fort Worth needed a "heart and soul."

As the long-term president of the Fort Worth Art Association, Bewley arranged visits by artists and lecturers on art and civic subjects for the clubwomen of Fort Worth. She also kept the federation women advised and involved in the art exhibits in the gallery space of the Carnegie Library, a space that had previously provided their meeting chambers.

Lucile Lyons served as a city federation representative to the Relief Association, Fort Worth's main charitable organization, and for years was the vice president of an otherwise male executive board. In 1912 she and Florence Shuman, wife of Adolph L. Shuman, advertising director of the *Fort Worth Star-Telegram*, started the Goodfellow Fund as a FWWC project.

Lyons arranged and sometimes directed musical groups for the federation's Fourth of July celebrations, the summer concerts, and fund-raisers. In 1916 Lyons helped found and was the first president of the Texas Federation of Music Clubs. She was an innovative and farsighted president of the National Federation of Music Clubs in the 1920s and went on to a career as an independent concert manager.

Anna Shelton was the city federation's main liaison from the state and national federations. She and friend Etta Newby, who was a chairman of the federation's lecture committee during this rich period, were increasingly aware of the need for an adequately-sized permanent home for the clubwomen. Mayor Davis had decided to get the women agitators out of his hair. He told them that their meeting chambers at city hall were needed to house the sanitary food inspector that the women had insisted upon and to whose salary they contributed. A subsequent effort to buy a downtown residence for conversion failed. When Anna Shelton was appointed the chair of a committee to establish permanent headquarters, she spied a bargain property on Pennsylvania Avenue. The U.S. government had seized the home of a German national in World War I and had offered it for sale for some time. A banker's widow, Etta Newby trusted Shelton's business sense and agreed to purchase the property in 1923 for a permanent home for the clubwomen of Fort Worth, insisting that Shelton be the first president of the Woman's Club of Fort Worth. Shelton's record as a realtor and home builder insured the energetic cooperation of local bankers who loaned as much as $100,000 as the Woman's Club was remodeled and expanded to fill an entire city block. The membership grew with the facility to a couple of thousand women. The Woman's Club of Fort Worth has remained one of the largest and most successful clubs for women in the Southwest.

Without these amazing "modern women," Fort Worth would not be the cultural center and the philanthropic city it is today.

BIBLIOGRAPHIC ESSAY

Though I was aware in general of the cultural contributions of clubwomen of Fort Worth, it was not until I became a member of the Woman's Club of Fort Worth that I truly awakened to the rich history of clubwomen and their role in the making and shaping of the city. My research about the Woman's Club and the lives of some of its founders became focused on the early clubwoman movement while assisting Hollace Weiner with her investigation of Fort Worth literary clubs and Jewish women as part of her master's thesis. The Woman's Wednesday Club and '93 Club kindly shared their scrapbooks and existing early records with both of us.

There are many clubwomen who were important in the history of their club and the larger community; however, space limitation did not allow for me to write about them all. The clubwomen featured attained state and/or national prominence. I included clubs in which these women had leadership roles. Some of the other early member clubs of the Fort Worth Federation of Women's Clubs and other women were mentioned if it contributed to the ongoing story of the featured women and the woman's club movement. Margaret Frazier of the Harmony Club and Michelle Cyrus of Sorosis Club were incredibly helpful about their club histories and Lucile M. Lyons and Anna Shelton, respectively. Fellow historians Hollace Weiner, Sherrie McLeRoy, and Jan Jones have generously shared their discoveries about clubwomen with me.

I spent many hours in the Woman's Collection at Texas Woman's University reviewing biographical profiles on clubwomen, reading minutes of the Fort Worth Federation of Women's Clubs, and deciphering the letters of Mary Y. Terrell.

Several collections and books in the Fort Worth Public Library local history and archives section were essential to piecing together the clubwomen's story from 1889 to 1923. The Club Yearbook Collection contained gems about the clubs and their members. The Tarrant County Historical Society's Collection had the only other known existing ledger of early minutes of the Fort Worth Federation of Women's Clubs. Newspaper articles about club histories and leaders in vertical files helped direct me to earlier sources. The Lucile M. Lyons Collection and the Florence Shuman Collection with their fantastic publicity photos of concert artists kept me enthralled for hours. Programs in the Sam Losh Collection helped me appreciate the achievements of Lucile M. Lyons and the Harmony Club even more. The original records of the Fort Worth Library Association and books about the Fort Worth Library and the Fort Worth Art Association were invaluable. City records from the mayor and city council proceedings had petitions and letters from the city federation.

My constant companions during the research and writing of this essay were *A History of the Woman's Club of Fort Worth* by Marion Day Mullins and *History of the Texas Federation of Women's Clubs*, volumes 1 and 2, by Fannie C. Potter. *Creating the New Woman* by Judith N. McArthur was, as ever, my best resource for women's organizational history in Texas.

Since I found no records of the Federation of Women's Clubs 1898–1902 and from the

Woman's Department Club, there were missing periods in the records of individual clubs, articles in the Fort Worth newspapers and the *Dallas Morning News* were critical to continuity of the story of these amazing women.

I was disappointed to find two photographs in such poor condition that they could not be reproduced—one of the 1906 Fort Worth Federation officers and some city commissioners on microfilm and the other a print of the Woman Wednesday's Club Room in the Texas Spring Palace.

Chapter 6

MUDHOLES, FAIRY GODMOTHERS, AND CHOIR BELLS

by Ruth McAdams

MARY KELLEY, WRITING in *The Foundations of Texan Philanthropy*, says that Fort Worth has enjoyed more philanthropic ventures per capita (primarily through charitable foundations) than any other community in the country. Everyone is familiar with the most famous names of Fort Worth's donors to charitable causes—Amon G. Carter, Sid Richardson, and the Bass family. True, most of the giving has been through the men of the city; women have been constrained from philanthropic ventures in their own right by law and custom until quite recently. Even so, the women of Fort Worth have managed to use their influence, their resources, and their own brand of feminine grit and grace to leave a legacy of purposeful use of wealth for public good. Seven women in this chapter represent the best charitable giving by Fort Worth women.

One of Fort Worth's earliest and most enduring philanthropic enterprises owes its existence to a lone woman's stubbornness—and a mudhole. Missouri Matilda Nail was born in Fannin County in 1858 of families who had migrated to Texas from Illinois and Tennessee. Her family

Missouri Matilda Nail Cook. *Courtesy the Collection of the Robert E. Nail, Jr. Archives of The Old Jail Art Center, Albany, Texas.*

ran cattle in Texas along the Red River and on into Oklahoma when it was still Indian Territory. After her marriage at age seventeen to W. I. Cook, her brothers and the Cook family joined forces, acquiring 7,760 acres for $49,000 cash from the Holstein family of Shackelford County, Texas.

Matilda's brother, James H. Nail, began to wheedle his sister, whom he called "Dude," to sell out to him. She refused. He insisted. But she was so adamant about not selling that she and her husband ended up buying out her brother, who bragged to family and friends about selling Dude "the sorriest piece of land in Shackelford County." He was sure she would go bust within a year. Cook was widowed in 1923, and in 1925 Fort Worth wildcatting partners Charles Roeser, Marshall Young, and Tol Pendleton made plans to drill on the piece of Cook's land that her brother had so coveted—this in spite of scads of dry wells and scant geological promise. In February 1926 on their way to the site they had selected, the vehicles carrying the drilling equipment got so bogged down in the mud that the partners, already flat broke and out of options, made the decision to begin drilling right then and there. The gusher they struck was the stuff of movies, making the partners and Matilda Cook rich, very rich.

The first well produced 1,000 barrels per day from 1,240 feet, making it for many years the largest shallow oil field in the world. By 1929 the Cook Pool was yielding 10,000 barrels per day. After bringing forth over 35,000,000 barrels of oil the Cook Oil Field still is producing oil as new wells continue to be drilled. Interesting enough, had the partners pressed on to their original site, according to a 1976 interview with surviving partner Marshall Young, they would have hit yet another dry hole!

Grateful she had kept the land and grateful for the unexpected fortune from oil, Cook made plans to fund a hospital in honor of her husband, who died in Fort Worth in 1923, and her daughter Jesse, who had died when Cook was only forty-six. Her intention was for this hospital to be operated "without individual profit and for benefit of working girls and women with limited or no means of medical treatment." Cook paid for the chosen site on West Lancaster, contributed $600,000 toward the building, and assigned one-fourth of her oil royalties to the trust running the hospital.

The W. I. Cook Memorial Hospital opened January 29, 1929, at 1212 West Lancaster Street in Fort Worth. Matilda Cook supervised the building's Italian Renaissance design. She imported many of the furnishings for the fifty-five-bed hospital from Italy. A 1932 *Fort Worth Press* article identified the room dedicated to Cook's daughter as one of the most beautiful in the hospital; it contained her daughter's portrait and the old piano on which Jesse had played.

Fittingly, Cook died in 1932 in the very hospital she had dreamt of and willed into being. And though the hospital has changed names, missions, and locations over the years, Fort Worth continues to benefit from Matilda Cook's vision and generosity.

One day in 1923 Anna Shelton woke from an appendectomy convinced that a "fairy godmother with [a] magic touch, had created … a new world" for her and fellow clubwomen. In the late 1890s and early 1900s middle and upper class women often were excluded from membership in the professional organizations formed and run by men. As women became increasingly independent, interested in social reform, and intent on developing their minds, they began forming clubs of their own, first to study literature, and, as time passed, such diverse topics as "natural resource conservation, home life, public affairs, international affairs, the arts, and Texas heritage." In Fort Worth, groups of women met in various homes for the Monday Book Club, the History Club, the College Women's Club, and so on. The City Federation of Women's Clubs, a collection of representatives from all the clubs, had entertained the notion of housing the groups under one roof as early as the late 1890s but dismissed the idea as financially impossible. After all, their husbands reminded them, they would need funds for buying the land and putting up a building. And then there would be continuous funds for maintenance.

In 1922 Shelton saw just the sort of dream house she wanted for Fort Worth clubwomen when she traveled to Atlanta, Georgia, and saw the excellent woman's club Georgians had built. In January of 1923, she met with members of the Fort Worth's women's clubs and formed a committee devoted to finding a suitable site for building a clubhouse such as she had seen in Atlanta. When it seemed their plans were doomed to suffer the financial difficulties predicted by the men of Fort Worth, a fairy godmother—Etta Price Newby—waved a magic wand and made their dreams a reality.

Newby was the wife of William G. Newby, president of the American National Bank in Fort Worth. Born in Enterprise, Mississippi, in 1862, she moved to Fort Worth in early childhood, marrying Newby in 1883. The 1924 publication of the Texas Federation of Women's Clubs, *Who's*

Etta Newby.
Courtesy of The Woman's Club of Fort Worth.

Who of the Womanhood of Texas, includes this fulsome description: "a helpful inspiration to her husband. Not every woman has proven a load star [sic] for her husband's ambition as has she. Tender and worshipful in her devotion, at his passing, she took the torch he had so bravely borne and resolved to carry on to the fulfillment his philanthropic ideals."

Though not a clubwoman herself, Newby was sympathetic to their aims of "the study of good books, the bringing together of friends, the making of a place where the stranger may be made to feel at home and the broader humanitarian efforts that engage the minds and hearts of good women everywhere." Accordingly she searched for a fitting memorial for her late husband and found it at 1613 Pennsylvania Avenue in the former home of the family of Heinrich Frerichs, a man suspected of heading German Intelligence in the Southwest. In 1914, when war in Europe broke out, Frerichs and his family fled to Germany. When the United States entered World War I in 1917, the government confiscated the Frerichses' handsome home to house army personnel. Mrs. Newby bought the home in 1923 and deeded it to the Fort Worth Woman's Club. The building was to be named the William G. Newby Memorial. The building still contains some of the dining room furniture the Frerichses abandoned when they left for Germany.

Under Anna Shelton's capable leadership the club purchased other lots and buildings adjacent to the original property for lectures, musical performances, and the carrying out of social projects; it was, though, Newby's gift that made possible all that has followed. The Woman's Club of Fort Worth now owns the entire block on which Etta Newby's original purchase resides, and it is all dedicated to the continued purpose of "fidelity to principle; concern for social welfare; love of Fort Worth and participation in all things for its betterment; enjoyment of fine literature; good fellowship, and delight in social contact with congenial friends; a keen appreciation of the beautiful, and pleasure in artistic surroundings."

Upon her death in 1936 Etta Newby's will established a trust that donated to a wide range of causes. She gave her library and $1,000 to her "friend and Sunday School pupil, Mary McAllister," and she established the Etta Newby Student Loan Fund at Texas Christian University for the "purpose of assisting poor boys and girls in the State of Texas who are ambitious

to equip themselves for professional pursuits, but who are without adequate means to do so." The loan is interest free, but recipients are asked to "make a contribution to the fund when their loan is repaid." She also endowed Pioneers Rest Cemetery, established a trust for the upkeep of the Newby Memorial Building, provided a building for the Fort Worth Lighthouse for the Blind, and furnished the chimes for the Fort Worth First Methodist Church, rung at her memorial service June 24, 1936. It is, though, the beneficiaries of the Fort Worth Woman's Club who remain most grateful for Etta Newby's magnanimity—every year the flag at the club flies at half-staff on Newby's birthday, May 28, and club members travel to Pioneer Rest Cemetery to place flowers on her grave on that day.

Kay Kimbell, husband of Velma Kimbell, used to tell a story about his wife's get-it-done attitude. An avid gardener her entire life, Kimbell was anxious for their two homes in Westover Hills to be landscaped to her specifications. A boulder on one lot stymied groundskeepers. She urged them to move the rock. They explained to her that its size made it immovable. She did not pull rank or fly into a rage. She, as Mr. Kimbell said, just got out there with the workers and pushed!

Born Velma Fuller in 1887 in Whitewright, Texas, she met Kay Kimbell in public school in Whitewright and attended Grayson College before marrying her high school sweetheart in 1910. Kay founded the Beatrice Milling Company, which grew into the Kimbell Milling Company, and led to his being head of more than seventy corporations, including flour, feed, and oil mills; grocery chains; an insurance company; and a wholesale grocery firm. Under Velma's influence, he began collecting art with the same perspicacity he applied to business.

According to Patricia Loud, curator of architecture and archivist of the Kimbell Art Museum, within five years the Kimbells had become serious collectors of art and formed the Kay Kimbell Art Foundation. They lent their treasures to local libraries, churches, colleges, and other institutions. By the time of Kay Kimbell's death in 1964, the Kimbells had amassed a collection of approximately 360 works. Motivated by a "long-felt ambition—to encourage art in Fort Worth and Texas by providing paintings and other meritorious works of art for public display, study, and observation in suitable surroundings," Kimbell left much of his estate to the foundation. Within a few months of her husband's death, Velma donated her share of the estate to the Kimbell Art Foundation.

The foundation's board of directors took Kay Kimbell's intention of establishing a museum "of the first class" to heart by selecting a site close to the Amon Carter Museum of Western Art and other nearby attractions with the idea of creating a museum district for the citizens of Fort Worth.

In 1966, the foundation, under Velma Kimbell's leadership, selected Richard Fargo Brown, director of the Los Angeles County Museum, as founding director of the new museum. Kimbell allowed Brown free rein in selecting an architect for the Kimbell Art Museum. Brown chose the celebrated architect Louis I. Kahn to design a museum where, as Brown said, visitors "would be neither specialists in art nor architecture, but representatives of the general public.... Their total experience of a visit to the museum should be one of warmth, mellowness and even elegance. Among other experiences education-

ally and personally enriching, a visitor to an art museum ought to be charmed."

Though Kimbell was the recipient of numerous awards for her benevolence to the people of Fort Worth, such as the West Texas Chamber of Commerce Cultural Achievement Award, the Fort Worth Patron of the Arts Award, and the Exchange Club's Outstanding Citizen of the Year Award, surely her most significant gift was the freedom she granted the Kimbell Art Museum's directors and architect. Edmund Pillsbury, the museum's director at Velma Kimbell's death, praised her for "guiding the museum through its construction and early development by always placing a minimum of restriction on the professional staff, giving maximum flexibility as to how the museum would develop."

Now seen as one of the world's great small museums, the Kimbell, which opened in October of 1972 at a cost of $7,500,000, was questioned by some as too avant-garde. Kay Fortson, niece of the Kimbells, recalls the board's early trepidations: "On paper, it really looked fine," she said. "It was just when we saw all those turned-over vaults and the concrete and everything that we became pretty scared. It all seemed so different from what it was on paper. In building it, they had to turn the vaults upside down, so we saw it as if it was completely inside out. And there were all these bits and pieces that didn't seem to go together. People would call me and say, 'You've got to do something. It's going to be the most horrible thing that's ever happened in Fort Worth.' But we did have faith in Ric Brown, and it just couldn't have turned out better. People seeing it for the first time still make remarks about the wonderful architecture. Mr. Kahn knew what he was doing."

Velma Kimbell.
Courtesy of Special Collections, The University of Texas at Arlington and The Fort Worth Star-Telegram
Collection, *Special Collections, The University of Texas at Arlington.*

Velma Kimbell's instinct for allowing the Kimbell Art Museum the freedom to evolve to meet each new generation's needs was sound. Today the museum offers "a full schedule of public programs to promote appreciation of the collection and special exhibitions, including symposia featuring guest speakers, regular lectures and gallery talks by the professional staff and regional artists, and storytelling for children. Workshops on the arts—especially designed to share the resources of the museum with all levels of the community—are held regularly for children, high-school students, adults, senior citizens, and the hearing-impaired and are based on the principle that increased understanding is the key to an expanded enjoyment of art."

Dr. May Owen decided when she was a young girl that she was going to be a physician, even though girls in those days rarely completed high school. She also decided that she was going to live to be 100 and was going to work every day until she died. Born into a rawboned German/Welsh family in Falls County, Texas, in 1892, May grew up knowing nothing except hard work—penning calves, chopping cotton, and doing the field work of a man. She also knew the feel of a quince bush switch on her bare legs when she did not do as she was told. Her family was, as she said, poor as Job's turkey; frugality was second nature, as was helping others. (Owen's medical career is covered in the chapter "Cracking the Glass Ceiling.")

Owen won many professional awards, but she was too busy and worked too hard to pay

May Owen receiving plaque from Joe B. Rushing.
Courtesy of Tarrant County College District Archives.

much attention to them. She said the only reason she ever accepted the awards was so she could use them for establishing funds and scholarships for deserving students. While president of the Texas Medical Association, for instance, she established the Physician's Benevolent Fund to aid doctors and their families in times of financial need by donating the funds set aside for her travel—she refused to accept travel monies and insisted on paying her own way. She created the May Owen Student Fund with $300,000 of her own money to send what she affectionately called "her boys and girls" to medical school. What is amazing about the amount she accumulated is that she always worked on salary and never earned the big dollars society often associates with the medical profession.

As important as her many accomplishments in the field of medicine was her work in helping to establish Tarrant County Junior College, now the Tarrant County College District. Owen had been involved for a number of years with the Fort Worth Town Hall movement, organized to promote citizen participation in city and county decisions. She supported their idea of a bond initiative for the purpose of creating a community college. With customary efficiency, she spent nearly a year drumming up public support for the idea, but no one was more surprised than she when members of the Chamber of Commerce Education Committee called to ask her to be a candidate for the first board of trustees. The nominees' names would appear on the ballot of the bond-issue vote. She was told that the people of Fort Worth so revered her that the issue was sure to pass if it had her support. She consented only if she did not have to do any campaigning. They agreed and, on July 31, 1965, Tarrant County Junior College was born. Owen was so thrilled that every year thereafter she threw a birthday party for the college at her own expense. She served on the board until the day she died.

According to Joe Rushing, founding president and first chancellor of the district, and C.A. Roberson, executive vice chancellor and later chancellor of the district, Owen was, from the very first, fastidious about safeguarding what she always referred to as "the people's money." In those early days of sizable construction costs, every check had to be signed by an officer of the board of trustees. Rushing and Roberson often depended on Owen to sign the checks because she lived downtown and was usually easy to track down. Rushing recalls Owen asking many, many questions before she signed each check, adding her endorsement only after she was satisfied the expense was warranted.

Roberson took on the job of finding a place for Owen to live when the Hotel Texas, her home of forty-five years, closed for remodeling. He tried to persuade her to get an apartment with perhaps a college-aged companion to live with her to take care of household chores. He remembers to this day her immediate reply, "Mr. Roberson, you don't understand. I have never owned a bed sheet, a towel, or any other household item in my life and I have no interest in owning such now. The less I have for myself the more I have to give away!"

Owen moved from the Hotel Texas to the residential floor of the Fort Worth Club. She was

never comfortable there, though. Rushing said it was just too fancy, too ostentatious, too rich for her. From the Fort Worth Club she moved to a two-room suite at the Rodeway Inn close to the hospital district. After the Hyatt Regency (formerly the Sheraton, formerly the Hotel Texas) was remodeled, she moved back there. The hotel had instituted a non-resident policy but made an exception in Owen's case. After she fell at the Hyatt she realized that, at age ninety-six, she could no longer live alone in the hotel. After a brief stint in the Westside Convalescent Center, All Saints Hospital provided her a room as a permanent resident. She died there in 1988.

Rushing's favorite May Owen story concerns a plaque. The TCC board voted to name the district's new downtown administrative offices the May Owen Center, much against Owen's wishes. She finally agreed to allow her name to go on the building when the other board members told her they chose her because she had the shortest name and the sign for the building would be cheaper that way. As Rushing recalls, they had a plaque made to present to Owen at the dedication ceremony in 1983, but what most pleased her was that they had salvaged some silver from the district photographic labs, taken it to Haltom's, and had them use the recycled silver for the plaque.

In keeping with her desire for educating young people, especially those destined for medical careers, in 1984 Owen endowed a nursing scholarship at Tarrant County Junior College for students with a "sincere interest in the profession of nursing and a keen desire to serve humanity in the capacity of a nurse."

Dr. May Owen died in 1988, three weeks shy of her ninety-seventh birthday. Surrounded by nurses who had earned their degrees at Tarrant County Junior College thanks in part to her generosity, she almost reached her goal of living and working until she was 100, putting into practice her goal of "trying to live my life in my work."

Ruth Carter Stevenson remembers her mother as a perfectly done-up dynamo in pink with size two-and-one-half feet, stylishly coiffed hair, and a knack for "letting you have her way, just gently." Nenetta Burton Carter developed her persuasive powers early on. Born in Texarkana in 1895, she was the oldest of four sisters, all spoiled by their parents. Breeze Burton, as they called Nenetta, attended Sweet Briar College, and was much admired by the young men of Virginia. Stevenson found six fraternity pins in her mother's safety deposit box after she died. She was even engaged to someone else when she met Amon Carter. She married him in 1918.

Divorced from Amon in 1941, Nenetta Burton Carter was living in New York when she received word that her son, Amon Carter Jr., was reported missing in action in 1943. Kneeling before the altar of the Blessed Mother at St. Patrick's Cathedral she made this promise: "If God will give me back my son, I will spend the rest of my life trying to help others." Ten days later she got word her son was alive in a prisoner of war camp. He was liberated in 1945. His mother set about making good on her promise.

She and Amon Sr., with whom she remained cordial after their divorce, established the Amon G. Carter Foundation in 1945 and funded it in 1947 with $8,511,712 from the sale of their Wasson Field oil interests. He donated sixty percent of that seed money while Nenetta added forty. Fort Worth residents then and now benefit literally every day from the work of the founda-

Nenetta Burton Carter.
Courtesy of Fredrieka Ankele.

tion, so much so that the 1972 publication of the Golden Deeds Award, honoring the foundation's trustees, posed the following questions: "Did you go to a hospital? Is your daughter or granddaughter a Girl Scout or Campfire Girl? Did a child from your family take part in an activity at the Fort Worth Museum of Science and History? Did one of the boys in your family play Little League ball under the lights? Do you have ties to Texas Christian University? To Texas Wesleyan University? To the University of Texas? To Texas Tech University? If your answer to any of these questions is yes, then Carter Foundation has been a part of your life."

The breadth and scope of organizations and individuals helped by Amon and Nenetta

Carter's largesse is endless; even in 1972 the Golden Deeds publication said the list could "stretch on literally over pages of this program." To date the foundation has made charitable gifts of over $335,000,000, among the most recent being the Nenetta Burton Carter building on the campus of Texas Wesleyan University.

The crown jewel of the foundation is the magnificent Amon Carter Museum. It was Amon Carter's desire, through the efforts of the foundation, that the "museum be operated as a nonprofit artistic enterprise for the benefit of the public and to aid in the promotion of cultural spirit in the City of Fort Worth and vicinity and particularly, to stimulate the artistic imagination among young people residing there." The museum hosts more than 22,000 children visits per year.

Cowboy and Indian art pieces, though, were not what Nenetta admired and were not displayed in her home. Ruth Carter Stevenson said the only western picture of her dad's she saw until she was nearly grown was *His First Lesson* by Frederic Remington that hung in Amon's office at the *Fort Worth Star-Telegram*. It is now displayed in the Amon Carter Museum. He kept the remainder of the collection at the Fort Worth Club. Nenetta Carter preferred to be surrounded by what her children always called "pretties." One of Ruth's early punishments was having to take a tissue and wipe off individual leaves of her mother's delicate jade trees.

Nenetta Carter loved flowers. She bought 15,000 wholesale tulip bulbs every fall from the Netherlands. One of Fort Worth's most splendid sights was when the pink and red flowers bloomed in front of her home in Westover Hills. The bulbs were shipped in September when it was still too warm to plant them, so Carter stored them in Koslow's Furs refrigerated vaults until the weather cooled enough for planting.

Carter's love of "pretties" figured prominently in the project closest to her heart, the Fort Worth Children's Hospital. She, along with Bille Bransford Clark, president of the Woman's Board of the hospital, hatched an idea for raising money for indigent pediatric patients in 1953. On January 30, 1954, the first Jewel Charity Ball was held at the Hotel Texas. The decorations were, predictably enough, pink—stuffed pink poodles with diamond collars and diamond ear clips, pink rose trees, pink centerpieces. Harry Winston—*THE* Harry Winston—attended, bringing with him the Hope Diamond, the 337-carat Catherine the Great Sapphire, and a necklace with 336 diamonds and fifteen emeralds dating from the Spanish Inquisition. The women sold raffle tickets for prizes like Justin boots, a parakeet donated by Amon G. Carter Jr., and a mink stole from Koslow's Furs. That first fling netted $9,000. The Jewel Charity Ball is still Fort Worth's hottest ticket, raising over $2,000,000 each year for the Uncompensated Care Fund of Cook Children's Medical Center.

Along with the Jewel Charity Ball, Nenetta Carter invested her time and money in an array of other projects. She was, for example, instrumental in the establishment of the *Star-Telegram* Employees' Fund and received their highest award. The fund, still in force today for those hired before 1974, provides retiree benefits and emergency aid for individual employees. She earned her thousand-hour volunteer pin from Fort Worth Children's Hospital, where she did anything that needed to be done, from weeding the flower beds to washing dishes. She gave generously to St. Joseph's Hospital, allowing them to redesign and equip the obstetrical department. She made possible the Frels organ, the largest tracker organ in Texas, at Holy Family Catholic Church.

Nenetta Burton Carter died May 18, 1983, scant months after the death of her son, the same child whom she feared lost in World War II and for whose safety she made the vow to spend the rest of her days helping others. She more than made good on that promise.

A 1980 *Fort Worth News-Tribune* article dubbed Anne Valliant Burnett Tandy "Fort Worth's First Glamour Girl." Her life was distinguished by a long line of firsts, hardly surprising given her bloodlines. Her great-grandfather, Captain Martin B. Loyd, founded the First National Bank in Fort Worth. Her grandfather was Samuel Burk Burnett, for whom the town of Burkburnett is named. Burnett went on to found the legendary 6666 Ranch, which became the largest individually owned ranch property in the state. Burnett was the first private citizen to have his own rail car as part of the Quanah, Acme & Pacific Railway. The first well brought in on the Texas Panhandle Field was on Burnett land.

Her father, who owned the Tom L. Burnett Cattle Company, taught his daughter to "make a top hand." She went on to manage both the 6666 Ranch and the Triangle ranch properties, a total of some 500,000 acres. Her interest in upgrading ranch animals led to the organization of the American Quarter Horse Association in 1940 at a meeting in her home. She developed such a keen eye for horses that when a group of Texans made plans to form a syndicate for the purpose of buying a son of Triple Crown winner Secretariat in 1976, they would not proceed

Anne Burnett Tandy.
Courtesy of the archives of Burnett Companies.

until Anne saw the horse and judged him to be superior.

Her marriage to Charles Tandy in Fort Worth in 1969 at St. Andrews Episcopal Church was a noteworthy affair even by Texas standards. It marked the first time the *Fort Worth Star-Telegram* had reported a local wedding on the front page.

Tandy was the first woman appointed to the board of trustees of the National Cowboy and Western Heritage Center in Oklahoma City and the first woman named to the executive committee of the West Texas Chamber of Commerce. She was the first female on the board of the Southwestern Exposition and Fat Stock Show. In 1980 she founded the American Quarter Horse Association's Hall of Fame. The State Fair of Texas selected Tandy as an inaugural member of the Heritage Hall of Honor in 1992 for her "significant contributions in the fields of ranching and agriculture."

Her many memberships and honors include service as a trustee of Texas Christian University and the Museum of Modern Art in New York. She and Charles Tandy won the Golden Deeds Award from the Fort Worth Exchange Club and the Patron of the Arts award from the Arts Council of Greater Fort Worth.

Upon Charles Tandy's death in 1978 his widow established the Anne Burnett Tandy and Charles D. Tandy Foundation, which has made grants totaling over $495,000,000. Local organizations have benefited most significantly. For instance, TCU is home to the Tandy Center for Executive Leadership. Other recipients of large gifts include $5,000,000 to support the endowment of the Modern Art Museum of Fort Worth's acquisition program, and $2,500,000 of the $10,000,000 raised in support of the community effort in 1990 and 1991 to purchase Thomas Eakins' *The Swimming Hole* for permanent ownership and exhibition in Fort Worth.

At her death in the early days of 1980 two things were especially fitting. First, her lifelong ranching roots were represented in the selection of pallbearers for her funeral: J. J. Gibson, foreman of the 6666 Ranch; Robert Thompson, foreman of the Burnett ranch near Paducah; Curtis Lightfoot, foreman of the ranch at Iowa Park; Herbert Propps, foreman of the ranch at

Panhandle; Jay Pumphrey, trustee of the Burnett Estates; and Charles Baudoux, pilot of Mrs. Tandy's plane.

The Matisse Backs, which she once called "the most beautiful things" she had ever seen, were purchased by the foundation she established in her memory and are on indefinite loan to the Kimbell Art Museum. They can be seen in the museum's Buffet Restaurant. Like so many other Texas women, Anne Burnett Tandy proved that a lady with pioneering blood could love the land and the arts and live a life dedicated to both.

Born Mary Eudora Fleming in 1913 in Whiteright, Texas, Mary D. as she was later called, was four years old when her father struck oil, ending the family's meager days forever. Realizing the word "rich" might rightly be applied to them produced such a sense of responsibility in Mary D. that she never got over it—it was the guiding principle for all she did.

The contributions by Mary D. and her husband, F. Howard Walsh, to the civic and artistic life of Fort Worth are legendary. In 1931, she began volunteering by helping to cook meals for hospital patients. She was a founding member of the Jewel Charity Ball. She donated astounding amounts to area schools and universities (including $3,500,000 to TCU for a performing arts center and all the land for TCC's Northwest Campus). She was an underwriter of the Fort Worth Ballet, the symphony, the opera, and the Texas Boys Choir.

Her special love, though, was the Dorothy Shaw Bell Choir. Mary D. and Howard met Dr. Lloyd Shaw and wife Dorothy in Colorado Springs, where Lloyd was an educator. Dr. Shaw had written a simple play, *The Littlest Wiseman*,

Mary D. Walsh.
Courtesy of F. Howard Walsh, Jr., Estate of Mary D. Walsh.

and had shared it with the Walshes. It had been presented at the Cheyenne Mountain School in Colorado Springs for many years, but in 1961 the Walshes moved the "nativity play pageant [that] brings beauty, music and enhanced meaning to the traditional Christmas season" to Fort Worth. According to longtime Walsh employee Sharon Ward, Mary D. Walsh decided to augment the rather short play with the Dorothy Shaw Bell Choir. She became so attached to the young people in the choir that she began traveling with thirty-two of them each year and ten or fifteen chaperones, at her expense, anywhere—from Texas to Europe to New Zealand. Choir members were expected to dress up each day and behave themselves—Walsh told a reporter, "I like children at their most awkward age, but I'm too old to put up with any trouble with them!"

Walsh loved music and dancing—and parties. She and husband Howard hosted what came to be known as the Winter Pilgrimage each year. They cheerfully bore the expense of a four-day round of Christmas parties, including the hotel bill, for a large group of friends from all over the country, culminating in a production of *The Littlest Wiseman*.

The Shaws introduced Howard and Mary D. to square dancing, another love of Walsh's life and another avenue for her generosity. She hosted weekly square dance lessons in their home for many years. The most enduring Walsh memory for many of the Fort Worth social scene was the sight of wheelchair-bound Mary D. being pushed around the dance floor, glitter in her hair and a

Mary Walsh square dancing, her favorite pastime. *Courtesy of F. Howard Walsh, Jr., Estate of Mary D. Walsh.*

smile beaming from her face, for one last square dance.

Mary D. Walsh died in 2005, after a long life filled with giving of her time and resources to others. Her legacy lives on. *The Littlest Wiseman* will continue to delight audiences in Fort Worth at no charge so that, as she said when named Patron of the Arts by the Fort Worth Arts Council for 1969–1970, "those coming into contact with the arts receive the fullest pleasure and enjoyment from them and become disciples for our programs and objectives."

Walsh once said when someone asked her about the millions and millions of dollars she gave away, "You don't get gold stars for helping . . . you just do it because you should."

Humble to the end, Mary D. Walsh's living room sofa sported a pillow proclaiming: "I know I'm efficient, tell me I'm beautiful!" By any meas-ure she was.

BIBLIOGRAPHIC ESSAY

I am indebted to *The Handbook of Texas Online*, the *Fort Worth Star-Telegram*, *Aura Magazine*, *Fort Worth Magazine*, and the *Fort Worth Press*. In addition, websites, publications, and archival materials from the Federated Women's Clubs, the Fort Worth Woman's Club, the Kimbell Art Museum, Cook Children's Medical Center, Tarrant County College District, Texas Christian University, the Amon Carter Museum, and Texas Wesleyan University have been helpful. Ted Stafford's biography of May Owen was a valuable source of information. Finally, the following individuals graciously granted interviews: Patricia Loud, C. A. Roberson, Joe B. Rushing, Ruth Carter Stevenson, and Sharon Ward.

Chapter 7

"IN THE INTEREST OF THE CHILDREN"

by Sherrie S. McLeRoy

*T*N THE LAST DECADE OF THE NINE-teenth century, new scientific notions about homemaking and child rearing, national events such as the 1893 World's Columbian Exposition, and the burgeoning number of study clubs introduced Texas women to social progressivism and the power of their combined numbers. As Fort Worth activist Belle Burchill wrote in 1896, "Reform, the great cry of the age, is heard along all lines of activity. Reform the drunkard, convert the fallen, stop this evil, do that, and there is such a cry that one is deafened by it." Dubbed by Victorian society as the virtuous moral guardians of home and family, women used that position to begin tackling gritty issues that affected their domestic sphere.

None was more important to Texas women in their "natural" role as mothers than to work "in the interest of the children," a popular phrase used to denote projects, events, and legislation that affected the well being of children.

In Fort Worth, efforts to help abandoned and neglected children began in the mid-1880s, and the Woman's Christian Temperance Union was the first to take practical, effective action. The city's young bootblacks and newsboys were poor and often lived on the streets without family support, sleeping in boxes and outhouses. Led by Belle Burchill and Delia Collins, the WCTU organized a small home for them in the fall of 1887 in a vacant storehouse at 302 Main Street, with a reading room and dormitory. "That [first] night five street waifs applied for shelter," Burchill later recalled; within days the number had quadrupled. (See "Duchesses with Hearts of Love and Brains of Fire.")

By the following spring, "the ladies found themselves compelled by the unwritten law of motherly kindness to [also] take in little girls" when two sisters and their brother sought refuge from an abusive and drunken father. Adding girls required more space, and the women asked Tarrant County Commissioners to purchase the large frame house on Cold Springs Road at Samuels Avenue that had previously served as "Madame Brown's" brothel. (The site is now Arnold Park.) Burchill, the home's superintendent, moved eighteen children there in June

1888. Known as the (Industrial) Home for Friendless Boys and Girls or simply the Orphan Home, it was incorporated later that year as the Fort Worth Benevolent Home.

Burchill kept the Benevolent Home in the public eye with frequent newspaper articles, and the city took the children to heart. The young "inmates" were treated to picnics, plays at Greenwall's Opera House, holiday meals, free transportation to events, and annual gifts from public school students. Still, like most orphanages, the Benevolent Home was constantly strapped for money and room, happy to break even and often in debt despite some support from both city and county governments. Burchill herself donated $800 over the years.

By 1896, more than 300 children had passed through the home's doors, and the Board of Lady Managers (who oversaw daily operations) was looking for stable financial help. They briefly allied with a National Children's Home Society based in Chicago, and Burchill was named superintendent of the new Texas Children's Home and Aid Society, which was intended to function statewide. But she resigned just four months later, and the Benevolent Home pulled out, leaving Reverend I.Z.T. Morris to take up the TCHAS and lead it in a different direction. (See below.)

The Lady Managers maintained a constant round of fundraising—teas, balls, and theater productions—to remodel, expand, and maintain the property. They struggled to accommodate children orphaned by the 1900 Galveston hurricane and the ever-growing numbers from Tarrant County. By 1901, the home was so overcrowded that both the Lady Managers and the male trustees began asking commissioners for a new facility. Lillie Dunklin and Adelphine Keeler

launched the women on a successful capital fund drive; long before construction finally began six years later, they had raised half the cost.

The new ten-acre home was in Handley (then in the countryside of East Fort Worth) and the Lady Managers acknowledged the commissioners' financial support by changing the name to Tarrant County Orphans' Home. When the county agreed in 1915 to take over the financially beleaguered facility, the Lady Managers became an advisory board that supervised the juvenile court officer who was now in charge of the home. That fall, however, the Federation of Women's Clubs urged that a new advisory board of both men and women be created to investigate applications and authorize adoptions; the five-member board included Dunklin and two other women.

But by the time the home moved to its last location at 3125 East Lancaster in 1931, Tarrant County and the juvenile court had completely taken over operations from the women who had nurtured it for more than four decades. The Tarrant County Orphans' Home closed in the late 1970s.

The origin of the Texas Children's Home and Aid Society—the modern Gladney Center—is complex and still being researched, but it now seems closely tied to Belle Burchill and Delia Collins. Persistent stories say it began with a group of ministers in the mid-1880s who rescued abandoned children. Indeed, J'Nell Pate in *North of the River* refers to an older newspaper article that stated the two women "frequently assisted a Methodist minister on errands of mercy in Hell's Half Acre and the North Side red-light district." A 1912 home newsletter reported that the Reverend I.Z.T. Morris, a

In 1907, Sam and Edna Gladney traveled to Havana, Cuba on business. While there, the philanthropically-minded Edna tricked her new husband into visiting a leper colony. "I thought he'd never quit scrubbing himself after that visit," she later recalled. *Courtesy of Mrs. Earl Chester.*

Methodist minister generally considered the founder, placed out forty children in 1887. But Morris did not arrive in Fort Worth until 1891; he was then assigned to the city mission, which would have taken him among the needy, so it is likely he began charity and rescue work immediately.

However the story of its beginnings may unfold, Texas Children's Home was officially formed in March 1896, by representatives of a Chicago-based Children's Home society; Belle Burchill was named state superintendent. Its purpose was not to be an orphanage where children lived until old enough to support themselves, as the Benevolent Home was, but to find, care for, and "place out" abandoned and needy youngsters into "carefully selected family homes."

Morris, who replaced Burchill in July, traveled widely across Texas and the Southwest, locating children in need, taking others to new homes, and checking on previous placements. For years, those awaiting new homes lived in the Morris house in Polytechnic Heights and were cared for by Belle Morris and the couple's seven children. During the twenty-five years that Morris, and, after his death, Belle ran the home, it grew rapidly, placing out thousands, opening various facilities in Fort Worth, and even developing field offices in other parts of the state.

At some point, the Morrises met a short, dark-haired dynamo named Edna Kahly. A

Milwaukee native, Kahly had moved to Fort Worth in 1905 for health reasons and lived with Arthur and Flora Goetz, relatives who were prominent in local business, society, and club circles. The Fort Worth connections she made through them would later prove invaluable to her work.

In 1906, Edna married flour miller Sam Gladney; after several years here, they moved to Wolfe City and then Sherman. She had helped children all her life, but it was in Sherman that she first became really active, working with others to clean up the county's poor farm. The children from there were sent to Fort Worth because Gladney knew the Texas Children's Home and Aid Society well from her previous residence; around this time, she also began volunteering for the home, possibly on an auxiliary board.

In 1927, five years after changes in the economy brought the Gladneys back to Fort Worth, Edna agreed to take the superintendent's position at the home, which was reeling from debt, staff turnover, and allegations of mismanagement. Working as a volunteer, she called on her network of contacts to "make the dirt fly." Her first move was asking Amon G. Carter to persuade Texas Electric head A. J. Duncan to buy a large house at Ballinger and El Paso for a new children's home. The deepening Depression meant endless fundraising, and Gladney was well known around town for the milk bottles she placed in businesses for donations. She often joked that the Home had the distinction of never having been out of debt.

Around 1933, Gladney began working with other social workers to change Texas birth certificates, which cruelly listed illegitimate children as such and remained unchanged through-

out their lives. The resulting legislation passed in 1935 but had to be revised several times to correct errors, a task she followed through despite the grief of losing her husband in the midst of it. Several decades later, she would go back to the state legislature to change inheritance laws for adopted children.

In 1940, a Metro-Goldwyn-Mayer scriptwriter who had adopted through TCHAS approached Gladney about making a movie of her life. *Blossoms in the Dust* with Greer Garson and Walter Pidgeon (released in 1941) made her internationally famous but had the unfortunate effect of also linking her name above all others in the public's consciousness with the Texas birth certificate law mentioned above. Decades after her death, open records advocates still blame Edna Gladney for the restrictions on access to these records that remain in place today, though she was only one of many supporters.

Despite poor health, Gladney stayed busy enlisting support for the home; her "weapon of choice" was the telephone, and few could deny her requests. Her work was featured in the *Congressional Record* (1941), *Woman's Home Companion* (1953) (reprinted in *Reader's Digest*, 1954), and *Christian Science Monitor* (1957). In 1953, poet Oswald Mueller dedicated a book of children's poetry to "humanitarian, Mrs. Edna Gladney, who has worked tirelessly and endlessly…[to assure]…that homeless children will be given a chance to take their rightful place in society." She appeared on *This Is Your Life* (1954), and MGM made a second film based on the home, *Those Wilder Years* (1956) with James Cagney. A New York literary agent asked Gladney to write a book, but she replied that she was much too busy.

After World War II, in acknowledgment of changing times, Gladney began moving the Texas Children's Home from an orphanage to a maternity home with its own hospital. In 1950, the board honored her by renaming it the Edna Gladney Home. Two years later, she celebrated her twenty-fifth anniversary as superintendent by forming the first Gladney auxiliary in Houston, which became famous for its star-studded annual Shamrock Ball. More awards came her way in the 1950s. The L. F. Shanblum Lodge of B'nai B'rith in Fort Worth honored her for "outstanding service in community and civic affairs," and Texas Christian University presented her with an honorary degree in 1957, noting, "Her ministry of mercy has captured both the imagination and the admiration of the nation."

Then in her seventies, Gladney maintained a hectic work schedule and voluminous correspondence as she tried to adjust to changing social work standards. More auxiliaries were established and a new hospital built, while she began the preliminary work that would eventually make the home a member of the Child Welfare League of America (1962). Abolishing "gray market adoptions"—private adoptions that verge on being illegal or unethical—was yet another battle.

Increasingly ill from diabetes and related problems, she became unable to climb the steps to the home's second floor. She retired as superintendent in 1960 but agreed to continue helping raise money for a new nursery. She died October 2, 1961, just two days after rallying to go over construction plans.

Nearly forty years after her death, Gladney was named one of the 100 most influential women of the twentieth century by the Women's Chamber of Commerce of Texas. Her name and legacy live on at The Gladney Center.

The third Fort Worth child care facility traces its roots to 1908 when, at the instigation of Gertrude Bloodworth, the Methodist women organized a city mission board for their church. One of the first projects they considered was establishing a "co-operative home" where working girls could live cheaply and safely. The women familiarized themselves with the operations of such a home and surveyed the city's female workers. They concluded that it was as yet "impractible," though they continued to believe there was a need for it.

Four years later, the Methodists invited their counterparts from other denominations to form what became the All Church Federation of Women. In December 1915, the group responded to a call for help from the Reverend J. H. Woodruff, who had opened a Fort Worth co-operative home a few months earlier. The All Church Women's Federation agreed to give "their fullest cooperation" and endorsement to this project they had advocated for years—no small matter given the social prominence and activism of many of the organization's members. Josephine Reed and Ida Jarvis were the first representatives elected to the board; soon after, the home's purpose was amended to also serve mothers with children. Jarvis immediately began petitioning the city for monetary help. But when Reed took over the finance committee in March 1916 the women discovered Woodruff had been misusing funds. The home was seriously in debt, and Reed, as she wrote later, "was given the dirty work to oust him" as superintendent.

Woodruff was gone, but the debt he had incurred continued growing despite stringent

Esther Wilson served as president of the All Church
Federation of Women for thirty-two years. Her
daughter, Emily Bird, followed her in that position,
while her husband, Judge James Wilson, volun-
teered on the advisory board for twenty-five years.
Courtesy of Fort Worth Star-Telegram *Collection,*
Special Collections, The University of Texas at
Arlington Library, Arlington, Texas.

Pecan, where it remained for fifteen years.

Early in 1923, the board incorporated as the
All Church Woman's Co-Operative Home,
"where dependent girls and women will be furnished room, board and maintenance at cost or
free until they secure work and become self-sus-
taining, and ... [to provide] ... the proper care,
support and maintenance of dependent mothers
and caring for their children while the mothers
are at work." Afterward, the board was reorganized, with all its members drawn from the All
Church Women's Federation.

The home enlisted support—both monetary
and in-kind—from the Community Chest (forerunner of United Way), churches, physicians,
and civic groups such as Kiwanis and Rotary.
The city paid a per diem for residents it sent
there, while Tarrant County contributed monthly.
By October 20, 1927, federation president
Esther Wilson was able to announce at a meeting that the home's debt of $10,000 had at last
been liquidated. Members rose in response and
heartily sang "Praise God from Whom All
Blessings Flow."

With the assistance of Fort Worth's
Children's Bureau, the board then changed its
focus to accept only school-age children:
"orphans, deserted children and children of destitute parents who would be otherwise handicapped by improper nutrition and lack of home
care." Many came from homes broken by separation, divorce, death, or illness. Because the aim
of the newly named All Church Home was to
help families "over rough spots," few of the children stayed for years but instead returned home
as soon as feasible.

By 1937, All Church had outgrown the
Pecan Street facility. Led by Wilson, the board

economy. WCTU member, home finance chairman, and former president of the Methodist's
City Mission Board, Bloodworth energized the
women into fundraising. One memorable "Tag
Day," for example, brought in $3,500, and a pen-
cil sale netted $1,000, which meant the board
could finally consider a larger building. (Tag Day
workers were stationed in businesses and on
street corners around town to solicit donations,
"tagging" those who contributed.) Around 1921,
with remodeling work donated by city labor
unions, the home moved from 401 West First to
the former Benno Smith residence at Bluff and

acquired the tile-roofed, Mediterranean-style mansion at 1425 Summit built by Frank Ball in the 1880s and later owned by oilman and rancher Samuel Burk Burnett. The property—still owned today by the home and supplemented by gifts of adjoining land from William Bryce and the Mary Couts Burnett Trust—sloped down to the Trinity River and included a historical marker noting it as the site of the last Indian attack against Camp Worth.

There, the children enjoyed their own skating rink, playground, gardens, recreation building, and woodworking shop. They attended public schools and nearby churches and had their own Scout troops. In the 1950s, the home became the first in the city to utilize cottages that moved the children from dormitory accommodations in the mansion to a family-type setting with individual rooms. The historic house itself was demolished after a 1963 fire and the site filled with several modern buildings.

Today the All Church Home for Children is a state-licensed child care facility and child-placing agency that maintains its sprawling headquarters on Summit Avenue, a separate residential campus in the Wedgwood area, and a ranch near Stephenville. In 2005, the home merged with the Bridge Youth and Family Services and now operates in nine counties.

A dying child's vision led to the last of Fort Worth's historic child care institutions. In his final days, seven-year-old Conrad Pope told his parents he was going to a mansion filled with children and that they should build one like it on earth. His mother, Louisiana-born Lena Holston Pope, buried him in Houston when he died of diphtheria just a few days after Christmas 1914. Sixteen years would pass before she could fulfill his vision.

The Popes and their two younger children moved to Fort Worth in the late 1920s and joined Broadway Baptist Church, where Lena found an outlet for her charitable interests in the Martha Sunday school class. The "Marthas" helped board homeless or needy children in temporary homes, even housing a dozen in the church basement.

Pope asked the Marthas to share Conrad's dream with her. They agreed, deciding it would be cheaper to have the children they served all in one location, and rented a small house at 1215 Washington in the Fairmount neighborhood.

"We planned to care for fourteen children of our denomination who were destitute, neglected, and dependent," Pope told the *Star-Telegram* in 1947. But when the first of January 1930 dawned frigid and sleety, the women found twenty-five youngsters waiting for them—the beginning of the Lena Pope Home.

With only $150 in the bank and the country entering the Great Depression, their first problem was money. Fort Worth Coca-Cola distributor C. A. Lupton, whose wife Marie was a Martha, provided money for a year's worth of groceries. Their second problem was the state Children's Bureau, which refused to grant a license because none of the women were trained social workers. Pope finally drove to Austin and brought back the assistant head of the Texas Welfare Department to see the need for himself; she got her license.

In its first year, the home moved four times in search of more space, ending at the W. T. Waggoner residence at El Paso and Summit (near the All Church and Texas Children's

Left to Right: Marie Lupton, Audie Evans, Lena Pope, and Thelma Rigg were among the members of the original Martha Class at Broadway Baptist Church who worked with class president Pope to establish the Lena Pope Home in 1930. *Courtesy of* Fort Worth Star-Telegram *Collection, Special Collections, The University of Texas at Arlington Library, Arlington, Texas.*

homes). By that time, Pope and the Marthas were caring for nearly 100 children, as the worst of the depression hit Fort Worth.

The board was composed of members of the Martha Class, with Pope as president, but now she felt they needed representatives from the business community to advise them through the tough economy. Through the 1930s, she enlisted C. A. Lupton, department store owners Will Monnig and Marvin Leonard, businessman Leo Potishman, and newspaperman Amon G. Carter.

In 1932, the home moved to a large granite mansion at 4801 Camp Bowie Boulevard. Even it became overcrowded, and Pope had to stop taking children for a time. The home now began to pay its staff, but Pope continued as a volunteer, working there while her own children were in school.

The home had grown so large, so rapidly, that it was now beyond the financial capabilities of either the Marthas or Broadway Baptist. Many of the children came from Tarrant's juvenile courts and its overcrowded orphans' home (see above), their care paid for by the county. To house them, Pope built new dormitories, with most of the labor and supplies donated.

The several hundred children who called the facility home—many of them until they graduated from high school, because the home did not do adoptions—enjoyed their own sports teams and Scout troops, an extensive playground, and even a goldfish pond built with rock left over from the dorms. They were not allowed to smoke or drink, only seniors could date, and everyone helped with chores. Pope took in families, too, when she could, in order to keep siblings together.

While many of the home's boys, past and present, served in World War II, Pope and the board looked for another site, settling on seventy acres across from Arlington Heights High School and fronting the proposed expressway. To help finance it, Carter, Lupton, Leonard, Monnig, and Texas Electric chairman J. B. Thomas pledged $250,000 over five years.

Despite opposition from area property owners, the home began clearing the twelve-block site in 1947—the same year Pope was named first woman honoree of the Exchange Club's Golden Deeds award—while fundraising continued. In the meantime, the postwar baby boom filled the separate infants' facility on

Collinwood, near the main house on Camp Bowie. It would be the first unit rebuilt on the new campus; the C. A. Lupton Memorial Babyland, with room for ninety infants, opened in time for Pope's seventieth birthday in December 1950. (The site was converted to green space after the building burned decades later.)

Less than a dollar was left in the building fund, but Pope pushed ahead with the main building. Construction stopped every time money ran out, so it took nine years to complete. The home finally realized its dream when the last of the children and operations moved from the dilapidated buildings on Camp Bowie in December 1960.

Seventy-nine-year-old Lena retired as board president that same year to care for her ailing husband, though she retained a seat and was named president emeritus. During this decade, the home was licensed and began placing children for adoption, was racially integrated, and followed All Church Home's lead by moving to cottage residences. Pope published her autobiography, *Hand on My Shoulder,* and, in 1967, was named Texas Baptist Mother of the Year and received the Sertoma Club's Service to Mankind Award.

The 1970s brought many regulatory changes to agencies such as the Lena Pope Home, few of which Pope liked. She tried to force a return to older methods through the courts, but the attempt failed, and, in 1974, she moved to Taos, New Mexico, to live with her daughter. She died there two years later.

The twenty-first century Lena Pope Home is no longer an orphanage but works with troubled and emotionally disturbed youngsters and families in need of counseling. With most of its high-way acreage leased for commercial development, its most visible landmark is now the striking Marty Leonard Chapel, designed by E. Fay Jones and built in 1990.

Genteel Victorian women were expected to oversee their children's education, a goal advocated by Mothers' Study Clubs. Fort Worth's club was organized in February 1896 with about a dozen women who believed it was "better to form than to reform." Their aim was establishing public school kindergartens in the city, then a new and controversial educational concept but one that supporters believed would help build better citizens and thus reduce crime and poverty.

The term "kindergarten"—literally, a garden of children—was coined by German educator Frederick Froebel in the 1830s. Froebel emphasized outdoor play and gardening, self-directed activity, and the use of games and songs to release a child's creativity and independence. Introduced to this country in the late 1840s, kindergartens did not become popular until featured at the 1876 Centennial Exposition. Even then, many middle-class parents were skeptical because it stressed the trained teacher over the mother in a child's development. Texas teachers did not begin seriously discussing the concept until the mid-1880s. El Paso opened the first free public kindergarten in 1893, but most early programs were private and required tuition.

Eliza J. Whitmore, who would later serve as matron of the Benevolent Home and, by 1896, operated her own kindergarten, led the Mothers' Study Club in its first action: to immediately form the Fort Worth Kindergarten Association. One member, physician Ellen Lawson Dabbs,

urged public acceptance: "[They] will find that it is cheaper to build handsome, well regulated kindergarten places than it is to build jails, court-houses and reformatories."

The women opened their first class in September 1896 at the corner of Main and Ninth in Fort Worth's infamous Hell's Half Acre. Two years later they expanded farther south, then opened two more facilities in 1900 and 1901 and a fifth at the Benevolent Home in 1903, when an average of 130 children attended the free classes, children "who would otherwise be left to drift about on the streets, subjected to all kinds of vicious and ignoble influences." Each location annually cost $600–$800 for furniture, supplies, and a teacher's salary of $50 a month.

The steadily increasing demand for public and private kindergartens brought an equal demand for trained young women to run them. So members of the city's association "commenced the gigantic task" and, in the fall of 1900, opened the Fort Worth Kindergarten Training School: the first in Texas specifically for kindergarten teachers. (The name was changed to Fort Worth Kindergarten College in 1903.) A two-year course, it soon associated with the prestigious Chicago Kindergarten College to train its faculty because "only a few members, ladies from the North, knew anything about the work." Martha Crombie was the first principal, Myra M. Winchester was her assistant, and seven young women from Fort Worth, Walnut Springs, Iowa Park, Corsicana, Sherman, and Hillsboro formed the first class. They adopted Froebel's motto, "Come, let us live with the children," and "the modest marguerite" as their class flower.

School tuition was $50; the Kindergarten Association underwrote expenses (salaries,

Sallie Capps (center) was association president in 1908 when this photo was made for The Club Woman's Argosy. Mrs. E. A. Watters (3) served as vice-president and Mrs. H. H. Cobb (10) as 2nd vice-president, while Mrs. A. J. Roe (4) was past president of both the Fort Worth and Texas Kindergarten Associations. Myra M. Winchester (2) was college principal in 1908. Other women pictured were Mrs. H. Brann (5), Mrs. Hunt McCalabe (6), Mrs. O. Lee Jones (7), Mrs. E. L. White (8), and Mrs. J. J. Nunnally (9). *Courtesy of Sallie Capps Collection, Special Collections, The University of Texas at Arlington Library, Arlington, Texas.*

rents, and supplies) through these fees, membership dues, donations, and special events. In 1901, the women petitioned city council to appropriate money for more kindergartens, a request supported in person by representatives of the Fort Worth Federation of Women's Clubs.

Students of the college were required to have a high school diploma or equivalent, a health certificate, and references for admission and were on probation for eight weeks. Afternoon classes met in a "little house" on Fifteenth and Calhoun streets (just east of the modern Water Gardens), and the students taught mornings at two schools in the Third and Fourth Wards, rotating through different classes to learn methods.

The faculty expanded their second year to include Mary P. Belden in domestic science and Elizabeth Hammers in art; a nature course, psychology, and music were soon added. The young women also studied children's literature, physiology and hygiene, and games and physical education. Their second year was more intense and included a sociology class to acquaint them "with some of the problems of a modern city and of the function of the school in relation to them."

Over the next few years, the college's class locations moved constantly. The association planned to buy a building near downtown to house free kindergarten classes in the morning and college classes in the afternoon, as well as a second floor dormitory for the women students. Though money was raised, it was apparently never built, and the college moved to special rooms in the new Fort Worth High School when it was completed. In 1910, the city Board of Education incorporated the college into the public system and soon added the position of supervisor of kindergartens and primary grades.

By this time, the school had an adjunct operation, the Social Settlement House at Crump and Eighteenth. Such services were established in the poorer neighborhoods of major American cities, with Jane Addams' Hull House being the most famous, and were often near free kindergartens. The Fort Worth women tried to operate theirs with volunteers but soon had to hire Margaret Grabill of Denver to run it. Settlement House offered mothers' study clubs, girls' sewing and housekeeping classes, boys' social and literary clubs, a circulating library, and a "penny savings fund."

Documentation for the college ends in 1919, and it is likely that the students transferred to either North Texas State Teachers College (now University of North Texas) or Texas Woman's College (formerly Polytechnic and now Texas Wesleyan University); these schools started kindergarten courses in 1919 and 1923, respectively. But the Fort Worth Kindergarten Association and its Alumnae Association, organized by the first graduating class, continued to operate well into the 1930s. In 1938, their representatives protested the elimination of free classes in the city's public schools. It was a powerhouse group that included Mrs. Henry King, Sallie Capps, and Jennie Scheuber. Association president King reminded the school board members that they had promised to include kindergartens in their recent bond issue, which the association had supported. "We had 500 members then," King said tartly, "and 500 women can do a lot of talking. Now they're letting us down." But despite the women's efforts, tuition was imposed, and kindergarten enrollment dropped from 727 children to 79.

Today the kindergartens they fought to establish are accepted as integral parts of a public or a private education.

Particularly responsive to Fort Worth's minority communities, United Community Center was created in 1971 from five Methodist-supported facilities and now serves thousands of residents each year.

But it all began in 1908 with a six-room cottage.

That September, twenty-seven delegates from Fort Worth's Methodist women's mission societies met to organize the City Mission Board. Carrie Boaz served as first president. The group

had several major goals: (1) to pursue evangelistic and mission work in North Fort Worth, where a booming but poor foreign population worked in the stockyards and packing houses; (2) to open a Sunday school in the same area; and (3) to consider establishing a co-operative home for working women.

The latter goal proved elusive. Boaz reported visiting all the telephone offices, where she found thirty-nine female workers, "but few of them [were] anxious to avail themselves of the advantages of this home." Other women reported similar findings from restaurants and hotels, so the idea was abandoned. Board members returned to it several times over the following years, for they still believed there was a need.

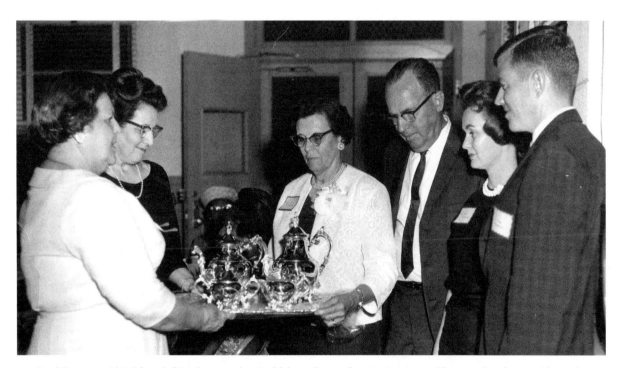

Pearl Feemster (third from left) volunteered at Bethlehem Center from its inception. She served as first president of its Board of Directors and as first president of Methodist Community Centers Council, forerunner of United Community Centers. In this 1964 photo, she receives a silver service from Dorothy Ashley and Frances Bickham, honoring her for her many years of service. To her right are husband Lee Feemster and son Rev. Ben Feemster with his wife Pat. Lee gave his own years of service to Bethlehem, keeping the building in repair. *Courtesy of Pat Feemster.*

Not until 1915 did others organize the Fort Worth Co-Operative Home; it would not have survived long without the eventual intervention of the Methodist women—who already had studied the concept—and their fellow members of the All Church Federation of Women. (See above.)

For the Stockyards work, the City Mission Board hired Laura Padgett at $39.50 per month. She made hundreds of home visits, distributed clothing and religious tracts, led prayer meetings, and opened a Sunday school in a six-room cottage on Weatherford Street near Samuels, where many immigrants lived. Padgett, exhausted by the demanding work, was replaced in 1910 by Lillie Fox, who was to receive $50 a month. Rarely, however, did either woman collect her salary in full, as the City Mission Board continually ran a deficit.

By 1911 the need for a "Wesley House" on the North Side had become clear. The board engaged Eugenia Smith, who had spent several years doing similar work among the multinational coal mining population in Thurber, west of Fort Worth. She rented a house and opened in December with a Christmas tree for the community's children, many of whom had never seen one.

In 1913 the board purchased a lot at 2131 North Commerce Street and erected the two-story Jerome Duncan Wesley House for $4,100. Its female staff operated a kindergarten and offered church services and sewing and cooking classes.

But close by Wesley House were three saloons that sold liquor to minors roaming the streets while their parents worked. In her "deaconess garb" of black dress with white collar and cuffs, and a black dress bonnet, Smith confronted the owners, threatening to report them to the city and have their licenses revoked. Sales to children stopped. It must have been satisfying to her in 1921 when the Mission Board purchased the corner saloon and tore it down, reusing the heavy timbers to build La Trinidad Church for the predominantly Mexican neighborhood.

At Wesley House, the Methodist women began a free clinic in 1928, opened a relief center in the floods of 1922 and 1949, and distributed government food.

Meanwhile, a biracial Methodist leadership conference in 1937 led delegate Dorothy Rollins Staten to open the Negro Day Nursery as a kindergarten and day care for children of working parents "in the largest Negro neighborhood in Fort Worth." Supported by both black and white women's groups, the nursery became an official project of the Central Texas Methodist Conference in 1942—the first west of the Mississippi River—and was renamed Bethlehem Center. The organization has had several strong women directors, including Josephine Beckwith, a polio victim who was the first black person commissioned as a Methodist home missionary.

After fifty-three years in the same location, Wesley House followed the city's northward population shift and moved to 3600 North Crump. Separately, a third facility, Maddox Community Center, opened in 1967. Three years later, the Methodist women voted to merge their operations as the United Community Centers. All three—Wesley, Bethlehem, and Maddox—would continue to be owned by the women's mission group, but their operations would be shared by the entire Methodist Church. Beckwith, recipient of United Way's Hercules

Award in 1968, was named executive director. She also began Fort Worth's Meals on Wheels program and oversaw development of UCC's Polytechnic Center in 1975.

Planning for a city children's museum began with the Fort Worth Council of Administrative Women in Education, a group of principals and other female school executives organized in 1934 with sixteen charter members. With a combined 244 years of teaching among them, and 333 years as administrators, these women knew a little something about education.

A 1937 program on "Preservation of Things Old and Rare" spurred them to begin thinking about museums. But it was member Ella J. Smith, principal of South Hi-Mount School in Arlington Heights, who proposed in 1939 that the CAWE focus on children. The council agreed, and Smith, appointed museum committee chairman, began corresponding with children's museums around the United States and in Canada to learn more about the subject. The women had several goals: to make learning more fun, to help children better understand the world around them, to educate students and their parents about the opportunities offered by museums, and, as a result, to build better citizens.

While gathering data and planning fundraising strategy, the council invited more than a dozen other groups—primarily women's organizations—to join them in this project, including American Association of University Women, Woman's Club of Fort Worth, Business and Professional Women's Club, and Zonta Club. With this impressive show of support, the CAWE then approached city officials. In the fall of 1940, the Fort Worth City Council agreed "to sponsor a $150,000 children's museum on the Centennial grounds [Will Rogers Coliseum] providing the fifteen women's organizations backing the project can raise the funds and work out a method of caring for maintenance costs." Ima Love Kuykendall, first president of the council, reported that the public library would help furnish exhibits from its collection of art and historical relics.

The group incorporated in 1941 as the Fort Worth Children's Museum and, while World War II precluded any major action, the women stayed busy gathering exhibit materials and pledges of support. Working with the city, they also drew up plans for a building. War's end brought preparation for commercial and infrastructure development in Fort Worth; to the women's delight, the bond issue to pay for these improvements included $300,000 for a children's museum.

Until postwar supply restrictions allowed construction, however, the museum board needed a site. They found one at DeZavala Elementary School, 1419 College Avenue, where the school board provided two large rooms. When the Fort Worth Children's Museum opened on Valentine's Day 1945 as the first such museum in Texas or the Southwest, the women of the CAWE were among the hostesses, and member Lulu Parker, (see "Cracking the Glass Ceiling") a recently retired principal, was the volunteer curator.

Their next move was inspired by Eleanor Roosevelt's newspaper column about John Ripley Forbes, director of New York's Hornaday Foundation and energetic advocate of children's museums. The council invited him to Fort Worth to advise their group; he would also secure gifts of materials and curatorial help from such prestigious collections as the American

Ima Love Kuykendall, first president of Fort Worth's Council of Adminstrative Women in Education, presents current president Fanjane Stovall with a pair of ceramics Kuykendall purchased in France for the Fort Worth Children's Museum. *Courtesy of* Fort Worth Star-Telegram *Collection, Special Collections, The University of Texas at Arlington Library, Arlington, Texas.*

Museum of Natural History. In an interview with the *Star-Telegram*, Forbes noted two more advantages of postwar children's museums: to help supplement the shortage of teachers and to teach children "to understand the habits and customs of other people as an antidote for the misunderstandings that lead to war."

Energized by his visit, the CAWE, the Junior League, and the Provarsu Club then led a campaign that raised more than $30,000 for operations.

The museum proved so popular that it quickly outgrew the schoolrooms. In September 1947, the collections—including a stuffed and mounted buffalo—were moved to the former R. E. Harding mansion at 1306 Summit (later demolished for commercial space). With Forbes' guidance, volunteers filled the twenty rooms, designated outbuildings for class and theater space, and developed a nature trail down the bluff to the Trinity River.

One of the most enduring figures associated with the museum soon arrived to teach astronomy and organize a pioneering Junior Astronomy Club. Charlie Mary Noble's innovative work at the Fort Worth Children's Museum would be copied by many other groups. (Read more about Noble in the chapter "Cracking the Glass Ceiling.") To honor Noble, the council asked the Junior League to donate a planetarium. Their 1949 gift of $1,000 made Fort Worth the first children's museum in the nation to own a modern Spitz Planetarium; it was installed under a homemade dome in a tent in the mansion's backyard. The league would also contribute to Noble's salary for many years.

The museum was filled every day with children taking classes in geology, drawing, and

leather crafts, hiking area nature trails, caring for the museum gardens, and watching movies in the old garage, now a playhouse. A popular exhibit was the live animal room, where children could interact with native Texas critters: possums, snakes, a de-scented skunk, and the museum's first animal, Limpopo the alligator.

Raising money was a constant battle, even with such generous donors as Anne Burnett Windfohr and Alice Davis. Mrs. Jack Furman headed the women's division of several campaigns to raise funds for a permanent, salaried staff, as the museum's rapid growth was becoming too much for volunteers alone. In 1948, Lulu Parker retired as founding curator and was succeeded by Ann Webb, formerly of the Boston Museum of Fine Arts. Visitation and services expanded even more, and the museum was featured in *Ladies Home Journal*'s July 1950 issue.

That same year saw several important financial and program developments. A Ladies Auxiliary was formed to promote the museum and encourage gifts; Nancy Lee Bass was elected president and later served on the board. (The auxiliary is now the Museum Guild.) Their first benefit was to host the "Court of Jewels," an $8 million exhibit sponsored by jeweler Harry Winston that included the Hope Diamond.

Also in 1950, the Fort Worth School Board appointed a fulltime teacher to coordinate the school district's curriculum with the museum. And the "Frisky and Blossom Club," now the Museum School, debuted.

A second bond issue in 1951 finally allowed construction of the new museum to begin on Montgomery Street west of the Will Rogers Coliseum. Director Anne Webb and donor Anne Windfohr were the only women to help break ground on October 24, 1952, though founding museum committee chair Ella Smith was acknowledged. The dedication ceremony sixteen months later, however, honored its women founders by featuring the museum's first two directors, Lulu Parker and Anne Webb (retired 1953), Josephine Kelly (then president of the Council of Administrative Women in Education), and Ella Smith.

Today the Fort Worth Museum of Science and History (renamed 1968) is the largest in the Southwest, with more than a million visitors annually, and boasts the first IMAX Theater in the Southwest.

A cold day in 1915 led to an act of charity that had long-lasting repercussions for Fort Worth. A young city doctor, his name long lost, found a baby girl abandoned in his office. But there was no children's hospital to care for her even though the Fort Worth Federation of Women's Clubs had donated $3,500 in 1913 for a children's wing at the city-county hospital (now John Peter Smith). Not knowing what else to do, the doctor decided to carry her home to his wife. At the streetcar line, he met Ida L. Turner, the city's former postmistress, who was appalled at the infant's story and condition: cold, malnourished, and ill-clothed.

Ida Turner was a woman of action. A Texas delegate to the 1893 Chicago Exposition and an energetic member of the WCTU, she helped found Fort Worth's Humane Society in 1904. But even with her contacts, she also could find no hospital that would take the child. Finally, a local minister appealed successfully on her behalf to All Saints Hospital.

Though this story had a happy ending when the baby was adopted several months later,

Turner knew other children were not so lucky. She enlisted Mrs. John H. Strayer, chair of the Fort Worth Relief Association's welfare committee and of Federation's social service committee, and Turner's good friend Jennie Scheuber, chair of the civic committee. For months, they investigated the city's high infant mortality rate to discover its causes. World War I had made jobs and food scarce, and hungry mothers could not produce enough breast milk for healthy babies. Cow's milk was not yet pasteurized, resulting in frequent epidemic diarrhea in babies. Meanwhile, the West Texas oil boom caused Fort Worth's population to explode, placing even more strain on the few public health services.

"Determined that this unholy holocaust must stop," the women decided Fort Worth needed a facility like Dallas' Baby Camp, opened in 1913 (now Children's Medical Center). Turner, Strayer, and Scheuber called a meeting of civic, fraternal, and women's clubs in March 1917 to begin soliciting money. "It was an appeal that touched all hearts," the Federal Writer's Project reported later. "The whole community answered this prayer."

Headed by Strayer, the newly formed hospital committee—all women—persuaded Fairmount Land Company to donate 2.5 acres on a hilltop in what is now Park Hill. (Later gifts would bring it to six acres.) Sanguinet & Staats, who designed so many landmark buildings in Fort Worth, drew up plans for a hospital and supervised the construction at no charge. Though workers were scarce and wages high as a result of the war, the building trade unions donated half the labor costs, and material suppliers all over town gave, too. A list of donors and gifts in the Fort Worth Public Library Archives runs six single-spaced pages—everything from Swiss curtains to steel and concrete to a Jersey cow. Organizations such as the Kindergarten Association donated beds, while the City Union of King's Daughters and Sons provided linens and gowns.

Work on the one-story frame structure began June 7, 1917, and was completed in August. To thank the laborers, Polly Mack organized women to make lunches for them most days. Meanwhile, Dr. H. K. Beall began assembling physicians who would donate their time, and the hospital board continued to raise money with a benefit baseball game, a carnival, and the first of many Tag Days. Their most successful event was Fort Worth's first charity ball, held at the elegant Metropolitan Hotel on January 9, 1918. Two thousand people crammed the ballroom, including hundreds of officers from Camp Bowie and the area's three aviation fields in full dress uniform. Famed stage dancer Vernon Castle, a captain in England's Royal Flying Corps stationed at Benbrook, entertained the guests in what would be his last stage appearance; he died several days later in a training accident.

The twenty-five-bed Fort Worth Baby Hospital opened at 2400 Winton Terrace West in March 1918, free of debt as a result of the women's hard work and supplied with food by its own cows, chickens, garden, and orchards. The entire property was held in trust by the City Federation of Women's Clubs from 1917 until 1943. Clubwoman and co-founder Jennie Scheuber succeeded Strayer as president, directing the hospital's activities from her executive desk at the public library and holding office until shortly before she died in 1944.

In 1923 a second floor was added to the building and the name changed to Fort Worth

Children's Hospital. Financially able families paid a minimal amount, but most were indigent and treated free.

By World War II, the hospital's physical plant and financial resources were sorely overtaxed. Scheuber had begun developing plans for a new facility, but the war and restrictions on building materials caused their postponement. To qualify for future federal money, the board incorporated in 1943 as the Fort Worth Children's Hospital, and the federation transferred the property to it. Three years later, they bought a lot on another hilltop at Ballinger, Thirteenth, and Collier Streets, just west of W. I. Cook Memorial Hospital (opened 1929), and authorized architectural plans.

But in 1947, the women made the tough decision to re-form as an auxiliary woman's board and establish a new governing board of both men and women. While the Winton Terrace building received a temporary remodeling, Margaret Ware, wife of the new board chairman, was named to head the campaign for a modern one—its thirty beds were now "woefully inadequate" for a city of 300,000 people.

Also that year, the hospital received its first major gift: half a million dollars from the estate of Josephine Harrold Barnes, whose father had been in the cattle business with Winfield Scott and Samuel Burk Burnett. Initially considered for the building fund, the bequest instead launched an endowment fund.

Construction money proved elusive, however, so the board was willing, in 1951, to entertain a proposal that it merge with Cook Memorial and the Crippled Children's Center. But negotiations broke down over who would manage the new medical center and who would be on the governing board. The Children's Hospital returned to its own building plans; meanwhile, Cook converted from a general to a children's facility in 1952.

To help raise funds, Nenetta Burton Carter, second wife of Amon G. Carter and daughter of oilman W. G. Burton, resurrected the old Assembly Ball begun in 1918 and renamed it the Jewel Charity Ball. Over the decades, it has raised millions of dollars for the Children's Hospital and its successor.

In the fall of 1959, the board finally broke ground at Sixth Avenue and Pruitt, close to Harris Hospital. During construction, safety considerations forced the hospital to sell the Winton Terrace building and move to a house at Sixth and Cooper until the new $1,116,000 structure opened in March 1961.

The Baby Hospital begun nearly a century ago by three determined women lives on today as the state-of-the-art Cook Children's Medical Center, the result—finally—of a 1985 merger between it and Cook Memorial.

Space does not permit more than mention these other child-related institutions:

World War I—"the Great War"—forced many women into the workplace and led to a need for reliable child care. Some two-dozen clubwomen launched the Day Nursery Association in 1920; founding president Carrie McFarland served in that office three decades. That same year, Olive Kuykendall of the Fort Worth Relief Association and Roseland Herren instituted a separate nursery to serve the North Side.

When the Great Depression hit Fort Worth hard in 1932, Alice Leavy organized a soup kitchen near Peter Smith School for hungry children. The first support money came from [Fort]

Worth Post No. 372 of the American Legion, composed of women war nurses, of which Leavy was president.

Mother-daughter team Elizabeth DeCory Vaughn and Hazel Vaughn Leigh organized the North Fort Worth Boys Club in 1935 to help combat juvenile delinquency. Leigh served as executive director and was active until the mid-1970s. (For more information on Leigh, see J'Nell Pate's excellent biography.)

BIBLIOGRAPHIC ESSAY

Several references were invaluable throughout the chapter: the *Dallas Morning News* Historical Archive (online), *The New Handbook of Texas; North of the River, A Brief History of North Fort Worth* by J'Nell Pate, and the Works Progress Administration's National Writers Project, Fort Worth City Guide in special collections at the University of Texas at Arlington. I also made use of the *Fort Worth Star-Telegram* archives in the UTA Special Collections.

In the genealogy and local history section of the Fort Worth Public Library, I used the local history collection, vertical files, historic newspapers on microfilm, Tarrant County Historical Society records, Mary Daggett Lake Collection, and city directories. I also consulted websites of those organizations still operating today.

I wish to thank my colleagues Ruth Karbach, who generously shared her research in the city records housed at the library and minutes of the Fort Worth Federation of Women's Clubs at Texas Woman's University, and Hollace Weiner, who lent material on the Kindergarten Association.

The section on the Texas Children's Home/Edna Gladney was largely drawn from my own research for an upcoming biography of Mrs. Gladney. My thanks to Mrs. Earl Chester and The Gladney Center.

The All Church Home graciously allowed me access to their archives, which date to the home's formation.

Additional research for the Lena Pope Home came from Mrs. Pope's autobiography, *A Hand on my Shoulder* and from *Beyond the Blue: Lena Pope Home, 75 Years: Caring for Children and Families Since 1930* (2005).

Additional sources for Fort Worth Kindergarten College included "A History of the Kindergarten Movement in Texas from 1886 to 1942" by Mary King Drew; catalogs of the college from the archives of the Association of Childhood Education International at the University of Maryland, and the Sallie B. Capps Papers and Fort Worth Kindergarten Association Collection at the University of Texas at Arlington.

The archivists at the Fort Worth Museum of Science and History provided much important material, including "The Charter Members of the Fort Worth Council of Administrative Women in Education" (1952) by Avis Roberson Collett, et al., "The Wonderful World of Children's Museum's" by Herbert and Marjorie Katz in *Woman's Day* (November 1967), and correspondence of Ella J. Smith.

Chapter 8

THE NORTH SIDE, LA FUNDICIÓN, AND EL TP

by Sandra Guerra-Cline

N HIS 2003 COLLECTION OF FORT Worth history, *Stories from the Barrio: A History of Mexican Fort Worth*, Carlos E. Cuellar explains the migration patterns of the city's earliest Mexican inhabitants. He recounts the stories of the men who came north looking for a better life, in some cases running from the death and destruction brought about by the Mexican Revolution. They came to Fort Worth seeking jobs and stability. Almost without exception, these men were scouts, coming to a strange land ahead of their families. If they succeeded, they would settle somewhere and save their money; then they would send for their wives and children, brothers and sisters, and many others.

To trace the early Mexican population in the city, Cuellar used U.S. Census figures and information from such sources as the Fort Worth City Directory. The first Hispanic woman listed in the city directory was Millie Mendoza. Mendoza is a bit of a mystery. Her profession is listed as "actress" at the Theatre Comique on Main Street in downtown Fort Worth. Despite her sur-

name, Cuellar says it is impossible to determine if Mendoza was indeed Mexican, Spanish, or an Anglo woman who had married a man with a Hispanic surname. In subsequent examples, also from the city directory, Cuellar finds Mexican women who worked in restaurants and as maids and laundresses.

By and large, the jobs Mexican men found in Fort Worth were hard ones. The Armour and Company and Swift and Company meatpacking plants drew these men and their families to the city's rambling and chaotic stockyards area, which would grow into a large and influential Mexican-American neighborhood known today as "the North Side." The Texas Rolling Mills, a steel foundry established in 1908 in a neighborhood to the city's immediate south side along present-day Hemphill Street, gave birth to another Mexican neighborhood, La Fundición. Another area on the west side of town with concentrations of Mexican families was called El TP, where families of Mexican workers at the Texas & Pacific Railway lived.

Esperanza "Hope" Padilla Ayala, who for thirty-three years worked as the secretary of All Saints Catholic Church, a social hub of the North Side, has fond memories of growing up with her family there in the 1930s, 1940s, and 1950s. Ayala is the daughter of Margarito R. Padilla and Maria Felan Padilla. The Padillas had six children, and Ayala was the oldest, born December 18, 1928.

"We were poor, but we never did lock our houses [on the North Side]. What could they steal?" she says, drawing a vivid picture of the close community. In the heat of summer, "sometimes, we would sleep outside in the back yard, all three of us girls. And we never had any fear."

While attending high school, the young Esperanza went to work as cashier and popcorn maker at the neighborhood's Rose Marine Theater.

"I made $10 a week, and the money went to my mother. She was the one [in the family] in charge of the money," Ayala says.

With the money, her mother bought material to make the children's clothes, paid the bills, and shopped for food at Lovelace Grocery Store. Ayala often accompanied her mother to the store, hoping her purchases would be many. "If you bought a lot, say $5 or $10 worth, the store would send you home in a cab," she says. "I loved that!"

She married Michael Ayala in 1949, and they had three children. Life on the North Side went on, with PTA meetings, festivals and feast days at the Catholic church, and, over the years, many, many family reunions.

"In my time I've seen a lot of contributions by women in the [North Side] community," says Michael Ayala. "Women who worked the *fiestas*

patrias; at the Wesley Community House, women who were always ready, as we say in Spanish, to *prestar su tiempo* (give of their time) to the community. Ayala hopes that these women—"ordinary women," he says—will be forever remembered in the pages of Fort Worth history.

But who indeed is an "ordinary" woman?

Certainly not Dionicia Pulido, who worked her entire life for the betterment of others and her family. When the Pulido's restaurants celebrated the company's fortieth anniversary in the summer of 2006 by rolling back prices to match the 1966 menus, the dishes they were honoring—the $1.35 enchilada dinner, the $1.20 combination plate and the hungry-man "Pulido dinner" for $2.25—were the ones created in the kitchen of Dionicia Pulido. They were her original recipes for enchiladas, tacos, tamales, and guacamole, and, of course, the rice and beans. They were the meals she prepared for her young, growing family over a wood-fired stove.

Dionicia Marquez, daughter of Mauricio and Eufemia Marquez, married Pedro Pulido in 1935. She had three sons, Vincent, Philip, and Shannon, and her new husband adopted them. Pedro Pulido worked for the Texas & Pacific Railway, which had a rail yard just southwest of downtown Fort Worth. As the Pulido family grew to seven children, Pedro and Dionicia moved to El TP, the small barrio on the north side of the rail lines. The barrio, or what is left of it, sits between Interstate 30 and Vickery Boulevard, and is bordered by University Drive to the east and Montgomery Street to the west. Robert Pulido, the Pulidos' youngest son who is known as Bobby, likes to tell people that he and his brothers and sister spent their summers

Dionicia "Mama" Pulido stands with one of her sons,
Bobby, at work on March 10, 1985.
Photo courtesy of the Pulido family.

dren staked the cows out to pasture on their way to school. After school, the young Pulidos retrieved the cows, bringing them back to the barn to join an assortment of animals, including horses and Dionicia's chickens. Pedro Pulido also had a garden that the children worked. And there was homework to be done before bedtime.

"Dad had his garden, but Mom always had her chickens," and her egg money, Bobby says.

The Pulido story is legend in Fort Worth: How the patriarch Pedro, or "Papa" as he came to be called, began sharing his lunches with his fellow railroad workers. How they clamored for Mama Pulido's tacos and enchiladas, to the point where several of the men would stop by the house after work to buy tamales to take home for supper.

"Mom was the entrepreneur," Bobby says. "Daddy brought his check home and always gave it to Mother. She was also the family disciplinarian, unless it went too far, and then, of course, it was going to Dad."

The family began selling hot lunches at the rail yard; the kids helped. Pedro and Dionicia began investing their extra money by buying houses and renting them. Bobby Pulido remembers his mother could add figures in her head, remember dates and names, and keep a running tally of loans people owed her. Intelligent, frugal, and goal-oriented, Mama Pulido eschewed banks and liked to keep her money in little buckets.

"She knew exactly how many coins she had," Bobby Pulido says. "And she'd tell me, 'I've got enough money to buy a house now.'"

Bobby remembers that, at one point, he and one of his brothers were attending Texas Christian University. Pedro Pulido was making only about $5,000 a year working for the railroad, and

beneath the lush, green trees of the nearby Botanic Garden.

In fact, it is quite likely that Bobby and his siblings—who, in addition to Vincent, Philip, and Shannon (Chano), now included Mary, Pedro Jr. "Pete," and Rodolfo "Rudy"—pastured the family's cows near there or down near the banks of the Trinity River.

The Pulidos bought a large two-story house on Spring Street in El TP, which they filled with their children while still having room left over for visitors from Mexico.

"My mother never let us run around with the neighborhood kids," Bobby recalls. "We had to work."

The Pulido children got up early to milk the cows, bringing Dionicia the milk, part of which she made into cheese and sold. Then the chil-

yet with Mama Pulido's enterprises and savings, the family managed to pay a tuition bill that was well over $2,000 a year.

"I don't know how she managed it, but she did," Bobby Pulido says. "She always knew how to handle her money."

Bobby Pulido married Carol Rodriguez in 1962, and they soon started a family. Mama Pulido had been talking about opening a family restaurant for years, and Bobby dropped his dentistry studies and began working at the El Chico restaurant managed by his brother-in-law, Edward Gamez. In 1965, the Pulidos broke ground on their own restaurant, across the street from their home in the old TP neighborhood. In *Stories from the Barrio*, Cuellar says the Pulidos used whatever materials they could get their hands on, including salvaged timbers from the T&P roundhouse that had been torn down. Bobby's older brother Pete, who had an upholstery business, refurbished the booths.

On July 1, 1966, the restaurant opened with Mama Pulido and Bobby Pulido running the kitchen. Mary Pulido Gamez and Bobby's wife, Carol, were the cashiers and hostesses; and cousins and other family members bused tables and waited on customers.

Few people predicted success for the family's business in the barrio, Bobby Pulido explained in a *Dallas Morning News* article August 18, 1983, headlined "Family's Mexican eatery becomes chain of success." "We proved them wrong within two weeks. Even the elite would come dine with us. They'd line up outside the door waiting to get in."

The restaurant proved to be a draw for Mexicans from El TP and the Anglos who lived in the nearby Arlington Heights neighborhood.

The Pulidos recognized a winning concept when they saw it; the year after the first restaurant opened, the family decided to incorporate. They opened their second restaurant on Highway 377 South in Benbrook. A new restaurant followed pretty much every year after that, until the Pulido's chain grew to thirteen restaurants and a tortilla, tamale, and chip factory with more than 300 employees.

In 1990, Dionicia "Mama" Pulido was named one of nine "Outstanding Women of Fort Worth" by the Fort Worth Commission on the Status of Women. The award recipients were honored by the Texas Legislature and feted at a public reception at the Amon G. Carter Jr. Exhibits Hall in the Will Rogers Memorial Center. In a 1990 *Fort Worth Star-Telegram* story, reporter Kara Rogge wrote that the Pulido's corporation generated an annual income of some $8 million, and that Mama Pulido, who was almost seventy-nine at the time, still reported for work each morning at the Pulido's commissary, or central kitchen, where she supervised production of the restaurants' rice, beans, and taco meat, among other products.

In fact, years earlier, Mama and Papa Pulido had moved to a large, brick home on two lots in Benbrook. Bobby and Carol also lived in the still vaguely rural neighborhood off Winscott Road. But little else had changed about the elder Pulidos' lives. Thanks to special permits acquired at Benbrook City Hall, Papa still kept a horse and Mama her chickens, except now she gathered eggs each morning to distribute among the workers at the tortilla factory, also located in Benbrook. Every morning the family would gather at the factory, and Mama would cook breakfast in a huge skillet with the fresh ingredi-

Dionicia "Mama" Pulido packs food to be sold at Fort Worth Mayfest in 1983.
Photo courtesy of the Pulido family.

ents at hand—chorizo and eggs, tortillas and salsa. Sometimes she made a big pot of menudo. With full stomachs, Bobby, Rudy, and the others would part ways, off to keep the chain's various enterprises running.

Always looking for ways to grow, in 1991 the Pulidos applied for and won, on their first try, the nacho chip concession for the Texas Rangers home games in Arlington. It was the year that Pulido's restaurants celebrated their twenty-fifth anniversary.

That year, Dionicia told *Star-Telegram* business reporter Worth Wren Jr., "My wish is that the company will progress, but mainly that the family will work as a unit, close together . . . and remain a satisfied family." Wren reported that, at the time, more than twenty Pulido family members, including in-laws, worked for the company, which was still generating an estimated $8 million a year at a time when restaurant sales were dropping across the board.

The following year, the Pulido's restaurant chain was ranked number two in *Tarrant Business* newspaper in a chart of Tarrant County's largest minority-owned businesses. The newspaper said the chain had reported a 1991 revenue of $9.6 million.

During those years, the Pulido family worked hard and played hard, too. At the family farm near Springtown, Mama and Papa Pulido presided over Fourth of July bashes and Christmas parties, and the company organized golf tournaments, usually benefiting a charity, and other community events.

As Mama and Papa Pulido entered their eighties and nineties, they continued to work, often beginning their days before dawn at the tortilla factory. But on July 13, 1999, after sixty-seven years of marriage, Mama lost Papa Pulido. He was ninety-one. His obituary in the *Star-Telegram*, which ran a separate story recounting the building of the Pulido's restaurant empire, includes this paragraph: "Less than three weeks ago, on June 25, Pedro Pulido worked his last day as quality control and operations overseer in the company's tortilla and chip factory in Benbrook." Mama was almost certainly by his side.

Four years later, on June 23, 2003, Dionicia Pulido died. She was ninety-two. The previous fall, she and her great-granddaughter, eleven-year-old Logan Pulido, had been featured in the *Star-Telegram*'s Hispanic Heritage Month special section "This is who I am. This is where I come from." In a photograph in which she is wearing a smart, winter-blue suit, the white-haired, bespectacled Dionicia leans ever-so-slightly to receive a sweet kiss from the young blonde girl, part of the third generation of Pulidos to live in the United States. There is a satisfied, almost mischievous, smile on Dionicia's face.

Dionicia told the reporter she is from Jalisco, Mexico, "where the pretty women are from," and said that she still made tamales for the restaurants five days a week, working from nine in the morning until noon.

In the days following her death, tributes published in English and Spanish hailed Dionicia Pulido as a humble and hard-working woman who treated all of her employees like family.

"We didn't call her Mama for nothing," longtime employee Gilbert Gutierrez is quoted as saying in the *Star-Telegram*'s Spanish-language newspaper *La Estrella,* in a tribute written after her death. "She was like a grandmother. She treated you well, but if you did something wrong, she was going to correct you."

Longtime Pulido's employee Frank Klein-wechter remembers, "In the kitchen, Mama ruled the roost. They did it her way, or no way."

He also remembers that he never left the tortilla factory without Mama Pulido's tucking a dozen tamales into his hands to take home to his wife and his son.

Listening to Bobby Pulido talk about his mother, it is easy to imagine her as being larger than life. It is somewhat surprising then, when he reveals that Mama Pulido never learned to read and write in English, did not like to shop, never learned to drive and, even as a young woman, was a petite woman "about 4 feet, 11 inches tall."

Dionicia Pulido dared to dream big, however, and she had the resourcefulness, intelligence, and work ethic to make those dreams come true. She was also a compassionate woman, and her door and her heart were always open to those in need.

"The first thing she would ask anybody was 'Have you eaten? Are you hungry?'" Bobby remembers. "That never changed."

Jacinta Saavedra Jara is another woman who devoted her life to bettering her community and her family. She was born in Cisco and raised in the small rural community of Eastland. Her father, Arnulfo Rocha Saavedra, had been a professor in Guadalajara, Mexico, before he immigrated to the United States. Teaching was the family profession. All of her father's brothers also were professors in Mexico. The understanding that education was of prime importance would inform her whole life and that of her children. Jara's father, who owned a store in Eastland that imported spices and other products from Mexico, worked tutoring children of Mexican immigrants in reading and writing Spanish.

Mutual friends introduced Jacinta to Manuel Jara in Fort Worth. He had served in the

Family friend Corrine "Rin" Kleinwechter, left, and
Mama Pulido, at the Pulido factory on
October 16, 1983.
Photo courtesy of Frank Kleinwechter.

Dionicia Pulido in an undated family
photograph, c. 1990s.
Photo courtesy of the Pulido Family.

U.S. Army and was working as a printer. It did not take long for her to understand that her young husband would never sit still in the face of injustice.

"My husband and I, and two of his friends—two soldiers in uniform—went to a cantina, or bar, near the Tarrant County Courthouse," she says, estimating the year to be either 1942 or 1943. "We were told they didn't serve Mexicans. Manuel said, 'Fine. Take me to jail if you want to.'" The police were called, Manuel refused to back down, and off to jail he went.

Manuel and Jacinta Jara would encounter example after example of discrimination against the Mexican community in Fort Worth. For a short while after their marriage, they lived with his parents, Alfonso and Maria Jara, in a duplex on the North Side. Their two daughters, Mary and Jo Linda, were born there.

The year Jo Linda was born, the young family moved to a house in the 1200 block of North Houston Street. It was only a block or so

away from what traditionally defined the border of "the North Side" in the years before World War II, but still it was considered a bold move. Their new house was across the street from H. B. Helbing Elementary School, where Jo Linda started her education. Few Mexican students attended there, but Jacinta Jara was soon involved in the parents' organization. It was typical of her willingness to walk through doors that had been previously closed to Hispanics and then hold them open for others to follow.

At home, the Jaras spoke Spanish, and the girls' social lives and religious instruction centered on All Saints Catholic Church, which at the time was predominantly Anglo. The Jaras took great pains to teach their daughters to succeed in school and in life, no matter what barriers others might try to put in their way because of their race.

As she and her sister grew up, Jo Linda Jara Martinez remembers her parents' becoming

Guest speaker Vincent Jimenez poses with the Jaras at a G.I. Forum event. *Photo courtesy of Jolinda Martinez.*

increasingly involved in the Hispanic community. More and more, Manuel Jara would speak out against the injustices that beset the Mexican— and increasingly Mexican-American—community. The Jaras plunged into parish work and Democratic politics. Despite that night in jail early in the Jaras' relationship, Manuel Jara's enduring reputation is that of a reasonable and intelligent negotiator, a communicator in both languages, in both worlds.

As part of a group of Fort Worth Hispanic leaders, the Jaras would meet Dr. Hector P. Garcia, who established the American G.I. Forum in the years after the world war. Garcia, of Corpus Christi, formed the group to fight the discrimination that war veterans of Mexican descent still faced in restaurants, theaters, housing, and education. Manuel Jara would become president and district chairman of the American G.I. Forum.

Manuel Jara, who by that time owned a successful printing company on Fort Worth's Pennsylvania Avenue, also was one of the found-

ing members of the Fort Worth Hispanic Chamber of Commerce. Cuellar, in his book, gives both Manuel and Jacinta Jara credit for helping organize the Fort Worth Chapter of the International Good Neighbor Council, a group that promoted trade and good relations between the United States and Mexico.

In photographs published in *Celebrating 150 Years: The Pictorial History of Fort Worth, Texas 1849–1999*, Jacinta Jara is always seen by Manuel's side, a small, beautiful woman with arching eyebrows. In one photo taken at a convention of the International Good Neighbor Council, she stands between her husband and U.S. Congressman Jim Wright, who would become the U.S. Speaker of the House. In another, she is at her husband's side as he accepts the 1973 Brotherhood Award from the Tarrant County National Conference of Christians and Jews from newsman Bob Schieffer. There she is, in a cluster of tuxedos, proudly, beautifully, and elegantly serene.

In a caption beneath a photograph of Jacinta Jara standing between two Anglo women at a 1964 Democratic fund-raiser for President Lyndon Baines Johnson, Jo Linda is quoted as saying, "Dad was more visible...but Mom has been, in her own quiet way, an equal influence on my sister and me."

Indeed, Jacinta's legacy to her daughters may well have been that they could be whoever they wanted to be, if only they worked hard enough and did not let anything stand in their way. Both their daughters would go on to graduate from college and become Fort Worth educators of distinction.

Mary Jara graduated from Texas Christian University in 1966. For a short time she worked

Above: Manuel and Jacinta Jara with Congressman Jim Wright at the International Good Neighbor Council Convention in Fort Worth.

Above Right: From left, Edna Martin, Jacinta Jara, and Mary Bradley host a Democratic Party fundraiser, "All the Way with LBJ," in 1964.

Right: Manuel Jara, second from left, receives the Tarrant County National Conference of Christians and Jews annual Brotherhood Award on March 29, 1973, with his wife, Jacinta. At left is newsman Bob Schieffer.

Photos courtesy of Jolinda Martinez.

as a bilingual secretary and then as an administrative assistant in the California corporate offices of Greyhound Bus Lines. This career, she soon decided, was not for her, so she came back to Fort Worth, and, on the advice of friends, began teaching mathematics at McLean Middle School. In the tradition of her mother's father, Mary found teaching to be a natural fit. And so began a thirty-four-year career in the Fort Worth Independent School District that would take her from the classroom to the principal's offices at

J. P. Elder Middle School and South Hills High School.

At J. P. Elder, Mary instituted programs that would spread across the district. She earned her master's degree in education from North Texas State University in 1976 and became known as a math specialist.

Married twice, Mary never had children but throughout her career she had thousands of students that she called her own. Mary Jara Wright was the principal of South Hills when

Above Left: Sisters and educators Jo Linda Martinez, left, and Mary Wright in December 2002. *Above Right:* A family portrait: from left, Jo Linda Martinez, mother Jacinta Jara, and Mary Jara Wright. *Photos courtesy of Jolinda Martinez.*

she died in June 24, 2003, after a battle with cancer.

"My sister gave her heart and soul to working with the kids and the teachers," Martinez said. "Sometimes, when I've organized a board or a workshop that involves some school principals, I can see her in them, because she taught them. And there's still a little bit of Mary up there."

One of Mary's trademarks was to have daily visits with a particularly troubled student every year. Often, this student had been identified by one of Mary's teachers who could see the child's intelligence and promise, despite his or her behavior.

"You wouldn't think it was much. A few words, a hug," Martinez says of Mary's custom, but it often worked. Mary made it work. And the next year, another child would be in her office every day.

Although she was very ill, Mary Jara Wright hugged and congratulated every graduate of the 2003 South Hills class who walked across the stage. There is a memorial garden dedicated to her at South Hills High School.

In a brief summary of Mary's career provided by her sister are these words, "Mary Jara Wright was a true servant leader. She often said of her positions in the school district, 'I'm here because this is where God needs me to be.'"

Martinez is herself an outstanding educator, though she came later to that career than did her sister. After marrying Jesse P. Martinez right after graduating from North Side High School, she spent the next twenty-three years raising four children. Finally, after the death of her father in 1985 (an elementary school is now named for Manuel Jara) and while she was working in the Student Placement Center of the Fort Worth Independent School District, she decided to take advantage of scholarships being offered by Texas Woman's University for bilingual education majors. She finally earned her bachelor's degree in Spanish, with bilingual certification, from Texas Wesleyan. In 1997, U.S. Congresswoman Kay Granger presented her with the Texas Woman's Power of One Award for her work with H.Y.P.E., Hispanic Youth Promoting Excellence. The innovative Fort

Jacinta and Manuel Jara join a North Texas delegation boarding the inaugural flight of Mexicana Airlines from D/FW Airport to Guadalajara, Mexico. *Photos courtesy of the Martinez Family.*

Worth school district program, which Jo Linda created and initially ran out of her house and car, is known today as Absolute Xcellence and encourages leadership skills in middle school and high school minority students and prepares them for success in higher education. Part of the program is a student competition in poetry, prose, solo acting, and prose interpretation in Spanish. Older students mentor younger ones in the program, and parent involvement is encouraged. Martinez also is the district's bilingual teacher program coordinator, recruiting, training, and mentoring an estimated fifty teachers a year. She is included in the *Who's Who Among American Educators.*

Longtime Fort Worth businessman and community leader Sam Garcia knows more people in the city's Hispanic community than almost anyone. His list of who should be included in this chapter on Hispanic women in the Fort Worth community is a long one, including these names that came up in a long interview in the fall of 2006.

Like restaurateur Dionicia Pulido, Jesusa "Mama Sus" Torres Garcia, of Joe T. Garcia's

fame, never lacked for media exposure during her lifetime. Hers is a name that still is well known throughout the city today.

Mama Sus was born in 1905, and she immigrated to the United States in 1914. She married Jose Tafolla Garcia in 1923. Garcia was a packinghouse worker on the north side of Fort Worth, and they began their family in the North Side neighborhood. Like the Pulidos, the Garcias made extra money by selling delicious Mexican-food lunches to Jose's co-workers. When Mama Sus and her husband opened a small grocery store, these people and many more came in asking for Mama Sus' food. It was a sure sign that a restaurant was the way to go.

Joe's Barbecue and Mexican Dishes opened July 4, 1935. With Mama Sus cooking, Jose grilling, and the entire family, including their five children—Josephine, Ralph, Pauline, Mary and Hope—working hard, the restaurant grew and grew into the famous North Side dining establishment Joe T. Garcia's is today. (Jose Garcia's last name was, in fact, Tafolla, but when he came to the United States from

Mexico, he signed his name in the Spanish tradition, Jose Tafolla Garcia, and Joe T. Garcia it
became.)

Jose died in 1953. After his death, Mama Sus
and her youngest daughter, Hope Garcia
Lancarte, kept Joe T.'s going and growing. Today,
the family still runs the restaurant, which
encompasses an entire block with its inside and
patio dining areas, as well as two other restau-
rant-and-bakery establishments in Fort Worth's
north and near-south neighborhoods. Mama Sus
Garcia died in 1988.

Elisa Acuña Cagigal was another North Side
entrepreneur. She married Orencio Doce
Cagigal, a Spaniard, in 1915 in San Antonio. His
work brought the couple to North Texas, and
eventually, to Fort Worth. They had four sons,
Artemio, Orencio Jr., Simon, and Francisco.
Francisco was the only son to be born in Fort
Worth, in 1924.

The Cagigals ran a grocery store from their
North Side home. Elisa managed both the business and her family with efficiency. She not only
ran the store (Orencio worked as a carpenter)
but also cooked and sold hot lunches to the
neighborhood's packinghouse workers. Orencio
died in 1965. Elisa Cagigal died in 1987. She was
ninety-three.

Yet another woman who used her treasury of
recipes to find entrepreneurial success was Lola
San Miguel Pineda, who with her husband,
Geronimo Pineda, opened The Original
Mexican Eats Café in 1930. The Pinedas are one
of the many Fort Worth families profiled by
Carlos Cuellar in *Stories from the Barrio.*

The restaurant, often described as the oldest
Hispanic-owned restaurant still in operation in
Fort Worth, stands at 4713 Camp Bowie

Boulevard. From the beginning, its clientele was
a surprising mix of Anglo businessmen and Fort
Worth society families. In fact, one of the restaurant's signature plates, the Roosevelt Special, is
named after U.S. President Franklin Delano
Roosevelt's son, Elliott, who lived in nearby
Benbrook and was a regular at the café in the
1930s.

Even after Geronimo's death, Lola and one
of her daughters, Ruth Pineda, continued to run
the restaurant. Ruth, who had contracted rheu-
matic fever as a child and suffered from ill health
her entire life, died September 12, 1966. She was
fifty-two. Lola Pineda died October 2, 1974. She
was ninety-three. The Pinedas sold their restaurant to their accountant in the 1960s, and it has
passed on to other owners since that time.

Sam Garcia says no recounting of the history of Fort Worth's Hispanic women would be
complete without a mention of Juanita
Hernandez Zepeda, who ran unsuccessfully for a
seat on the Fort Worth City Council in 1971.
She was the first Hispanic woman to do so. (See
"Braving the Smoke.")

Juanita was born in Fort Worth in 1917.
Every bit as activist-minded as her husband, J.
Pete Zepeda, a well-known Fort Worth business
and political leader, Juanita was determined to
bring change to her community and did so
through volunteerism and civic service. She
served on the city's parks and recreation board
for six years, was second vice president of the
Community Action Agency, and served on the
board of the North Side Community Center.

In a 2002 interview, Gilbert L. Zepeda, one of
the Zepedas' four sons (they also had a daughter,
Connie), described his father Pete as an organizer
who loved to lead by building a consensus and

employing his famous sense of humor. His mother was just as much a leader, he said, but she was more of a firebrand, someone who was quick to take action, especially if she perceived any injustice.

Like the Jaras, the Zepedas moved in Anglo society and on the Texas political scene with confidence and aplomb years before it was considered a common thing for Hispanics to do.

When Juanita Zepeda died in December 1978 following a traffic accident, a headline in the *Star-Telegram* described her a "Fort Worth civic leader." The family established a memorial fund at Texas Wesleyan College in honor of a woman who encouraged others to educate themselves so that they might better serve as advocates for yet others in need someday.

Juanita Zepeda's contributions are still remembered today by people like Sam Garcia. For decades, Garcia, a decorated veteran of World War II who became a U.S. citizen after the war, worked tirelessly to organize the Hispanic community to fight discrimination, to create jobs and educational opportunities where none had been offered before. He published a newspaper, *Community News and Events,* and a phone book for the Hispanic community. With his first wife, Maria, and a small group of women who were concerned about the high dropout rate of girls in the Hispanic community, he established the Hispanic Debutante Association, which raised scholarship money for the girls' college education. In the summer of 2006, Garcia donated his vast collection of "papers," including photographs, minutes of meetings, and other irreplaceable documents to the Fort Worth Public Library.

Like author Carlos Cuellar, who found a dearth of documented history of the Hispanic community in Fort Worth, Garcia worries that important people, their lives, and personal histories will be forgotten.

He fears that some of the first to be forgotten will be those of Hispanic women, who, like women of other ethnic groups, stood proudly by their men, worked by their sides and kept the home fires burning while their husbands initiated the social, political, and economic change of the 1960s and 1970s.

"A lot of these men would not have been successful if not for their women," he says. "In those days, if you had a man in the trenches, the woman was right behind him, fighting in those same trenches."

The women in this chapter—homemakers, dynasty builders, entrepreneurs, and trailblazers—along with countless other Hispanic women helped make Fort Worth a vibrant city for all of us.

BIBLIOGRAPHIC ESSAY

I could not have done this work without the assistance of Esperanza "Hope" Padilla Ayala, who provided names, phone numbers, and introductions to several subjects in my chapter on Hispanic women in Fort Worth. Her reminiscences of growing up on the city's North Side proved invaluable and informative and were essential to capturing the essence of the close-knit community of more than half a decade ago.

Thanks to Mrs. Ayala I was able to meet and interview Jacinta Jara and her daughter, Jo Linda Martinez. Mrs. Jara spoke candidly about her life, and Mrs. Martinez opened her home to me so that I might interview her mother. She also was generous in sharing books from her personal library and many family photographs.

The story of Dionicia Pulido would not have been possible without several interviews with her son, Bobby Pulido, at the Pulido's chip factory in Benbrook. Another invaluable resource was the Pulido family's scrapbook, a large collection of newspaper clippings, menus, photographs, and other memorabilia that have been lovingly assembled over the years by longtime family associate Frank Kleinwechter of Benbrook. The family allowed me to keep the scrapbook for as long as I needed it. Mr. Kleinwechter also consented to be interviewed and shared many stories about Mama and Papa Pulido.

Fort Worth businessman Sam Garcia allowed me to read many of his historical papers,

many of which he has given to the Fort Worth Public Library. He shared copies of personal histories and consented to a long interview about the history of the Hispanic community in Fort Worth. He proved to have a treasure trove of information and contacts.

Finally, this chapter would not have been possible had it not been for news stories from the *Fort Worth Star-Telegram* archives and Carlos Cuellar's book, *Stories from the Barrio: A History of Mexican Fort Worth,* published by TCU Press in 2003. As I did, Mr. Cuellar discovered that the histories of Fort Worth's Hispanics are largely oral, and his assemblage of names, dates, and details was a treasure trove of information for this chapter.

Chapter 9

THE JEWISH WOMEN'S AMERICANIZATION SCHOOL

by Hollace Ava Weiner

A TRIO OF ARAB BUSI-nessmen who moved to Fort Worth in 1968 enrolled in English-language classes at a Baptist church but quit because the teachers delivered more doctrine than diction. Instead, the Muslims attended the Council of Jewish Women's Americanization School and content-edly learned in a non-sectarian classroom.

Likewise, the Italian nuns running Saint Teresa's Home for Children studied English at the Americanization School, headquartered in a synagogue. The sisters, who wore habits to class, learned not only the vernacular but also enough streetwise tips to pass their Texas driving tests.

Another student, a longtime Fort Worth res-ident from Greece, yearned to take her citizen-ship exam but could not comprehend America's three branches of government. At the Americanization School, her teacher compared the United States' executive, legislative, and judicial branches to an old-fashioned kitchen stove. The oven was the legislative branch; the broiler, the judiciary; and the stovetop, the chief executive. Each branch functioned separately,

yet together as a unit. The metaphor helped the immigrant pass her naturalization test.

The teacher, in each instance, was Amelia Levy Rosenstein, a master of metaphor and the Americanization School's unofficial dean from the 1930s until the school's closing in 1973. Without textbooks—or tuition—Rosenstein taught year after year, first at the Hebrew Institute and later at Beth-El Congregation, using intuition and common sense to teach adults from more than a score of foreign nations. Along with a corps of changing volunteers, she cut pictures out of grocery ads and catalogues and pasted them on construction paper to simu-late a trip to the store. She hosted potluck sup-pers in her home to sample dishes from exotic lands. She scheduled after-school conferences to untangle bureaucratic snarls resulting from the ever-changing maze of immigration statutes and naturalization requirements.

The Council of Jewish Women opened the Americanization School in 1907, during an era when democracy's melting-pot theory prevailed. At that time, Fort Worth was a booming stock-

Feeling right at home. Around her dining room table in 1965, Amelia Rosenstein gives an English lesson to Sister Alesandra (left), Sister Anna Pia, Mother Superior Rinaldina, and Mother Superior Elia. The four Italian nuns were members of the Missionary Sisters of the Sacred Side, which staffed Fort Worth's Saint Teresa's Home for Children. *Courtesy,* Fort Worth Star-Telegram *Photograph Collection, Special Collections Division, The University of Texas at Arlington Libraries.*

yards and packinghouse town, beckoning immigrant families from Greece, Poland, Mexico, and at least fifteen other nations. With the promise of jobs, foreigners arrived to work in the city's two meatpacking plants, one operated by Swift and Company and the other by Armour and Company.

In the early twentieth century there were few restrictions on European or Latin-American immigration. However, the increasing visibility of foreigners with varying complexions led to mounting xenophobia and, by 1921, to immigration quotas based upon country of origin. The general populace believed the Anglo-Saxon heritage to be the strongest, purest, most civilized strain. Popular public speakers and best-selling books advised that instilling immigrants with

Anglo-Saxon values and customs would "convert" them to the American work ethic and turn them into patriotic citizens. The Council of Jewish Women's Americanization School met a need, both practical and psychological, helping to homogenize newcomers through lessons not only in language but also in etiquette and hygiene. The Americanization School also reassured the city's Jews, whose families had immigrated to the United States a generation or so before, that they too were looked upon as 100 percent American.

The Americanization School's 1907 opening also corresponded with the start of the Galveston movement, which, over a seven-year period, brought 10,000 Yiddish-speaking refugees to Texas. From the port of Galveston,

Top Right: Sisterhood. Amelia Rosenstein chats in 1968 with Sister Alessandra, left, and Mother Superior Elia of Saint Teresa's Home for Children. The Italian-born nuns learned English at the Americanization School. *Courtesy,* Fort Worth Star-Telegram *Collection, Special Collections Division, The University of Texas at Arlington Libraries.*

Below Right: "Dean" of Americanization School. Amelia Rosenstein stands at a chalkboard at the Hebrew Institute, where, throughout the 1940s, she taught classes three times a week to immigrants learning English and studying for U.S. citizenship tests. Rosenstein directed the National Council of Jewish Women's Fort Worth Americanization School from the 1930s until her retirement in 1973. *Courtesy,* Fort Worth Star-Telegram *Collection, Special Collections, The University of Texas at Arlington Library, Arlington, Texas.*

these East European immigrants dispersed across Texas and the Middle West as far north as the Dakotas, with an average of eight refugees a month settling in Fort Worth. Local rabbis served on the refugee-resettlement committees.

Some of those refugees were unsavory types—prostitutes, pimps, and political extremists. The Americanization School rarely enrolled such undesirables. Indeed, Jewish clubwomen shunned them. When Fort Worth Rabbi G. George Fox heard ranchers whispering about "Jew whores…huddled together in a district known as the 'Levee,'" he consulted his wife and learned that "our women's committee wouldn't even speak to them." Twenty Jewish prostitutes were arrested and eighteen of them deported. The two who stayed married their pimps, moved

into respectable lines of work, and, a century later, remained an item of gossip and conjecture.

Also anathema to the clubwomen who operated the Americanization School were radical refugees who spouted socialism and anarchism. Schoolteacher Flora Weltman Schiff, an active member of the council, described these radicals as "negative, down-with-the-monarchy" types.

Above Left: Night School, 1940. Amelia Rosenstein, back left, instructs Annie Rutlader while a class full of immigrants read an assignment. Janet Teter, another volunteer teacher, stands at right. The students, with their native countries, are, first row, front to rear: Theresa Zulouf, Poland; Erwin Wolf, Austria; Mrs. T. Bergman, Poland; and Annie Rutlader, Poland. Second row: Erwin Richker, Germany; Rosie Snofsky, Russia; Mrs. A. Haller, Poland; Ida Star, Russia. *Courtesy,* Fort Worth Star-Telegram *Collection, Special Collections, The University of Texas at Arlington Library, Arlington, Texas.*
Above Right: A photo of Beth-El Congregation, where the Americanization School classes convened from 1951 to 1973. This photo was shot in 1948 .The congregation sold the building in 2000. It remains vacant. *Courtesy,* Fort Worth Star-Telegram *Collection, Special Collections Division, The University of Texas at Arlington Libraries.*

Such refugees threatened the hard-earned status of the city's acculturated Jews. The Americanization School's good works served to counterbalance the negative side of the Jewish immigrant tide.

The Council of Jewish Women was an upscale social-service club that asserted itself mainly in secular and civic affairs. Founded nationally in 1893 and in Fort Worth in 1901, its local members tended to be American born, if not native Texans. Most belonged to the city's Reform synagogue, Beth-El, where worship was almost entirely in English, rather than to the Orthodox congregation, Ahavath Sholom, where the liturgy was in Hebrew and minutes were taken in Yiddish. The clubwomen in the council were the wives, mothers, sisters, and daughters of attorneys, land appraisers, downtown haberdashers, dry-goods merchants, and cigar and liquor wholesalers. As affluent, enlightened, twentieth-century females, they viewed communal problems through the lens of social science. They were disinclined to become "Florence Nightingales" tending to one charity case at a time. Rather, they were "new women" of the Progressive era, determined to equip immigrants with lifetime skills. The mission of the Americanization School, according to council president Pauline "Polly" Sachs Mack, was to help immigrants "master the English language [and] to assimilate American ideals."

The school opened with six teachers—three women from the council and three men from the local B'nai B'rith lodge. It enrolled around twenty students—so-called "scholars" ranging in age from fourteen to forty-five. Evening classes initially convened in a prominent location—the Tarrant County Courthouse, a landmark that symbolized the school's importance and the women's connections. "Through the kindness of Judge R. E. Bratton," announced the council's Polly Mack, "we were permitted to use his courtroom…for our semi-weekly sessions."

The Fort Worth Council of Jewish Women—along with sister chapters in Detroit and New York—was among the earliest Jewish women's groups to organize a school to "help the foreign born." As the grassroots effort caught on, the council's headquarters in New York issued a policy statement in 1911 urging that every chapter help Americanize immigrants who were resettling in their cities. Eventually, Americanization Schools opened in dozens of cities across the United States including El Paso, Houston, and San Antonio. To assist the network of adult-education schools, the council's national office published instruction manuals, sponsored regional institutes, and worked so closely with the U.S. Immigration and Naturalization Service that it had its own special code number—#116—for requesting documents, tracking lost paperwork, and helping immigrants cut red tape. As the organization's influence expanded, it added the word "National" to its letterhead, in 1923 becoming the National Council of Jewish Women.

Fort Worth's Americanization School was well established by 1925, the year that Amelia Levy, a Houston schoolteacher, visited the city to attend the Jewish Chautauqua Society's southwest regional meeting. Her role was to present a "model Sunday school lesson" during a special program following Friday evening worship services at Beth-El. Her appearance and her presentation so captivated congregant Abe Rosenstein, an auditor with the Rock Island Railroad, that a two-year courtship ensued.

As two working professionals, Amelia Levy and Abraham Moses Rosenstein shared much in common. Both were native Texans, the children of Polish immigrants who had come to the United States as youngsters. His father, Max, who died in January of 1925, had operated a dry-goods store; her widowed mother, Rachel, ran a grocery. His mother, Sarah, was a founding member of the Fort Worth Council of Jewish Women; her mother was the first state president of Hadassah, the women's Zionist organization, and had traveled the country with Hadassah's founder, Henrietta Szold. Both families had deep feelings for Judaism and strong ties to European Jewry.

Abe Rosenstein, born February 28, 1899, in LaGrange, had grown up in the Reform Jewish tradition at Fort Worth's Beth-El. Amelia Levy, born November 15, 1897, in Houston, was raised at Beth Israel, also a Reform congregation, where she taught Sunday school. For two years, Amelia Levy had attended Rice Institute, now Rice University, graduating with a certificate that qualified her to teach in the primary grades. She went to work as a first-grade teacher at Houston's Hawthorne Elementary, an inner-city school, where the principal, Edith D. Wright, praised her as "efficient,. . . cooperative. . . and genuinely interested in the welfare" of her pupils and those around her. Abe Rosenstein's sister, Millie, also was a public school educator, a mathematics teacher at Fort Worth's Jennings Avenue Junior High.

With so much in common, Abe and Amelia

The old Ahavath Sholom Synagogue on Taylor Street. Next door is the Hebrew Institute where the Americanization School held classes. The photo is from 1952. *Courtesy Beth-El Congregation Archives.*

and their extended families bonded. The couple married in Houston in June of 1927 and moved in with his family in a house at 2511 Fifth Avenue. By then, Abe was helping his mother in the family dry-goods store, Rosenstein's, at 106 Houston Street.

In that era, marriage was deemed a fulltime role for women. Female teachers lost their classroom positions when they wed. The Fort Worth school board, however, relaxed the rule if there was a teacher shortage—and there was. Amelia Rosenstein was hired at an annual salary of $900 to teach first grade at Hi-Mount Elementary, a four-room, red brick building, now a community center, at 4125 Lafayette Avenue. She also taught at Arlington Heights Elementary at 5100 Camp Bowie Boulevard. The school district's employment policy granted exceptions to married women, but not those expecting children. Amelia Rosenstein apparently stopped teaching at the start of the 1931 school year. On

December 7, 1931, Amelia and Abe Rosenstein's only child, Bernard, was born. Because teaching was Amelia's calling, as soon as she was able, she began to substitute in the Americanization School.

By then, the school for immigrants had experienced some ups and downs and was at a low point. Libby Simon Ginsburg, president of the Council of Jewish Women (and a cousin of Max Rosenstein), made it her priority, according to her annual report, to restore the "school of adult education" to its prior position of prestige. This was during the Great Depression, and funds were scarce. Classroom space was donated by the Hebrew Institute, the three-story Jewish community center at 819 Taylor Street that was operated by Ahavath Sholom, the Orthodox synagogue next door. A recruitment drive for students went into high gear. Among the "difficulties to overcome was getting married women to attend classes." By the end of the spring semester, however, the Americanization School once again had a reputation "as a school of real merit." Ginsburg reported that the Fort Worth "Board of Education became cognizant of our excellent work…[and] furnished us a highly qualified teacher." Among the volunteer teachers listed in the council's annual report for 1934 was "Mrs. A. Rosenstein."

The more Amelia Rosenstein volunteered at the Americanization School, the more she took charge. When the school district's teacher moved on to another position, Rosenstein stepped in and received a small salary. In the late 1930s, the Works Progress Administration began funding English-literacy classes, and the Americanization School received some of that

New Deal money, funneled through the Fort Worth school board. Gradually, Rosenstein became the school's unofficial dean.

"I went to help, and I liked it so much," Rosenstein told the *Fort Worth Press*. On another occasion, she wrote, "To me, all teaching is a thrilling and romantic adventure, but teaching in our…Americanization School is a very definite adventure. You just lose yourself so completely in…these people who come from all over the world…It's a challenge to help." The most challenging students were those who had never been to school and were illiterate in their native language. By contrast, students with formal schooling—whether in Japanese or Swahili—realized that there were patterns to discern, and they grasped more quickly where the teacher was headed.

The stream of students enrolling at the Americanization School throughout the late 1930s and early 1940s was mainly from Europe, where Hitler and the Nazi Party were rising to power. After World War II, the War Brides Act of 1945 facilitated immigration for spouses and families of returning American soldiers who had been stationed in the Philippines, Japan, and across Europe. In 1948, the Displaced Persons Act allowed admittance of many refugees uprooted by the war and unable to enter the United States under standard immigration policies. The 1953 Refugee Relief Act loosened restrictions for still more. With the onset of the cold war, the Hungarian Refugee Act of 1956 and Cuban Adjustment Program of the 1960s kept Rosenstein's classes full and diverse. Fort Worth's Americanization School became a veritable United Nations, a diplomatic meeting ground, that annually enrolled up to thirty students from Siberia to the South Pacific and South America.

One rule at the school was "English only"—a trial indeed for Eulalia and Petra Zamora, sisters-in-law from south of the border who had failed their citizenship tests three times during a nineteen-year period. After one semester in Amelia Rosenstein's classroom, they made the grade.

More difficult than the Zamoras was an Asian student who resisted using capital letters at the start of sentences. His native language had but one set of letters—all the equivalent of lower case. Another challenging student was a Swiss chef who needed to learn culinary terms. Rosenstein's students roared with laughter as she contorted her body to illustrate the word gizzard. "As long as we have…pantomime, we're all right," she chuckled. Rosenstein also utilized Braille to assist a blind student and speech therapy to help an adult who had so few teeth she could not pronounce Massachusetts.

One year, the FBI came looking for Rosenstein. The reason: an Austrian war bride married to a Saginaw, Texas, judge, had heard about the school but had no idea how to locate it. Her only clue was that a woman named Eeemelia from a Jewish organization ran the classes. Out of frustration, the war bride, Margueretha Hess Luedke, asked her husband's chum, the Saginaw chief of police, to track down the school. He turned the request over to his friends at the FBI. One evening, a startled Amelia Rosenstein picked up the telephone receiver and heard a man's voice announce, "Mrs. Rosenstein? This is Agent _____ with the

FBI. We've been looking for you." A short time later, Margueretha Luedke passed her citizenship test.

Another, much larger, success story involved a Hong Kong war bride, a former teacher who not only became an American citizen but also enrolled at Texas Wesleyan College, graduated magna cum laude, studied on scholarship at Texas Woman's University, and became an East Coast research chemist.

Most Americanization students had more modest goals. Annie Rutlader, a pre–World War II immigrant, fulfilled her dream on December 1, 1940, when she smiled and raised aloft her naturalization papers for a *Star-Telegram* photographer. Polish-born Rutlader had arrived in Fort Worth in 1931 to join her husband, Sam, who had immigrated a decade before to join a brother. By 1938, despite seven years in Texas, Annie's English skills were virtually nonexistent. With her relatives, she spoke Polish and Yiddish. Her husband's English also remained rudimentary, because he rarely heard it; he operated a grocery store in a Mexican neighborhood. "He had to learn to speak Spanish, because his customers weren't going to learn to speak Yiddish!" observed his daughter, Bess Rutlader Gaines, who was born in 1932.

When Bess started first grade in the fall of 1938, her mother enrolled in the Americanization School. "We were learning to read English at the same time," she recounted. "I would help her with some of the work. I remember so well asking her the questions that might be on her citizenship test: 'Can anybody be a president?' She would shake her head, 'No,' and say, 'You have to be born in the United States.'"

Bess remembered riding the bus with her mother to the Hebrew Institute, where classes convened until 1951, when the building was sold. Neither of Bess' parents ever learned to drive a car. During her mother's afternoon classes, the child waited in the lobby on a marble bench in front of a white-marble slab inscribed with the names of eighty-one Jewish servicemen from Fort Worth who had fought in World War I. Bess read and re-read their names—Tony Bergman…David Greines…Leo Potishman…S. Sankary. "It was cold on that bench," Bess recalled. Whenever Annie Rutlader stayed after class to confer with her teachers, Amelia Rosenstein invited the child into the classroom.

More than half a century later, Bess recalled Amelia Rosenstein as a "tiny" but commanding woman with "big, round brown eyes, like Betty Davis," and wavy, graying hair loosely pulled back into a bun. She often wore high heels, white gloves, and a necklace that matched her dress. A cordial yet formal presence, she could communicate with anyone, whether or not they spoke the same language. Bess remembered Rosenstein especially well because her family subsequently moved into a one-story brick house with a front porch a block away from the Rosensteins' home at 2717 Hemphill Street.

The Rutladers were among the more fortunate immigrants who had departed Europe before the outbreak of World War II. Later students at the Americanization School were not as blessed.

Livia Schreiber, a survivor of the Auschwitz death camp, arrived in Fort Worth in 1945 and moved in with her first cousin, physician Eugene Steinberger. He had sponsored her immigration to America. Pretty and animated, the twenty-

New American citizen. Annie Rutlader shows off
her prized citizenship certificate, earned in 1940.
Rutlader, a native of Warsaw, Poland, immigrated
to the U.S. in 1931 and joined her husband, Sam,
who had previously settled in Fort Worth. *Courtesy,*
Fort Worth Star-Telegram *Photograph Collection,*
Special Collections Division, The University of Texas
at Arlington Libraries.

Headline news. Livia Schreiber Levine, a survivor of
the Auschwitz Concentration Camp, made the front
page of the *Star-Telegram* when she became an
American citizen in 1950. The Czech native grad-
uated from the Americanization School. Livia
Schreiber Levine, personal papers. *Courtesy,* Fort
Worth Star-Telegram *Collection, Special Collections
Division, The University of Texas at Arlington Libraries.*

year-old refugee picked up English with a lilting
Czech accent. The National Council of Jewish
Women nominated her as its 1947 candidate for
Presentation, a Jewish debutante ball held at
Thanksgiving time. Within a few years, Livia
married Texan Sam Levine, enrolled in the
Americanization School, and applied for U.S.
citizenship. On June 19, 1950, Livia Schreiber
Levine stood before a federal district judge,

renounced allegiance to any "prince or poten-
tate," and recited the oath of American citizenship. Her success turned into a front-page headline in the next morning's *Fort Worth Star-
Telegram:* "Citizenship Helps Blot Out Concentration Camp." Levine's empathy and optimism
led her to return to the Americanization School
as a volunteer teacher. (In later years, she taught
Hebrew and Holocaust studies at Beth-El.)

Each Jewish woman to graduate from the Americanization School received a year's membership in the National Council of Jewish Women. Amelia Rosenstein encouraged Livia Levine to attend a meeting. Following the introductions, Levine was asked to describe her wartime ordeal, from her 1939 deportation from Czechoslovakia to her seven-year trauma at the Auschwitz and Bergen-Belsen concentration camps. "My English was so bad, I am afraid I hit it off wrong with the women," Levine recalled fifty years later. Some of the women were skeptical of her narrative. "One of the ladies said, 'You know we had it hard too. We had to have special coupons for gasoline and tires for a car.'…I was talking to them about bread….Some of these women really and truly did not know what had gone on under the Nazis. I was so hurt." Although the trauma of the death camps had been in the headlines, many chose to deny it or blot it out.

Americans were even less aware of Louis and Ann Kirschner Bogart's nightmare. This Polish couple—he, a textile designer from Lodz, and she, a fashion designer from Beilsko-Biala— met and married in Uzbekistan after spending much of the war in Stalinist labor camps in Siberia. "Nobody talked about people in Russia starving to death. It was never publicized," maintained Ann Bogart, who immigrated to Fort Worth in 1950. "In Siberia, we were eating grass. If we did get food, it was corn mush three times a day. I can't eat cornbread to this day. It tastes bitter to me. In Siberia, during the winter we cut down trees for fuel. In the summer, we planted potatoes. You couldn't run away. You would freeze to death." At the outbreak of World War II, both Ann's and Louis' families had fled east to

escape the advancing Germany army, only to be taken prisoner by the Russians. When Germany attacked Russia in 1941, the Soviets joined the Allies and eventually released Polish prisoners, many of whom journeyed by cattle wagon across the Ural Mountains to Uzbekistan. There, Ann and Louis met in January 1944 at the home of her cousin, also a war refugee. The couple married on March 8, 1945. Postwar, the Bogarts spent five years in a displaced persons camp in the Bavarian town of Landsberg. From there, they applied to immigrate to Israel, Norway, and the United States. "We waited to see what came first," Ann Bogart explained. Visas for Norway and the United States arrived on the same day. The Bogarts chose America, "because Norway was too close to Russia."

The couple traveled by ship to New Orleans and by train to Fort Worth, where they received one month's rent for an apartment stocked with food and located on St. Louis Street close to Beth-El Congregation, which they began to attend. Once in Texas, they put the past behind them. "It's good to know where you came from," Ann Bogart acknowledged, "but you can't think about the things that happened. You have to go forward or you will just wilt away."

In Fort Worth, Louis Bogart went to work as a shipping clerk at S. Herzfeld Sportswear, a ladies' ready-to-wear manufacturer on Jennings Street. Owners Sello and Frieda Herzfeld, German immigrants who had fled to the United States in 1938, were Americanization School graduates themselves and good friends of Amelia and Abe Rosenstein. In fact, when Sello Herzfeld passed his naturalization exam in the 1940s, he celebrated by giving the Rosensteins' son a $50 U.S. savings bond.

During the months that Louis Bogart worked at S. Herzfeld Sportswear, his wife, Ann, earned extra money at home, stitching clothing alterations on her Singer sewing machine. It was Amelia Rosenstein who introduced Ann Bogart to pinking shears—the saw-toothed scissors that keep edges of fabric from easily fraying.

"I didn't go very long to the Americanization School," Ann Bogart recalled. "Because I knew more languages than one, it was easier for me to grab it." At the Americanization School, Ann and Louis Bogart received instruction in U.S. history, the Bill of Rights, and the Constitution. Ultimately, none of those civics lessons came to bear when Ann Bogart took her citizenship exam. "All I remember about my test is that… the man asked me why a woman cannot be a president of the United States." Quizzically, she stared back at the examiner, unaware that he was teasing her with a sexist joke. "He said, 'Because a woman won't say her age.' That was my test. He never asked me about history."

Toward the end of Ann Bogart's second year in Fort Worth, she designed a coat for a school-teacher. A buyer with Meacham's Department Store saw the teacher wearing the coat, asked where it was purchased, and subsequently contracted with Ann Bogart to sew for the upscale store. "I started to make skirts," she recalled. "Louis took an order for the skirt—five dozen. He went to Dallas, where he bought leftover fabric. I sewed them." The couple's eye for business and fashion soon led them to apply for a loan from the Hebrew Free Loan Association—also called *Gemilus Chasodim*, Yiddish for "deeds of kindness." This lending institution, common in Jewish communities and dating to 1907 in Fort Worth, extends interest-free business loans upon

Ann and Louis Bogart, 1944, in Uzbekistan. The Bogarts, post-war immigrants with expertise in textiles and fashion, resettled in Fort Worth in 1950.
Photo courtesy Ann Bogart.

the recommendation of two co-religionists. "That's how we started," Ann Bogart recalled. (The Herzfeld Sportswear company had also begun with a Hebrew free loan.) Bogart Industries eventually employed 1,000 people in factories in Fort Worth, Jacksboro, Cleburne, Dublin, and Mexico. Ann Bogart designed clothing for Sears, Roebuck and Co., and J.C. Penney. She also sewed custom-made bathing suits and evening gowns for contestants in the Miss Texas and Miss America pageants. For many years, the Bogarts served on the board of directors of the Miss Texas Pageant, which is headquartered in Fort Worth. For Ann Bogart, and many other immigrants, the Americanization School was one important step along the path toward a new life in Texas.

Rosenstein's leadership at the Americanization School turned her into a role model for other Jewish women. In 1943, she was elected president of the Fort Worth Council of Jewish Women, the city's premier Jewish women's organization because of its interaction with the secular community. During Rosenstein's two-year term, a record number of new members—108—joined the council, increasing its roster to more than 250 women. Many of these new NCJW members were congregants at Ahavath Sholom, the more traditional synagogue. Under Rosenstein's leadership, the NCJW became less elitist and more inclusive. To her credit, Rosenstein expanded the annual "Council Shabbat," a Friday evening in which women conducted a service at Beth-El, to include a second worship service at Ahavath Sholom.

Although the Jewish population of Fort Worth was less than 3,000, the work of the NCJW gave the Jewish community visibility and clout. To expand the council's influence, Rosenstein initiated the practice of placing NCJW members on the boards of social-service organizations with which the group was involved. She termed this a "gesture of sharing and giving towards a better and more human community." When, in the mid-1940s, Fort Worth's charitable organizations formed the Council of Social Agencies, Rosenstein made certain that the NCJW sent a delegate. In her annual report of 1944, she explained, "We are…

giving this group a definite picture involving the problems of child guidance, child delinquency, the inadequacies of child labor laws in Texas."

Rosenstein also wrote about the council's card parties, its rummage sales on the north side of town, its Red Cross canteen work at the Santa Fe Station, and its panel discussions about postwar plans for Europe. She described an "emotional" ceremony on World Government Day in memory of "our beloved boys, Harold Gilbert and Alvin Rubin," two young Jewish soldiers who perished during World War II.

Of course, Rosenstein also wrote about her pride and joy, the Americanization School, which in 1944 helped "six New Americans [who] acquired. . . citizenship status." She recounted the tale of "a Greek woman, who until she learned about our school, continued to fail her citizenship examinations." That student was Fotini Nixon, an illiterate Greek Catholic who had sailed to America in 1921 with her husband, Harry Z. Nixon, a veteran of the Balkan Wars. Rosenstein related the rest of that story to journalist Edith Guedry, a reporter with the *Fort Worth Press* who devoted a column dated June 1, 1942, to Fotini Nixon. "She had been raised in an area of Greece where boys, not girls were educated," the article explained. "The first time that Mrs. Nixon laboriously wrote her name, 'Fotini,' she was as happy as a child. When she could read the sentence, 'Five and one make six,' her eyes lighted up with a strange new joy." To study for her U.S. citizenship test, she wrote questions and answers on large sheets of paper and tacked them up all over her kitchen walls so she could study while she washed the dishes.

The day Fotini Nixon recited the oath of American citizenship in a ceremony at Fort

Worth's federal courthouse, Amelia Rosenstein and her eleven-year-old son, Bernard, were among the official witnesses. Bernard recalled that the last major classroom hurdle for Fotini Nixon was comprehending America's three branches of government. "Mamma said to her, think about your kitchen stove. You boil water on top on the burners; broil steaks in the oven inside of it; and can also bake a cake. The three parts of the stove are like three branches of government."

To Bernard Rosenstein, another of the Americanization School's most unforgettable graduates was Rosie Snofsky (pronounced Schnapfsky). A Polish immigrant, she visited the Rosensteins' home one day for help with filling out her application for U.S. citizenship. "Mama said, 'Where'd you come from?' 'Pinsk.' 'When's your birthday?' 'Auch Purim,'" she responded, meaning on the Jewish holiday of Purim, the Feast of Esther, which can fall in February or March, depending upon the vagaries of the Jewish lunar calendar. The year that Rosie Snofsky applied for U.S. citizenship, Purim fell on March 17. Therefore, Amelia Rosenstein wrote March 17, 1882, as her birth date. "It became a family joke," Bernard recalled. "The birthday of Mrs. Snofsky"—hardly an Irish-sounding name—"was on St. Patrick's Day."

Besides helping immigrants fill out forms, teaching English, training volunteers, and leading the Council of Jewish Women, Amelia Rosenstein also taught first-grade Sunday school at Beth-El Congregation. For forty years, Rosenstein worked with a succession of seven rabbis—Harry A. Merfeld, Samuel D. Soskin, Eugene Lipman, Ernest S. Grey, Milton Rosenbaum, Abraham J. Brachman, and Robert

En route to citizenship, 1949. Amelia Rosenstein, standing, instructs Agnes Igdolsky, left, a Dachau concentration camp survivor who spent the post-war years as a displaced person in Rumania, and Helena S. Davis, a native of Athens, Greece. Davis immigrated to the United States after marrying a Texan. *Courtesy,* Fort Worth Star-Telegram *Collection, Special Collections Division, The University of Texas at Arlington Libraries.*

J. Schur. Annually, her students decorated the walls of her classroom with crayoned pictures of animals, two by two, entering Noah's ark.

The first-grade curriculum began with the creation of the world. "This is pertinent to a six-year-old," Rosenstein told a reporter from the *Fort Worth Press.* "He can see clouds, the sea, the trees…Year after year, children love and enjoy the 'in the beginning'…which celebrates the joy of Creation." Rosenstein's creation-story lessons culminated with the celebration of the Sabbath, with several Sundays devoted to a "Sabbath

Rosenstein's first priority. As the longtime first-grade teacher at Beth-El Congregation, Rosenstein prepared scores of children for Consecration, the ceremony that initiates youngsters into Jewish learning. The 1963 Consecration Class stands on the altar at Beth-El, located at 207 West Broadway Avenue, in front of Rosenstein, Rabbi Robert Schur, who is holding a Torah scroll, and student assistant Carol Goldman (Minker). The youngsters, who hold mini-Torahs, are, row one: Jerrald B. Smith, Felise Antweil, Alyson Wolens, Marty Stenzler, Jon Siegel, Kirsten Wilson, Joel Baker, Charlotte Bronstein, Michelle Cristol, and Stuart Rosenthal. Second row: Craig Poster, Sherri Evans, Suzy Bronstein, Marcia Alenik, Monica Freed, Richard Haas, Salvador Hanono, and Layne Alan Berman. Don Barnett Photography. *Courtesy Beth-El Congregation Archives, Fort Worth.*

Table Program." Over and over, the first graders rehearsed Hebrew blessings for lighting candles, sipping the fruit of the vine, and breaking bread until they had internalized the sanctity of the seventh day. They baked challah, a traditional braided egg bread, in the temple kitchen. The course of study ended with an annual Model Sabbath Table Demonstration—a Sunday morning when each first grader set his or her place at an elegant table covered with fine linen. From home, the students brought a setting of china, silver, and crystal, as well as fresh flowers, candlesticks, and a Kiddush cup—a special silver

chalice for ritual wine. The children's beaming parents attended, as did the rabbi. One parent sent her son with a paper plate instead of fine china and received an admonishment from the teacher.

Rosenstein's final Model Sabbath Table Demonstration was celebrated in the fall of 1972. That November, she turned seventy-five. By the end of the school year, her sister-in-law Millie had died, and her husband Abe was in declining health. Amelia Rosenstein announced her retirement.

Rabbi Schur began planning a Sabbath serv-

Surrounded. Americanization School alumnae surprised their longtime teacher, Amelia Rosenstein, seated at center, with a party in December 1968. Photo by Norman Bradford.
Courtesy, Fort Worth Star-Telegram *Collection, Special Collections,*
The University of Texas at Arlington Library, Arlington, Texas.

ice in her honor. Rosenstein's adult students, however, begged her to continue. The NCJW looked for a successor. The school's top two volunteers were Clara Levy, a Beth-El congregant who worked at General Dynamics, and her close friend Pat Riddell, an Episcopalian. "They asked me if I would take over the school," recalled Riddell, whose volunteer work had earned her "honorary membership" in the National Council of Jewish Women. Although Riddell enjoyed teaching English to foreigners, she declined the job because she was unfamiliar with the labyrinth of rules governing immigration and naturalization. That was Rosenstein's area of expertise.

Thus, Amelia Rosenstein's 1973 retirement brought to a close the Americanization School,

which, under her guidance, had graduated more than 600 students. By then, area public schools offered adult-education classes to help foreigners transition to life in Texas. The NCJW's Americanization School no longer filled an unmet community need. Clara Levy unofficially revived the school in the 1980s when she tutored waves of Russian "refusniks" who resettled in Fort Worth. Levy said that she sought to emulate her mentor, whose classes "began with a very comfortable, homey atmosphere."

At the Sabbath service honoring Amelia Rosenstein on September 7, 1973, several generations of worshippers gathered to praise the beloved Sunday school teacher and Americanization coach. When the legendary educator died a decade later, on December 19, 1983, Rabbi

Schur noted in his graveside eulogy that Amelia Rosenstein had taught students from Vietnam to Venezuela and from first grade to retirement age. Her lessons live on.

BIBLIOGRAPHICAL ESSAY

The best nuggets about the Americanization School were gathered during oral-history interviews with two alumnae—Livia Schreiber Levine (on June 4, 2003) and Ann Bogart (on July 5, 2006) —as well as a telephone interview (October 25, 2003) with volunteer teacher Pat Riddell, who is not Jewish but was best friends with another teacher, Clara Levy, who recruited her. Bernard Rosenstein, whose mother, Amelia Levy Rosenstein, was the "dean" of the school for decades, shared his memories and his collection of newspaper clippings from the *Fort Worth Press*, *Fort Worth Star-Telegram*, and *Texas Jewish Post* during my visit to his Dallas home on June 6, 2003. Those articles date from 1942 to the school's closing in 1973. The Americanization School was frequently written up in the newspapers, with lengthy news features about colorful graduates and small blurbs about registration deadlines. Marcia Melton, at the *Star-Telegram*, opened up the newspaper's library for my research. Also of invaluable help were earlier clippings, which are part of the *Star-Telegram* Collection housed in the archives at the University of Texas at Arlington. The latter includes a wealth of black-and-white photographs used to illustrate this chapter.

All of the news clippings consulted, as well as notes from oral-history interviews, have been photocopied and incorporated into the National Council of Jewish Women Collection at the Fort Worth Jewish Archives at Ahavath Sholom. This archive, which is funded by the Jewish Federation of Fort Worth and Tarrant County, includes fifteen boxes of materials about the Fort Worth NCJW and ten scrapbooks. The materials were collected, sorted, and arranged as I worked on my master's thesis, "The Jewish Junior League: The Rise and Demise of the Fort Worth Council of Jewish Women, 1901–2002." The thesis has been revised into a forthcoming book by the same name that is to be published by Texas A&M University Press.

References in this chapter pertaining to Rabbi G. George Fox, who rounded up Jewish prostitutes from Hell's Half Acre, came from his autobiographical essay, "The End of an Era," in *Lives and Voices: A Collection of American Jewish Memoirs*, edited by Stanley F. Chyet (Philadelphia: Jewish Publication Society of America, 1972), 279–81. The material was incorporated into an earlier biographical essay, "G. George Fox: Fort Worth's Front-Page Rabbi," in my book *Jewish Stars in Texas: Rabbis and Their Work* (College Station: Texas A&M University Press, 1999), 80–101.

To put the Fort Worth Americanization School into context, research was conducted at the Library of Congress, home to the NCJW Administrative Collection, 1893–1975. Key sources in that collection are *The Immigrant Monthly Bulletin of Department of Immigrant Aid*, published by the NCJW; "Making Americans," a pamphlet by the Council's Cecilia Razovsky; and the NCJW's "A Guide for Teaching English to Foreigners," a booklet published in 1942. Also helpful was the NCJW's 1941 "Glossary of Immigration Terms."

Another primary source was the Reverend Josiah Strong's rabidly patriotic *Our Country: Its Possible Future and Its Present Crisis,* published in 1891. Written for the American Home Missionary Society and published with New York's Baker & Baylor Company, the volume was a bestseller for three decades. It warns of the perils of Catholics, "Romanism," and Mormonism, and led to a myriad of Americanization Schools in pre-World War I America.

Among the secondary literature, most helpful was Seth Korelitz's journal article, "'A Magnificent Piece of Work': The Americanization Work of the National Council of Jewish Women," *American Jewish History* 83, no. 2 (1995): 177–203. Korelitz's broad overview and interpretative framework are insightful, particu-larly his conclusion that these schools helped American Jews reassure themselves, and others, of their U.S. credentials.

Other secondary sources of immense help were Michael R. Olneck's "Americanization and the Education of Immigrants, 1900-1925: An Analysis of Symbolic Action," *American Journal of Education* 97 (August 1989): 398-417; Edward George Hartmann's *The Movement to Americanize the Immigrant* (New York: AMS Press, Inc., 1967), and Lauren Berlant's *The Anatomy of National Fantasy: Hawthorne, Utopia, and Everyday Life* (Chicago: University of Chicago Press, 1991), particularly Chapter Four, "On Americanization," which demonstrates how clubwomen interacted with the ideologies pertaining to turn-of-the-century womanhood.

Chapter 10

FOR THE PRICE OF A GOOD CIGAR

by Susan R. Petty

IN EARLY FORT WORTH THE ACTIVITIES of women and men split along gender lines. The city was growing out of its frontier status, the Indian wars were over, and civilization was advancing on the Lone Star State. Men, for the most part, were building the economic base of the city—establishing railroads, drilling oil wells, forming banks.

Women took on the more genteel, civilizing activities. Indeed, the rich arts scene of twenty-first-century Fort Worth owes its existence in large part to the persistence of several nineteenth- and early-twentieth-century visionary women who were determined to nurture the arts in their raw new city despite the many restrictions put on them by convention.

In the late 1870s, there were women artists in Fort Worth, but their work generally adhered to the hierarchy of artistic endeavor mandated by the European academies. Women could paint so-called "genre" scenes, domestic interiors, or small-scale still lifes, but it was frowned upon for them to attempt large-scale history painting.

Women were especially talented at painting miniatures and at china painting. This was the height of the Victorian period in America, and American women were influenced by work that came out of the academies in England and Germany.

One of the earliest known artists in Fort Worth was Elizabeth M. Carter, who came to the city in the late 1870s to teach art at the Clara and Arnold Walden Institute, located in the 600 block of West Fourth Street. She established her own private studio on upper Houston Street in the midst of the business district, where she taught drawing and painting to young ladies and a number of older residents. In fact, some of her more advanced students exhibited and received honorable mentions in the New Orleans Exposition of 1885–1886. Carter took classes in Cincinnati with Frank Duveneck, who had studied in Germany and became known as a master of American naturalism. Carter's teaching methods were unusual for the time as she and her female students worked from live models, something not allowed at any of the American academies. Her oil paintings and watercolors were described as grounded in fine draftsmanship and "smooth and beautifully worked out in the style of that time."

In 1881, drawing began to be taught in Fort Worth public schools, offering more opportunities for women to earn a living using their art. Private studios were another good way for single women artists to earn their living and to maintain respectability. Fort Worth city directories of the 1880s list several private studios. Dalla Marks, a graduate of Northern Illinois Seminary, opened her studio at 407 West Second Street in 1887; Mattie Melton, who was the principal of art at the old Polytechnic College, established her Anaero Art School in either 1904 or 1907 (sources conflict) and maintained it until 1921. Medora Rowley taught art in the mid-1890s at the old Fort Worth University and then moved to Galveston just in time to endure, and survive, the 1900 hurricane.

Blanche Goodman Brazelton Stillman succeeded Rowley as art teacher at Fort Worth University in 1896 and stayed there until 1904. She then taught at Carlton College, Bonham, until it closed in 1916. Brazelton painted a portrait of Adelphine Keeler, an early founder of the Carnegie Library and Fort Worth Art Association and one of the most important early forces in shaping the arts in Fort Worth.

Ida Loving Turner was a contemporary of Elizabeth Carter, teaching drawing from plaster casts using charcoal, oil, and watercolor. She also copied from photographs and taught china painting. One of her most advanced students, Josephine Barnes, became famous throughout the country for her china painting.

Turner was born in Carrollton, Mississippi, in 1858 and moved with her mother and two sisters to Fort Worth when she was fifteen. She was delighted to see the first train arrive in Fort Worth on July 19, 1876. Her family's initial home was a log cabin located at Fourth and Main streets. The family quickly became friends with some of Fort Worth's prominent families including the Peaks, the Scotts, and the Van Zandts. Ida Loving Turner studied art at the Cooper Union School of Art, New York, and took portraiture classes with Otto Vineno in New York as well. Around 1885, she started giving private art classes in Fort Worth.

In 1888, Polytechnic College created its first art department and chose Turner as its teacher. Turner also taught art at the Warren Female Institute, where she was named manager by President Grover Cleveland. Cleveland later appointed Turner as postmistress of Fort Worth. She was active in the women's work of the Texas Spring Palace Association in the late 1880s and in the Daughters of the American Revolution. One writer credits Turner with conception of the Fort Worth Children's Hospital. Turner was actively involved in the establishment of the Fort Worth Art Association and was directly responsible for one of the association's early acquisitions, Gilbert Stuart's *Portrait of Miss Clementine Beach.*

Christina MacLean was considered the dean of Fort Worth art teachers. She succeeded Brazelton in the art department at Fort Worth University in 1904, remaining there until May 1911, when it moved to Oklahoma. MacLean stayed in Fort Worth and taught at the Arlington Heights College for girls and also conducted private classes at her studio in her home at 1620 Washington Street.

MacLean was born in 1853 in Glasgow, Scotland, where she studied art with David Murray, who later became president of the Royal Academy of Art. She must have craved adventure, because for five years she taught art in the Good Hope Seminary and at the Dutch Reformed School for Boer Girls at Cape Town, South Africa. She got out of Africa just before the Boer War erupted. During the 1890s she attended the St. Louis Art School and the Chicago Art Institute and moved to Fort Worth to assume the position at Fort Worth University.

MacLean is described by one of her peers as "having an eager face and tremendous energy, and a driving spirit." This driving spirit led her to membership in the Old Painters Club and the Woman's Club of Fort Worth, and a listing in *Who's Who of the Womanhood of Texas* (The Texas Federation of Women's Clubs, 1923–24). Most importantly, she formed an association with Ida Loving Turner and Virginia "Jennie" Scott Scheuber in pioneering the art gallery in the Carnegie Library. Her association with Scheuber and the beginnings of the Carnegie Art Gallery must have linked her with that most pivotal figure in the history of Fort Worth art— Mrs. D. B. Keeler.

Adelphine Keeler was a public relations genius who began a lively campaign to raise money for a new library. She had the chutzpah to ask industrialist Andrew Carnegie for the seed money to build a library, and he was so taken by her boldness that he offered $50,000, provided, of course, the women could secure the land and raise $4,000 a year to maintain the facility. Part of Keeler's plan to raise that money consisted of accosting cigar-smoking gentlemen on the street, asking them to donate the price of a good cigar for the cause.

Portrait of Jennie Scheuber by Robert Vonnoh. This was one of the first paintings purchased by the newly formed art association in honor of Scheuber, who was instrumental in its founding.
Courtesy The Fort Worth Public Library.

Keeler and Scheuber made a formidable team—Keeler was keenly aware of the civilizing effect of the arts on a community, while Scheuber was among the first to realize both the civilizing *and* the economic power of a lively art scene.

On April 2, 1892, at a meeting at Scheuber's home, twenty Fort Worth women formed the Fort Worth Library Association; the charter for the group was established on April 25. Keeler and Scheuber arranged for the Jennings family to donate the property for the library at the corner of Ninth and Throckmorton streets. Thus was born the first art museum in Texas. The group began a series of "entertainments" to raise the operating money Carnegie had specified. By April 1893, the group had raised $224.63 from these entertainments, and it was at this point that Keeler began her assault on the cigar-smoking population.

The Texas Federation of Women's Clubs had a hand in bringing the library/art gallery to completion. One of the organization's first efforts was to secure a collection of photographs of masterpieces of art, which then circulated throughout the state. For a small fee, any club in the state could obtain the collection, which was in the care of a "conductor"—a curator who not only carried the slides from place to place but also "conducted" the classes in which they were shown. Other women's organizations helped as well—in 1898 the Women's Wednesday Club, along with other clubs in the city, made arrangements with the Art Institute of Chicago to bring Mrs. John Sherwood to town for a course of lectures that had a great influence in awakening the city's interest in the arts.

The circulating photographs and the extension lectures were among the activities generating public awareness and interest in the arts that encouraged the women to form the first organization that later became the Fort Worth Art Association. The new library building opened to the public in 1901, and the Fort Worth Art Gallery Association, led by Scheuber, began to focus on the day-to-day operations of the gallery and the association's goal of a free museum that offered educational programs for the public. In 1904 the group, under Scheuber's aegis, authorized the purchase of the first important work for the gallery's permanent collection, George Inness' painting *Approaching Storm* (1875, o/c,

19.5" x 19.5", collection of the Amon Carter Museum of Art). Other items purchased were Alexander Compera's *Evening* and Blanche Brazleton Stillman's *Portrait of Mrs. D. B. Keeler.*

In 1909 Scheuber made arrangements with the newly formed American Federation of Arts, Washington, D.C., to assemble and tour a collection of American oil paintings. The "First Annual Exhibition of Selected Paintings by American Painters" came to Fort Worth on December 20, 1909, and more than 5,000 people viewed the exhibition before it closed on January 10, 1910. The exhibition generated enormous enthusiasm in the city and culminated in the purchase of several paintings for the association, including *Mañana Point* by Paul Dougherty and the Gilbert Stuart that Ida Loving Turner was so eager to obtain. This seminal event gave birth to the Fort Worth Art Association, a group that still exists today, and whose goals were to establish a free public art museum, to promote the visual arts through exhibitions, lectures, and classes; and to create a fund for the purchase of art.

In 1901 the museum was known as the Art Gallery of the Carnegie Public Library. In 1910 it became the Fort Worth Museum of Art; in 1954 it was christened the Fort Worth Art Center. In 1971 it was renamed the Fort Worth Art Center Museum, and in 1974 the Fort Worth Art Museum. On November 1, 1987, it became the Modern Art Museum of Fort Worth. Today the Modern's outstanding collection is housed in a stunning building designed by Japanese architect Tadao Ando. The museum's world-renowned status is the culmination of the vision of those twenty women gathered in Jennie Scott Scheuber's living room in 1892.

But at the time, those women were thrilled

A view of the art gallery showing the typical "skyed" arrangement of paintings, a holdover from the nineteenth century.
The lighting at the time was considered state of the art.
Courtesy The Fort Worth Public Library, Local History and Genealogy Collection.

to have the gallery in the library. One of the first accomplishments of the Fort Worth Art Association was to outfit the gallery with sophisticated lighting, wall treatments, and woodwork to show off the collection to its best advantage. The association pledged to acquire at least one good painting each year and to continue the tradition of a comprehensive exhibition of American art at least annually.

Beginning in 1910 the association presented two shows a year: an exhibition of American art in the winter and an exhibition of Texas artists in the spring. It was this Texas annual that helped shape the lively and innovative Fort Worth art world. The Woman's Wednesday Club and the '93 Club supplied the association with supporters and volunteers whose enthusiasm and interest were a testament to the growing appreciation of the arts in Fort Worth.

Ella Ray Ledgerwood and two gentlemen gave free art classes on Saturday mornings in the new gallery. Ledgerwood was born in Dublin, Texas, and attended Polytechnic College as well as TCU in Fort Worth. She studied at the Art

Academy of Chicago, the New York School of Art, and with Robert Henri and Irving Wiles of New York. She exhibited at the Three Arts Club, New York; the Southern Exhibition of New York; the Dallas Forum; The Waco Cotton Palace; The Fort Worth Museum of Art; and other Texas cities.

Ledgerwood's free art classes, the traveling exhibitions, and the beginnings of an important permanent collection by the Fort Worth Art Association were responsible for the development of a new generation of Fort Worth artists.

Margaret Martin Littlejohn was one of the first local artists to be recognized in a *Fort Worth Star-Telegram* article touting the establishment of an art gallery in Fort Worth. Littlejohn was a painter, muralist, and art teacher who was born in 1876 in Jefferson, Texas. She studied in Venice, Italy, and graduated at an accelerated pace from the Boston Museum of Fine Arts School. In 1912 she moved to New York to study with William Merritt Chase and at the Art Students League. Littlejohn spent time painting in Woodstock, New York, at the University of Colorado at Boulder, and at the National Academy of Design, New York. She taught art abroad briefly and then taught in the Fort Worth public schools and also at TCU. But her career took root in the free art classes at the library. She died in 1954.

Other noted artists who came out of the free classes were Pattie R. East, Sallie M. Gillespie, Sallie Blythe Mummert, Blanche McVeigh, and Evaline Sellors.

Pattie R. East was born in 1894 in Hardesty, Oklahoma, but after living eighty years in Fort Worth should be considered a native. East was a painter, graphic artist, muralist, and teacher who chose as her subject the landscape of Texas and New Mexico, painting in Abilene, the Big Bend, and Santa Fe. She graduated from TCU and studied under Jose Arpa, Sven Binger Sandzen, Harry Anthony DeYoung, and Joseph Amadeus Fleck. She took courses at the Art Institute of Chicago and the Broadmoor Art Academy at Colorado Springs. In 1926 East attended the Texas Artists Camp where her instructors were Xavier Gonzalez and Sally Haley Russo. East exhibited and taught in Fort Worth for more than fifty years and was a frequent exhibitor at the Carnegie Art Gallery. One of her finest paintings, *High Desert Blooms,* an undated oil on canvas belonging to the A. C. Cook family and the Hockshop Collection, was featured in the exhibition catalogue *First Light: Local Art and the Fort Worth Public Library 1901–1961, A Centennial Exhibit.* She owned and operated Pattie R. East Art Studio and Gallery and also gave lessons in her home in Benbrook, where she died in 1994.

Sallie Meredith Gillespie, landscape painter, teacher, and lecturer, became one of the prime scions of the Fort Worth Circle and her roots can be traced to her days studying under Ella Ray Ledgerwood in the Saturday morning free art classes. Gillespie was born in Fort Worth in 1898; her father was a four-term U.S. congressman. She graduated from Sophie Newcomb College in 1920 and attended the University of Chicago and Pennsylvania Academy of Fine Arts. Gillespie first taught in Philadelphia public schools, then later at Montana State University, Missoula. She studied abroad for a year in France and Italy and returned to Fort Worth to teach in the public schools and at the Fort Worth School of Fine Arts from 1932 to 1933.

Gillespie was one of the founders of the Fort Worth School of Fine Arts. She also taught advanced teachers' classes at Our Lady of Victory School. From 1942 to 1945 she was head of the art department at Texas Wesleyan College and became secretary of the Fort Worth Art Association. Gillespie was an enthusiastic supporter of the Fort Worth Museum of Art, now the Modern Art Museum of Fort Worth, serving as a volunteer there for almost twenty years. In addition to her work with the public schools, the Fort Worth Art Association, and Texas Wesleyan, Gillespie maintained a private studio in Fort Worth and in Taos, New Mexico. She died in Taos in 1991.

Blanche McVeigh was born in St. Charles, Missouri, in 1895 and moved to Fort Worth as a child. She graduated from Washington University in Missouri and returned to Fort Worth, where she taught elementary school for several years. She then decided to become a professional artist and attended the Pennsylvania Academy of Fine Arts for one summer and the Art Institute of Chicago for another. She attended the Art Students League in New York and spent a year in Europe, where she discovered aquatint, a kind of etching. McVeigh died in 1970.

In 1932 McVeigh and Evaline Sellors, along with Gillespie and Wade Jolley, established the Fort Worth School of Fine Arts at 1100 Lipscomb Street, where McVeigh taught figure drawing and etching. Sellors and McVeigh also established the Fort Worth Artists Guild, the first local organization to support and exhibit local artists.

Evaline Sellors is one of the few sculptors besides Electra Waggoner Biggs to make her living and name in Fort Worth. Sellors was one of the founders of the Fort Worth School of Fine Arts, out of which grew the Fort Worth School or Circle of artists. Reared and educated in Fort Worth, Sellors attended the Pennsylvania Academy of Fine Arts and exhibited there. A 1927 catalogue from PAFA features one of her sculptures. Known mainly as a sculptor of animals and portrait busts, Sellors is described by one source in this way: "Pluck, perseverance, and hard work have won for Evaline Sellors recognition as a sculptor of high rank." Sellors died in 1995.

Carrie McLeod Greathouse was born in 1870. She moved to Fort Worth about 1904. She taught china painting, tapestry weaving, and commercial art. She taught in regular sessions from 1912 to 1920 at TCU and in the 1915 summer session as well. She also gave private lessons in her studio. Greathouse studied at the Chicago Art Institute, the Broadmoor Academy of Fine Art, and under Katherine Cherry and Frank N. Hendenschu in St. Louis. She also took classes with Frank Reaugh in Dallas. One of her paintings, *Madonna and Child* (1902, o/c, 80" X 45", collection of Thompson's Harveson Cole Funeral Home) was exhibited in the St. Louis World's Fair and at the Louisiana Purchase Exposition.

Greathouse was also a force in the women's club movement, serving as chair of the First District Federation of Women's Clubs and State Chair of Art Exhibits for the Federation. She organized the Arts and Crafts Club, which was still active in 1939 Fort Worth. In 1944 Carrie Greathouse died of injuries received when an automobile struck her.

Dura Brokaw Cockrell was another artist influenced by the offerings of the Carnegie Library. She was principal of the art department at AddRan Christian University in Waco in 1900 and also taught French there until the university moved to Fort Worth in 1910. She started the art department at AddRan with one pupil. Cockrell remained head of the art department at TCU until 1924. During her teaching years, she also received her master's degree in art from TCU, in 1917. She helped to organize the Fort Worth Painters Club, which later changed its name to the Allied Artists Club.

Cockrell was born in Iowa in 1877 and was educated at the Art Students League in New York, the Art Institute of Chicago, and with Robert Henri and William Merritt Chase, as well as F. Luis Mora. In 1924 she and her husband moved to Fulton, Missouri, where he obtained a teaching position. Cockrell taught art in Fulton and found the time to write two art textbooks, *Introduction to Art* and *Masterpieces of Painting with Religious Subjects* (both New York: R. R. Smith, Inc., 1930). In 1934, Dr. Cockrell died, and Dura Cockrell moved back to Fort Worth, where she remained associated with TCU until her death in 1961. In 1937 she became house-mother in a TCU residence hall. In 1939 she was a member of the Missouri Advisory Committee on Women's Participation to the New York World's Fair. She died in Edinburgh, Texas, and is buried in Fort Worth.

Other, lesser-known, artists were influenced by the growing appreciation for art coming out of the Carnegie Art Gallery or exhibited there in the Texas annuals. Belle Austin was the third cousin of Stephen F. Austin. Although born in Smith County in 1880, Belle Austin lived most of her life in Fort Worth. She exhibited often in the Texas annuals and was noted for her "charming landscapes and Texas bluebonnet pictures."

She died in 1980. Louise Jez was a very popular painter in the annual exhibitions of selected Texas paintings at the Fort Worth Carnegie Public Library; her canvases of bluebonnets appeared every year from 1928 to 1937. Jez was born in Brenham, Texas, in 1897 and moved to Fort Worth about 1920. She studied art at the College of Industrial Arts, now Texas Woman's University, in Denton. She died in 1981. Ella Beall Behrend also exhibited frequently at the Carnegie gallery. She was known as a landscape and still-life painter and was also a master framer. She died in 1982.

Nell Pierce Dow was born in 1893, grew up in Weatherford, Texas, and began exhibiting at the Carnegie Library in 1924. She founded the Dow Art Club. Dow also exhibited her paintings in the new Fort Worth Public Library exhibitions in 1939 and 1941. This painter, musician, and teacher left a long line of artists who still live in Fort Worth and own Dow Art Galleries. She died in 1976. Mary Jane McLean Bullock was born on a farm in North Fort Worth in 1898 and became a regular exhibitor at the Carnegie gallery. She also was an excellent painting instructor. She died in 1978.

Dura Cockrell left a legacy of students from her years at TCU; among them Mary Sue Darter Coleman. Coleman was born in 1893, graduated from TCU in 1915 and then attended the Art Students League, where she studied with George Brandt Bridgman, Dimitri Romanowsky, F. Luis Mora, and Edward Penfield. She studied three summers in Woodstock, New York, and taught at Midland Christian College from 1916 to 1917. She taught at TCU in the years 1917–1918 and also 1924–1925. In 1925 she married Harvey B. Coleman, who was also an artist, and the couple moved to Los Angeles, where Mary Sue Darter Coleman died in 1956.

Mignon Mastin began showing at the Carnegie Library when she moved to Fort Worth in the 1920s. Mastin studied at the Art Students League in New York and later at the Fort Worth School of Fine Arts. Records show that she took painting classes in Wellfleet, Massachusetts, La Jolla, California, and Taos and Santa Fe, New Mexico. Mastin might be considered the unofficial impetus for the founding of the so-called "Fort Worth Circle of Painting" because she was the first person to make completely abstract images. Mastin died in 1960.

The Fort Worth School or, more properly, the Fort Worth Circle was a loose association of artists working in different styles and media around the beginning of World War II. They grew out of the Fort Worth School of Fine Arts, which was instrumental in bringing to local artists' awareness the current trends in European art. Flora Blanc Reeder, co-founder with her husband Dickson of the Reeder School, often spent time in New York and Paris and brought the latest trends home to Texas to explore in the FWSFA classes. The faculty of the FWSFA even organized an exhibition program, which brought the work of cutting-edge European artists like Picasso, Matisse, Braque, and Derain to Fort Worth. The Reeders were perhaps the most influential members of the FWSFA and the Fort Worth Circle of artists because their home became a salon and a forum for the exchange of new ideas and techniques, especially print making.

The heyday of Fort Worth School or Circle was between 1945 and 1955, during which time the associated artists worked in a variety of more-or-less contemporary modes. Although the group was considered avant-garde in Fort Worth, they were working in styles that had blossomed in New York and Europe almost forty years earlier. Most members worked in a realistic manner with imagery drawn from either Cubism or Surrealism. They were, however, among the first artists in Texas to experiment with these difficult approaches and thus the first to bring these artistic innovations to the attention of the Texas public. Some of the group (Flora Blanc Reeder and Veronica Helfensteller along with four of their male colleagues) were invited to exhibit together in a New York gallery in 1944. The art critic of *The New York Times* particularly cited Helfensteller's work for consideration and described the group as ". . . at once individualized and congenially related. I understand that these Fort Worth painters are, so to speak, inseparable. . . . Creatively, the artists have still far to go, but some reveal not negligible promise. And the joyousness of the ensemble effort proves infectious."

One woman who was not able to benefit from the burgeoning downtown art scene was Manet Harrison Fowler. Fowler was an African-American artist, musician, and educator from Fort Worth. She was born in 1895, graduated from Tuskegee Institute in 1913, and studied at the Chicago College of Music. She taught at Prairie View State Normal and Industrial College and became president of the Texas Association of Negro Musicians. She also taught art in Negro schools in Fort Worth. In June 1928 Fowler founded the Mwalimu School in Fort Worth, which she later relocated to Harlem in New York City. The Mwalimu School was an integral part of the Harlem Renaissance, and, as

Manet Harrison Fowler, who founded the
Mwalimu School in Fort Worth, then moved it to
Harlem, where the school and Fowler became an
integral part of the Harlem Renaissance. Fowler
taught art and music in Fort Worth schools for
black children. *Courtesy Fowler Papers, Manuscript,
Archives, and Rare Book Library, Emory University.*

it expanded its scope, became known as the
Mwalimu Center for African Culture. Noted faculty members of the Mwalimu School include
author and historian Carter G. Woodson, the
father of the black history movement. Fowler
died in 1976.

Sweetie Ladd's delightful approach to her art
endeared her to generations of Fort Worth artists
and art aficionados alike. "Just paint poorly, my
dear," was the advice Ladd gave to one struggling
artist who took herself a bit too seriously. It was
her "folk" style and her dedication to preserving

historical accuracy that made Ladd's paintings of
Fort Worth buildings and events so sought after.
Born in Bonham, Texas, in 1902, Sweetie was
the fifth child of Edgar and Lou Kerr. Cissy
Stewart Lale, in her book *Sweetie Ladd's Historic
Fort Worth,* says that one of her older sisters
insisted the baby be called "Sweetie" because she
was so sweet. Her legal name was Ileta, but no
one ever called her anything but Sweetie, which
Ladd regretted, thinking it led people to believe
she was not sophisticated.

Her family moved to Fort Worth in 1905,
and they were somewhat well to do, with a nice
house on Hemphill Street. She lived during a
time when Fort Worth's buildings were beautiful
"monuments to the builders," and she faithfully
reproduced the tiniest details of buildings, clothing, and animals. Ladd graduated from TCU in
1932 with a degree in English and Spanish. She
had already married Homer Ladd and borne her
only child, Homer Ladd Jr. She was in her sixties
when she decided to take art lessons. She joined
the art department of the Woman's Club of Fort
Worth and studied under Bror Utter, a luminary
of the Fort Worth Circle. Ladd's work is often
compared with that of Grandma Moses, but her
viewpoint is more sophisticated than Moses'.
Ladd described herself as an "eclectic primitive."
She painted to the day of her death in 1991 and
is buried at Mount Olivet Cemetery in Fort
Worth beside her husband, who died in 1978.
Most of her work is in the collection of the Fort
Worth Public Library.

Josephine Mahaffey was another lively force
in the Fort Worth art scene. This painter,
teacher, businesswoman, and gallery owner was
born in Hopkins County, Texas, in 1903 and
reared in San Marcos. She studied art at the

College of Industrial Arts, now Texas Woman's University in Denton. Mahaffey continued her artistic explorations with Sallie Mummert in Fort Worth, where she had moved following her marriage to Mark Mahaffey. After Mummert's death in 1938, Mahaffey studied with Clinton Blair King, Octavio Medellin, Kathleen Lawrence, and John Erichser. She received her B.A. from Texas Woman's University later in life. The Mahaffeys had eight children and maintained a farm and art gallery near Azle. She taught watercolor classes all over the Fort Worth area. Watermelons were her favorite subject, and she sometimes painted on old newspapers. She was a beloved teacher and, in 1968, the State Fair of Texas declared a Josephine Mahaffey Day. She died in 1982.

Another noted teacher was Kathleen Goodman Lawrence. She was born in 1906 and began painting at the age of eleven. She was recognized for her ability to capture the effects of rain on canvas. Lawrence exhibited at the Annual Texas Artists Exhibition of Fort Worth from 1933 to 1937; the Southern States Art League Annual Exhibitions in 1937, 1939, and 1941; the 1938 National Exhibition of American Art at Rockefeller Center, New York; the Golden Gate International Exposition in San Francisco in 1939 and 1940; and the Annual Fort Worth Local Arts Show in 1940 and 1941. She died in 1983.

Lia Cuilty was born in Chihuahua, Mexico, in 1908. She fled the Mexican Revolution with her family and came to Fort Worth in 1917. She enrolled in the Fort Worth School of Fine Arts in the mid-1930s under the tutelage of Blanche McVeigh and became an important member when the Circle coalesced in the 1940s. Cuilty was best known as a graphic artist and painter. In addition to the Fort Worth school, she studied at the Dallas Art Institute art school of the Dallas Museum of Fine Arts. One source describes Cuilty as a "competent painter in gouache and oils." In 1946 she embarked upon a printmaking career, making etchings and lithographs. She participated with Veronica Helfensteller and Bror Utter in weekly experimental printmaking sessions at Helfensteller's studio. She died in 1978.

Emily Guthrie Smith began sketching in correct perspective at age five and took her first art lessons at age eleven. Smith was born in Fort Worth in 1909 and attended Texas State College for Women (later Texas Woman's University) in Denton, 1927–1929; she graduated from Oklahoma University in 1931. As many women artists of Fort Worth did, Smith attended the Art Students League in New York but returned to Fort Worth to teach, paint, and exhibit in the Tarrant County Annuals, in exhibitions sponsored by the Fort Worth Art Association and the Texas Fine Arts Association, among the many organizations that awarded prizes to Smith's works.

She had developed an interest in portraiture at the University of Oklahoma and over the span of her career painted more than 2,000 portraits, including pictures of actress Mary Martin and former Speaker of the House Jim Wright. Her preferred medium was pastels, because they allowed a quick "take" of the subject, but she was highly proficient in watercolors, oils, acrylics, sculpture, and mosaic. Smith was given several solo exhibitions and in fact died while preparing work for her third retrospective exhibition mounted by the Longview Museum and Art Center, which opened on September 21, 1986.

Emily Guthrie Smith, *Summer Breeze*, 1999 , Oil on Canvas, 31 x 50 inches.
Courtesy Longview Museum of Fine Arts, Longview, Texas.

After her death in 1986, a scholarship in her name was established at TCU.

Veronica Helfensteller was one of the leading lights of the Fort Worth Circle. Helfensteller was born in Fort Worth in 1910 and grew up here. She studied with Sallie Blythe Mummert, became president of the Fort Worth Artists' Guild in 1939, and was affiliated with many arts organizations throughout the country. In addition to the Fort Worth School of Fine Arts, Helfensteller attended the School of Fine Arts at Washington University, St. Louis, and the Colorado Springs Fine Arts Center. In 1937 she

Emily Guthrie Smith, *Young Mulatto*, 1942,
Oil on canvas.
Dallas Museum of Art, Lida Hooe Memorial Fund.
Courtesy Dallas Museum of Art.

Veronica Helfensteller, *Council of the Birds*, 20th century, Gouache, 22 x 28 inches.
Courtesy The Modern Art Museum of Fort Worth.

toured Europe and spent time studying art at the Budapest International School of Art. Later she traveled to Guatemala. Helfensteller made her living as a secretary in Fort Worth until 1946. She was adept in most artistic media and was one of the few in the Fort Worth Circle to study the lithography and engraving processes in depth. In 1947, Helfensteller moved to Santa Fe, where she lived, painted, and taught until 1954 when she moved to Tucson, Arizona. From 1961 to 1964 she taught art history and art appreciation at the Valley School for Girls in Tucson. She died in there in 1964 after a long illness. She was affiliated with Allied Artists Club in Fort Worth;

the Baltimore Watercolor Society; the California Watercolor Society; Southern Printmakers; the Southern States Art League; Texas Printmakers; the Printmakers Guild; and The Tucson Art Center. Her realistic style is characterized by flowing line and dramatic contrasts of light and dark. It has a haunting, lyrical quality and still seems current today.

Marjorie Johnson Lee was an alumnus of the '30s-era Fort Worth School of Fine Arts. Lee was a good friend of Veronica Helfensteller and a sketching partner of Bror Utter. She was noted for broad, flat planes of color delineating abstracted landscape forms. During World War II,

Lee enlisted in the WAVES (Women Accepted for Volunteer Emergency Service), and in 1949 was invited by the Fort Worth Art Association to mount a one-woman exhibition at the Fort Worth Public Library. She died in 1997.

Electra Waggoner Biggs, a socialite turned sculptor, was born in Fort Worth in 1912 and named after her illustrious aunt, Electra I, and her maternal great-grandfather, Electius Halsell. "Electra" means shining star in Greek, and both Electras lived up to that prophetic name. Electra II grew up in her parents' home at 556 Summit Avenue, across the street from "Thistle Hill," Electra I's former home. The family moved back and forth between Fort Worth and the Double Heart Ranch in North Texas. Electra developed her lifelong love of music listening to the player piano that was part of ranch life.

In the summer of 1918, the Waggoners moved back to Fort Worth, purchasing a house at 1212 Summit Street owned by Electra's grandfather, Dan Waggoner. Electra's mother, Helen, and Mrs. Bernie Anderson organized a kindergarten for eight children and hired three English sisters, Clara, May, and Gertrude Marsh, to teach music and dance, among other subjects. Electra attended Bryn Mawr College in Pennsylvania and Columbia University, New York. She also spent some time at the Sorbonne in Paris and with Arnold Geissbuhler in Boston. Electra said she had always wanted to be a sculptress and even worked in a foundry in New York to learn more about the casting process. Her most famous work is a sculpture of Will Rogers on his horse, Soapsuds, commissioned by Amon Carter Sr., after Rogers' death in a plane crash. A dedicated technician, Biggs destroyed the first casting of the work, entitled *Into the Sunset*, and started over,

completing the work in 1942. It was installed on the Will Rogers Complex grounds in 1947. She also made three full-size castings of *Into the Sunset* and ten maquettes, or miniatures. She died in 2001. (See "Ranch Women, Cowgirls, and Wildcatters.")

Beth Lea Clardy was a painter, showgirl, draftsperson, printmaker, and teacher. Born in Fort Worth in 1918 or 1919 (sources conflict), Clardy was valedictorian of the 1936 Polytechnic High class and graduated from TCU, where she studied painting under Samuel Ziegler. In 1941 she attended the Pennsylvania Academy of Fine Arts summer school in Chester Springs, Pennsylvania. While Clardy was in college she worked summers for Billy Rose's Casa Mañana as one of the Tall Texas Beauties. After she returned from Pennsylvania, Clardy began teaching Spanish and art at Oakhurst Elementary School and later became the art specialist for the Fort Worth Independent School District. During World War II, she was a drafter at the Convair plant. Clardy encouraged artists and opportunities for artists to exhibit their works, including the annual Art in the Metroplex juried competition at TCU. In 2003 the Fort Worth Arts Council bestowed upon Beth Lea Clardy the Distinguished Texas Artist Award. She died in 2004.

A longtime art teacher in the Fort Worth public schools, Beatrice Dunning began her career in 1936 at Alice Carlson Elementary School. In the 1940s she taught at McLean Junior High School and was the first art teacher at R. L. Paschal High School after it moved to Forest Park Boulevard. In 1967, Dunning was named Paschal's Teacher of the Year.

Dunning's obituary in 2005 describes her

this way, "Bea's students were her children. A hard taskmaster, mediocrity was not in her vocabulary and certainly was never acceptable. Everyone and everything in her life was 'special.' She lived in an era when travel was more grand, having traveled around the world, once spending several nights in a tent at the foot of pyramids."

One of the last great Fort Worth painters of the twentieth century, Cynthia Brants managed to blend art, family, equestrian pursuits, and historic preservation into a satisfying career and life. Brants was born in Fort Worth in 1924, attended South and North Hi Mount Elementary schools, and graduated from the Madeira School in Fairfax, Virginia. In 1945, she earned her B.A. from Sarah Lawrence College, New York, and also studied printmaking with Stanley William Hayter at Atelier 17, probably with Flora Blanc Reeder and Veronica Helfensteller. Brants taught art at Sarah Lawrence for six years and owned a home in Maine. She exhibited at the Fort Worth Art Museum, the Bodley Gallery in New York City, and galleries and museums around Texas. Brants' obituary in 2006 describes her as an "avid horsewoman," taking part in hunter/jumper and dressage competitions. In her later years she moved to Granbury, Texas, where she was involved in the restoration of the property on the square. She also maintained a studio and gallery in Granbury, where she continued to paint and make small metal castings and models until her death.

Unlike the artists described above, Fort Worth writers had to depend on themselves for support and inspiration. No writers association of Fort Worth sponsored readings; no benefactor created a place for writers to learn and practice. The sole exception was *The Bohemian,* an illustrated quarterly of "Our Literary Club in Bohemia," or the Bohemian Club. The club was organized in 1898 and met every second and fourth Fridays at the "Nest," home of Henrie C. L. Gorman, at East Belknap and Harding streets. Out of these meetings grew five editions of *The Bohemian* and a special souvenir edition.

Gorman, author, editor, and proprietor of *The Bohemian,* wrote as Clara Leclerc. She described herself as "an Alabamian by birth, a Georgian by education, and a Texan by adoption." Her goal for *The Bohemian* was "to prove to the world that the South has brains as well as brawn." Gorman/Leclerc wrote romances, "descriptive writings," essays, and was especially noted for her children's writing. In an article in *The Bohemian* ("Texas Authors, Prose Writers, and Poets"), Judge C. C. Cummings opines that her particular expertise at children's writings came from her many years as a teacher. Other contributors to *The Bohemian* include Mattie Warren, who was among the first women to write for Gorman; Sarah Luce Larimer, Margie Brantley, and Mamie E. Lochridge. *The Bohemian* discontinued publication in 1907, according to a 1916 letter Gorman wrote for the Texas Press Women's Association scrapbook, with the souvenir edition. (Read more about Gorman's journalism career in the chapter "High-heeled Times in the Newsroom.")

Laura Nettleton Brown was associate editor of *The Bohemian.* She was married to author Charles Montresor Brown. Brown's only copy of an unpublished novel and a work of philosophy were burned in a fire at the Marfa train depot. Sources describe her writing as elegant and learned.

Ethel Bostick was another writer featured in Judge Cummings' article. Bostick was a journalist who graduated from college in Tennessee. She was the society and literary editor and dramatic and musical critic of the *Fort Worth Morning Record*, as well as responsible for the daily woman's department and the weekly "Boys and Girls" column. Born in Kentucky, Bostick was raised in Tennessee and, like Henrie Gorman, considered herself a Texan by adoption.

Forrest Tucker graduated from Baylor University, Waco, Texas, and then attended the Boston School of Oratory. She established Miss Tucker's School of Expression, Elocution, Reading, and Physical Culture in Galveston, Texas, which apparently was well known throughout the state. Although Judge Cummings does not indicate what Tucker did in Fort Worth, he lists her as an "elocutionist and writer, Fort Worth, Texas." Other early literary figures were Cora Melton Cross, who was a historian of the cattle drives and trail drivers; and was noted for her biographies of these colorful figures (See "High-heeled Times in the Newsroom"); and Fanny L. Armstrong, an important figure in the WCTU, a friend of Frances Willard, and a charter member of the Texas Woman's Press Association. Cummings' article says that Armstrong never married because there was only one man for her, but he lived in another country and another time. It was Martin Luther, "the greatest of all reformers," and the only person who could have won her own reforming heart. (See See "High-heeled Times in the Newsroom" and "Duchesses with Hearts of Love and Brains of Fire.")

Clare Ogden Davis, along with her husband, Burton Davis, wrote mysteries under the pen name of Lawrence Saunders. Davis was on the staff of the *Fort Worth Record*. The Davises lived in North Fort Worth and later moved to New York. Their novels include: *Smoke Screen*, 1930; *Columnist Murder*, 1931; *Six Weeks*, 1932; and *Devil's Den*, 1933.

Known for compilations, essays, and *belles lettres*, Mabel Major was a member of the TCU English department beginning in 1919. Her best-known work is *My Foot's in the Stirrup, My Pony Won't Stand*, written in collaboration with Rebecca W. Smith, another Fort Worth writer. Major and Smith wrote under the pseudonym of W. S. Bartlett. Major and Smith also put together an anthology of writing about the West in 1929. Entitled *The Southwest in Literature*, the anthology served to introduce high school students to western writing. They also published scholarly articles such as "British Ballads in Texas," for *Texas Folklore Publications* 10 (1932).

Mary Daggett Lake was born in Fort Worth in 1880. She became a guiding force in the botanical world of Fort Worth. She majored in botany and music at Cottey College in Missouri and was research assistant at a private herbarium for twelve years. From 1935 until her death, Lake was educational director of the Garden Center of Fort Worth. She established nature classes for children, began a gardener's library, and was a supporter of innovation in soil conservation and highway beautification. She wrote a weekly column for the *Fort Worth Star-Telegram* and was also garden editor from 1937 to 1955. Her interviews with Fort Worth old-timers, "Among Tarrant County's First Hundred," for the Texas Centennial, were serialized in the *Star-Telegram*. She also wrote *The Legend of the Bluebonnet* and *Cotton Superstitions*. She died in 1955.

Margie Belle Boswell taught in the Fort Worth public schools until 1897, when she married W. E. Boswell. She was a member of many poetry societies including serving as president of the American Poetry League and the Poetry Society of Texas. Beginning in 1937 Boswell wrote a column for the *Fort Worth Press*. She taught verse technique, contributed to literary journals, and published eight books of poetry. Among the most notable are: *The Mockingbird and Other Poems,* 1926; *Scattered Leaves,* 1932; *Wings Against the Dawn,* 1945; *The Light Still Burns,* 1952; *Sunrise in the Valley,* 1959; and *Selected Poems and Little Lines,* 1962. In addition to her literary output, Boswell produced a poetry program on radio station KFJZ. She and her husband had eleven children. A grateful recipient of many poetry prizes, she established the Boswell Poetry Prize at TCU. She died in 1963.

Pulitzer Prize-winning author Katherine Anne Porter was born in Indian Creek, Texas, in 1890 and spent her early years in Texas. Considered by many to be the "only star in the Texas [literary] firmament," Porter went head to head with her famous novel *Pale Horse, Pale Rider* against J. Frank Dobie for the 1939 Texas Institute of Letters Literary Prize, which Dobie won for *Apache Gold, Yaqui Silver.* Dobie's reputation has waned in modern days, while Porter's has increased in stature, and the TIL prize is even today a source of literary argument. Porter's love-hate relationship with Texas extended even to denying that she ever worked for the *Fort Worth Star-Telegram*, which she did. (See "High-heeled Times in the Newsroom.") She also took part in the Vagabond Players, Fort Worth's answer to the little theater, a theatrical group to which Porter's friend, reporter Kitty Barry

Crawford, introduced her. Porter was involved with the group from its debut performance in October of 1921 for the entire season, playing various roles in the group's digs over the horse stalls in Lotta Carter Gardner's barn on Alston Avenue in Fort Worth.

From such inauspicious beginnings Porter went on to produce stories and novels, including the widely acclaimed *Ship of Fools,* which brought her a modicum of fame and fortune, but not the critical notice that *Pale Horse* had achieved. However, *The Collected Stories of Katherine Anne Porter* (1965) won the National Institute of Arts and Letters' Gold Medal for Fiction, the Pulitzer Prize, and the National Book Award. An article in the *Atlantic Monthly* from 1975, "Notes on the Texas I Remember," talks about religion, racial tension, and Mexican food, but gives her time in Fort Worth short shrift. A final indication of her difficult relationship with Texas is the thwarting of her intention to leave her papers to the University of Texas if the university would name a library after her. The university declined, and Porter's papers reside at the University of Maryland. Porter died in 1980.

Mary Whatley Clarke was a western historian, newspaper editor and reporter, and author. She was born in Palo Pinto, Texas, in 1899 but moved to Fort Worth in 1946 after her marriage to Albany banker Joe Clarke when he was named executive vice president of the Fort Worth National Bank. Before her marriage to Clarke, Whatley had been married to James Dunbar, publisher of the *Norwood Press* in Winnipeg, Canada. After his death, she ran the *Press* for four years and in 1927 sold it in order to buy the *Palo Pinto Star,* a one-woman operation.

She was the first female president of the West Texas Press Association.

After moving to Fort Worth, Clarke published her first book, *Palo Pinto Story* (1950), a history of Palo Pinto County. In 1956, she published a collection of her columns for the *Palo Pinto Star* entitled "Sunbonnets." Clarke's interests were wide ranging: she wrote a history of the Texas Cherokees, a history of the Texas and Southwestern Cattle Raisers Association, some ranch histories, and a children's book. In addition, she contributed more than 150 features for *The Cattleman* magazine between 1943 and 1982 and a monthly column for a magazine published by the Fort Worth Children's Hospital, where she was also a volunteer.

Clarke and her husband were among the founding organizers of the Van Cliburn International Piano Competition and the Jewel Charity Ball. They were avid travelers and happened to be on the maiden voyage of the Italian luxury liner *Andrea Dorea*, the ship that several years later collided with another vessel and sank in the Atlantic. Somehow Mary Clarke always managed to include some kind of cattle operation on the couple's travels, but they always got back to Fort Worth in time for the annual convention of the Cattle Raisers Association. She died in 1990.

Patricia Highsmith, author of such psychological thrillers as *Strangers on a Train* and *The Talented Mr. Ripley*, had, like Katherine Anne Porter, a love-hate relationship with Texas. Like Porter, Highsmith's reputation has continued to grow in the years after her death, and even though she did not consider herself to be a "Texas" writer, she is one of Texas' finest. She was, however, incontrovertibly Texan, feeling most at home in Levis, eating cornbread and collard greens, even in France.

Highsmith was born in Fort Worth in 1921, into an unhappy marriage. Her mother was beautiful, elegant, and narcissistic. Mary Coates Plangman Highsmith was not what one would call a doting mother, especially to an essentially awkward, intensely moody, and gangly young girl who from her earliest memories felt herself to be an outsider. For all of Patricia Highsmith's life she pursued relationships with women who were like her mother, in vain attempts to recreate or remold that primal relationship into something that would give her the happiness that always eluded her.

Highsmith actually was the daughter of Jay Bernard Plangman, Mary Coates' first husband. The couple was divorced soon after Patricia's birth, and Highsmith was raised by her much-disliked stepfather, commercial artist Stanley Highsmith. It was not until later in life that Highsmith discovered she was not Highsmith's natural daughter. She and Plangman met as adults and developed a peculiar, ongoing relationship. Mary Coates was married to Plangman only a year, divorcing him after becoming pregnant with Patricia and being unsuccessful in aborting the baby. Throughout her life Patricia Highsmith was painfully aware that her mother had tried to abort her.

Highsmith was closer to her grandmother, Willie Mae Coates, and the three of them, Patsy, as Patricia was called then; Mary, and Willie Mae, often lived together in the house on West Daggett Street when Mary's fortunes were on the wane. Patsy attended schools in Fort Worth off and on and developed an early interest in bizarre, macabre subjects. She was fond of Edgar

Allen Poe, the paintings of Francis Bacon, and Dr. Karl Menninger's *The Human Mind,* an account of deviant behavior, such as schizophrenia, kleptomania, and pyromania. The compilation of anecdotes for Dr. Menninger's book was undertaken by Robert Ripley, who later created "Ripley's Believe It or Not!" Interestingly, Highsmith's psychopathic protagonist in *The Talented Mr. Ripley* is named Tom Ripley.

Mary Coates and her second husband moved to New York when Patsy was six years old, then moved back to Fort Worth a year later. This pattern would recur several times during Patsy's young life. She hated school in Fort Worth but loved it in New York. She hated classmates in New York, but loved her playmates in Fort Worth. Her grandmother's house on West Daggett was in a neighborhood in transition and her closest running mates were "Negro children" who lived in a shanty behind Willie Mae's house. Mother Mary did not care that her daughter played with black children, but Willie Mae was horrified and did everything she could to keep the friends apart. Willie Mae would have been even more horrified to learn that her beloved granddaughter was a lesbian and had her first affair in a New York school when she was in her early teens. This was a time when lesbianism was even more repugnant to the majority of people than male homosexuality. Highsmith was aware of these attitudes and suffered terribly from the grotesque portrayals of female homosexuals in literature and film and the attitudes of her contemporaries.

As Highsmith grew more famous, she spent more time in Mexico and abroad, away from the judgmental eye of American morality. Her affairs often caused her great pain, but her relationship with several lovers served to inspire her writing. Highsmith died alone in 1995. Only in her work did she find the joy and satisfaction she missed in life.

BIBLIOGRAPHIC ESSAY

The local history and genealogy department of Fort Worth Public Library provided no end of advice and services during my research for this chapter. Librarians Donna Kruse and Betty Shankle pointed me in the direction of unpublished manuscripts such as "Art in Fort Worth"; "Art: A Tentative Course of Study for Grades 4, 5, 6, 7, & 8" (Fort Worth: Fort Worth Public Schools Curriculum Bulletin #130, 1933); and Peak, Aline, "Beginning of Art in Fort Worth." The microfiche resources yielded treasures in the form of articles from *The Bohemian*: Brantly, Mrs. F. M., "Texas Musicians, Vocalists and Artists"; Cummings, Judge C. C. "Texas Authors, Prose Writers, and Poets"; or on the Fort Worth Artists Guild, from the Federal Writers Project. The *Fort Worth Star-Telegram* obituaries yielded background information on Cynthia Helen Brants, Beth Lea Clardy, and Beatrice Dunning. Charles R. Fuller's contributions to the Federal Writers Project gave a lively sense of the developing Fort Worth scene and his discussion of the early, middle, and modern periods gave me a loose structure with which to organize my notes. The library's archives of reference books, theses and dissertations, and clippings gave me glimpses into the art and literary worlds of former days.

TCU Mary Couts Burnett interlibrary loan specialists helped locate articles and long out of print materials such as: Porter, Katherine Anne,

"Notes on the Texas I Remember," *The Atlantic* 235, no. 3 (March 1975): 102–106; Porter, Roze McCoy. *Electra II: Electra Waggoner Biggs, Socialite, Sculptor, Ranch Heiress* (Vernon, Texas: Red River Valley Museum, 1995); Ross, Grace, and Mabel Kuykendall. *Poetry Out Where the West Begins: A Collection of Poems by Fort Worth Authors* (Dallas: Kaleidoscope Press, 1949); and Swank, Patsy, "Deep in the Arts of Texas," in *Texas Celebrates! The First 150 Years* (Dallas: Southwest Media Corporation, 1985).

The Albany Old Jail Museum archives were an essential source for material on Evaline Sellors: Sellors, Evaline Clarke. Papers. Robert E. Nail Archives, The Old Jail Art Center, Albany, Texas.

The staff at the Emory University Library were helpful in obtaining the image of Manet Harrison Fowler and their online Guide to Manet Harrison Fowler Papers was a model of organization.

By far the most important online reference materials are at the Handbook of Texas Online, http://www.tsha.utexas.edu/handbook/online/index.html, a treasure beyond compare.

In addition, I would like to thank my colleagues on this project, many of whom volunteered a source here, an article there, to help give life to the artists and writers with whom I became acquainted. These are the women whose lives will be explored in *Grace and Gumption II*, I guarantee.

Chapter 11

"THERE'S NOTHING SO USELESS AS A SHOWGIRL"

by Jan L. Jones

ANY OF FORT WORTH'S first "ladies" of the stage were members in good standing of the local demimonde and vied, sometimes in bouts of hair-pulling and fisticuffs, for top billing in Hell's Half Acre's raucous variety theaters. These prima donnas of the ribald, actresses with such colorful appellations as Rowdy Kate, Baby Murray, and Kitty Devine, took to the boards in bawdy musical turns and melodramas. Between shows, they retired with free-spending admirers to private rooms in the theaters or in nearby "female boardinghouses."

But it was leading ladies and histrionics of a different sort that tamed Fort Worth's early reputation as a wild and wooly cowtown and shaped its long-range cultural vision. Evans Hall, the city's first legitimate performance space, debuted in 1876. The hall's rudimentary stage attracted professional touring companies and fired theatrical fervor among local thespians. Within months the Home Dramatic Club organized. Its first production, *The Streets of New York,* took to the

boards in June 1877 featuring Lucy Souter and Lula and Isabella Beall. *The Fort Worth Democrat* noted that the women "performed in an almost faultless manner, lending a peculiar charm to the play."

A second, more significant group formed later that same year, taking its name from its meeting place, the recently completed El Paso Hotel. The El Paso Literary and Music Society grew steadily, counting in its ranks such leading citizens as Dr. Julian T. and Sarah (Ferguson) Feild and General James J. and Lilly (Loving) Byrne. To raise money for a city library, the club staged *The Lady of Lyons* in February 1881 with a cast that included Annie Berry, Elizabeth Priest, and Nellie Bennett, daughter of D. C. Bennett, vice president of First National Bank.

The completion of the Fort Worth Opera House in 1883 brought local thespians together for the city's first community-produced operetta, *The Chimes of Normandy,* produced in February 1884. The musical, involving forty singers and musicians, became "the social event of the season," playing to large crowds. Anna Pettus, driving force behind the production and stepdaughter of G. M. Otten, company music director, assembled the town's finest talent for the event with Pettus herself taking the lead role of Serpolette. Fannie Murphy, daughter of Southside Baptist Church pastor John Decatur Murphy, sang the part of Germaine.

Within a year, the city also gained its first female impresario when Agnes Benton became the opera house's third manager. Benton previously had worked as business manager of the Dallas Opera House, a hall managed since around 1882 by her husband, Charles Benton. She had other talents besides a head for business. In about 1883 she had mounted a "fairy" production (children's company) of H. M. S. Pinafore for theater mogul John H. Haverly, nationally known for his touring minstrel and operetta companies. In 1884, shortly after her husband acquired the lease of the Fort Worth Opera House, she became business manager of the recently completed hall.

The Bentons' multiple business ventures, which also involved management of touring theatrical companies, led to a division of responsibilities later that same year. Charles Benton took to the road, while Agnes Benton assumed full control of the opera house. Hall directors later extended her lease by an additional three years, but just months after this vote of confidence she abruptly vacated the agreement. She followed her husband to New York, where both continued in theatrical management for several years. In 1897, she directed Cinderella, a weeklong charity event involving three casts and more than 3,000 children staged in the Metropolitan Opera House.

In Fort Worth, increasingly ambitious amateur productions continued to serve as important catalysts in the city's artistic development. Such events became meeting points for cultural resources, showcasing the area's finest actors, singers, and musicians. Women figured prominently in these often-lavish theatricals. Sallie Huffman, wife of opera house majority owner Walter A. Huffman, organized several events between 1883 and 1890, including an 1886 production of Gilbert and Sullivan's Patience, starring Fannie Bridges in the title role.

The Pirates of Penzance, staged in 1888 by the recently organized Fort Worth Musical Union, featured twenty-year-old soprano Maud Peters. A Missouri native, Peters had arrived in Fort Worth around 1887. She became the city's most sought-after performer after she "carried the audience by storm" with her "pure soprano voice and perfect conception of character." She became a featured artist in the Texas Spring Palace expositions of 1889 and 1890 and over the next twenty years remained in demand as a soloist for churches, music societies, and civic organizations in both Fort Worth and Dallas.

In 1891, Peters married another prominent area singer, Louis H. Ducker. Following her marriage, she sang the title role in Esther the Queen (1892) in Dallas, and in Fort Worth starred in a revival of Pirates of Penzance (1897). She played opposite her husband in stagings of Ben-Hur (1898), and The Sorcerer (1905). By the early 1900s, she had become one of the city's leading vocal instructors, serving on the faculty of Polytechnic College and drawing private pupils from among Fort Worth's leading families. Around 1903, she organized the St. Cecilia

Choral Society, becoming its director and first president.

At the turn of the twentieth century, vaudeville bills featuring an eccentric hodgepodge of comedy, dance, circus, and musical acts were upstaging extravagant musicals and operettas in popularity. Edna Burchill, daughter of the city's second female postmistress, Belle Burchill, parlayed an unusual baritone singing voice into a show business career that took her to some of Chicago and New York's leading vaudeville houses and roof gardens. Interstate Amusements unveiled the Majestic, the city's first high class vaudeville theater, in 1905, drawing such crowds that by 1911 the company abandoned its original site on Jennings Avenue to build a much larger Majestic at Tenth and Commerce.

Fourteen years later, the Majestic had become the city's preeminent live performance hall. Lela McMath Rogers, entertainment columnist for the *Fort Worth Record,* covered the weekly vaudeville bill, often accompanied to the theater by her young daughter, Virginia. Virginia hung out with performers, listening to backstage gossip and picking up bits of business. She took dance lessons from Norene Thrash, a local veteran of both nightclubs and the circuits, and from Eddie Foy Jr. Foy, who toured in a song-and-dance act with his younger siblings, taught her the Charleston. During the Foys' Fort Worth stop, one of Foy's sisters became too ill to perform one night. Foy quickly taught Virginia the act, and she went on for the evening performance.

In 1925, the fourteen-year-old entered a Charleston contest sponsored by the Interstate Circuit. Grand prize was four weeks of appearances in the circuit's Texas theaters. On

Ginger Rogers, c. 1925. *Courtesy,* Fort Worth Star-Telegram *Collection, Special Collections, University of Texas at Arlington Libraries.*

November 6, in the Texas Hotel ballroom, the teenager danced away with the local title easily. Three nights later, she bested entrants from across Texas to win the state finals, held at Dallas' Baker Hotel. The precocious teen opened in Waco several weeks later using her stepfather's last name in a dance turn billed as Ginger Rogers and the Dancing Red Heads. The act played Fort Worth the week of December 13, 1925. Rogers' dance skills stretched her original booking into three years of appearances across the country. Already appearing on Broadway in 1930, she signed her first motion picture contract, an event that led to pairings in several movie musicals with dancer Fred Astaire and eventual stardom.

Norene Thrash, whom some sources credit as one of Ginger Rogers' earliest dance instruc-

Norene Thrash, left and Lena Viehl, the dancing "Warren Sisters," on vaudeville's Interstate Circuit, c. 1925.
Courtesy Olin Clyde "Tex" Eddleman.

tors, had herself spent several seasons on the vaudeville circuits. Born in Eastland in 1899, she grew up in Fort Worth. Her parents, Nora and Sidney J. Thrash, sent her to New York to train with Theodore Koslov, formerly of the Diaghilev Ballet. From him she received a classical veneer, gaining experience dancing small parts in the company of the old Metropolitan Opera. In the early 1920s a scout for New York theater moguls the Shubert brothers, "discovered" her, and by 1925 she was dancing in the company of famed "shimmy queen" Gilda Gray. She toured the Interstate Circuit with another Fort Worth dancer, Lena Viehl, as the Warren Sisters; and with Frank Mack and other male partners, she performed exhibition ballroom dancing billed as Fernandez and Lolita and Francois and René in major nightclubs, including Havana's Casino Nationale. Returning to Fort Worth in the 1930s, she taught dance, operating her own studio at 4567 Meadowbrook Drive for thirty years. Following World War II, she also danced in productions of the Fort Worth Municipal Opera.

As vaudeville hit the zenith of its popularity in the years after World War I, the little theater movement was gaining momentum as live performance halls all across the country switched to motion pictures. Little theater became the new frontier in live performance, its proponents advocating smaller, less commercial productions staged by self-supporting, community theater groups. Fort Worth's Vagabond Players organized in 1921 led by Rosalind Gardner, daughter of wholesale grocer Hunter E. Gardner and former Fort Worth society belle Lotta Carter Gardner.

Rosalind Gardner's interest in dramatics emerged during her school years at Nashville's Ward-Belmont School and National Park Seminary in Washington, D.C. She gained production experience in California with Hollywood Community Theater. In 1921 Gardner returned to Fort Worth, where she and other little theater enthusiasts, including Lotta Gardner, Marguerite Kerr, Mary Hartmann, and Rosalind's brother Hunter Gardner erected a small stage in a barn on the Gardner property in the 1300 block of Alston Avenue.

The Vagabond Players debuted October 12, 1921, with *Suppressed Desires*, a one-act comedy featuring Gardner, Kerr, and Walker Moore. Among audience members that evening was a struggling young journalist from Indian Creek, Texas, Katherine Anne Porter, staying with local friends. Porter soon joined the company, acting in several productions through the fall and winter and writing a piece for the *Fort Worth Star-Telegram* about little theater's power "to free the artist from conventionalized forms." (See "High-heeled Times in the Newsroom.")

Rosalind Gardner left the Vagabond Players after just one season to pursue a professional acting career, but her mother held the group together. Lotta Gardner, from the beginning, had been the force driving the organization behind the scenes. She provided the $800 needed for start-up expenses, served as both ticket agent and house manager, and cajoled wealthy friends into supporting the effort.

Gardner's enthusiasm for the project probably derived, at least in part, from her own unrealized theatrical ambitions. Born in Longview in 1876, she grew up in Fort Worth society circles. Her parents, E. H. and Belle Carter, moved to the city about 1882, where Carter established Fort Worth Grocery Company, and, later with Charles Battle, Carter-Battle Grocer Company.

Intent on a theatrical career, Lotta attended Boston's Sargent School in the 1890s, where she studied dramatic arts. She shelved those plans, however, in 1897 to marry Hunter E. Gardner, a bookkeeper with her father's firm.

From 1921 through World War II, Lotta Gardner remained the little theater's most avid booster. The organization officially incorporated in 1923 as the Fort Worth Little Theater and moved to its own building at 609 West Fourth. Gardner was elected president of the association in 1925 at the same time her son, Hunter Gardner Jr., became the company's first paid director. Gradually, she shifted from strictly behind-the-scenes work to playing occasional character roles, even as she continued to enlist new supporters for the organization. Largely through her efforts, the Little Theater moved to the music building of the Fort Worth Woman's Club in 1927 with sponsors that included such influential businessmen as Amon G. Carter, H. C. Meacham, W. C. and W. K. Stripling, E. E. Bewley, W. P. McLean, and E. A. "Ed" Landreth. In 1928, the club added a children's theater division headed by Katilee Fender.

Gardner withdrew from local theater work from 1929 to 1932 but not before the Little Theater recognized her many contributions. In 1927, the organization named her honorary president, a title she retained until the company ceased production in 1935 under the deepening effects of the Depression. As the organization struggled against declining support, Gardner returned to active little theater participation in 1932 after spending several years in New York, where her children were pursuing acting careers. That same year she helped establish the Theater Guild, an organization that continued to sponsor

live performances for several years after the little theater closed its doors.

In 1938, Gardner attempted to revive the theater she helped found, once again sponsoring play performances in her garden. Interest had waned, however, and little came of the event. The movement seemed on the brink of a resurgence in 1941 under a new board that included Rosalind Gardner, who, in the meantime, had married Dr. Harold J. Shelley. Several plays followed through 1941 until America's entrance into World War II finally brought down the curtain for good. Lotta Carter Gardner, little theater's most devoted advocate, died in 1949.

Paralleling the development of little theater in Fort Worth's white neighborhoods, a similar movement was underway in the black community. A network of small amateur theatrical groups, including the Smarter Set, Northside Dramatic Club, and the Utopian Dramatic and Versatility Club presented plays and provided a creative outlet for local actors during the 1920s and 1930s. Among women promoting dramatics was Maelene Norfleet, who with her husband Charles led the Century of Progress Dramatic Club and later the Globe Entertainers Dramatic Club. The Fort Worth Negro Little Theater's production of DuBose Heyward's *Porgy* in 1935 included cast members Emma Lillian Greenwell, Ruby Williamson, and Demaris V. Scott, all local teachers; Mutelle Flint, wife of Dr. Clarence Flint; Idelle Enge, caseworker for the Tarrant County Board of Relief; and Bennye LaFrancelle Reeves, dance instructor and leader of a troupe that performed in area revues.

A performance of the *Queen Esther* cantata in March 1906 brought together students from the city's segregated black schools and featured twenty-year-old soprano Lillian B. Jones. Jones, who later married J. Gentry Horace, became English teacher and dean of girls for I. M. Terrell High School in 1911. (See "These Women Lived!" and "Cracking the Glass Ceiling.") She established the school's debating program and in 1922, with Miss E. M. Benton, organized a theater club and department of dramatics. Students that first year presented Benton's original operetta, *The Stolen Princess.*

In the broader African-American community, women led in both theatrical training and performance. Mabel Hallowell Echols taught classes in dramatic expression and presented readings and impersonations for concerts and recitals. Mrs. W. H. Humphrus conducted a school of dramatics that regularly furnished actors for plays performed in black halls, schools, and recreation centers.

In March 1936, Fort Worth business leaders announced the hiring of New York showman Billy Rose to stage the Frontier Centennial and a Broadway-style revue as the city's contribution to the Texas centennial celebration. Rose dubbed the exhibition's centerpiece, a 4,000-seat outdoor cafe-amphitheater with a revolving stage the size of a city block, Casa Mañana. The Casa Mañana Revue, anchored by bandleader Paul Whiteman and fan dancer Sally Rand, premiered July 18, 1936, to national acclaim.

Strutting in their own fast-paced production numbers between star turns were Rose's hand-picked chorines, forty-eight dancers and twenty-four showgirls selected during local auditions that attracted star-struck applicants from across the Southwest. One local girl to make the cut literally stood head and shoulders above her peers. Lanky North Texas State Agricultural

College student Mary Dowell stood six foot two by age twenty-one. She had stuttered since childhood, an impediment that combined with her height to set her uncomfortably apart from classmates and made her the butt of schoolyard jokes. She was born in North Platte, Nebraska, on December 14, 1914, but moved to Fort Worth in 1920, where her father, Arthur Dowell, joined the police force. By 1936 he had risen to captain of detectives; in 1937 he became chief of police. Mary Dowell grew up doing farm chores on the family's still-remote property in North Fort Worth.

Dowell's insecurities became her greatest assets after she blundered into one of Rose's dance auditions, hoping to land a job. Angry at the intrusion, Rose stormed off the stage. "What do you want?" he demanded. Dowell strained to reply but could not utter a syllable. As the five-foot-two Rose took in her improbable height and obvious inability to speak, he softened. Handing her a pad and pencil, he commanded, "Write it."

"Please give me a job in your six-foot chorus," she managed to scrawl. Rose hired her on the spot, but it was stage director John Murray Anderson who tagged her with the epithet that ultimately became her trademark—Stutterin' Sam.

Over the course of the summer, Anderson transformed the gawky farm girl into a standout showgirl gliding through elaborate production numbers that often required her to maneuver heavy, unwieldy costumes and oversize headdresses. As the Symbol of Peace in 1937's sequel to the centennial, the Frontier Fiesta, Dowell ascended a four-story-tall staircase under the combined weight of a ten-foot-wide pair of wings, full-length white satin gown, and

a train seventy-five feet long and sixty-five feet wide.

Dowell's show business career continued to flourish after Billy Rose left Fort Worth at the end of the 1937 season. She followed him to New York, becoming a top showgirl in both his Casa Mañana and Diamond Horseshoe night-clubs. And though she stammered, she was never at a loss for words. She bylined her own column filled with insider tidbits about Broadway personalities and backstage doings for the hometown *Star-Telegram. Collier's* noted her "posse" of ringside admirers, and Walter Winchell and Ed Sullivan quoted her. Suitors courted her with jewelry and furs, but she brushed them all off, snapping at one reporter, "[I] know what I've got and what I haven't got. The phonies give themselves away telling me I'm beautiful."

By her late twenties, Dowell was growing increasingly disillusioned with show business. She walked out on Rose a dozen times, craving a real world job and what she called a "normal existence." "There's nothing so useless as a showgirl," she complained to an Associated Press correspondent in 1940. She seized the opportunity to quit for good in 1943 after Warner Brothers optioned her backstage jottings about showgirl life and offered her a job as a screenwriter in the bargain. When her contract expired a year later, she fled Hollywood as well, this time to marry New York broker Sigmund Hindley.

Dowell never returned to show business except for one brief stint as press agent for the George S. Kaufman–Cole Porter revue, *Seven Lively Arts.* Hindley died in 1950, and for several years after Dowell worked as a toy company

Opposite: Mary "Stutterin' Sam" Dowell performing in Billy Rose's Casa Manana Revue, 1937. *Courtesy, Texas/Dallas History and Archives Division, Dallas Public Library.*

Right: Flora Reeder and student performers of the Reeder School, 1950. *Courtesy, Reeder Collection, Special Collections, University of Texas at Arlington Libraries*

executive. At age thirty-nine she remarried, to advertising mogul Guild Copeland. In 1963, twenty years after abandoning the show world, she succumbed unexpectedly to a blood disorder. Nationally syndicated Broadway columnist Earl Wilson paid tribute, remembering her "gift for words" and calling her "beloved on Our Street."

Two organizations sharing similar artistic goals, both founded by women, helped lay the groundwork of Fort Worth's postwar theatrical community. The Reeder School and the Fort Worth Civic Opera began within months of each other in 1946. (See "For The Price of a Good Cigar.")

The Reeder School, established by Flora Blanc Reeder and her husband, Edward Dickson Reeder, became the city's most influential children's theater academy in the decade following World War II. Between 1945 and 1958, the school established a national reputation for both its methods and the excellence of its yearly productions.

The school had its origins in Flora Reeder's childhood. Born in 1916 to Edward Blanc and Martha Elliot King in New York City, Reeder attended the King-Coit School, renowned for immersing young students in diverse cultures as they prepared for theatrical performance. Her ambition to become an artist took her first to New York's Art Students League and eventually to France. While studying in Paris, she met Dickson Reeder, a young Fort Worth artist. The pair married in 1937. In 1940, the couple moved to Fort Worth, where they taught and painted while establishing themselves in a group of artists who became known as the Fort Worth Circle.

This close-knit group, including, among others, Cynthia Brants and Evaline Sellors, became Reeder's artistic allies in productions staged by the Reeder School. Flora researched music and source material, adapted scripts, directed productions and taught; Dickson led painting classes and sketched plans for lavish sets and costumes. Circle artists created scenery and costumes from Dickson Reeder's designs. Pupils, ages four to fourteen, studied mythology, art, mime, dance, painting, and acting two or three days a week. Every aspect of instruction immersed the children in a single classic tale, bringing them, over eight months, to a thorough understanding of the story's time period, music, customs, and dress. The school year culminated with performances of the play.

The Reeder School's first "official" production, *The Rose and the Ring*, was staged in June 1946. (Flora had directed *Aucassin and Nicolette* in 1945 as part of a class project at Texas Christian University.) Between 1945 and 1958, the Reeders staged fourteen plays at various locations using only children as performers. Productions became known as much for the Reeders' exacting standards of artistry and authenticity as for the abilities of their young players.

In 1958, the school closed, ostensibly to give the couple more time for study and painting. Flora continued to teach occasionally, but Dickson Reeder's health had declined, and no more public productions were attempted. He died in 1970. From 1981 to 1986, Flora reopened the school on a limited basis, with Dickson's nephew, D. Jefferson Reeder, reproducing his uncle's designs for several productions. The school finally closed for good in 1986. Flora Reeder died in 1995.

In 1946, a pair of opera singers and a concert pianist conceived the idea of forming a local opera company. With the backing of key business leaders, Eloise MacDonald Snyder, Betty Berry Spain, and Jeanne Axtell (Walker) filed a state charter on May 29, 1946, to incorporate the Fort Worth Civic Opera Association.

Snyder and Spain had both experienced firsthand the travails of young, would-be opera singers. Snyder, the daughter of Wilbur MacDonald, a concert pianist and fine arts dean of Fort Worth's Polytechnic College, studied voice with Paul Althouse, Frank LaForge and Queena Mario, but gave up performing to raise three children. Her postponed professional debut finally came in 1944 with the New Orleans Opera. One year later, she sang Arsena in *The Gypsy Baron* with the New York City Center Opera. Axtell, third member of the triumvirate, was born in 1905 in Kansas City, Missouri, to

George and Elizabeth Newfield Jobe. She trained as a concert pianist, but moved to Texas after marrying Herbert S. Axtell, whose father, F. W. Axtell, founded one of the Southwest's leading windmill and well equipment manufacturers. In Fort Worth, she taught and worked with both the Theater Guild and Reeder School.

Both Snyder and Spain appeared in several of the Fort Worth Opera's earliest productions, which, by 2007, its sixtieth season, was the longest continuously active municipal opera association in Texas. In November 1946, Snyder sang the role of Violetta in the company's first opera, *La Traviata*. She became a key figure as well in the formation of the Opera Guild in 1948 and helped reorganize the Fort Worth Symphony in 1957.

Fort Worth produced several actresses of note in the decades following World War II. The Fort Worth Community Theater and the second Casa Mañana, constructed in 1958 near the site of Billy Rose's original theater, became important proving grounds for such local talent as Eugenia "Gena" Sleete Ferreira, who followed her mother Norene Thrash into show business. She became a staple of local theater, first as a charter member of the Fort Worth Community Theater and later as a regular performer for Casa Mañana Musicals. In later years, she acted in both television and motion pictures, most notably in Peter Bogdonavich's *Texasville*.

Joy Garrett also achieved considerable professional success before her premature death. Garrett, daughter of Clarence and Kathleen Garrett, graduated with honors from Texas Wesleyan College in 1967. She landed her first New York job as a singer in the famed Latin Quarter theater/nightclub that same year, shortly after winning a two-year scholarship to the American Academy of Dramatic Arts in national auditions.

Garrett had first received professional notice while still a teenager. She won the Miss Fort Worth Pageant in 1963 at age seventeen; although she did not become Miss Texas, she attracted the attention of both Mason Johnson, director of TWC's theater program, and Melvin O. Dacus, general manager of Casa Mañana Musicals. That summer, Dacus cast her as the shy, younger sister in *Wildcat*. Johnson offered Garrett a scholarship, and over the next four years she performed featured roles in several TWC musicals, including Mama Rose in *Gypsy* (1967). About the same time, she earned a spot in the Dallas Summer Musicals ensemble and played the title role in *Gypsy* for the Oklahoma City Lyric Theater. She also continued to appear at Casa Mañana, taking lead roles in *Gypsy* (1968), *How Now, Dow Jones* (1969), and *Sugar* (1974).

Her first Actors' Equity job came in an off-Broadway production *Gertrude Stein's First Reader* (1969). Reviewers generally panned the show, but *New York Times* critic Clive Barnes singled out Garrett, applauding her "panache." Other off-Broadway plays followed. Her first Broadway role came in 1971 in the short-lived, but critically praised *Inner City*. She followed this in 1972 with a major Broadway success, *Grease*, in which she played likeable tough-girl Betty Rizzo.

By the late 1970s Garrett had turned her sights to steadier work in California's television industry. She appeared in made-for-television

Joy Garrett in Texas Wesleyan College's 1964 production, *Bells are Ringing*.
Courtesy, Fort Worth Star-Telegram *Collection, Special Collections, University of Texas at Arlington Libraries.*

movies and did series work, including *Dynasty, Magnum P. I., Three's Company, Charlie's Angels,* and *Star Trek*. From 1986 to 1993 she was a regular on the long-running soap opera, *Days of Our Lives*. In 1993 at age forty-seven, she succumbed to a liver disorder.

Fort Worth's de facto "first couple of theater" in the latter decades of the twentieth century was Katy Dacus and Melvin Dacus. Katy Dacus was born Kathryne Louise Peirson on July 25, 1928, in Kansas City, Missouri, where her mother, Louise Lena Peirson, and her maternal grandmother, Mikala Neuer, raised her in a culture-conscious atmosphere. She took piano lessons on a grand piano once played by Ignacy Paderewski and trained with Constance Eberhardt at the Kansas City Conservatory. By age nine she was already performing solo parts in adult church choirs. She gained professional experience singing in hotel and club engagements before moving to New York to continue her schooling at the Juilliard School of Music. There she sang with the school's vocal ensemble, conducted by Robert Shaw, and as a soloist for the Riverside Church. She graduated with a B.A. degree in vocal performance.

It was at the Riverside Church in the late 1940s that Peirson met another young soloist, Melvin O. Dacus, a Fort Worth singer and World War II combat veteran, who was studying at the American Theater Wing. Following their marriage in 1949, the young couple sang in the resident company of New Jersey's Paper Mill Playhouse until Melvin Dacus was recalled to active military duty in 1951 during the Korean War. While assigned to the Marine Corps school at Quantico, Virginia, they continued to perform. Melvin Dacus organized the Quantico

Katy and Mel Dacus in Fort Worth Theater's 1985 production, *On Golden Pond.* *Courtesy, the Dacus family.*

Players, and the couple sang the leads in the company's first production, *Roberta*.

At war's end in 1953, the Dacuses relocated to Fort Worth, where both took jobs with WBAP-TV, which that same year launched *Carousel . . . With Katy and Mel*, a live studio program featuring music, reviews, and interviews with entertainers and local personalities. Melvin Dacus left the station a year later to become the first full-time general manager of the Fort Worth Opera, a position he held from 1954 to 1958. Katy Dacus, meanwhile, made concert appearances, appeared in commercials, and taught voice part time at TCU while raising the couple's three children, Kim, Mindy, and Brent.

In 1958, Melvin Dacus became co-founder, along with opera president James Snowden, of Casa Mañana Musicals, Inc., an offshoot organization formed to capitalize on the popularity of Broadway musicals. The second Casa Mañana attracted national attention both as the first permanent theater in-the-round devoted to musical presentations and for its unusual aluminum geodesic dome roof. Melvin Dacus left the opera to become general manager/producer of the company, a position he held from 1958 to 1974. Katy Dacus took occasional roles in productions while also starring in American Handicrafts' nationally syndicated television show, *Crafts with Katy,* for three years, from 1971 to 1973.

Throughout her marriage, Dacus never actively pursued stardom, content seemingly as a supporting player in her husband's higher profile career. This did not change when, in 1974, the Casa Mañana board abruptly ousted Melvin Dacus after seventeen seasons. In typical fashion, the Dacuses segued to the next phase of their careers together, shortly joining forces with director Buff Shurr in Dacus/Shurr Productions. They spent two years managing the Country Dinner Playhouse in Round Rock and toured on the dinner theater circuit in *The Sound of Music* and *Fiddler on the Roof,* shows in which they could perform together. In a moment of supreme irony, Casa Mañana invited the couple to return to the Casa stage in 1979, showcasing them as dairyman Tevye and his wife Golde in *Fiddler on the Roof.*

Over the next two decades, the couple continued to appear at Casa Mañana and other area theaters both separately and together. Between

roles, Katy Dacus taught voice and audition technique and conducted workshops in musical comedy for Circle Theater, while researching the lives of George and Martha Washington for a two-person show. One of her most memorable performances came in 1985 when Bill Garber, director of Fort Worth Theater, cast the couple as long-married Ethel and Norman Thayer in Ernest Thompson's poignant drama of aging and familial love, *On Golden Pond.*

In 1994, the Live Theater League of Tarrant County honored the Dacuses' forty-five years together in theater with the Elston Brooks Award for lifetime achievement. Melvin Dacus died in 1999 with Katy following in 2001. After their deaths, TCU continued to honor the couple's legacy, establishing the Melvin and Katy Dacus theater scholarship and in 2002 dedicating the Melvin and Katy Dacus Acting Studio in Ed Landreth Hall.

BIBLIOGRAPHIC ESSAY

Fort Worth's theatrical events and the women who participated in them are well documented in local newspapers, starting with the *Fort Worth Democrat, Standard, Daily Gazette,* and *Register* in the nineteenth century and continuing into the twentieth century with the *Record, Star-Telegram,* and *Press. The Galveston Daily News* and the *Dallas Morning News* also covered many early Fort Worth events and served as additional sources when local editions did not survive. Another invaluable source was the Federal Writers Project for Fort Worth and Tarrant County, which during the 1930s and 1940s collected many local records, newspaper accounts, and oral histories. Information on Katherine Anne Porter's activities in Fort Worth came both from the *Fort Worth Record*, for which she wrote several articles, and from Joan Givner's 1991 biography, *Katherine Anne Porter: A Life*. Ginger Rogers' break into vaudeville and life in Fort Worth is chronicled in her 1991 autobiography, *Ginger, My Story*. Accounts of Mary "Stutterin' Sam" Dowell came both from the *New York Times* and from Dan Parker's profile of the showgirl in *Colliers Magazine*, July 10, 1943. Interviews with a number of individuals, including retired I. M. Terrell administrator and teacher Mrs. Hazel Harvey Peace; dancer/choreographer Olin Clyde "Tex" Eddleman; longtime Fort Worth Opera board member Mrs. Ahdel Chadwick; former Fort Worth Community Theater director William Garber; and Kim Dacus Reynolds, daughter of Katy Peirson Dacus, provided additional personal insights.

Other important sources included the Flora and Dickson Reeder Collection, University of Texas at Arlington Library; Fort Worth city directories, Fort Worth Little Theater and Fort Worth Community Theater programs, Frontier Centennial and Frontier Fiesta scrapbooks 1936–1937, the Lilliam B. Horace papers, and the *Fort Worth Mind*, all held by the Fort Worth Public Library, Local History and Genealogy.

Chapter 12

THESE WOMEN LIVED!

by Phyllis Wonjou Allen

EXAS DID NOT GET WORD OF THE 1863 Emancipation Proclamation until two years after it had been signed. On June 19, 1865, Union general Gordon Granger and 2,000 federal troops arrived at Galveston with word that "all slaves are free." William Ewart Gladstone said, "Justice delayed is justice denied." This delay in restoring freedom to an enslaved people had an effect on the state as well as the former slaves. Those two years meant that some African Americans were forever denied freedom, and the state, like the nation, still is recovering from the legacy of slavery.

In Texas as in the rest of the South, slavery was followed by Jim Crow laws that greatly restricted the freedoms granted the newly freed blacks. Yet despite all the strictures of race and gender, some African-American women born in the late nineteenth and early twentieth centuries were destined to become leaders whose impact would carry into the twenty-first century. Even though these women were born into a world not prepared to recognize their ability to

formulate plans for themselves and their people or their power to implement such plans, they boldly lived lives filled with courage and vision as well as charm and grace. They were not content to be passive onlookers at the transformation of a society. They were mothers and wives, but they also were nurses, journalists, chiropractors, teachers, and politicians. Some were born into slavery, most were only two generations removed from slavery, living under the restraints of segregation without any models upon which to fashion their aspirations. Even so, they were successful in changing their lives and leaving lasting impressions on the history of Fort Worth. These women lived!

Mary Keys Gipson was born into slavery in Mississippi in 1854. She went on to become the first black graduate of an accredited nursing school to work in the South. In 1872, at eighteen, the newly married Mary Keys Gipson moved to Fort Worth with her husband, the Reverend Franklin Pearce Gipson. She credits her husband with encouraging her to pursue nursing as a career. In 1903, she entered the Chautauqua School of Nursing in Jamestown, New York, and got her nursing certificate on March 2, 1907. She was fifty-three years old. She must have been very good, because in the segregated Fort Worth of the early 1900s she worked with prominent white doctors such as Isaac L. Van Zandt and Elias J. Beall. She also worked as a midwife. She founded the National Association of Colored Graduate Nurses. She was an ardent anti-segregationist who worked successfully for the integration of the American Nursing Association, one of the first professional organizations to admit African Americans.

In Fort Worth in the 1920s many African-American women owned small businesses. One example is Ethel Chappelle, who owned a hairdressing, massage, cutting, fitting, and sewing shop on West Thirteenth Street—a kind of early spa. Other women made their mark in spite of being unschooled. One such woman was Ella Mae Shamblee, who left behind a building named in her honor. Opal Lee, the coordinator of Fort Worth's Juneteenth celebration and a social activist, remembers Shamblee, who was a maid at the downtown library in the twenties. Shamblee persuaded her employers to allow her to take books on the Interurban train to the African-American neighborhood of Lake Como. Every two weeks she would take books out and pick up the ones that the residents had read. Lee says that Shamblee never lost a book. In the 1930s, when Lee was a little girl, she remembers going to a house on the southeast corner of Humboldt and New York streets where Shamblee, with the help of the Carnegie Library, had started a library and after-school program for the neighborhood children.

"I went every afternoon and did my homework. Every time we took a book she gave us these journal-like books to write about what we read," Lee said.

The library operated in the house on the corner of Humboldt until it moved into the Bethlehem Community Center in the late 1950s or early 1960s. In 1982 a new library was built at 959 East Rosedale and named the Ella Mae Shamblee Public Library.

Lenora Rolla was born March 4, 1904. She began writing the story of her life this way: "My grandmother was a slave, given to Massa's daughter as a wedding present, came with the couple from South Carolina to Texas." In her long life, Rolla was a funeral director, burial association manager, the dean of women at Jarvis Christian College in Hawkins, Texas, an editor at the *Dallas Express,* the oldest black newspaper in Texas; and in the insurance business for twenty years. Rolla always said that her most important asset was her marriage to Jacob Rolla, a railroad employee, for he allowed her room to follow her passions.

When her name is mentioned, it is always as a great historian, tireless fundraiser, and committed genealogist, but Rolla was also active in Democratic politics. In January 1961 she received a letter on the stationery of the U.S. Senate from a young senator, John F. Kennedy, thanking her for her efforts on behalf of the Democratic ticket in the 1960 presidential election. Another letter on stationery of the U.S. House of Representatives, dated April 11, 1968, reads: "I am writing to because you are such an understanding friend. There are times when a fellow really needs one, and this is such a time for Me...if you can, and to the extent that you

Lenora Rolla and LBJ. *Courtesy of the Tarrant County Black Historical and Genealogical Society and the Fort Worth Public Library.*

are willing, I'd earnestly appreciate your trying to help me protect my flanks from the attacks that are likely to come and saying a good word for me in this regard if you conscientiously can." The letter is signed, "Sincerely, Jim Wright," and it was written the day after he voted for the Civil Rights Act of 1968. On March 17, 1971, Lenora Rolla's name was read into the *Congressional Record* by that same Jim Wright in recognition of her work in establishing the East Hattie Street Haven, a community center that provided services to people of all ages. But Fort Worth knew Rolla best as executive director of the Tarrant County Black Historical and Genealogical Society. In reality, she *was* the Tarrant County Black Historical and Genealogical Society. She willed it into being and breathed life into it. Asked in the early 1980s if a separate black history society was necessary, Rolla responded, "Perhaps by 1990 or the year 2000 there will be no need for the 'black' in Tarrant County Black

Historical and Genealogical Society....This black-white situation erases familyhood and we can't deny it and we can't change it." Rolla recognized that the story of the African Americans in Fort Worth was not different from any other residents in Fort Worth—it was all a part of the same history. But without it, Fort Worth's story would be incomplete. That belief fueled her commitment to ensuring that the African-American page of Fort Worth's history book would not be blank.

Rolla never got over the demolition of the mansion on the corner of 1201 East Terrell that had belonged to African-American banker William "Gooseneck" McDonald. She vowed that no other historical treasures in the black community would be lost if it was up to her. She worked tirelessly to make sure every ladies luncheon, political gathering, or church meeting shared her dream of a museum about the African-American community in the African-

Principals of Good Publishing Company. Second from left, George Levitan, Publisher;
third from left, Adelle Martin, Editor.
*Courtesy of the Tarrant County Black Historical and Genealogical Society
and the Fort Worth Public Library*

American community. Rolla persuaded families to donate their heirlooms to the genealogical society rather than risk their being sold at flea markets or, worse, being disposed of in the local landfill. In 1980 the society purchased the Reverend A. L. Boone's home at 1120 East Humboldt for $4,000 as a repository for its collected artifacts. Rolla again hit the luncheon circuit with a goal of raising funds to restore the house and archive the collection. But in spite of her long life, she ran short of time. At her death at age ninety-seven on June 29, 2001, her dream still had not been realized. The Boone House remained in disrepair, and the collection was in danger of being irreparably damaged by water, rodents, and decay. Some of the collection now resides safely in an acid-free, climate-controlled environment at the Fort Worth Public Library. The Tarrant County Black Historical and Genealogical Society is still attempting to complete restoration of the Boone House. Rolla's vision may have been for a museum on a street restored to the elegance that she remembered from her youth, where people could visit her collection and reminisce. What she got instead was the legacy to the city of Fort Worth of one of the finest collections of early African-American life in the country.

In the 1950s and 1960s when "journalist" nearly always meant "male writer," African-American women were in positions of authority in the Fort Worth publishing world. Good Publishing Company produced true-confession style magazines with a sepia tone, both in color and voice, for the African American community. These magazines depicted characters and stories with which the readers could identify, even more so than did the Chicago-based *Ebony* magazine.

Good Publishing evolved from *Negro Achievements,* a magazine founded at the close of World War II. Horace J. Blackwell, an African-American businessman and Texas Negro Baseball League officer, created the magazine to give voice to African-American autobiographical stories, usually with a moral. The magazine was also sprinkled with shorter features of church and social news from throughout the South Central states.

Blackwell's assistant was Adelle Conner Jackson Martin. After Blackwell's death in 1949, Martin knew that in order to save her job, she had to save the magazine. She searched for a financial rescuer. After months of negative responses Martin finally convinced George Levitan, a white businessman, to assume the magazine's debts and continue to publish. Levitan would agree only if he could have sole ownership and full editorial control. Martin, realizing this was her only choice, acquiesced, and Levitan became publisher of what was to become the Good Publishing Company. Within a year, Levitan hired a young white couple from New York, Seth and Anne Kantor, to edit the magazine. It was the Kantors who changed the magazine's format to a more urban one in an effort to capture emerging young, black urban readers. New layouts and graphics completed the change from *Negro Achievements to Sepia Record* and finally *Sepia.* The true-confession stories moved into sister publications such as *Bronze Thrills.*

In spite of these sweeping changes, several black women from the original staff were retained. Possibly in an effort to further improve the quality of his magazine, Levitan brought in a college instructor to teach these women journalism skills and arranged for them to take journal-ism classes at Texas Christian University at a time when TCU did not accept black students. For most of these women this was their first glimpse into possibilities for an African-American woman beyond being a teacher or a maid. As a result, each went on to expand her role in the publishing world. Martin worked at Good Publishing from 1946 to 1962, while at the same time raising a son. (See "High-heeled T imes in the Newsroom.") Her legacy helped give voice to an entire community. Travis Geraldine Dearman-Wilburn worked with her husband as co-editor of the *Lake Como Monitor,* one of many African-American neighborhood newspapers in the city in the1940s that covered stories their readers could not find in other papers. Her responsibilities at the *Monitor* included making decisions on the look and tone of the newspaper as well as content. She was also a co-editor at Good Publishing.

Celestine Hawkins, a graduate of I. M. Terrell High School and Bishop College, was a businesswoman in her own right, operating the Harris Mimeograph Service before going to work for the Department of Engineering in Washington, D.C. After working as a secretary for the *Fort Worth Press* for fifteen years, she became an editor at Good Publishing and an enthusiastic membership recruiter for the YWCA.

But the superstar of the Good Publishing team was Beatrice Pringle. Pringle started to work at Good Publishing in the shipping department in 1945. She advanced quickly, learning every aspect of the magazine business. By 1975 she had worked herself out of shipping into the comptroller's office and then into the publisher's seat, all the while raising three daughters, planning sweet sixteen parties, debuts, and weddings.

These women helped to build Good Publishing into a national company distributing more than three-quarter million copies worldwide every month. They learned to overcome the constraints of color and gender to perform well in a world that was not only male, but also largely white male. In 1977, Pringle and Edna K. Turner, the creative director of Good Publishing, received the Margaret Caskey Award for outstanding service in the field of communication presented by the Fort Worth Professional Chapter of Women in Communications, Inc. Pringle, Wilburn, and Martin also had broad interests in their community. Each worked on projects near to her heart. Pringle was one of the early members of the Sickle Cell Anemia Association that worked to educate the community about a disease that at the time was a silent killer. Wilburn gave freely of her time and energies to her church, Grace Temple Seventh Day Adventist, where she was an active member. Martin wanted other minorities to benefit from the opportunities that she had enjoyed, so she helped found Minority Business Development, Inc., to aid in the growth of African-American businesses.

These women were raised in a time when women, especially black women, were confined to well-defined roles. When black women of this time attempted to expand or step outside those roles via education, travel, or military service, they frequently found conflicts between the world in which they were living in school, in the military or overseas, and the real one to which they would one day return.

Aurelia Harris, the first African-American chiropractor in Texas, wrote while she was serving as a lieutenant in the U.S. Army in 1945,

"I've been wondering of late if some of the nice things that the Negro WAC Officers are exposed to is a good thing or bad? It makes us more conscious of our lot and restless . . ." In 1952 Harris was newly arrived in Fort Worth and setting up a practice in the relatively unknown medical field of chiropractics at a time when most black people could not afford to see any doctor. Harris knew there were more than backs to be straightened. She may have been restless and unsure of her place in the world, but she was absolutely certain about the contributions she could make to the community. She knew that attracting patients would require more than competency, so she advertised in local weekly black newspapers and was a pioneer in direct-mail advertising, mailing letters to people within her target demographic area. The letters always began, "Dear Friend." Then they went into detail, citing statistics on the number of patients who had been helped by chiropractic treatment. This was before the days of mailboxes crammed full of shiny mailers, so people actually read the letters. Harris' practice flourished.

Harris was a proven leader and an organizer, accustomed to creating those social structures she found missing. In a biographical sketch submitted to *Who's Who of Texas*, Dr. Harris says that while at Kansas State University, she founded and was the first president of the only teachers' sorority west of the Mississippi. She also tells that in the course of setting up her chiropractic practice she discovered that young African-American women who found themselves unwed and pregnant had no place to turn. Harris took this as a mandate to establish a maternity home. She offered a comfortable place for these young women to have their babies without fear of discrimination. Harris never married and maintained strong familial ties to the Harris clan that she left back in Kansas, her birthplace. She maintained a narrow definition of who was and was not a Harris, in spite of adopting a daughter, Edwardean. In her handwritten will she dealt with the question of a piece of heirloom furniture that her adopted daughter wanted by pointing out that the furniture must stay in the Harris line, and Edwardean was not a Harris.

Harris was involved early on with Lenora Rolla in the formation of the Tarrant County Black Historical and Genealogical Society. In the late 1960s and 1970s, when the African-American vote became critical in the elections of candidates from city council members to the nation's president, Harris became a key player in the political scene. The chiropractor, social midwife, and political insider all peacefully coexisted inside one woman with a desire to bring some of the "niceness" that she had seen as a WAC officer to her people.

When civil rights leader Dr. Martin Luther King came to Fort Worth in 1959, he visited Harris' house in southeast Fort Worth before funeral director Herbert Baker drove him to the Bellaire Drive West home of the Reverend Alberta H. Lunger and her husband, the Reverend Harold L. Lunger of Brite Divinity School, for coffee with a group called Operation Fellowship. (The Lungers had started a rotating dinner with African-American pastors.)

In spite of the efforts of these women, however, nothing much changed in Fort Worth's race relations until the turbulence of the 1960s. Then, in Fort Worth as in the rest of the nation, it seemed everything started to change—and

women were often the catalysts. In Fort Worth, integration of city hall happened without a single march and with no rocks thrown. Vera Jenkins simply sat down at her desk and began to work. Jenkins was the first African-American clerk-typist hired by the city of Fort Worth. She and another African-American woman, Ethelia Hall, were hired as clerks in the warrant division and went to work without a single incident. Today almost twenty percent of the workforce at city hall is African American, almost exactly the percentage of the city's population that is African American. The city has had an African-American city manager and several department heads are African American. This is a result of trailblazers like Jenkins and Hall.

In 1964, the city hired Bertha Knox Collins, a woman whose name was to become synonymous with youth advocacy in Texas. Born in Waco in 1914, Bertha Collins and her mother moved to Fort Worth in the early 1930s. Bertha worked at a dress shop, a bank, and as a substitute teacher. In her fifties she received a degree from Paul Quinn College, which was at that time in Waco. In 1960, while employed as an instructor and testing specialist for education services of the 4123rd Strategic Wing (SAC) at Clinton-Sherman Air Force Base in Oklahoma, Collins practiced on young airmen the teaching skills she would later use so effectively on other young people. Collins asked the airmen to write a paper entitled, "What School Has Done for Me." Thomas Welch wrote, "I like the way Mrs. Collins, our teacher, teaches the whole class and is able to get to the bottom of things. Then she is able to bring things out to the utmost level." Each of the airmen who turned in papers on that exercise said essentially the same thing: "Mrs.

Collins has helped me not only in class but in my social life." "Mrs. Collins has helped me achieve what I know I should have done long ago, get my high school diploma." This ability to reach young men who were looking for direction later made Collins effective in dealing with disenfranchised urban youth.

In 1963, when Collins was hired to direct the Harmon Field Recreation Center adjacent to Butler Housing, one of the city's public housing communities near downtown Fort Worth, she was best known for the pots of beans that she personally cooked to feed "her kids." She was devoted to the Harmon Field facility and worked tirelessly to raise funds to modernize her center and make it more attractive. Less than nine months after going to the Harmon Field center, she was named as the district recreation supervisor, a post in which she oversaw several of Fort Worth's public recreation centers.

Collins was a tireless advocate for the children of Fort Worth, working with the Boy Scouts, YMCA, YWCA, and the Fort Worth Police Department, establishing recreational outlets for urban youth. Her 1966 divorce from Pinkie Collins did nothing to slow her down. She rejuvenated the Harmon Field Recreation Center, built programs that benefited her beloved youth, and even started a popular ceramic class at Harmon Field.

In 1969, the city caught up with Collins, finally turning its attention to the needs of its youth. Collins was named the director of the Mayor's Council on Youth Opportunity. Her duties included coordinating youth activities with a focus on employment opportunities, education and training, recreation, and cultural enrichment activities. One of her gifts was the

ability to motivate young people unfamiliar with museums, symphonies, and operas to not only go to these places and performances but also to appreciate them. Her kids knew what to look for when they entered a museum or heard Tchaikovsky's Fifth.

But Collins never lost sight of who she was. A real estate agent once approached her and told her that her current residence did not match her new, higher paycheck. He said he had the perfect house for her, with rolling hills and the proper cachet. Collins replied, "These [her neighbors] are the people that I knew before [when] I didn't have this job." That was her way in all things. She was the same Bertha Collins she had been when she came to town in 1935. She didn't want anyone to treat her differently because she was making more money or seemed to have more power. The early 1970s brought her numerous awards and recognition—she was given an honorary degree from St. Stephens College, Fremont, California, and named Newsmaker of the Year for 1975 by the Press Club of Fort Worth.

In 1976 a new Human Resources Department was created by the city and the Mayor's Council on Youth Opportunity was incorporated into the new department under the direction of Ramon Guajardo. Collins was never considered for the job and because she felt discriminated against, she filed suit in federal court. Collins felt she had been unfairly stripped of a job she loved only to see it given to someone she considered unworthy. On the margin of one of the notes she made on a meeting to discuss city officials taking their charges against her to the news media was the written wail, ". . . stripped and given to a man that most people don't know and in no way relates to our children or community." Even in the midst of her personal disappointment and distress her primary concern was for the children and her community.

In spite of letters and petitions from the community Collins did not prevail in her suit, and on January 31, 1980, she turned in her notice of retirement. The work situation had become so rancorous that she made her effective retirement date five months earlier than she planned, citing adverse working conditions she said were detrimental to her physical and mental wellbeing.

But Collins was not one to into seclusion. She opened Bertha Collins Enterprises, selling unique Fort Worth and Texas souvenirs. On February 20, 1981, she held a preview for invited guests at the Press Club of Fort Worth in downtown Fort Worth. But the business was not to be the third act of her life that she had planned. By March 25, 1981, she was dead. Her death certificate lists the cause of death as myocardial infarction due to heart disease, but anyone who knew the pain of her final years with the City of Fort Worth had to believe that she simply died of a broken heart. Many said upon her death that Bertha Collins was successful because she was never bureaucratic—red tape frustrated her—and her only interest was in the people she served. Years passed, wounds healed and the city renamed her beloved Harmon Recreation Center the Bertha K. Collins Recreation Center. It was too late for Collins to stand on yet another dais, smiling as she was being lauded, but her center is still here, a testimony to the contribution that she made to her city.

While Collins and others are easy to find in the city's history, other women who made signif-

icant contributions to Fort Worth and the African-American community are less well known, even when the contributions they made so thoroughly transformed their community that it was hard for people to realize things hadn't always been this way. Every year in schools across the city young people stand up in auditoriums filled with their parents and classmates. These students speak of one of the most significant moments in the civil rights movement—a woman arrested because she refused to give up her seat on a city bus. Heads in the audience nod and most of the parents' lips silently mouth the name Rosa Parks. But four years before Parks took her seat and refused to budge, there was a woman in Fort Worth, tired from work and years of obeying unjust rules without question, who refused to yield her bus seat upon threat of arrest or worse. Sadly, few remember her name.

On December 14, 1951, Essie Sturges was removed from a Fort Worth city bus for refusing to relinquish her seat to a white passenger. From all accounts Sturges was a strong woman. She could pour concrete, build a house, and paint. At the same time she was a musician, a writer, and a member of Zion Missionary Baptist Church. That cold December afternoon, Sturges was headed to Lake Como. She stood all the way until all the whites left the bus, leaving a vacant seat in the front. Sturges took the seat near the door, next to other African-American passengers. The ride was uneventful until a white girl boarded the bus and sat on the opposite end of the same seat. Two people, one black woman and one white girl, sharing a seat on a bus does not sound very radical in today's world, but in 1951 that incited the bus driver to demand that Sturges get up. When she refused, the driver first made a gesture as if to strike her, then stopped and called police. Sturges was arrested. The city ordinance at the time required that Negroes fill buses from the rear forward. In a uniquely Fort Worth settlement, both sides agreed that Sturges had complied with the law and could not move backward because there were no more unoccupied seats behind her. The case quietly went away, but Sturges filed suit against the Fort Worth Transit Company. History has erased the outcome of the civil suit, but somewhere there is a white woman who still does not understand why the "nice" lady could not sit on the seat beside her when she was a girl.

Lillian B. Horace also quietly contributed to her community. She was a graduate of Prairie View College and Simmons University and did graduate work at Columbia University and the Universities of Chicago and Colorado. She came to teach English in the Fort Worth schools in 1911 after teaching in both Mansfield and Handley schools. In 1928 she became dean of girls at I. M. Terrell High School, a position she held until the need for a full-time librarian arose. Actually, it was Horace who conceived of the library and breathed it into life. The Terrell student newspaper, *Terrellife*, also was Horace's brainchild. It was the first newspaper to give a byline to Bob Ray Sanders, now a columnist and the first African-American vice president of the *Fort Worth Star-Telegram*. Other Horace innovations at I. M. Terrell include the annual "soiree" for the parents of graduating seniors and the annual senior play. By most accounts, the amphitheater that was built to stage the senior play was also her idea, even though it was not built until after she had retired. Horace also was a member of the board of the YWCA, the Order of the Eastern Star, Alphin Art and Charity Club, and Progressive Women's Club. Furthermore, she was a talented writer. Her journal includes poems, musings, and ideas so fresh and relevant that they could be published today. Horace lists the basic rights of every person in a poem in her handwritten journal entitled *Freedom or Fantasy, Why?*:

> Parents—care and love of intelligent
>   parents
> Right to be well born
> Moral and intellectual training
> Education—liberal
> Full participation in government
> Parks, theaters, all amusements
> A job for which he can qualify
> A home that he can afford where
>   he chooses

After forty-two years of service, Horace retired from teaching and moved to Evanston, Illinois, to join her husband, the Reverend J. G. Horace, who was the pastor of the Second Baptist Church in Evanston. (For more about Horace, see "Cracking the Glass Ceiling" and "There's Nothing So Useless as a Showgirl.")

Dynamic women were a staple at Terrell. Women such as Hazel Harvey Peace, who continues to be a force in the Fort Worth community, taught alongside teachers such as LaBerta D. Miller Phillips, an English and journalism teacher at Terrell. Phillips has been cited by Bob Ray Sanders as the person who first interested him in journalism. For more than forty-four years Phillips instructed students in the intricacies of sentence diagramming, the complexities of *Julius Caesar*, and the process of putting together a

Mary Frances Turner Blanche.
*Courtesy of the Tarrant County Black Historical and
Genealogical Society and the
Fort Worth Public Library.*

never …," was not likely to forget it.

After leaving Terrell, Peace was dean of women at Bishop College in Dallas. In 2005, when she was more than 100 years old—her age is a closely guarded secret—Peace was given the University of North Texas President's Honorary Alumna Award. The award is presented to "individuals who never attended UNT, but who have exhibited outstanding devotion, service and support to the university." Texas Wesleyan University awarded her an honorary doctorate in 1992. She was an Olympic torchbearer as the torch came through Fort Worth on its way to the 2002 Winter Olympics in Salt Lake City. Peace is probably best known for her work encouraging reading with small children. The Hazel Harvey Peace Youth Center at the Fort Worth Central Library is named in her honor. In 2004, the UNT School of Library and Information Sciences created the $350,000 Hazel Harvey Peace Professorship in Children's Library Services to continue Peace's devotion to literacy by producing future educators of children's librarians. It is the first professorship at a four-year state-funded institution in Texas named for an African American. Peace is a much beloved figure in Fort Worth and often turned to for stories of the African-American community.

In addition to LaBerta D. Miller Phillips, Peace taught with another outstanding teacher at I. M. Terrell, Mary Frances Turner Blanche. Blanche had been in the first graduating class at Terrell (1928) and returned there to teach after earning a degree from Wilberforce University in Ohio in 1932. At Terrell she was known for never being without her trademark white gloves and black leather pocketbook. She earned a master's degree from Prairie View A&M

newspaper. She went on to become dean of women and a remedial English teacher at the Southwestern Christian College in Terrell, Texas.

Hazel Harvey Peace began her teaching career at Terrell, her alma mater. She graduated from Howard University in 1926 with a bachelor's degree and got a master's of art degree from Columbia University. She served as counselor, dean of girls, and vice principal before retiring. Many women who attended Terrell in the 1950s and 1960s have anecdotes of how Peace influenced their lives. Any high school girl who received a Hazel Harvey Peace lecture on deportment that began, "Young lady, a lady

University in 1951. She retired from Terrell in 1966. Blanche taught English for thirty-two years while also operating the Blanche Day Center and Private School. Blanche and her husband Sherman opened the day care center for Negroes in Fort Worth in 1946—at the time it was one of the few Negro private schools certified by the State of Texas and is still operating today. In November 1986 the Day Care Association of Fort Worth and Tarrant County honored Blanche and her late husband for their dedication to education. In 1987, she was among the honorees at an exhibition of the history of black women presented by the Tarrant County Black Historical and Genealogical Society titled *They Showed the Way*. She was ninety-one when she died in 2004. In Blanche's obituary in the *Star-Telegram*, Peace gave her old friend the supreme accolade: "She was a very good and dedicated teacher and a good scholar. She knew her subject matter."

Viola Pitts came to Fort Worth in the 1940s, cleaning houses for twenty-five cents an hour. She was still cleaning other people's homes when she first became politically active. She was named *Fort Worth Star-Telegram* Woman of the Year for 1992. She had parlayed her knowledge of the local government system into improvements for her neighborhood. Like most of the women who worked for their community and city, Pitts cited her belief in God and her daily commune with Him as the basis for her success in becoming a West Side power broker.

Pitts was the undisputed authority on the needs and the moods of her Como neighborhood. Her mentor, the late Sopora Hicks, who was at that time the political kingmaker of Como, trained her in the ways of Fort Worth government. Pitts was an able protégée. Upon Hicks' death, Pitts was ready to step in and the fill the void for her beloved neighborhood. During the late eighties and the early nineties when Como, like other black communities, was under siege from drug dealers and users, Pitts would walk her streets identifying the problems and seeking aid from her powerful friends.

She was the Democratic Party chair of Precinct 1120 and through sheer force of will consistently turned out "her" voters. Pitts contended that Como voters carried the $49.5 million bond issue in 1982. That bond issue paved the way for the expansion of John Peter Smith Hospital and its services. "When I showed up at that courthouse the night of the bond election— I'm bringing in 705 votes and 700 of them are for the bond issue—that's the proudest thing I've ever done for that hospital," Pitts said. It is no wonder that in 1992 the Como Multipurpose Center got its first health clinic. That clinic has since outgrown its space at the center and is now a freestanding clinic open daily to serve the entire community. Since 2000 it has operated under the name Viola M. Pitts JPS Health Center.

Pitts was eighty-nine when she died in 2004. A horse-drawn hearse carried her casket through her beloved neighborhood to the Como Community Center while hundreds lined the streets. Former president Bill Clinton sent a tribute and Congressman Martin Frost read a commendation of Pitts on the floor of the House of Representatives. (Read more about Pitts' political career in "Braving the Smoke.") Pitts bequeathed many of her trademark hats, photographs, letters, and other political memorabilia to the Tarrant County Black Historical and

Genealogical Society.

Emma Janet Vivian Guinn operated an orphanage with about fifty bright boys and girls in North Fort Worth. Guinn was born in Alabama in 1879. The 1911 City Directory shows her as principal of North Fort Worth Colored School, and her husband, James P. Guinn, as principal of South Fort Worth Colored School. Records show that in 1920 she was a teacher at J. P. Guinn Elementary School, named for her husband after his death. She died on February 16, 1949, at age seventy.

Whenever a young African-American woman achieves her dream, big or small, the spirits of these great women certainly must smile and say, "You go, girl! It was for you that we lived!"

BIBLIOGRAPHIC ESSAY

This chapter would have been impossible for me to write were it not for the exceptional assistance of key persons. First I want to thank Ruth Karbach, a fellow contributor to this project, for it was her generosity of spirit and information that pointed me in the right direction to access these women's lives. Ruth answered each of my questions enthusiastically and with a wealth of information and introduced me to the Fort Worth Public Library's history and genealogical department.

The staff at the library tutored me on the use of collection guides for the Tarrant County Black Historical and Genealogical Collection. Opening the boxes in this collection allowed me an opportunity to sit down and chat with women who are no longer here. Because of Donna Kruse and the other archivists I was able to hold the death certificate of Bertha K. Collins, the holographic will of Aurelia Harris, and the marriage license of Lenora Rolla, whose foresight was responsible for the collecting of these items.

Additional information was gathered from an online printing of a research paper, "Sepia Record as a Forum for Negotiating Women's Roles" by Sherilyn Brandenstein. This document filled in gaps on the evolution of the Good Publishing Company and the women's careers it spawned.

Also, I interviewed a living legend in her own right, Opal Lee, a community activist and historian as well as a founding member of the Tarrant County Black Historical and Genealogical society.

I have been fortunate enough to experience firsthand the wisdom of some of these women, including Hazel Harvey Peace. Also, thanks to another fellow contributor, Ruth McAdams. Only she knows what she gave me.

H. J. Res. I.

Sixty-sixth Congress of the United States of America;

At the First Session,

Begun and held at the City of Washington on Monday, the nineteenth day of May,
one thousand nine hundred and nineteen.

———

JOINT RESOLUTION

Proposing an amendment to the Constitution extending the right of suffrage
to women.

———

*Resolved by the Senate and House of Representatives of the United States
of America in Congress assembled (two-thirds of each House concurring therein),*
That the following article is proposed as an amendment to the Constitution,
which shall be valid to all intents and purposes as part of the Constitution when
ratified by the legislatures of three-fourths of the several States.

"ARTICLE ———.

"The right of citizens of the United States to vote shall not be denied or
abridged by the United States or by any State on account of sex.

"Congress shall have power to enforce this article by appropriate
legislation."

F. H. Gillett

Speaker of the House of Representatives.

Thos. R. Marshall

Vice President of the United States and
President of the Senate.

Joint Resolution by the Sixty-Sixth Congress of the United States, Proposing the 19th
Amendment to the U.S. Constitution, May 19, 1919.
Courtesy National Archives and Records Administration, Washington, D.C.

Chapter 13

BRAVING THE SMOKE

by Cindy C. Smolovik

SMOKE-FILLED ROOMS, DEALS AND double deals—the world of politics before the late twentieth century was almost entirely the purview of men. Even so, women had a very keen interest in community and political affairs. This is evident in the activities of various women's clubs and organizations, in movements for suffrage and temperance, promotion of public schools, the building of libraries, and other organized movements for social and political change. However, the actual holding of political office and participating in the behind-the-scenes machinations was forbidden territory for women. Any women braving this male domain had to make a decision on how to operate—did they have to behave like men to be taken seriously in this realm? But first, they had to get in the door.

On August 26, 1920, the U.S. secretary of state declared that the Nineteenth Amendment to the U.S. Constitution had been ratified by the legislatures of thirty-six of the forty-eight states. Women finally had succeeded in obtaining the right to vote. (The ratification by all the states was not completed until Mississippi ratified it March 22, 1984, after having rejected it on March 29, 1920.)

After achieving this milestone, women started finding ways to enter the world of public service by running for elected offices, holding public office, and being appointed (by men) to various boards and commissions. While the ranks of women in public office, even in the twenty-first century, is a relatively small number, it would be even smaller without the courage of a few women to make a difference and to fill a need. Their willingness to serve emboldened them to push open the doors of the smoke-filled rooms, making it possible for women with a similar calling to follow.

Fort Worth women began actively seeking public office as early the 1920s but would not be fully successful until the 1950s. Some of those brave enough to take the cigar smoke smack in the face were Clarice Spurlock, Reecy McKnight, Edith Alderman Deen, Margret Rimmer, Walter B. Barbour, and others elected to the Fort Worth City Council. Betty Andujar and Chris Miller took on the Capitol in Austin—Andujar serving as state senator and Miller serving as state representative. Eva Barnes literally held court as a Tarrant County judge. Others like Juanita Zepeda, Viola Pitts, and Margaret Carter worked behind the scenes, while several others held political appointments or positions within government service.

In 1933 Edith Alderman Guedry (later known as Edith Alderman Deen) used her column in the Fort Worth Press to call for a woman on the city council. She stated in her December 20, 1933, column, "why not a woman for the next vacancy on the City Council . . . women [can] play other roles than that of sheltered homemaker."

This call remained unanswered for nineteen years, until Clarice Spurlock was elected to the council in 1952. Spurlock was born in Thorndale, Texas, in 1913. Politics was in the Spurlock household; she was married to Judge Joe Spurlock, Second Court of Appeals. Her first attempt at a political post was in 1944 when she ran unsuccessfully for county treasurer. Spurlock did not give up. She turned her sights toward the city council. Another woman, Mrs. Landgrave T. Smith, had campaigned unsuccessfully for a place on the council in 1949.

Spurlock's 1952 platform included hiring more police officers, installing traffic signals around schools, creating recreation centers for teenagers, and reducing water rates. Upon being elected, Spurlock quickly became the council's point person for youth issues because she was a former schoolteacher and public school principal at Smithfield Elementary. When the council created the Youth Board to deal with juvenile delin-

quency and vandalism, Spurlock became its first chair.

The Fort Worth Star-Telegram reported May 12, 1953, that she proclaimed at the Youth Board's first meeting, "In many Fort Worth homes there are parents with broken hearts. The dreams they had for their sons and daughters have been shattered. . .if our board can reduce the number of parents who see their boys and girls go astray. . .then we will not have served in vain."

During her four years on the council, Spurlock became an advocate for the Fort Worth police and firefighters. When the Dallas–Fort Worth Turnpike was proposed and constructed, Spurlock fought a losing battle for toll-free use of the western portion and state legislation that would lift the toll twenty years after the road opened. (The toll was finally lifted in 1977.) Spurlock ran unsuccessfully for a third term in 1956. She died in Tyler, Texas, on April 24, 1977.

There were two women serving on the council for a short time prior to Spurlock's defeat. The second woman was Reecy McKnight. Her husband, Councilman Mansfield McKnight, died in early August 1956. Several days later Reecy was nominated by Clarice Spurlock to fill her husband's seat. The council approved, and McKnight was asked if she would accept the nomination to serve.

She agreed on August 7, 1956, saying, "I consider this a great honor....We all realize I can't take my husband's place, but I will serve the city to the best of my ability, and of course to be some company for Mrs. Spurlock up here."

Spurlock and McKnight faced the varied community, economic, and cultural issues of the 1950s. Controversial topics included fluorida-

Clarice Spurlock with other members of the Fort Worth City Council: Joe B. Ellis, T. L. Carleton, Edgar Deen, Buddie Thomas, M. M. McKnight, Thomas A. McCann, Ed Kane, and J. F. Tarlton, *Fort Worth Star Telegram*, April 22, 1953. *Courtesy* Fort Worth Star-Telegram *Collection, University of Texas at Arlington Library, Arlington, Texas.*

tion of the city's water supply and improvements of poorer areas of town. Regional issues were also a priority with the construction of the turnpike connecting Dallas and Fort Worth and early discussions for a regional airport. The Dallas–Fort Worth Turnpike, now I-30, and the regional airport, now Dallas/Fort Worth International Airport, continue to serve the area well. Examples of cultural improvements the council dealt with include art museum bids in 1952 and support for the Fort Worth Zoo in 1953. Present-day Fort Worth has a world-class cultural arts district and internationally renowned zoo in part because of these visionary leaders.

McKnight was born one of fourteen children in May 1907 in Comyn, Texas. Her father was William David Weeks, a farmer and champion old-time fiddler. She grew up in Proctor, Texas. She trained and worked as a nurse at Scott &

White Hospital in Temple from 1923 to 1927. She moved to the Fort Worth area in 1927 to work at a variety of jobs to support herself during the Great Depression. During World War II she became a timekeeper for aircraft manufacturer Convair. She worked for the company from 1942 to 1945. While at Convair, she and others formed a union. She met Mansfield M. McKnight at a dance given by the printers union and they were married in 1944. Mansfield and Reecy McKnight were active supporters of the Texas labor movement and the Typographical Union in particular.

In the 1950s, women formed auxiliaries as a way to support union activity. For years prior to and after her service on the city council, McKnight served the Women's Auxiliary, Number 44 of the Typographical Union 198 in various capacities, including president in 1954.

Reecy McKnight, *Fort Worth Star-Telegram*, August 8, 1956. *Courtesy* Fort Worth Star-Telegram *Collection, University of Texas at Arlington Library, Arlington, Texas.*

She was public relations chair and called on union members to take part in the Mothers' March on Polio in 1952. Organized labor at this time was keenly aware of the necessity of having supporters in political office. McKnight worked to create lists of candidates in local, state, and national elections who were favorable to labor. In 1953 McKnight was a representative to the Texas State Federation of Labor Convention. At this convention she urged union people to be diligently conscious of labor laws being passed in Texas. McKnight was instrumental in promoting the purchasing of goods with the union label and the stocking of union label goods in department stores in downtown and elsewhere in the city. She created a scrapbook depicting as many

union labels as she could find to use as exhibit material.

Newspaper articles at the time portrayed her as a simple "housewife, who depended on her [recently deceased husband] for many things" pointing out that "she can't drive the family car." A *Fort Worth Press* headline from August 9, 1956, admonished, "Councilwoman Must Learn to Drive Her Car."

Although she was managing her husband's insurance company and fully intended to keep it going after his death, she was portrayed as a typical American housewife, and articles suggested that she was appointed because "she is familiar with her husband's program and philosophy of government." It may have been the councilmen's intention that McKnight sit as a place holder in her husband's seat, but McKnight quickly showed that she meant to do more than sit and smile. At the end of her appointed term, McKnight campaigned for a term of her own, and successfully won three future elections. She even presided over a council meeting in November 1960, when Mayor Tom McCann and Mayor Pro Tem John Justin were out of the city. According to the *Star-Telegram*, it is believed to be the first time a woman presided over the council. In 1961 she received the Distinguished Citizen Award from the Fort Worth Chamber of Commerce.

Organized labor was her base of support and McKnight often was seen as the labor candidate. Despite this, she was determined to be seen as someone working for the whole community and for the general public welfare. The Fort Worth Trades Assembly recognized her efforts by unanimously passing a resolution endorsing McKnight's campaign in 1957, saying that she "seeks to serve neither business nor labor when she goes to the council table but rather the good and welfare of the whole community." Labor issues were high on her list of concerns, however, and she supported the interests of city employees, police and fire associations in particular.

Her time on the council was not without conflict. In 1958 political in-fighting on the council resulted in the replacement of Joe B. Owens with Robert Driskell. The controversy arose out of the development of the Ridgmar neighborhood, an area that was not quite within the city limits. The *Fort Worth Press* quoted McKnight April 24, 1958, as saying that replacing Owens "was a frame up to keep real estate interests on the council." McKnight announced on February 6, 1963, that she would not seek reelection for a fourth term. At the end of her last term she had served for fourteen years in Place 7.

For the rest of her life McKnight worked for better working conditions, support for union company products, and recognition of the contributions of organized labor to the American way of life. McKnight also served as secretary of the Fort Worth–Tarrant County Tuberculosis Society and National Multiple Sclerosis Society, Fort Worth chapter. Her desire to ensure that the history of labor activities was preserved is evident by her assistance with the establishment of the Texas Labor Archives and Manuscript Collections at the University of Texas at Arlington Library Special Collections. This collection serves as one of the building blocks for the archival collections at the university. Reecy McKnight died Christmas Eve 1998, at the age of ninety-one.

With the 1963 departure from the council by McKnight, the council was again without a woman member until Edith Alderman Deen was elected in 1965. Deen is best known as a journalist, author of religious literature, and the wife of Mayor Edgar Deen. Her political and social viewpoints were often expressed in her work as women's editor and columnist for the *Fort Worth Press* from 1924 to 1954. (See "High-heeled Times in the Newsroom.") Prior to her election to the council, she twice served on the Fort Worth Library Board of Trustees—from 1957 to 1961 and from 1964 to 1965. Deen already was well known and the recipient of many honors prior to running for office. So in seeking election she was not necessarily out to make a name for herself. She basically believed that the council needed a woman, as illustrated by this quote from the *Star-Telegram* of April 7, 1965: "I simply do not see any reason women should not have something to say about the course of city affairs." It was her opinion that it was not enough to sit back and let others decide the course of the city.

In considering politics Deen noted, "You must never forget that human dignity, economic freedom and individual responsibility are the characteristics that distinguish a democracy from all forms of government." Her time on the library board gave her the opportunity to be involved in the politics of the city as well as promote her own love for books.

Deen served only one term on the council. Fort Worth politics was entering a new phase in the late 1960s. The formation of the Good Government League by area business and professional leaders began a new political chapter by officially backing candidates that, according to the *Dallas Morning News*, added "spice" to campaigns. City politics began to focus on real estate development and zoning controversies between commercial and residential land use. Support of the new Good Government League did not necessarily mean getting elected. Deen had the support of the Good Government League but lost her bid for reelection in a hotly contested race with Harris Hoover. Deen may have miscalculated by challenging Hoover in Place 2 rather than running for her Place 4 seat. Deen continued to be noted as a literary figure from Fort Worth and stayed involved in community affairs until her death in January 1994.

This time the defeat of a woman candidate did not leave the council without a woman. In the same election in which Deen met defeat, Margret Rimmer was elected. Rimmer, a former television commentator and owner of a dress shop, ran against Good Government League candidate Bill Sarsgard. After winning a run-off election Rimmer began her service on the council that would last for ten years, even rising to the level of mayor pro tem. Her focus was beautification of the city and environmental issues. In 1974 Rimmer chaired the Committee for a Greener, Cleaner Fort Worth with the purpose of improving the environment through increased green space, beautification projects, and anti-air pollution practices. With her husband, Dr. Raymond Rimmer, she donated seventy-five globe locust and eleven purple-leafed plum trees that were planted on Bellaire Drive West and West Berry Street near the Texas Christian University campus. She made a fervent appeal to expand the city's paper recycling efforts.

Other issues facing the council included ending the toll on the Dallas–Fort Worth Turnpike, the much-anticipated opening of the Dallas/Fort Worth Regional Airport; and calls for single member districts.

The year 1977 saw two milestones in the increasing participation of women in city politics. Rimmer was defeated in 1977 by another woman, Shirley Johnson, and community activist Walter B. Barbour became the first African-American woman elected to the council.

During Rimmer's tenure, Juanita Zepeda ran for council in 1971 but was not elected. She was the first Hispanic woman to run for council. Zepeda is best known as a volunteer and community activist for the North Side and Poly neighborhoods of Fort Worth. Her goal was to encourage people not to be afraid to ask questions at city hall. She firmly believed that, whatever the problem or issue was, it could be conquered through being informed and going to the source. Although she did not serve in an elected capacity, Zepeda played an important role as the first community coordinator of the Fort Worth Teacher Corps Project, a cooperative partnership between the federal government, Fort Worth public schools, and Texas Christian University School of Education. Graduate students from TCU worked with students at J. P. Elder Middle School in order to raise their academic level. Zepeda was born in Fort Worth. Her mother was from Mexico and her father from Rhome, Texas. Her husband, Pete, encouraged her volunteer work in the community. In addition to the Fort Worth Teacher Corps Project, Zepeda's civic service included the Fort Worth Parks and Recreation Board, Mayor's Commission on the Status of Women, Community Action Agency, hospital district Mental Health Advisory Board, and Adult Basic Education and Bilingual Education Advisory Boards.

Fort Worth women found their way into politics on the local level in the 1950s, but it was not until the 1970s that Fort Worth would finally send two women, Betty Andujar and Chris Miller, to serve in Austin. Texas women had entered state politics as soon as possible, beginning with Edith Wilmans from Dallas in 1922 and Mary Elizabeth "Margie" Neal from Carthage in 1923. Their numbers increased through the decades, and even gained national respect in the case of Barbara Jordan, who was the first African-American woman to serve in the Texas Legislature. She was in the Texas Senate from 1967 to 1973. She was elected to Congress in 1972.

Women found serving in this forum raised an interesting conundrum. What was the best way to handle the typical "good old boy" network? How to get around the patronizing manner and be more than the "little lady"? (Not all the problems the women faced were philosophical. The Senate chamber had to add a woman's restroom for the first time when Jordan was elected.) A report from a national conference of women state legislators held May 18–21, 1972, stated: "Family considerations and traditional attitudes regarding women's roles in the family loom large for women holding elective office. Society in general imposes barriers by still dictating that a woman's place is in the home. If she wants to work outside, particularly in such a highly visible and competitive arena as politics, she has to justify herself."

In 1972, Betty Andujar was elected to the Texas Senate, becoming the first Republican woman to do so. The same year, Democrat Chris Miller was elected to the Texas House of Representatives. Both may owe some of their

Juanita Zepeda, *Fort Worth Star-Telegram*, December 12, 1975. *Courtesy* Fort Worth Star-Telegram Collection, University of Texas at Arlington Library, Arlington, Texas.

election success to the voters' response to scandal. The early 1970s included the Watergate scandal, which eventually brought down President Richard Nixon, and a separate scandal that resulted in the resignation of Vice President Spiro Agnew for tax evasion. Federal and state investigations and subsequent criminal charges swirled around many state and former state officials in Texas in 1971 and 1972. The center of the scandal was a stock fraud scheme involving state attorney general Waggoner Carr, former state insurance commissioner John Osorio, Dallas businessman Frank Sharp, and a handful of others. The scandal became commonly known as the Sharpstown Scandal because of the involvement of Sharpstown State Bank. By the time the dust settled, hints of bribery and other suspicions of corruption had cast shadows on Governor Preston Smith, state Democratic chairman Elmer Baum, House Speaker Gus Mutscher Jr., Fort Worth representative Tommy Shannon, and others. The whole group became known as "The Dirty Thirty." When election time came around the voters were in the mood to clean house and elect new faces.

Elizabeth "Betty" Richards Andujar was born November 6, 1912, in Harrisburg, Pennsylvania. She was a graduate of Wilson College with a bachelor of arts degree in English and history. She came to Fort Worth in 1938 with her husband, Dr. John "Andy" Andujar, a pathologist. She was short in stature—slightly over five feet tall—but tall on courage and humor. Andujar believed that being a woman should not be a factor in whether or not someone could be effective in politics. A few times she barged into the men's restroom because she knew important decisions were being made there

instead of in the Senate chambers. Most of the time, however, she felt it was important not to give up being a lady and that being polite was essential. She said, "Women really are the backbone of all political campaigns, all the men know it. These women are familiar with current issues and know why they prefer one party or particular candidate; they are articulate and effective, but you cannot be abrasive."

Texas was a one-party state, and that party was Democrat—conservative Democrat. For some like Andujar the Democrats were not conservative enough. In her eyes, the Republican Party represented the future conservative path in Texas. However, there were a few areas where she deviated (at least a little bit) from the conservative viewpoint. She was a supporter of abortion rights and opposed an amendment to the Texas Constitution in 1976 that would have barred abortion. She also was in favor of birth control, which, oddly enough, was considered a political issue. When asked her opinion about abortion and sex education in public schools, most of her letters included statements that indicated support while still showing her conservative opinion that government should not be directly involved in social welfare.

"I consider both these subjects to be essentially personal and family matters, and I wish the government were not involved with either. Unfortunately, our federal government has long been in the baby production business by supporting countless thousands of illegitimate children born apparently for the financial benefits of the mother. I personally would prefer to reduce the incentive for such births. Personally, I don't like abortion and fully expect a far better birth control method to be marketed in the relatively near future. Meanwhile, the Supreme Court has ruled that tax funds can be used for abortion only in certain, very limited circumstances, and I would abide by that decision."

Andujar enjoyed a variety of high points in her ten-year career in the Senate, including serving as "governor for a day" in 1977. One particularly proud personal moment occurred on January 29, 1973. Andujar introduced a resolution honoring President Richard M. Nixon for negotiating for peace in Vietnam. The resolution also honored military personnel in Vietnam, families of prisoners of war, and those missing in action.

Andujar voted in favor of providing driver's license examinations in Spanish for persons unable to take the examination in English. She voted to require a two-thirds vote of the legislature to impose a state income tax. The overall vote failed, possibly because it was seen as unnecessary. Suggesting a state income tax in Texas was (and maybe still is) political suicide and would never receive a simple majority, let alone a two-thirds vote. Andujar supported a bill to exempt disabled veterans from college fees if federal resources did not pay the fees. Her other achievements include the expansion of the Texas College of Osteopathic Medicine, now University of North Texas Health Science Center.

During the 1970s and 1980s the national economy, high inflation rates, and the energy crisis significantly influenced Texas politics. Showing her truly conservative side, Andujar asserted "that the most pressing problem in this country today is our nation's fiscal matters." She was convinced that the government had to stop overspending. In speeches and letters she blamed organized labor, saying, "Our country is being

Betty Andujar, date unknown. *Betty Andujar Papers, AR 272, University of Texas at Arlington Library, Arlington, Texas.*

emasculated by overspending by the government and this will ruin all our lives, yours and mine, if it is not stopped. Contributing to this is Labor. The labor movement is out of control in this country."

The attempt to adopt an Equal Rights Amendment to the U.S. Constitution was an important issue during this time period. Section 1 of the proposed amendment states: "Equality of rights under the law shall not be denied or abridged by the United States or by any state on account of sex." While seen as something women would likely support, the ERA was not necessary, according to conservatives like Andujar. In many letters Andujar wrote, "[The]

Civil Rights Act of 1964 provided equal treatment on the basis of sex, so both government and industry are now far more alert about hiring and paying women on an equal basis. Great progress is being made, and I believe women now have more opportunities than ever before and will gain ever greater recognition....I think most of the goals of ERA are being achieved without the tremendous government and bureaucratic interference which would follow passage of the amendment."

Andujar often was asked if being a woman posed any problems for her as a senator. She answered that her biggest obstacle was not being a woman—it was that she was not an attorney. In letters she indicated, "A woman candidate is especially good if she has worked professionally as a teacher, lawyer, or other type work, or has been active in any community, club or church work." On the flip side, she always felt compelled to point out that her husband financially supported her. Andujar often received letters requesting advice from young women who were interested in going into politics. She typically responded that being informed and studying the issues from both sides was critical. Andujar considered herself a legislator first and a woman second. "I have no problem regarding myself as a legislator rather than the special champion of women's issues only. . . . I do not consider myself a women's lib in the current sense of the word. I do believe in equal pay for equal work and other economic gains women have enjoyed. The interpretation of 'pure equality' will remain in the hands of our courts and only time will tell what that might mean."

Andujar defeated Roy English to win a second term in 1978. In 1979, debate over H.B. 856 proved most unfortunate for Andujar. The bill, known as the Barrientos Bill (named for then-Representative Gonzalo Barrientos), focused on the denial of emergency hospital services based on the ability to pay for those services. However, the debate also focused on non-English-speaking patients because they were most likely to be unable to communicate with hospital staff. Andujar opposed the bill and used a political maneuver known as a "tag" to kill it. The "tag" was a forty-eight-hour delay on the vote when the session had only twenty-four hours left. Her reasoning was that the bill was flawed, that it would have increased the economic difficulties already faced by hospitals, and that existing laws already provided that services cannot be denied. In letters and newspaper quotes she defended her position, saying: "[The] Barrientos Bill would have caused doctors, nurses, and other medical professionals to spend up to ten years in jail as a result of a misunderstanding or inability to communicate with a patient. The language of the bill reflected [a] vengeful attitude towards honest hospital employees, who in the course of their duties have no intent to harm anyone or to commit any criminal act."

There was a huge backlash, with critics claiming she was racist and in league with doctors and insurance companies.

Poor health forced her decision not to seek a third term in 1982. She remained active in the community until her death in June 1997 at the age of eighty-four. In a September 2006 interview, Kathleen Shaw, a former aide in Andujar's senate office, said what impressed her most about Andujar was that she truly tried to serve everyone regardless of party affiliation or whether or not they contributed campaign funds.

At the same time that Fort Worth sent a very conservative Republican to the Texas Senate, liberal Democrat Chris Miller was sent to the Texas House of Representatives. Miller was born Dorothy Chrisman on June 15, 1926, in Boston, but was raised primarily in New York. Her parents were the Reverend Charles and Dorothy Noyce Chrisman. Miller attended Wheaton College in Massachusetts and later Fort Worth's Texas Christian University. She married in 1944 and moved to Fort Worth in 1948. Miller divorced in 1965 and began her political life.

Finding herself a single parent, Miller also found that a great deal of discrimination existed for single women and single women with children in particular. The center of her politics became the fight against social injustice and inequality. And she was a fighter. Her son said, "She saw a lot of injustice in the world.... She had a lot of obstacles to fight." Miller described her venture into politics as "my journey to personhood."

Miller focused her political energy on the rights of women. In a 1971 letter she wrote, "An incredible amount of talent and ability is being over-looked and a vital portion of the American resource is often lost because of the legal and social status of women in the U.S. today." She was one of the founders of the Texas Women's Political Caucus in 1971, as well as the North Central Texas Women's Political Caucus. The Women's Political Caucus organizational flyer stated its purpose as: "We must organize to screen all candidates, follow their voting records and lobby effectively for women's concerns. We must prepare to support and elect qualified women candidates, if necessary, to represent the women's viewpoint...."

Miller's other activities for the advancement of women included the Mayor's Commission on the Status of Women from 1972 to 1973, American Women in Radio and Television, Women in Communications, Texas Federation of Business and Professional Women, League of Women Voters, Press Club of Fort Worth, Fort Worth Chamber of Commerce, Operation Diploma, Women's Haven, Institute for Women, and Zonta.

Miller served as secretary of the Fort Worth Human Relations Commission. She was a public relations consultant and worked for the Greater Fort Worth Housing Opportunity, Inc., the 1997 American College Theatre Festival, and the Minorities Cultural Arts Association. Miller was the moderator for Channel 11 Voter's Digest in 1965, advertising manager of the Fort Worth Chamber of Commerce from 1967 to 1968; a member of the Tarrant County Community Action Agency from 1968 to 1969. To top it all she owned her own business, Chris Miller Public Relations, from 1969 to 1972.

In the 1972 Democratic Party primary, Miller's opponents and the press contended that Miller's support came from various groups including aging hippies, women, and minority communities. Ethics were a huge issue because of the Sharpstown Scandal. A flyer from the Citizens' Association for Reform states: "The last regular session of the Texas Legislature was the grimmest in modern Texas history. Public officials were convicted of conspiracy to accept a bribe. Worse yet, the Texas House of Representatives did nothing to clean this blot from our state. On vote after vote, the so called representative of the people refused to lift a hand to investigate Mr. Mutscher and his dealings . . . ."

Chris Miller, date unknown. *Chris Miller Papers,
AR381, University of Texas at Arlington Library,
Arlington, Texas.*

A 1972 Miller campaign slogan was "For
Honesty and Responsibility." Her opponent,
Cordell Hull, did not take Miller seriously, not
because she was a liberal Democrat, but because
she was a woman. Hull often quipped, "a woman
would have to be Joan of Arc to win." So upon
defeating Hull by 12,000 votes Miller said, "I
became Saint Joan." Miller went on to win the
1972 general election to become the first woman
from Tarrant County to win election to the Texas
House of Representatives, taking office in 1973.
When the Press Club of Fort Worth named

Miller co-winner of the 1973 Newsmaker of the
Year award, the plaque read "Chris Miller,
Tarrant County's Jeanne d'Arc."

During Miller's three terms in the Texas
House she supported a Texas constitutional
amendment allowing homestead exemptions for
single adults, which was later approved by voters
in 1973. Miller worked for campaign finance
reform and prison reform. She served on the
House Human Resources Committee, Reappor-
tionment Committee, and the Joint Subcommittee on Public Health. She was vice chair of the
Pollution Subcommittee of the Environmental
Affairs Committee.

Miller supported keeping abortion rights
available. She believed that the decision of
whether or not to have an abortion should not
be up to lawmakers. In many of her letters she
stated, "My own conviction on this issue is that
no legislator is competent to make such an
important decision for another human being and
that the matter should rest between God, the
mother, and her doctor."

Unlike Andujar, Miller was a supporter of
the women's liberation movement: "Unfortunately, most people visualize woman's lib as nothing more than a fanatical bunch of bra burners
and nothing could be further from the truth . . .
I think the most important thing is to communicate with non-working women and explain just
what the whole thing is really about. Most working women understand the lack of equal rights,
but homemakers seem to fear the movement as
lowering their prestige."

Miller wrote a letter to Governor Dolph
Briscoe dated September 28, 1973, requesting
that a woman be named to the Public Welfare
Board. In it she declared, "It seems ridiculous

Chris Miller, date unknown.
*Chris Miller Papers, AR381,
University of Texas at Arlington
Library, Arlington, Texas.*

that the Public Welfare Board which deals mostly with women on welfare because they are incapable of earning enough money to support their children or in nursing homes because they live longer than men or on old age assistance because as elderly widows they have little or no further income or the many reasons that cause women in our society to be dependent on the state—has not had even one woman among its members for the past sixteen years!!!"

The governor answered that there were no openings on the Public Welfare Board, but he wanted Miller to send a list of names for consideration for future openings.

Miller was named Legislator of the Year by the national and Texas press in 1977. However,

she lost the election in 1978, largely due to redistricting. Miller described herself this way: "I was always accessible, outspoken and honest in all that I did, particularly with those whom I felt had not been represented, the elderly, the working corps, women, and minorities, and various handicapped and children who are abused by adults or neglected by their nation."

This is a fine epitaph for a woman who took on the Texas House without bending to the pressure to be the "little lady," to step aside, or avoid topics because they were controversial or difficult. After her service in the House she remarried and remained active in civic activities, including donating her legislative office to the Women's Center of Tarrant County. She eventually started her own travel agency. Miller died in March 1995 at the age of sixty-eight. Her son described his mother in the *Star-Telegram* as a "trailblazer." He also said, "Her opponents accused her of being a miniskirted, cigar smoking liberal, and she was."

The judiciary is another bastion of male domination. In fact the barrier was so large when it came to courts that women were not even allowed to serve on juries in Texas until November 1954. This barrier did not stop Eva Barnes—that's Judge Eva Barnes.

Barnes was born Eva Bloore in Birmingham, England, in 1909. Her father was an Anglican priest. After living in Canada, Maine, and Connecticut, the Bloore family moved to Texas when Eva was fourteen. Her father continued his studies at Southwestern Baptist Theological Seminary. As a teenager Eva became interested in the law while working at the First Baptist Church of Fort Worth as a temporary typist. In 1926, the pastor of the church, J. Frank Norris, was charged with shooting D. E. Chipps. According to newspaper accounts, Chipps, a friend of Mayor H. C. Meacham, was upset by comments Norris made about the mayor during a sermon. Chipps threatened to kill Norris, who then shot Chipps. The case caused an increase in letters to the church office, so Barnes was hired temporarily to assist. While there, Barnes met attorney Chester Collins, Norris' defense attorney, who hired her to work in his office after her job at the church ended.

Barnes was young and slight of build, so the people in Collins' law office dubbed her "Little Eva." The nickname stuck with her the rest of her life. But "Little Eva" went on to do big things. She became so fascinated by the law that it was all she could talk about. When the Jefferson University School of Law in Dallas announced the opening of a campus in Fort Worth, "Little Eva" went to law school at the age of nineteen. She worked her way through school by doing bookkeeping for the school. Barnes graduated with the Class of 1932. She passed the bar on her first try and became one of the youngest lawyers in the state. She was twenty-two.

In the mid-1930s having a law degree and passing the bar was not enough for a woman to be taken seriously as a practicing attorney. Eva decided to try her luck in New York City but once again had to settle for a job as a legal secretary. Homesickness and her mother's illness brought her back to Fort Worth. She married Marvin Barnes in 1942 and worked as a legal secretary in the offices of Canty and Hanger and then as a law clerk with Arthur Lee Moore. While waiting for her chance to practice law, Barnes fed her interest in politics. She worked for the Young Democrats in the 1930s and was selected as one of twenty Fort Worth residents to meet President Franklin Roosevelt in his private railroad car when it stopped in Wichita Falls. She worked on the gubernatorial campaign of W. Lee "Pappy" O'Daniel in 1938.

Barnes finally was given her chance in 1945. Al Clyde offered her a job as an assistant district attorney in 1945. She accepted, becoming the first female assistant D.A. in Tarrant County. While working for the district attorney, Barnes challenged the wording of adoption laws. Domestic cases were her passion from the beginning of her career. Soon after getting her degree she started talking about the need for a domestic relations court, one that could specialize in family problems. As an assistant D.A. she was frequently assigned juvenile court cases, custody suits, and family law cases.

After they left the district attorney's office, Clyde and Barnes opened a law office together. In 1949 Clyde and Barnes represented Arthur C. Hester in a highly publicized murder case. Hester was charged and convicted of murdering his guardian, Texas Christian University professor Dr. John Lord. The case was moved to Cleburne, Texas, and drew so much statewide attention that proceedings, including Barnes' summation, were carried by radio. This was her first full-fledged jury speech. Accounts say her summation moved spectators and jurors to tears.

Her life as an elected official began in 1962 with the creation of the Tarrant County Court of Domestic Relations. Barnes won the election held for the court, making her the first woman in Tarrant County to win an elected judgeship. (Other women had been appointed to serve as judges.) Even though she was well known and highly respected as an attorney by now, reporters writing about her campaign could not resist mentioning that her "profession never interfered with her role as wife, housekeeper and mother," and asking how her husband felt about her campaign. By all accounts, Marvin Barnes proudly supported her candidacy. Barnes was reelected to four consecutive terms and retired from the bench in 1979. However, she continued for many years to serve as a visiting judge when needed.

When asked if she felt discriminated against as a woman, she said, "I have always tried to keep from feeling that some men were prejudiced against me in any way." She had a reputation for being strict and tough but also fair and inventive. In some ways, she stuck to female tra-

Eva Barnes, *Fort Worth Star-Telegram*, May 13, 1962. Fort Worth Star-Telegram *Photograph Collection, University of Texas at Arlington Library, Arlington, Texas.*

ditions. She was a lover of pillbox hats. She insisted that women attorneys and/or caseworkers in her court wear dresses or skirts. No pants were allowed, no matter how nice or expensive. Children were her biggest concern. In her eyes children were the main casualties in divorce, and it was her job to help where she could. Adoption also remained a strong passion for Barnes. In August 1987, *The New York Times* reported that when a power failure forced the evacuation of more than 500 court and county employees, visiting judge Eva Barnes completed an adoption proceeding by flashlight.

Barnes received many honors from the legal profession and women's organizations. She died in April 2001 at the age of ninety-one. Eulogies portrayed her as a fabulous storyteller with a great sense of humor, and always a lady.

No political scene conjures up cigar smoking, salty talk, and "no place for a lady" assertions more than back rooms and behind-the-scenes deals. Viola Pitts, Democrat and outspoken self-appointed community spokesperson for the Como area of Fort Worth, and Margaret Carter, political devotee, campaigner, and organizer for the liberal arm of the Democratic Party, entered politics with strong hopes for change, not only for women, but also for the country and their local communities. "Smoke-filled rooms" did not intimidate them.

Viola Pitts is one of the best known of Fort Worth community activists. She was born Viola Marie Hamilton in Winnsboro, Texas, on September 8, 1914. She graduated from high school in Pittsburgh, Texas. She often was quoted as saying she held C.S. and M.W. degrees—Common Sense and Motherly Wit. She came to Fort Worth in 1941, left for San Antonio in the 1950s, and returned to Fort Worth in the 1960s. She claimed she voted for the first time in the late 1950s by picking out candidates whose names appealed to her. According to an article in the *Dallas Morning News*, Pitts changed this attitude in 1962 when she returned to Fort Worth. Another well-known community activist, Sopora Hicks, became her mentor and introduced her to politics and political responsibility. Pitts became legendary in Fort Worth as an advocate for her neighborhood of Como, located on Fort Worth's West Side.

Lake Como was built in 1889 and named by the developer for the famous resort in Italy. The area contained a man-made lake with an amusement park and dancing pavilion. Picnics and other social events were held there through the early 1900s. However, the real estate developer's dream turned out to be just that—a dream. The lots remained vacant through World War I. The amusement park was dismantled, and the neighborhood was used as a base hospital for the U.S. Army's Camp Bowie. In the years between World Wars I and II, predominantly African-American working-class families began purchasing the lots because the price was affordable. As the land boom began in the western part of Fort Worth, Como became an enclave surrounded by wealthier neighborhoods. Joyce Williams, a resident of Como, describes the neighborhood in her doctoral thesis for Texas Woman's University as "the servant's quarters for the affluent West Side of Fort Worth."

City improvements and services were just not made available in Como. Pitts made it her life's work to make sure the needs of her community were not forgotten. She was a fixture at council meetings. She wrote letters, made phone calls, and encouraged others from the community to do the same. While not all residents agreed with her on all things, she was recognized by most as the leader. The city's established political leaders called her "the unofficial Mayor of Como." She worked to ensure that the Como community received proper funding, elementary school improvements, and medical facilities. In 2000 Tarrant County officials renamed an area medical clinic in her honor.

Pitts held many political appointments, including precinct chair, member of the Tarrant County Hospital Board of Managers, the State Board of Hospitals, and the Charitable Solicitations Commission for the City of Fort Worth. She was vice president of the Neighborhood Action Commission. She also served on the 1989 Texas State Senate Advisory Commitee on the Creation and Expansion of Minority and

Women Owned Business Owner-ship and Opportunities.

Pitts was a strong campaigner for candidates she supported. She is quoted in the *Dallas Morning News* and *Star-Telegram* as having simple criteria for supporting a candidate: "They must be Democrats, they have to offer hope to poor and middle-income voters, and they had better keep their word. If I feel they're not going to be responsive to my people, I don't fool with them." She gained a reputation for being able to organize voters in her neighborhood; so much so that candidates would seek her support, including such well-known political figures as U.S. House Speaker Jim Wright. She also gained their respect and friendship. In 1992, Hugh Parmer, former Fort Worth mayor and state senator is quoted as saying, "Mrs. Pitts' influence can carry 500 to 1000 votes."

The Fort Worth City Council proclaimed February 10, 1998, as Ms. Viola Pitts Day. She died April 15, 2004, at the age of eighty-nine. She received a letter of tribute from President Bill Clinton and a commendation on the U.S. House of Representatives floor from Congressman Martin Frost. In his remarks Frost said, "Mrs. Pitts' determination, tenacity and honesty earned her the respect of many top elected public officials in North Texas." The Texas House and Senate also passed a concurrent resolution in her honor. Part of this resolution reads: "WHEREAS, this 'unofficial mayor of Como' fearlessly walked the halls of power, and became the political conscience of an area once overlooked, providing a voice for those who were dispossessed and long unheard; and WHEREAS, her fiery spirit was fueled by love, charity, and an unerring sense of fairness; . . . Her memory will live on in the hearts and minds of the countless people whose lives she touched . . . ." (See "These Women Lived!")

Margaret Carter was another Fort Worth woman for whom party politics held no fear. Carter was born April 18, 1909, in Sherman, the daughter of Walter and Mae Banks. Carter graduated from Baylor College for Women, (now called Mary Hardin-Baylor University) in 1928. She married Jack Carter in 1934. She took graduate courses in American history at Texas Christian University from 1937 to 1939. Carter was a schoolteacher from 1928 to 1942, starting her career as an elementary schoolteacher. She later taught high school social studies.

Carter became interested in Democratic Party organization in the late 1940s. She traveled the state organizing for the Young Democrats and served as the president of the Tarrant County Democratic Woman's Club. In the 1950s she served as a member of the National Democratic Advisory Council. In 1956 she was the first woman to be elected a delegate from the Twelfth Congressional District to the Democratic National Convention. Throughout the 1960s and 1970s she developed her skills and was known as the 'best political strategist in this [Tarrant] county, possibly all of Texas." Carter was volunteer secretary to Tarrant County Democratic Chairman from 1944 to 1946. She was president of the Tarrant County Democratic Women's Club from 1947 to 1951 and legislative chair for many years. She was the director of a countywide anti–poll tax campaign in 1949. She served as member of the State Democratic Executive Committee for the Twelfth Senatorial District in the 1970s.

For most of her career, Texas was a one-party

state with two party ideologies: Conservative Democrat and Liberal Democrat. Carter argued that it was better to have two distinct parties. Clearly on the liberal side, she opposed the tendency for politicians with what she saw as Republican ideas and voting patterns to remain in the Democratic Party, as illustrated by her letter to Senator Lyndon Johnson, on March 25, 1953. She refers to "Republican" leanings of legislators whose voting patterns supported oil and real estate interests: "Our opposition who chooses to fight the Democratic Party from within have been diligent in sponsoring changes in the election code which would make the development of responsible two-party government in Texas virtually impossible."

Carter described her career as "a lifetime as a volunteer campaigner for candidates and measures that would keep the political structures flexible enough to permit responsible leaders to function, while preventing arbitrary exercises of personal and economic power." She often found herself as an outsider because she was a liberal when conservatives ran the Democratic Party, at least in Texas. She was often at odds with Lyndon Johnson, and felt that Hubert Humphrey was too conservative. She was a major supporter of John F. Kennedy. She supported Jimmy Carter in 1976, but Ted Kennedy in 1980. Letters exchanged with fellow Democrat congressman Jim Wright show a lifelong friendship, but Carter and Wright were not necessarily in sync when it came to politics.

The Vietnam War and the civil rights movement in the late 1960s made being in politics difficult. In an oral history interview at the University of Texas at Arlington, Carter spoke about the tough politics of 1968. She said, "You know, you were considered a traitor if you suggested that perhaps some of the things going on at General Dynamics and Ling Temco Vought [major defense contractors and major employers in the Dallas-Fort Worth area] were not in the best interest of the human race. . . . They wrap the flag around anything the president says."

She felt that the powerful always tried to prevent the opposition from being heard and encouraged "people to be active, to take part and have their say." She constantly wrote letters to the editor of the *Star-Telegram*, many of which were printed. On December 6, 1979, in response to Ronald Reagan's proposal to make the Shah of Iran a permanent resident of the United States, she wrote, "When are we going to stop depending on alliances with thieves and tyrants, [and] then assuming an air of innocent surprise when their overthrow involves ugly cruel rebellion?"

Carter's position on women in politics was clear. There was no choice but to get involved, because public policy impacts women in particular. Carter felt political participation was an obligation to "the philosophers, pamphleteers and constitution makers." She wrote that she was motivated by the struggle of those women who came before her, to whom she paid tribute: "My grandmother, who having been divorced in a time when divorce was disgraceful and widowed after a second marriage, kept her courage and her sense of humor . . . in spite of the accepted wisdom that consigned widows and orphans to exemplary suffering; to my mother, who kept her Quaker principles intact while doing an office job when decent girls were expected not to work outside the home and died of too frequent child bearing when family planning was handicapped by ignorance and social disapproval, to my great

Margaret Carter (center), pictured with Drew Clifton (left) and W. V. Myres (right) *Fort Worth Star-Telegram,* January 29, 1940 at the opening drive of the Tarrant County Young Democratic Club. *Courtesy* Fort Worth Star-Telegram *Collection, University of Texas at Arlington Library, Arlington, Texas.*

aunt who took over my upbringing . . . put herself through school when higher education was considered superfluous for females."

She went on to say that being active was important in an "open society where civil liberties are cherished and there are no unimportant people." Carter said, "There is no off season." In her opinion there was "always a letter to write, a voter to register, a precinct leader to recruit, a boundary to check, a hearing to attend, a bureaucratic maze to thread, an issue to explore." Margaret Carter died in 1988. She was eighty-nine.

Mrs. Ollie Hargrave was one of Fort Worth's first female probation officers and police matrons. Her job included supervising the transport of young girls. An article in the *Dallas Morning News* of March 7, 1918, mentions

Hargrave in an article concerning moving Gertrude Ulrich, a thirteen-year-old girl who entered a plea of guilty in the murder of her father. Ulrich was sentenced to the Gainesville Training School until she reached the age of twenty-one. Hargrave is mentioned again in October 1917 in a brief article indicating a crackdown on girls under the age of twenty-one entering cabarets and dance halls without a chaperone. It is also noted in September 1925 that Hargrave was on the advisory board for a hotel for "destitute persons and paroled convicts" on Main Street in Fort Worth run by the Volunteers of America.

Fannie Card Coffey was elected district clerk for Tarrant County in 1918 and served two terms. Coffey was born in Denton County, circa 1885. She graduated from Kidd-Key College and

Fannie Coffey, *Fort Worth Star-Telegram*, November 22, 1955. *Courtesy* Fort Worth Star-Telegram *Collection, University of Texas at Arlington Library, Arlington, Texas.*

Mary Manchester, *Fort Worth Star Telegram*, March 14, 1963. *Courtesy* Fort Worth Star-Telegram *Collection, University of Texas at Arlington Library, Arlington, Texas.*

briefly taught school. She married G. Frank Coffey in 1903. Her husband, a police captain, was killed in the line of duty in 1915. Left with four children, Coffey took a four-month course in stenography and went to work. She worked as a clerk in the justice court and in the office of the county clerk. She also held a job in the county commission court. She died in 1957.

Almita Robinson represented the African-American community at a meeting held by citizens concerned over racial tensions in the Riverside area of Fort Worth in November 1953. This is the only mention of Robinson; she is described as a social worker.

Mary Manchester held an amazing position in the U.S. Department of State beginning in 1949, rising after fourteen years to hold a title

with diplomatic rank. Manchester served in Jakarta, Indonesia; and Seoul, South Korea; Japan, Germany, Ethiopia, and New Delhi, India. Manchester was a graduate of Pascal High School and went on to attend Arlington State College, and Barnard College of Columbia University where she obtained a degree in psychology.

Women around the world have always found various ways to make a difference, and taking part in politics is just one of them. Women will continue to follow those mentioned in this chapter into politics, clearing the air in those smoke-filled rooms in order to make a difference in the life of their community.

BIBLIOGRAPHIC ESSAY

The Special Collections of the University of Texas at Arlington Library were incredibly full of valuable information including the Betty Andujar Papers; Margaret Carter Papers; Texas Labor Archives; M. M. and Reecy McKnight Collections; Chris Miller Papers; a dissertation by Richard Donnell entitled "Life and Times of Margaret Carter," and the transcription of oral histories of Margaret Carter and Reecy McKnight. All photographs in this chapter are courtesy of the *Fort Worth Star-Telegram* Photograph Collection, also at the University of Texas at Arlington. The Jim Wright Papers, Series II, 1938–2001, at Texas Christian University Library in Fort Worth, and the Edith Alderman Deen Scrapbook Collection at Texas Woman's University in Denton also were full of interesting information.

The newspaper collections of the Fort Worth and Dallas public libraries provided resources from the *Fort Worth Star-Telegram*, *Fort Worth Press*, and the *Dallas Morning News*. The *Handbook of Texas Online*, published by the Texas State Historical Association, was used as a source for insight into the political history of the

state.

Two other published sources, *History of Fort Worth Legal Community*, by Ann Arnold (Austin: Eakin Press, 2000); and *Texas Female Legislators, 1923–1999: Capitol Women*, by Nancy Baker Jones and Ruthe Winegarten (Austin: University of Texas Press, 2000), provided historical context.

The research for this chapter was accomplished through the assistance of Ann Hodges, Gary Spur, and other staff members at the University of Texas at Arlington Library Special Collections; Michael Strom with the Jim Wright Papers at the Texas Christian University Library; Dawn Letson and her staff at the Women's Collection at Texas Woman's University in Denton; Tom Kellum of the Fort Worth Public Library; Doug Jones, records manager for the City of Fort Worth; and Carol Roark at the Dallas Public Library, Texas/Dallas History and Archives.

In addition, a special thank you to Dr. George Green, Kathleen Shaw, and Judge Pat Andres for sharing their personal reflections with me on their relationships with Reecy McKnight, Betty Andujar, and Eva Barnes, respectively.

Chapter 14

CRACKING THE GLASS CEILING: ENTREPRENEURS AND PROFESSIONALS

by Carol Roark

BEFORE WORLD WAR II IN Fort Worth as in the rest of the United States, a woman needed an exceptional amount of drive to succeed in a profession or business. Some women worked alongside their husbands and family in a business, but rarely held public leadership roles in the company. During the late nineteenth and early twentieth century, women who worked outside the home often were driven by economic necessity—the death or absence of a husband—that left them with a family to support. A few, who frequently remained single, were led by a desire to serve or make their mark in an arena other than home and family management. The number of women who worked outside the home was small, and most women chose jobs in fields that became traditionally identified as "woman's work"—teaching, nursing, librarianship, sales clerk, or secretarial work. The search for professional women in Fort Worth turns up a handful of well-known figures whose names have become icons: baker Ninnie Baird (Mrs. Baird's Bread), pathologist Dr. May Owen, and restaura-

teur Jesusa "Mama Sus" Garcia (Joe T. Garcia's). Many more worked without publicity in the mainstream media. They supported each other through organizations such as the Fort Worth chapters of Business & Professional Women, founded in 1922, and the Zonta Club, which gave awards for outstanding achievement. Tellingly, however, membership lists from the early years of the Fort Worth B&PW chapter show that the majority of members worked as stenographers or sales clerks.

Among the professions, some job categories were easier to enter than others, even though the total number of women working in them was small. Medicine, particularly osteopathy, was more welcoming and supported by a tradition of family service. Architecture and law, however, proved difficult even for those who had received training in the profession. Several women who passed the state bar exam ended up working as legal secretaries because they could not find professional employment in their field.

For each of the women discussed here, there

Members of the Fort Worth Chapter of Business &
Professional Women enjoy the atmosphere at the
1958 state convention held in Fort Worth.
Courtesy, Business & Professional Women
Collection, Texas Woman's University.

are many others who could have been included. For some, little information was available about their life and work. Others worked in Fort Worth for only a few years or took over their husband's business for a short time after his death but then remarried and left the business world. The women in this chapter are early and significant practitioners in a variety of fields who made a sustained contribution to their business or profession over a number of years.

Clara Peak Walden was born in 1854 in one of the old fort buildings when the town of Fort Worth consisted of only a few hundred souls. Educational opportunities were spotty at best—particularly during the Civil War—even though

her father, Dr. Carroll M. Peak, led efforts to establish the town's first public schools. John Peter Smith, who lived in the Peak home, supplemented Clara's education with studies in Greek, Latin, and mathematics. Captain John Hanna, a Confederate veteran, established a private school in 1866 in the old Masonic Hall at Jones and Belknap that Clara attended before becoming an elementary teacher there.

Clara Peak married fellow teacher LeGrand Walden when she was sixteen, but both of the couple's children died at an early age, and she returned to teaching at the school established by Addison and Randolph Clark (which eventually became Texas Christian University). In 1875, when the Clark brothers moved their school to Thorp Spring, Clara Walden opened the first of a series of private schools. The longest lived of these was the Arnold-Walden Institute, founded about 1877 and, by 1878, housed in a new school building built by Walden at the west end of Fourth Street.

About this time, Dr. Peak and others renewed their efforts to establish a public school system. Twice voters approved funding only to have opponents obtain rulings that invalidated the results. After the third election in 1881, the public school system in Fort Worth was finally established. Sue Huffman (later Mrs. Frank Brady, an active clubwoman), who had taught with Clara Walden at John Hanna's school, was named the first superintendent of schools. Her tenure did not survive yet another challenge from school opponents, and over the summer recess in 1882 the school board hired Alexander Hogg as superintendent. Both Walden and Huffman were hired to serve as principals in the new system.

Clara Peak Walden. *Courtesy Fort Worth Independent School District Archive.*

Lily B. Clayton. *Courtesy the Fort Worth Independent School District Archive.*

Walden leased the building she had built to the school board and continued to run the school—essentially a girls' high school, because boys and girls were taught in separate buildings—until 1890 when a new Central High School (Fort Worth High School) was built. She then moved to the new high school as a teacher where she worked until she left the school system in 1896.

In a February 1940 *Fort Worth Star-Telegram* article recalling Walden's career, longtime educator R. L. Paschal stated that between 1875 and 1900 more than half of the teachers in the Fort Worth school system had either had Walden as a teacher or served on the faculty with her. After her retirement, Clara Walden was active with

the Sunday School movement, religious education, and missionary work. Tragically, she was struck and killed by an automobile in October 1914.

Lily B. Clayton, interviewed by Edith Guedry for a March 1935 column in the *Fort Worth Press,* recalled an early encounter with Clara Walden. She had just been promoted from the First Ward School where she had taught the elementary grades to the high school where Walden was principal. Walden, who was "very much provoked," told Clayton that she did not want a "young woman" because both of her previous assistants had married and left teaching after working for only a short time. Clayton reassured Walden saying, "Well, don't worry, I'll never leave you. I am like Tennyson's 'Brook.'" The two became close friends.

Clayton, who was born in Columbus, Mississippi, in 1862 and raised in Kentucky and Alabama, came to Fort Worth with her mother in the fall of 1884. By the next spring she had secured a teaching position in the Fort Worth schools. She spent the next fifty years in the classroom, most of it teaching high school Latin, and became one of the city's best-loved teachers. In 1922, the head of the Parent-Teacher Association at the new elementary school in Mistletoe Heights and other supporters asked that the school be named in honor of this esteemed teacher. Lily B. Clayton Elementary School was the first Fort Worth school named for a woman. By the time Clayton retired in 1935, the list of her former students included many of the town's leading doctors, lawyers, judges, and educators. More than 800 people attended her retirement ceremony, and the crowd included representatives from every class that she had taught during her fifty-year career.

Following her death in 1942, Monsignor Joseph O'Donohoe, a priest at St. Patrick Catholic Church, told a story that likely recalls the origin of the phrase "Sweet Lily B.," which is still used to describe the school named for Clayton. "Those of us who were privileged to know Lily B. Clayton were so accustomed to her goodness and sweetness that we were spoiled into taking her for granted," he wrote. Most people are tempered through the trials and tribulations of life, "whereas Miss Clayton seems to have been born that way [good and sweet], as none of us can ever remember her being otherwise."

The first principal of Lily B. Clayton

Lulu Parker. *Courtesy,* Fort Worth Star-Telegram *Collection, Special Collections, University of Texas at Arlington Libraries.*

Elementary School was Lulu Parker, who was credited with making it a model elementary school for the city. Born in 1879 in Athens, Texas, Parker received her teacher training at the Bruce Academy in Athens as well as the University of Colorado and the Teachers College at Columbia University in New York. After teaching in Athens for three years, she moved to Fort Worth in 1910 with her brother E. G. Parker, a banker, and taught at the Chambers and Van Zandt elementary schools. In 1922, she was named principal of Lily B. Clayton, where she served until her retirement in 1944. Parker oversaw the school's growth from four rooms and 79 students to a building with fifteen classrooms with 325 pupils. She had her hand in all aspects

Charlie Mary Noble. *Courtesy Fort Worth Independent School District Archive.*

museum when it first opened in DeZavala Elementary School in 1945 through its first years at the 1306 Summit Avenue location from 1947 to 1948. The Altrusa Club named Lulu Parker as their 1947 "First Lady of Fort Worth" for her work with the city's youth. She died in 1963.

Another educator who became involved with the Fort Worth Children's Museum was Charlie Mary Noble, a contemporary of Lulu Parker but one with a penchant for science rather than civics. Noble headed the mathematics department at Fort Worth High School (renamed Paschal High School in 1935) between 1918 and 1943.

Noble was born in 1877 in Giddings, Texas, and moved to Fort Worth with her family in 1888. She graduated from Fort Worth High School and quite likely rubbed shoulders with Clara Walden and Lily B. Clayton. After completing her undergraduate and graduate education at the University of Texas and Texas Christian University, Noble began teaching at Fort Worth's Seventh Ward School.

Although mathematics occupied the majority of her teaching career, it was astronomy—her personal passion—that secured Noble's place in Fort Worth history. Her obituary noted that she would take her math students outside at night "to show them the relation between mathematics and astronomy," and she campaigned tirelessly for more science and astronomy classes in schools. During World War II, Noble taught celestial navigation to naval officers training at Texas Christian University. In 1947 she began teaching junior astronomy classes at the Children's Museum as well as evening astronomy classes for adults at TCU. She even developed a "telescope rental library" at the Children's

of the school, from overseeing the removal of fifty carloads of rocks from the new school grounds and subsequent landscaping efforts, (which won a prize in a city-wide improvement contest), to the creation of a first-class library, to the promotion of the ideals of good citizenship for all students. Everyone who described Parker noted her neatness and perfect sense of taste.

After she retired from the Fort Worth school system, Lulu Parker began a second career in museum work. She was one of the fifteen founders of the Fort Worth Children's Museum (now the Fort Worth Museum of Science and History), when the idea was first promoted as a project of the Fort Worth Council of Administrative Women in Education. Parker ran the

Lillian B. Horace. *Tarrant County Black Genealogy and Historical Society Collection, Fort Worth Public Library.*

Irma Marsh. *Courtesy Fort Worth Star-Telegram Collection, Special Collections, University of Texas at Arlington Libraries.*

Museum that allowed children and their parents to check out telescopes for backyard use.

Charlie Noble received an honorary doctorate from TCU in 1950, and in 1956 the Astronomical League honored her as "a beacon of light in the field of astronomy" for her work with children. Fittingly, the Children's Museum named its planetarium for Noble. Late in life, her sight dimmed by macular degeneration, she liked to sneak into the planetarium late at night to visit the stars. Summing up her career, she said, "When I first hitched my wagon to a star, I had no idea my wagon would give so many children a joy ride." She died in 1959.

From the same generation, but miles apart in terms of resources and opportunity, was Lillian B. Horace, who served for thirty-four years at I. M. Terrell High School, Fort Worth's segregated school for African Americans, achieving the celebrated status that Hazel Harvey Peace holds today. Born in Jefferson, Texas, in 1886, Lillian Akard moved to Fort Worth with her parents when she was two years old. She graduated from I. M. Terrell and did her undergraduate work at Prairie View College and Simmons University. She taught for six years in Handley and Mansfield before returning to I. M. Terrell as a teacher in 1911. Lillian Horace began her career there as an English teacher, but that was just a starting point. She established the school newspaper, *Terrellife,* in 1924, began the journalism and dramatics programs, started the tradition of the "Soiree" banquet for graduating seniors, and was named dean of girls in 1928. Horace not only undertook additional graduate training at the University of Chicago and the University of Colorado but also attended a course for school librarians offered by the American Library

Association. By the mid-1930s, she had established the school library and was serving as librarian, having organized the donated volumes collected in her English classroom. Horace was also an author. She wrote a biography of the Reverend Lacey Kirk Williams and two novels, *Five Generations Hence,* which was privately published, and an unpublished work, *Angie Brown.*

A 1936 article written for *Terrellife* celebrating her first twenty-five years of service to the school noted that Horace had "woven her exemplary personality into the warp and woof of the lives of our students." She continued her work at Terrell, retiring in 1945. Throughout her career and in retirement, Horace also was active in club and civic endeavors, most notably chairing a committee that fought for equalization of black and white teachers' salaries in the Fort Worth public schools and serving as vice president of the Texas State Teachers Association. She died in 1965. (See also "These Women Lived.")

Although many women taught and a handful became principals, mostly in elementary schools, very few rose to the ranks of school administration or became superintendents. Sue Huffman was the first school superintendent in Fort Worth, but she served only six months, and no other female held the position until Melody Johnson was appointed in 2005.

However, one Fort Worth woman did run a Texas school district. Irma Marsh served as superintendent of the Castleberry Public Schools from 1958 until 1972. Born in 1900, she was one of seven children of a North Side dairy farmer. She graduated from North Side High School and in 1921 married her classmate, D. R. Marsh. Irma Marsh began her teaching career in 1922 at W. J. Turner Elementary in the Rosen Heights

school district, but moved to Castleberry Elementary School in 1924 as one of only two teachers in the one-school district. Not content to let her career languish, Marsh went back to school and earned her bachelor's degree in education from Texas Wesleyan College in 1932 and a master's degree in administration from Texas Christian University in 1941.

Her degrees, as well as her long tenure in the growing school system, stood Marsh in good stead. She was named principal of Castleberry Elementary in 1937, only a few years before the area it served began to grow with World War II and the establishment of Convair (now Lockheed-Martin) and Carswell Air Force Base (now the Naval Air Station—Joint Reserve Base, Fort Worth). When Fort Worth expanded its city limits in 1946 the Fort Worth school district did not take in the new territory, so the Castleberry system did. In 1952, Castleberry opened its first junior high school, named for Irma Marsh. Castleberry incorporated as an independent school district in 1956, and in 1958 added high school to its program. Marsh assumed the superintendent's position, acknowledging that it was "just something I grew into."

She ran the system for fourteen years, and many of the district's buildings were constructed while she was either principal or superintendent. Marsh quipped in a 1980 interview in the *Fort Worth Star-Telegram,* "I should have been an architect." She took particular pride in the district's building program. Her unassuming manner made Marsh easy to work with, but her colleagues acknowledged that she had "a head for business and a knack for diplomacy." After retirement, Marsh devoted her efforts to civic projects, including the River Oaks senior citizens

Harriet Griffin. *Courtesy* Fort Worth Star-Telegram
*Collection, Special Collections, University of Texas at
Arlington Libraries.*

bachelor's and master's degrees in education from Texas Christian University before she went to work for the Fort Worth school district in 1935. She initially taught English but took on a host of other roles including counselor (where her desk always piled high with papers became something of note), evening school director, and administrator.

Griffin was not—in 1970s terms—afraid to buck the system, but she also worked within it, serving in 1965 as president of the Texas State Teachers Association and named in 1975 the Texas Classroom Teachers Association's Administrator of the Year. In 1976, the year she retired as director of professional relations for the Fort Worth Independent School District, Griffin began a second career as a civic activist.

She worked for women's rights, mental health, retired teachers, senior citizen and aging issues, and politics—always with an eye toward shaping policy for the future. She served as president of the Retired School Employees Association in 1977–1978, lobbying for better retirement benefits for teachers. In 1981, Griffin was a delegate to the White House conference on aging, and in 1983, she was the first "senior citizen intern" in the district office of Jim Wright, then the majority leader. The Fort Worth Independent School District recognized her accomplishments by naming the district's professional development center for her and establishing the Harriet Griffin Human Relations Award, given to a school employee who promotes the understanding of different cultures, equal opportunity, and better relations among staff. Judith Carrier, president of the Southeast Campus of Tarrant County College, summed up her work saying, "Wherever there was a need or hurt, there was Harriet Griffin." She died in 2001.

club and the local American Association of Retired Persons chapter, which she helped to organize. She died in 1987.

If Irma Marsh represented the "modern" teacher in terms of organization and administration, Harriet Griffin embraced the future in her civic activism. She was one of eight children, born in 1911 on a farm near Aledo, Texas. She attended school in Aledo. Griffin completed all of the courses offered at the local high school by her junior year, so she set her sights on Fort Worth, graduating from Fort Worth High School (also called Central High School) and earning both

Jennie Scott Scheuber always referred to herself by her married name, Mrs. Charles W. Scheuber, but in most other respects she approached her endeavors with a single-mindedness and independence that led one reporter to refer to her as a "scrapper." Although her life as a clubwoman and civic activist is discussed in greater detail in the chapters "For the Price of a Good Cigar," and "The Modern Woman," she is included here for her thirty-eight years of service as Fort Worth's first public library director.

Scheuber was involved in efforts to found the library before the untimely death of her husband in 1895. Shortly after he died, she and her son moved to Boston, where she worked in a bookstore to learn the book business. Upon returning to Fort Worth, Scheuber opened a bookstore that failed, reportedly because local citizens were not interested in the intellectual fare that she kept in stock. She and her son then returned to Boston, where he attended Harvard. As plans for the Fort Worth Public Library developed, supporters asked Scheuber to assume the head librarian position when the library opened. She returned to school and became a student of library science at Amherst, returning to Fort Worth to open the new library in 1901.

As library director, Scheuber added children's and branch services as well as extending library service to county residents. She filled the Carnegie Library building and grounds with pieces ranging from a World War I torpedo to a plaster-of-Paris cast of a Chinese rickshaw and driver. Scheuber also was active in professional library activities, serving two terms as president of the Texas Library Association in 1907–1908.

By the late 1930s, the library building (which also housed the Fort Worth Museum of Art between 1910 and 1937) was overcrowded, and some citizens questioned the seventy-eight-year-old director's ability to run the library and build a new facility. The library board wanted to build the new building on the site of the Carnegie Library and move the museum out of the library. Scheuber and her supporters wanted to build the new library in another location and preserve the Carnegie Building to house the art museum. The board prevailed, and Scheuber was forced to retire in March 1938. She died in 1944.

There were a surprising number of female attorneys in early Fort Worth, but few of them were actually able to practice law. Edith Conner was the second woman in Texas—and the first from Fort Worth—to pass the bar exam, but she never worked as a lawyer. Conner was born in Kansas in 1887 and moved to Texas with her family when she was six weeks old. She married Robert Baker in 1909 and passed the bar examination in 1911. After Mr. Baker died, she married E. R. Conner, who ran an office supply store. He died in 1937, and Edith Conner managed the office supply business until 1942. Conner died in 1946. Willie Mae Ross, who passed the bar exam in 1916, and Minnie B. Phipps, a teacher who attended night classes at the North Texas Law School and joined the bar in 1938, were two other women who had the credentials to practice law but apparently never did. Phipps did, however, maintain her bar certification.

Effie Redmond was Fort Worth's "petticoat pioneer," a title awarded her by a *Fort Worth Press* columnist. Born in Brownwood in 1885, Redmond moved to Fort Worth with her family about 1895. After high school, she took a job as a secretary to Judge W. P. McLean and studied law under both him and his son. She passed the bar exam in 1919, while she also was serving a term as county treasurer. A 1959 *Fort Worth Press* profile of her career notes that, "although she had a small legal practice of her own, she usually worked as a legal secretary, took depositions and, on special cases served as a court reporter." Redmond worked for a time for the firm of Foster & McGee but ended her career where she had started, with the McLean family firm. She died in 1951.

Three women attended Fort Worth's short-lived law school, the Jefferson University School of Law, and graduated with the first class in 1932. Helen Huff did not practice law but instead worked for the Fort Worth and Denver Railway. Eva Barnes was probably the best known of the three. She went on to become a family court judge, serving Tarrant County for many years. (See more about Barnes in "Braving the Smoke.")

Gladys Shannon was the third female graduate of the 1932 charter class at the Jefferson University School of Law. Born in Burleson in 1895, she lived her entire life in Johnson and Tarrant counties. Shannon first trained as a teacher, attending Texas Christian University. After a short time in the classroom, she joined the firm of Phillips, Trammel, Chizum, Price and Estes and worked as a legal stenographer while attending law school. After graduation Shannon became an attorney with the same firm, handling probate and income tax law. During the 1940s, she made partner and the firm became Phillips, Trammell, Edwards & Shannon, (later Edwards, Shannon & West). After the firm closed about 1963, Gladys Shannon opened her own practice. She died in 1997.

Fort Worth was fortunate to have one of the few medical schools operating in Texas during the late nineteenth and early twentieth centuries, the Fort Worth School of Medicine (also sometimes called Fort Worth Medical School or Fort Worth Medical College), which was affiliated with Fort Worth University. The school was established in 1894 and trained physicians until 1918 when it merged with Baylor University College of Medicine.

Daisy Emery Allen was admitted to the 1894 charter class after pointing out that the entrance requirements did not specifically prohibit women students. Allen was born in 1876 in Kaufman County, and her family moved to Fort Worth when she was in her teens. She had wanted to be a physician since she was four years old, an ambition her father fully supported. She became the first woman to complete medical school in Texas when she graduated in 1897, ranking second in her class of sixteen students. Following post-graduate training, teaching, private practice, and marriage to Dr. James W. Allen in 1903, Dr. Daisy Allen practiced with her husband in Oklahoma and Texas. After he died unexpectedly in 1913, she moved her two young daughters back to Fort Worth and joined the faculty of the medical school that she had attended, teaching pediatric medicine. When the school closed, she opened a private practice that focused primarily on treating women and children, working until she retired in 1950. She died in 1958.

Dr. Anna M. Greve was born in 1884 and came to Fort Worth from Iowa with her family in 1902. She graduated from the Fort Worth School of Medicine in 1911, the only woman in her class. She spent her almost fifty-year career practicing in Fort Worth as a physician and surgeon. She was on the staff of St. Joseph Hospital.

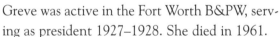

Left: Dr. Helene Kenney. *Courtesy,* Fort Worth Star-Telegram *Collection, Special Collections, University of Texas at Arlington Libraries.*
Above: Dr. Catherine Kenney Carlton.
Courtesy Fort Worth Star-Telegram *Collection, Special Collections, University of Texas at Arlington Libraries.*

Greve was active in the Fort Worth B&PW, serving as president 1927–1928. She died in 1961.

Even though there was no training facility for osteopathic medicine in Fort Worth until the Texas College of Osteopathic Medicine was established in 1970, the city had several female osteopathic physicians practicing here during the early twentieth century. Among the earliest was Dr. Helene Kenney, who practiced with both her husband and her daughter. Helene Larmoyeux was born in 1874. She first trained as a nurse but after several years of work in that field decided to enter the American School of Osteopathy in Kirksville, Missouri, where she graduated in 1910.

She first set up practice in Alice, Texas, just west of Corpus Christi but moved to Laredo within a year. Dr. Charles Kenney, who also grad-uated from the ASO in Kirksville, joined Helene in Laredo after their marriage in 1911, and they had a joint practice there until the couple moved to Fort Worth in 1920. The Kenneys' office was located in their home at 1301 Lipscomb Street, on the corner of Magnolia and Lipscomb. The couple had two daughters, Catherine and Emilie, both of whom became osteopathic physicians. Catherine Kenney Carleton graduated from the Kirksville College of Osteopathic Medicine in 1938 and returned to Fort Worth to practice with her parents. Emilie graduated a few years later and moved to England to practice with her husband, Dr. Philip A. Jackson. After Charles Kenney died in 1943, Helene continued to practice with her daughter Catherine, until her own death in 1948. Eventually the family home and office was demolished and replaced with a clinic

Dr. May Owen, left. *Courtesy Fort Worth Star-Telegram Collection, Special Collections, University of Texas at Arlington Libraries.*

building where Catherine and her husband, Dr. Elbert Carlton, practiced.

Kenney was a charter member of the Fort Worth chapter of Business & Professional Women, and both she and her daughter served as president of the local Zonta Club. Each also held a leadership role in osteopathic organizations. Both women were devout Catholics and attended St. Mary's Church, which was located only a few blocks east of the family office. As the church congregation became predominately Hispanic, Carlton—who spoke fluent Spanish—reached out to offer care to those who attended church with her. For decades, she was well known for offering free and low-cost services to those who could not afford to pay, and she made house calls throughout her career. Carlton died in 2005.

Dr. May Owen is perhaps Fort Worth's best-

known female physician, in part because her name appears on the Tarrant County College administration building. Born on a ranch in rural Falls County in 1891, Owen spent her formative years around animals. Like many female physicians, she decided to become a doctor at an early age—despite opposition from her hardscrabble poor family. Eventually her older brother offered to help her finish her education at Texas Christian University's high school academy, so Owen left the farm for Fort Worth in 1913. She started high school at age twenty-one and worked as a dorm monitor in Jarvis Hall to earn her tuition, room, and board, wearing her dead mother's threadbare work dresses. Dr. and Mrs. Truman C. Terrell mentored the young doctor-to-be and gave her a job delivering messages and caring for animals in their Terrell Laboratories. Owen graduated from TCU in 1917 and became the first female accepted at Louisville Medical School. She graduated in 1921 before undertaking postgraduate training at Bellevue Hospital in New York and the Mayo Clinic in Minnesota. In 1928, she returned to Fort Worth and again went to work for Terrell Laboratories, this time as a pathologist. During her early career, Owen made several important discoveries that changed care for both people and animals, including the finding that a type of non-absorbable talcum powder used in surgeon's gloves could cause inflammation if it escaped into surgical wounds and the discovery that a sheep food with a high sugar content from molasses induced diabetic coma and often killed feedlot sheep during warm weather.

Pathology is an exacting science that requires many hours working alone in the lab. Dozens of articles describe May Owen as being shy and unassuming, but the overall picture that emerges is that of the consummate professional. Owen did not make progress by meeting critics head on but rather by working harder and longer and letting others confirm her results. She was willing to forego most aspects of a personal life and devote her waking hours to her medical practice and the advancement of medicine.

Accolades and honors piled up alongside the hours that she worked. Owen was the first female president of the Tarrant County Medical Society (1947), the recipient of the society's Gold Headed Cane Award (1952), named the Medical Woman of the Year by the American Medical Women's Association (1955), given the George T. Caldwell Award from the Texas Society of Pathologists (1958), elected the first female president of the Texas Medical Association (1960), and named to the Texas Women's Hall of Fame (1986). The Texas Medical Association acknowledged her contributions with their highest honor, the Distinguished Service Award.

Owen worked well into her nineties and leveraged the savings accumulated by her frugal lifestyle (she never had a home of her own, but lived with friends and then in a single room at the downtown Hotel Texas most of her life) into support for young men and women who wanted to become doctors. This and her other philanthropic efforts are discussed in greater detail in the chapter, "Mudholes, Fairy Godmothers, and Choir Bells." Owen died April 12, 1988, at age ninety-six, at All Saints Hospital after working a full day the day before.

Another Fort Worth "medical family," Blanche and Caleb Terrell, focused on pediatrics. Blanche Osborne Terrell was born in Utah in

Blanche Terrell. *Courtesy* Fort Worth Star-Telegram *Collection, Special Collections, University of Texas at Arlington Libraries.*

1906, trained as a nurse, and moved to Fort Worth in 1929 as the surgical supervisor at the "new" Methodist hospital, now Harris Methodist Hospital, a division of Texas Health Resources. In her 2004 obituary, Paul Bourgeois noted, "she opened the operating room, ran the delivery room, and gave back half her salary to keep the place open."

Working at the hospital, Blanche Osborne met Dr. Caleb Terrell, a widower and one of Fort Worth's first pediatricians. The two married in 1931 and raised three sons. Caleb Terrell encouraged his wife to go to medical school, and she entered the University of Texas Medical Branch, School of Medicine in Galveston in 1941.

Above: Evelyn Loya, left. *Courtesy* Fort Worth Star-Telegram *Collection, Special Collections, University of Texas at Arlington Libraries.*

Right: Arlene Tinkler in the drafting room at Parker-Croston & Associates. *Courtesy* Fort Worth Star-Telegram *Collection, Special Collections, University of Texas at Arlington Libraries.*

Blanche Terrell chose to specialize in pediatrics so that she and her husband could practice together, which they did until his death in 1951. Terrell became chief of pediatrics at Cook Children's Hospital in the late 1950s.

In 1967 she left private practice and served for four years as health administrator for the Fort Worth Independent School District. After another stint in private practice, she joined the staff of the Texas Christian University Student Health Center in 1975, where she practiced with her son, Dr. Jack Terrell, until she retired in 1984.

Although nursing was the primary venue for women working in medicine, other fields did have female practitioners. More women, however, worked as physicians than pharmacists. Evelyn O'Conner Loya chose a career in pharmacy specifically because men told her that it "was not a woman's job."

Born in Dallas in 1908, she and her family moved to Fort Worth when she was a child. She worked at a South Side pharmacy while attending Central High School and Danforth Pharmaceutical College, where she met and married fellow pharmacist Joseph G. Loya.

After graduation, Evelyn Loya returned to the South Side pharmacy during the early years of her pharmacy career, working part time during the depression while she raised three sons. Shortly after World War II, Evelyn and Joseph Loya opened Loyal Pharmacy located at 1730 College Avenue, which they operated together until the late 1960s. After that, they worked at other pharmacies. Evelyn Loya died in 1998.

Female architects were a rarity, not only in Fort Worth but also throughout the United States. It was difficult to become established in a business where clients chose you based not only on your designs but also on your ability to follow a job through the construction process. Most business owners—the clients who commissioned the more lucrative commercial building projects—were male, and they preferred to deal with architects with established track records. Male architects got that experience by working in the office of an established architect, but it was difficult for females to secure such a position.

Facts about one of Fort Worth's earliest female architects, Barbara Tocker Friedman Eggert, are sketchy. Barbara Tocker is listed in the records kept by the Texas State Board of Architectural Examiners as holding license number 394. The architectural licensing system was not instituted until 1938, and Tocker was "grandfathered" into the first class, meaning that she already was practicing architecture at that time. She is not listed in the Fort Worth city directories as an architect, however, until 1941. By 1948 she is listed in the Architectural Examiner records as Barbara Friedman, but her name does not appear in Fort Worth city directories under the list of architects. By 1952, she had married, was known as Barbara Friedman Eggert, and had moved to Albuquerque, New Mexico. She maintained her Texas architectural registration through 1964 but then disappeared from the scene.

Arlene Tad Tinkler took a more unusual approach to architecture, particularly for a woman, by specializing in hospital design. Born in Gypsum, Kansas, in 1927, Tinkler received her master's degree in architecture from Kansas

State University in 1952. She was the first registered female architect in Kansas and either the fifteenth or sixteenth in Texas, holding Texas license number 763. In Fort Worth, Tinkler first worked during the late 1950s in the drafting room at Wyatt C. Hedrick's firm and then moved to a position at Parker-Croston & Associates. A colleague there described her as being "competent and very quiet." Among the buildings she helped design are a facility at the Scott & White Hospital in Temple, a veteran's administration hospital in Houston, the south campus of Tarrant County College, the Federal Office Building in Fort Worth, and a hospital at an air force base in Iceland.

During the early 1970s, Tinkler became an architect for the federal government's General Services Administration. There, she designed federal buildings, most notably the Bastrop, Texas, Federal Correctional Institute. This facility contained not only the usual prison cells but also classrooms, a hospital, athletic facilities, and housing for workers. It reportedly became a model for the design of other federal correctional facilities. Tinkler was a longtime member of both the American Institute of Architects and the National Association of Women in Construction.

She died in 2002. The College of Architecture, Planning, and Design at Kansas State University honored Tinkler posthumously in 2003, presenting her their Distinguished Service Award.

Economic necessity and personal drive motivated Fort Worth women to accomplish amazing things in fields where—at the time—no one would have expected them.

Florence Colston worked for forty-five years as the brand recorder for the Texas and

Florence Colston. *Courtesy Business &*
Professional Women's Club Collection The Woman's
Collection, Texas Woman's University.

Southwestern Cattle Raisers Association. She
was born in Kentucky in 1875 and as an infant
moved to Texas with her family. The Colstons
settled in Young County on a ranch adjacent to
a spread owned by J. C. Loving, the first secretary
and general manager of what was then called the
Stock Raisers Association of Northwest Texas.
J. W. Colston, Florence's father, assisted Loving
with the work of the association and became its
first brand recorder—the person who kept the
records of the cattle brands used on each ranch
that allowed cattlemen to identify the animals
they owned.

Living on a remote ranch, Colston was
schooled at home by her mother, but she later
attended high school and a normal college in
Graham. She taught school for a short time
before joining her father as an assistant in the
brand recording office. The association moved
from Graham to Fort Worth in 1893, and the
Colston family moved with it. About 1895, J. W.
Colston was promoted, and Florence Colston
became the brand recorder. During her tenure,
more than 8,000 brands were recorded in the
brand books she maintained. In March 1921,
when Florence Colston had been with the
Cattle Raisers Association for twenty-five years,
The Cattleman magazine said that she "knows
the brands and range of more cattlemen than
any other person." A few years later, a 1938 *Fort
Worth Star-Telegram* article noted that she could
"read a brand better than any man in Texas." In
1940, Colston retired to her farm near
Kennedale. In addition to her work with the
Texas & Southwestern Cattle Raisers
Association, she was also active with the
Business & Professional Women's Club, serving
as president 1931-1932 and serving on the Fort
Worth Public Library Board for many years. She
died in 1948.

Mary Louise Phillips' career with the Fort
Worth Chamber of Commerce was a classic case
of a woman in a stable and supportive marriage
entering the job market after her husband died
and her children were old enough not to need
her full-time presence at home. Born in Houston
in 1890, Mary Louise Young graduated from
Austin High School and entered the University
of Texas in 1906. She left school in 1910 to
marry attorney Edwin T. Phillips, and shortly
thereafter the couple moved to Fort Worth.

Phillips spent her years as a young matron
raising the couple's four sons and participating in
social and civic affairs. Her husband's early
death left her with the responsibility for the children, and she remained at home until the fall of

1932 when the youngest sons were in high school. At that point, she joined the staff of the Fort Worth Chamber of Commerce, putting her volunteer experience to use in the business world. That was unusual, as other women would likely have continued their club, social, and civic activities as volunteers. Most of her career with the chamber was spent managing the Civic Affairs Department, but at times she also headed the Wholesale and Manufacturers Development Division. During the depths of the Depression in 1933, President Franklin D. Roosevelt named Phillips to the national women's committee for the mobilization for human needs. Among her colleagues on the committee were Jane Addams, Frances Perkins, and Ida M. Tarbell. She was characterized as a "tireless worker" whose "dynamic personality and practical grasp of public matters established her as an authoritative source of information."

In 1934, Phillips was appointed to the Fort Worth Board of Education, on which she served until 1941. During World War II, she headed the Chamber's Housing Bureau, helping the hundreds of families who moved to Fort Worth to work in the defense plants find a place to live. She also was the only female member of the Round Table Club, an organization of civic leaders and city council members.

In 1947, Phillips developed cancer and died a year later. In the April 1948 issue of the organization's magazine, chamber officials noted, "Mrs. Phillips had the confidence of the city's leaders who respected her judgment on business matters. Almost every cultural or civic activity at one time or another was fortunate in having the guiding hand of Mrs. Phillips, willing and ready." In 1948, Mary Louise Phillips Elementary School was named to honor her service on the school board and her other civic endeavors.

Edna Gardner Whyte had heart bypass surgery when she was eighty-six years old and, for the first time in her life, failed to meet Federal Aviation Administration requirements to continue flying. At that point, her aviation career had spanned more than sixty years. Edna Gardner was born in Minnesota in 1902. She originally trained as a nurse but fell in love with aviation, spending $35 of her $75 monthly salary to take flying lessons. She had to show up at the airport at dawn and dress in men's clothing for her practice flights. She soloed in 1926 and

earned her pilot's license in 1928. During her flying career, she logged more than 30,000 hours of flight time and taught thousands of pilots how to fly.

In 1935, Gardner quit her job as a U.S. Navy nurse and moved to Louisiana where she opened the New Orleans Air College. She moved to Fort Worth in 1941 and taught Army and Navy pilots to fly at Meacham Field. After World War II ended, Gardner married fellow flight instructor and aircraft mechanic George Murphy Whyte, and the couple operated Aero Enterprise Flight School at Meacham Field. Edna Gardner Whyte was licensed to fly seaplanes, helicopters, and gliders in addition to airplanes, and she gave flying lessons in all of them. She also was a saleswoman for Channelchrome, a chrome-plated airplane engine cylinder barrel that avoided rust problems found in engines with steel cylinders.

In 1970, Whyte closed the twenty-four-year-old business at Meacham Field and moved to a plot of rural land close to Roanoke and near where Alliance Airport now stands. When the bank would not loan her money, she sold three of her own airplanes and built the Aero Valley Airport herself, with help from an assistant. She continued to train pilots until the FAA grounded her and was still trying to regain her pilot's license two weeks before she died.

Whyte received many honors during her aviation career, including the Charles Lindbergh Lifetime Achievement Award and induction into the Air Space Hall of Fame. She also served as president of the 99s, the International Organization of Women Pilots, and was elected to the Texas Women's Hall of Fame in 1985. Her 1991 autobiography, *Rising Above It*, chronicles Whyte's unusual career. In a 1992 interview, her

longtime assistant Kelly Bryan said, "She...
learned the tricks and psychology of flying. An
hour of her instruction was like two weeks with
any other instructor." She died in 1992.

Claudia Benge's interest in drama, her talent
as a great storyteller, and her early work in radio
all inspired her career in advertising. Claudia
Elliott was born in 1914 in Dallas, where she
graduated from Oak Cliff High School and the
Cocke School of Expression. Her teaching certificate from Mrs. Cocke's school landed her a
job teaching drama in the Texas Panhandle town
of Wellington, where she met and married Lester
Benge.

In 1940, the couple moved to Pampa, where
Claudia Benge found an unpaid job doing book
reviews for KPDN, the local radio station. She
parlayed that into a weekly talk show sponsored
by Wrigley Chewing Gum and also did some
writing for the local newspaper. The Benges
moved to Fort Worth during World War II, and
Claudia went to work for KFJZ radio as a copywriter. As more male station employees left to
join the military, she began to sell ads, which
gave her a start in advertising. KFJZ fired Benge
after the war when a returning serviceman
needed a job.

It took her a few years to find another position, but in 1948 she was hired by Roland Broiles
Advertising (later Goodman & Associates) as a
receptionist and copywriter, and it was there that
she found her niche. By 1951, Benge had been
named a company officer—she would eventually
work her way up to vice president—making her
the first female advertising executive in Fort
Worth. Her career at Goodman & Associates
covered print, radio, and television work for
clients such as Texas Electric Service Co. (now

Claudia Benge. *Courtesy* Fort Worth Star-Telegram
*Collection, Special Collections, University of Texas at
Arlington Libraries.*

TXU), Ridgmar Mall, Shannon's Funeral
Chapels, and several subsidiaries of the Tandy
Corporation (now Radio Shack). During the
early 1970s, she produced a television show,
Crafts with Katy, featuring local actress Katy
Dacus, for American Handicrafts Company that
was shown in more than twenty television markets. In a 1974 interview for *Fort Worth* magazine, Benge summed up her approach to marketing a client's product: "The basic tenets of good
advertising have always been to discover your
benefits and present them to the public." She did

not believe in negative ads or quirky gimmicks. Benge was active in many professional organizations, serving two terms as president of the Fort Worth chapter of Business & Professional Women and as president of Theta Sigma Phi, the Fort Worth chapter of Women in Communications. In 1972, the American Advertising Federation named her one of the Top Ten Advertising Women of the Year, and in 1978 she received the Fort Worth Ad Club's Silver Medal Award, its highest honor. After retirement, Benge returned to her first love, drama, appearing in local theatrical productions, films, and television commercials. She died in 1997.

Female entrepreneurs seem to have one characteristic in common—they are driven to succeed. Many in Fort Worth got their start working in a family business, but for others the absence of family support was the impetus that pushed their careers.

Fort Worth's best-known female entrepreneur, Ninia Lilla "Ninnie" Baird faced both situations during her career. Ninnie Harrison was born in Tennessee in 1869 and faced family instability early in life. Her mother died when she was five years old and her father when she was thirteen, so she lived with an aunt who taught her how to bake. In 1886, she married a fellow orphan, William Allen Baird, who was in the restaurant and bakery business. The couple moved to Fort Worth in 1901 with their four children. William sold fresh popcorn downtown and raised money to open a restaurant, variously called the Santa Fe Restaurant—for its location near the Santa Fe Depot—or Mrs. Baird's Restaurant. Ninnie served as the baker and proprietress; William Baird, as the manager. Eventually the couple had eight children, and

the oldest worked alongside their parents in the restaurant.

Only a few years after opening the restaurant, William Baird became ill with diabetes and was unable to work. This made operating the restaurant much more difficult, so in 1908 the Bairds sold it, and Ninnie established Mrs. Baird's Bread in her home, relying on the reputation she had developed for producing good bread and baked goods at the restaurant. When William Baird died in 1911, she and the children were on their own.

Mrs. Baird's quickly developed into a family enterprise, as the children assisted with the fledgling business. "All I wanted to do then," Ninnie Baird recalled, "was make a home and living for my children." Ninnie Baird's eldest son Dewey became an assistant baker, and the three younger sons delivered bread. The business grew, and by 1918 Baird was able to build a separate bakery at Sixth and Terrell avenues and start selling bread to grocery stores.

A decade later Mrs. Baird's began to expand, building a plant in Dallas managed by son Roland Baird. In 1938, a new Fort Worth bakery was built at the corner of Summit and Lancaster avenues with the firm's trademark plate glass windows that allowed passersby to observe the breadmaking operations. Texas Christian University students were even hired to provide evening tours. The old Sixth Avenue plant was used to bake cakes. Baird's sons also managed expansion plants in Houston and Abilene. By the late 1930s, Baird had largely turned over company operations to her sons. She remained chairman of the board, however, and directors meetings were held in her home. She also was the firm's living trademark, and marketing efforts

Ninnie Baird, front left, Beth Baird Beitman, front right. *Photo Courtesy of Margie Reynolds.*

wisely revolved around her character and the firm's humble beginnings. The family-run company still celebrated the woman who founded it by presenting Ninnie Baird with a traditional birthday gift of a loaf of bread wrapped in a white box tied with blue ribbons.

By the 1950s, Mrs. Baird's Bakeries, Inc., was the largest independent bakery operation in the United States. At the time of Baird's death in 1961, the company operated nine baking plants. Mrs. Baird's was purchased by the Mexican baking conglomerate Grupo Bimbo—Bimbo Bakeries, USA—in 1998.

Snack food was at the center of another woman-owned Fort Worth food production business. Esther L. Grubbs began making potato chips in her home about 1927 while her hus-

band, Clifton M. Grubbs, was working as a salesman for Mrs. Baird's Bread. She started by frying her chips in a tiny wash pot—working until she perfected the recipe—and then packed the chips in paper bags for delivery. Her mother was the firm's first "employee." There were setbacks, some of them weather-related, when rain would drench the paper sacks and make the potato chips soggy.

In 1932 the Grubbs enlarged the garage of their Townsend Street home to make room for chip production equipment. Despite the economic problems of the Great Depression, the firm was successful enough that they were able to move to a separate plant in 1934, and in 1947 build a modern production plant at 3561 McCart Avenue. Production methods at this

Lucille Smith demonstrating her hot roll mix in a grocery store. *Courtesy, The Woman's Collection, Texas Woman's University.*

plant were a far cry from the old wash-pot frying vat. Automatic cookers and stainless steel conveyor belts moved the potato from whole spud to packaged chip without it ever being touched by human hands. With the new plant, the product line also expanded to include pigskins, salted nuts, and corn nuts.

Grubbs remained involved in company oper-

ations, building a basement room for the firm's employees in her new home across the street from the old home and garage-based production facility. In this basement room, the employees held monthly sales meetings and company parties.

Clifton Grubbs managed the McCart Avenue plant until his death in 1965. By 1967, the firm had grown from an output of fifty pounds of chips per day to production of 24,000 pounds of chips during an eight-hour shift. In 1969, Mrs. Grubbs Potato Chip Company was sold to Pamex, a firm owned by Pulido's Mexican Restaurants. Although the brand name was used for a few more years, it eventually disappeared during the course of conglomerate mergers. Esther Grubbs died in 1988.

Yet another Fort Worth food entrepreneur was Lucille Bishop Smith, renowned for her hot roll mix and her signature "chili biscuits." Born in Crockett, Texas, in 1892, Smith moved to Fort Worth with her husband, Ulysses S. Smith, about 1912, shortly after graduation from Samuel Huston College in Austin and their marriage. For several years, she made her living as a seamstress, but she also cooked for private clients. A contact made when Smith catered a Fort Worth dinner led to a job running the kitchen at Camp Waldemar, an exclusive girls' camp near Kerrville.

In 1927, Smith was named as the teacher-coordinator of the Fort Worth Public School's vocational educational program for African Americans, which focused on domestic service training. That led, in 1937, to an invitation to begin a college-level household service training program for teachers at Prairie View A&M College where she developed five service training manuals.

In 1941, Smith capitalized on her most popular recipes and created a card file cookbook, *Lucille's Treasure Chest of Fine Foods*, which ran through three editions. In 1943, while recovering from a difficult illness, she hit upon the idea of making a hot roll mix for busy housewives. She set up a business, Lucille B. Smith's Fine Foods, Inc., and began to market her products. Photographs from the era show her marketing the hot roll mix at grocery store demonstrations flanked by lines of eager customers—both black and white. About this time she also became the first African-American woman to join the Fort Worth Chamber of Commerce. In 1952, Smith decided to close the business and return to Prairie View A&M to set up the school's commercial food training curriculum. Throughout her career, Lucille Smith's programs included an aggressive job placement effort. She took pride that the skills she taught others helped them to succeed and help others in turn.

Like many entrepreneurs, Smith juggled a number of activities at one time. Between 1942 and 1956 she returned to Camp Waldemar to head up food service operations, served as the first food editor of *Sepia* magazine, and catered for such notables as Eleanor Roosevelt. Although Smith received many awards throughout her career, they began to flow in after her retirement in the mid-1960s. In 1966 the City of Fort Worth celebrated Lucille B. Smith Day, and both African American and white city leaders honored her. Governor Preston Smith appointed her to the governor's commission on the status of women in 1970. City councilwoman and journalist Edith Deen summed up Lucille Smith's career, calling her a "pioneer in education, humanity, and civic service." She is, Deen said, "a woman who has used her time wisely." Smith died in 1985.

Landscape architect Nell Whitehead Strong was another strong-willed woman whose skill and determination helped her bridge difficult personal times. Strong was born in Douglass, Nacogdoches County, in East Texas in 1895, but moved to Fort Worth when she was very young. The family was poor, and she left home at the age

Top: Whitehead's landscaping and nursery operations at 901 University Drive.
Above: Nell Whitehead at the planting of the first tree at the United States Public Health Service
Hospital in Fort Worth about 1938. *Courtesy the Whitehead Family.*

of thirteen and moved to New Orleans to work in a factory. There, she fell in love with the city's gardens—especially those laid out in a formal manner. Family accounts about Nell's training in landscape design differ. Her stepson, Chuck Whitehead, remembers that she studied somewhere in the Midwest, while other family mem-bers believe that she was largely self-taught, learning about the plants that would flourish in a particular environment from library books. Both may be true.

Shortly after World War I, Nell married Chauncey B. Whitehead, who had moved to Fort Worth from Alabama. Her landscape work during this time period primarily involved residential design. She designed the grounds of well-to-do Fort Worth and Westover Hills homeowners. During the early 1930s, Nell Whitehead applied for and received many contracts for state highway beautification projects. Work was a family effort, her stepson Chuck Whitehead recalls. Nell Whitehead laid out the landscape plans, while his father coordinated the workers handling the installation, and he dug holes. Whitehead's designs during this time period were done under the name Mrs. C. B. Whitehead. In addition to her continuing work in Fort Worth—she designed the Bandy Gardens off Anglin Road, now Weston Gardens—she also worked in East Texas. Two of her most notable projects also occurred during the 1930s. She coordinated the implementation of Hare & Hare's landscape plan for the University of Texas at Austin campus, and she designed the reflecting pool and landscaping for the San Jacinto Monument near Houston.

In September 1939, the Fort Worth Chamber of Commerce magazine ran a notice: "Mrs. C. B. Whitehead, well known landscape architect, has opened a landscape office and garden supply shop at 901 University Drive." She worked out of the University Drive office for the next decade and also branched out into real estate. She acquired a home on Eagle Mountain Lake, a cabin around which she planted extensive gardens featuring her favorite flower—the rose. She loved being outdoors, and family members recall the Eagle Mountain Lake home as the center for hunting and fishing trips where everyone participated.

During the late 1940s, after twice divorcing C. B. Whitehead, Nell married oilman Alan T.

Alice Miranda Barber.
Courtesy John Sproles and the Barber family.

"Zeke" Strong. After a short period, the couple moved to Graham, Texas, where she continued her landscape practice and began another rose garden around their home. She became an active clubwoman and was honored by the Woman's Club of Graham and by the Graham Chamber of Commerce as an Outstanding Citizen of Graham. Family members all recall Nell Whitehead Strong as an attractive woman who did not hesitate to use her appearance to advantage as well as a "tough as nails" lady who "didn't know how to not work hard." She died in 1983.

Alice Miranda Barber founded a Fort Worth

Barbara and Irene Evans in Barber's Bookstore. *Courtesy John Sproles and the Barber family.*

institution that outlived her by more than thirty years. Barber was born in 1890 in North Platte, Nebraska, a farming community without a public library. She loved reading so much that she talked her way into using the library at the local YMCA, where her brother was a member. That love translated into Barber's Book Store, founded in 1925 by Alice and her husband Bert six years after the couple moved to Fort Worth.

Bert and Alice Barber divorced during the early years of the Great Depression, and family members recall that she retained ownership of the bookstore in the divorce settlement. Alice Barber continued her passion for reading—she read several books at one time and kept current volumes that she was reading scattered throughout her home. She especially relished new books "hot off the press." That love made her bookstore a haven for readers. Barber's catered to eclectic reading tastes and featured both new

and used books. She also was an active member of the Fort Worth chapter of Business & Professional Women, a group that gave her a great deal of support.

Barber retired and sold the store to longtime employee Irene Evans in 1945, and Evans continued to bring Barber all the new books. In 1960, Evans retired, selling Barber's Book Store to Brian Perkins. Alice Barber died in 1965. Barber's Book Store closed in 1997, and its contents were sold in 1998.

Sanny Sue McCleery was not so much interested in buildings or what was in them as she was in the land they occupied. Her father, W. J. Bailey, was a land developer, but Sanny Sue Bailey's education at Hockaday School in Dallas and at Sophie Newcomb College in New Orleans did not foreshadow her career as an industrial real estate developer.

During the early 1940s, as the United States

was gearing up to fight World War II, McCleery began to help her father coordinate the accumulation of land parcels for the sites that would become Tarrant Field (later Carswell Air Force Base and now Naval Air Station—Joint Reserve Base, Fort Worth) and Convair (now Lockheed-Martin). After his death in 1949, she took over the family's real estate operations, Bailey Realty Company and Realty Enterprises, Inc. Initially she worked to develop the Near West Side of Fort Worth along White Settlement Road and Bailey Avenue.

Then, she began to develop a parcel of land north of White Settlement Road bounded by North University Drive, Henderson Street, and the railroad tracks as an industrial park. Her father had originally sold some of the land for housing, but she bought it back, had the entire parcel rezoned, laid out streets and utilities, and built three warehouse facilities. Space in the warehouses was leased, and other parcels were sold to industrial users. McCleery also built an office building for her company at the corner of Sixth and Bailey. This work led to her election as the first woman member of the Society of Industrial Realtors.

During this period she also was active in the arts in Fort Worth, primarily as a founder and supporter of the Reeder School, a children's theater run by Flora and Dickson Reeder. McCleery even provided a home for the group for its first seven years in a log cabin located behind the family home on White Settlement Road. McCleery moved to Taos in the late 1950s, where she maintained her interest and involvement in arts organizations. She died in 1992.

Although few are household names, these women and their remarkable careers contributed

to the fabric of life and culture that helped make Fort Worth the city it is today. Most of the women operated without the traditional network of support available to men in business and the professions, but they supported each other through organizations such as the Business & Professional Women and Zonta clubs. There are doubtless many others whose stories are appropriate for inclusion here, but the record of their achievements is at present elusive. The challenge is to unearth and incorporate the contributions each of these women made into the overall ongoing story of Fort Worth.

Bibliographic Essay

Few books have been written about the lives of Fort Worth's professional women and entrepreneurs. Ted Stafford's biography, *May Owen, M.D.: The Authorized Biography* (1990) and Edna Gardner Whyte's autobiography, *Rising Above It: An Autobiography of Edna Gardner Whyte* (1991) are the exceptions.

Newspapers have proven to be the most voluminous, if not always the most reliable, source of information. Information from newspaper sources should always be corroborated. The biographical clipping files in the Fort Worth Public Library's Genealogy and Local History Department contain articles from both the *Fort Worth Star-Telegram* and the *Fort Worth Press*, as well as occasional magazines on many of the women profiled in this section. The *Fort Worth Star-Telegram* "morgue" or clipping files in Special Collections at the University of Texas at Arlington also proved to be very valuable.

Online newspapers offer the advantage of

keyword searching, but the *Dallas Morning News* is the only regional paper available with historical coverage, from 1885 to 1977 and, in a separate database, from September 1984 to the present. It does contain a number of articles on Fort Worth women. Free access to these databases is available through many local libraries and for a fee via the *Dallas Morning News* website. The "America's Obituaries & Death Notices" database, which contains *Fort Worth Star-Telegram* obituaries from 1991 to the present, is available through many local libraries.

Fort Worth magazine at the Fort Worth Public Library is useful because it is indexed, although few women were profiled in its pages during the early years.

Writer Edith Deen, who is profiled in this volume, wrote a women's column for the *Fort Worth Press*, and her articles are a particularly rich source of information. They are available at the Fort Worth Public Library in the clipping files and on the microfilm version of the *Press*, as well as in Deen's papers in the Woman's Collection at the Texas Woman's University Library. TWU also holds the papers of the Fort Worth Business & Professional Women's Club, which contains membership directories, photographs, and other useful information, and the archives generated during research for the "Texas Women: A Celebration of History" exhibit, which contains information and photographs on Lucille B. Smith. The Fort Worth Public Library holds a collection of materials related to Lillian B. Horace. The Billy W. Sills Center for Archives of the Fort Worth Independent School District contains a wealth of information about local educators.

Family sources are often the best source of information to clarify or confirm the details of a life story, when they are available. Most families have not organized the materials related to their relative because they do not think that anyone outside the family will be interested. With luck, this book may encourage family members to consider donating their records to a local archive so that the story of these women's contributions can more easily be included in future writings on Fort Worth.

Chapter 15

HIGH-HEELED TIMES IN THE NEWSROOM

by Katie Sherrod

T HE LATE TEXAS GOVERNOR ANN Richards often reminded people that Ginger Rogers did everything Fred Astaire did, except she did it backward and in high heels. Fort Worth newswomen have done everything Texas newsmen have done, only they did it wearing high heels, hose, hats, and gloves. They called what they did "newspapering," and they loved it enough to defy local ideas of what constituted proper "women's work" to do it.

Some of these women took up newspapering to support themselves and their families after their husbands died. Others were single and worked to support themselves. Many took advantage of opportunities that opened as men left newsrooms to fight in various wars. More than one was affected by the polio epidemics of the early twentieth century. With one exception, these women supported the various social justice movements that sought to expand opportunities for those at the margins. Like all pioneers, they were ahead of the cultural curve. In expanding opportunities for women, they made Fort Worth a better place for all people.

Mary R. Walton, who often used the byline "Mrs. M. B. Walton," was born in New York but spent the years of her marriage in Mississippi. She came to Fort Worth from Mississippi sometime around 1876, apparently after the death of her husband, a physician. Her writing career began as one of the editorial staff at the *Fort Worth Gazette*. She worked there until 1894. According to an 1896 story in the *Dallas Morning News*, while at the *Gazette*, "Mrs. Walton did much contributive work, and over time edited an evening paper, and for nearly two years, edited, unassisted, a weekly devoted to social and literary topics and business interests."

When she left the *Gazette*, she published under her own name a weekly devoted to the interests of women. It was a success, but the work took a toll on her health. Her friends told her she needed a change, on the interesting theory that for an "energetic soul" a change is as good as a rest. She took the position of matron of the "state lunatic asylum" in Austin but continued her interest in writing.

She was a charter member of the Texas Women's Press Association, founded May 10, 1893, at the Windsor Hotel in Dallas. She was its second president and served several terms as vice president. In 1896 she became the editor-in-chief of the women's portion of the *Press Bulletin*, the official publication of both the Texas Press Association and the Texas Women's Press Association. Pauline Periwinkle of the *Dallas Morning News* reported, "This 'press department' was a matter of venture on the part of the latter association, and that it has already proved a factor for progress speaks for the efforts of Mrs. Walton to aid in unifying this large body of earning women and maintaining existing pleasant relations. Mrs. Walton's force as a writer has gained her recognition on numerous occasions before women's clubs, and such bodies as the two press associations and the Texas Women's Council."

Mary Walton represented the TWPA at the 1894 Texas Woman's Congress convention. She served as president of the TWPA for a second time in 1897. Walton was a member of the Fort Worth Equal Rights Club. By 1894 there were seven equal rights clubs in Texas—in Fort Worth, Dallas, Denison, Granger, Belton, Taylor, and San Antonio. Getting the vote was very important to women journalists across the country, as evidenced by the fact that more than half the papers presented at the 1894 Pacific Coast meeting of the Women's Press Association had as their subject women's suffrage. Indeed, the Texas Equal Rights Association, dedicated to securing women's suffrage, was founded on the same day,

by the same group of women and in the same hotel as the Texas Women's Press Association.

In a 1901 Yearbook of Texas article on the TWPA, Dora Fowler Arthur wrote that Walton was "one of the most successful newspaper women of the State." At some point Mary Walton moved back to Fort Worth from Austin, for a 1905 article about the Women's Press Association meeting in Marlin listed her as "Mrs. Mary R. Walton, special writer, Fort Worth."

Henrie C. L. Gorman was another charter member of the TWPA. In 1899 she founded a Fort Worth club called Our Literary Club in Bohemia that met at "The Nest," her home at East Belknap and Harding streets. She also began publishing a magazine called *The Bohemian*, which she claimed was the "first and only literary magazine, not of Texas alone, but of the South." She edited articles contributed by business and professional men, including teachers, as well as other amateur writers. *The Bohemian* published news articles, poetry, and fiction. Gorman highlighted Texas history for the World's Fair Edition published in 1904. She wrote that the last issue of *The Bohemian* appeared in November 1907, "as I was forced to discontinue the work on account of a serious accident, and could never find anyone who possessed *grit* and *stickability* sufficient to attend to the *outside* work. Had I been able to secure a competent worker, my magazine, 'The Bohemian,' would be *flourishing* today," she wrote in a 1916 letter included in the TWPA scrapbook. In that same letter, Gorman said that her first story appeared in *The Temperance Crusader* of Atlanta when she was fifteen years old, and that she was the social page editor of the *Fort Worth Gazette* "during Walter Malone's administration." She mentions that she has published three books and has four more ready for publication; and that she wrote stories for children as "Aunt Clara" in *The Bohemian*. She also mentions an article on "The Women Writers of Fort Worth" written for *Fraternity*, which may have been a Fort Worth publication. She also served as president of the TWPA. Henrie Gorman died in 1919 at the age of seventy-two.

Other Fort Worth women who were charter members of the TWPA included Ellen Lawson Dabbs, M.D., a writer for the *National Economist,* a National Farmers' Alliance newspaper located in Washington, D.C., and author of articles and editorials in the *Dallas Morning News* supporting women's suffrage and an industrial school [college] for girls; and suffragist Fanny L. Armstrong, who lived in Fort Worth, Denton, and Dallas during her six-year stint as editor of *White Ribbon,* the Woman's Christian Temperance Union's state organ. Armstrong also wrote *The Children of the Bible* and the unpublished "Story of Martin Luther." Other Fort Worth women who were early members of the TWPA were Nora B. Walton, who wrote in the TWPA scrapbook in 1925 that she had been assistant editor of the *Texas Railway Journal,* and Cora B. Melton, later Cross, who wrote for the *Texas Farm and Ranch* magazine, the *Fort Worth Record,* and the *Fort Worth Star-Telegram,* and was a weekly contributor of farm news to the *Dallas Morning News* from 1916 to 1918. Cross wrote in the TWPA scrapbook that many of her articles were about home economics or agriculture, because "it is, largely, potatoes and not poetry that the public wants." She also wrote that she earned her biggest money writing for *The Country Gentleman,* a magazine published by the Curtis

Publishing Company, which also published *The Ladies Home Journal* and *The Saturday Evening Post. The Country Gentleman* always paid her "$10.00, sometimes more, the rate being 5 cents per word" for each article. Another early TWPA member was Ida Van Zandt Jarvis, who along with her work with the WCTU was also editor of the *Christian Courier,* the Texas publication of the Disciples of Christ. (Read more about Jarvis' WCTU work in the chapter "Duchesses with Hearts of Love Brains of Fire.")

In 1893 a writer named Sue Greenleaf was gaining recognition in North Texas for her articles in various publications. She was from Missouri and taught for several years there. She moved to Fort Worth in 1890 determined to make her living as a writer.

"She makes it her business to sell everything she writes," reported the *Dallas News* in an 1893 news story. "She sends her manuscripts to all classes of papers and magazines and invariably sells her wares to the highest bidder."

Greenleaf and Corolin Williamson owned and edited the *Texas Columbian Journal,* described as the "official organ of the World's Fair" in the 1892–1893 Fort Worth City Directory. An enterprising freelancer, Greenleaf wrote news articles, romances, children's stories, and commercial pamphlets, such as one about the Dallas business community published in 1894. But her most successful work was her series of short humorous articles about everyday life and occurrences, often offering helpful hints about how to cope with life's surprises.

Today Greenleaf would be called a blogger, for she sent out these columns weekly to a large number of subscribers. The income from this enterprise apparently formed the basis of her livelihood. Her first book was *Through Texas on Foot,* a collection of her humorous articles, published in 1893. Greenleaf was resourceful, writing in numerous areas. In 1895, a Chicago firm agreed to publish an illustrated book on a scientific subject by Greenleaf.

She was a feminist, delivering a paper entitled "Equal Suffrage Means Purer Laws" at the 1894 convention of the Texas Equal Suffrage Association meeting in Fort Worth.

Not all Fort Worth newswomen were feminists. Ida M. Darden would have been insulted to be so labeled. Her career as an archconservative lobbyist and journalist has been traced by Elna Green in a 1999 article in *The Journal of Southern History.*

Ida Mercedes Muse was born in Cleburne in 1886. She married Bert Darden in 1904 and they moved to Fort Worth. In 1908 their daughter Helen was born. Bert died the very next year. Forced to support herself and her child, Darden moved in with her mother and took a job as a stenographer with the Texas Businessmen's Association. Soon she was private secretary to James A. Arnold. The TBA worked against prohibition, woman suffrage, and opposed protective labor laws such as the eight-hour workday. Darden soon worked her way into a job as a lobbyist. Her political mentor was Senator Joseph Weldon Bailey, an archconservative.

Through Bailey, Darden met Pauline Wells, wife of rancher and South Texas political boss James B. Wells of Brownsville. Pauline Wells had joined the National Association Opposed to Woman Suffrage in order to begin anti-suffrage organizational efforts in Texas. Wells enlisted Darden, appointing her publicity director of the Texas Association Opposed to Woman Suffrage

in 1916. Darden's job was to write and distribute anti-suffrage literature.

"Personally, I do not think that women, as a rule, have enough sense to cast a ballot. It has always been my observation that they are unable to discuss a subject intelligently without displaying those feline qualities which are, unfortunately, a characteristic of our sex," Darden wrote in 1917 to Maybelle Blessing, a Fort Worth suffragist.

Darden's arguments against the vote are astonishingly similar to that of the anti-ERA groups that sprang up to oppose the passage of the Equal Rights Amendment in the decade between 1972 and 1982: voting would degrade women's status, not enhance it; women already wield political power by raising children and "managing" men; without women in the home, civilization would wither and die; feminists were socialists. Darden and Wells also never hesitated to play the race card, warning that if women got the vote, only two kinds of women would vote— "Socialists and the negro women."

Darden's conservative political work paid well, and she soon bought a small farm. She married Walter Frank Myrick of Fort Worth in 1920. In 1932, she announced her candidacy for Congress. This involved some mental gymnastics. Many anti-suffragists justified voting because "they had a duty to counterbalance the votes of the ignorant, the immigrant and the former slave." Darden's conservative male supporters justified supporting her bid for Congress by pointing out "she had the mind of a man . . . her knowledge of the Constitution and her devotion to its cardinal principles was not surpassed by that of any man." Even so, Darden lost the Democratic primary of July 1932. Around this same time, she divorced Myrick.

Ida Muse Darden, at her typewriter, edited *The Southern Conservative* newspaper for thirteen years during the the height of the Cold War. *Courtesy,* Fort Worth Star-Telegram *Collection, Special Collections Division, University of Texas at Arlington Libraries, Arlington, Texas.*

Darden became increasingly cynical about politics, and in 1936, she wrote and published *Gentlemen of the House,* described as "a cynical, witty attack on the Texas legislature," by Green in her article in *The Journal of Southern History.* Darden also became increasingly concerned about socialism, a fear fanned in the 1940s by the New Deal. That and the growing influence of organized labor and the increased militancy of African Americans' seeking their civil rights caused Darden to start a newspaper "to serve as a medium of expression for those in Texas who believe in sound governance." *The Southern Conservative* was published from 1949 to 1961 in Fort Worth. Darden had complete ownership and control. It gave her an outlet for views she had been developing for decades in her political work.

She had no formal journalistic training and was proud of her lack of higher education, writing in 1946, "scratch a graduate of any of our institutions of higher learning and you will find a Communist."

Darden had a strong antipathy for Eleanor Roosevelt (she wrote a column in *The Southern Conservative* entitled "My Night," a take-off on Roosevelt's syndicated "My Day" column) and "New Deal Socialism," Truman's work toward integration, the increasing power of the federal government, labor unions, and all reform movements. She insisted the civil rights movement was Communist-led, railed against foreign immigration, and blamed women "for the decline of politics and the emergence of the socialistic welfare state."

Darden's definition of "womanhood" was synonymous with conservatism. She particularly supported the Minute Women of America, a woman's group whose members took it upon themselves to ferret out Communists from school boards, libraries, and other such places.

Darden's daughter, Helen Thomas, had been very active in the Houston Minute Women chapter. When Helen died in 1962, Darden was devastated. She ceased publication of *The Southern Conservative* and retired from political activism.

While her grief was certainly a factor, the paper had been in financial difficulties for years. But it had served to give Darden national visibility and prestige in conservative circles. *The Southern Conservative* was not simply a local paper. Darden's wealthy supporter George Armstrong and others mailed copies to all members of Congress, all governors, and to the entire legislatures of eight southern states.

Darden retired, and in 1980, at age ninety-four, she died. She had outlived the McCarthy era, the Red Scares, and the civil rights movement. Her death got almost no notice in Texas.

Kitty Barry was among the first newspaperwomen in Texas. She had a B.A. degree from Kidd-Key College in Sherman, and, unusual for that time, she considered herself a career woman. She also was to have a profound influence on the career of Katherine Anne Porter.

Barry came to Fort Worth in 1911 from San Antonio, where she had worked for the *San Antonio Express.* She was first female city reporter for the *Fort Worth Star-Telegram.* In addition to her writing skills, she was a gifted musician and was knowledgeable about literature. In 1913, she married J. Garfield Crawford, another *Star-Telegram* reporter.

She and her husband founded the *Fort Worth Critic.* Kitty Barry Crawford contributed two columns, "This Week at the Theater" and "This Week at the Hippodrome," and also covered art, music, and social events.

Then she contracted tuberculosis and resigned to seek treatment. She was admitted to the Carlsbad Sanatorium just outside San Angelo in West Texas. In 1915, Katherine Anne Porter arrived as a patient. The two young women became fast friends. Joan Givner, in her excellent biography of Porter, traces their friendship over Porter's lifetime.

Crawford was the older of the two and the mother of a daughter. She soon became something of a mentor to Porter, while Porter regaled Crawford with extravagant stories of her life, nearly all of which were invented out of whole cloth. But Crawford did not know that and accepted the tales as true. Years later she would relate them to Porter's biographers, unwittingly contributing much erroneous information, according to Givner.

Crawford's college roommate, Jane Anderson, was also influential in the life of Katherine Anne Porter. Anderson was not at the sanatorium, but her letters and articles filled the long boring days for both Crawford and Porter. Anderson was a fearless journalist who covered the war in both England and France for the London *Daily Mail*, and her exploits thrilled the two women.

In 1916, Porter left the Carlsbad Sanatorium and was admitted to the Woodlawn Hospital in Dallas as a patient and employee. She was given the task of looking after the children with tuberculosis. She apparently loved the job, and her health improved dramatically enough that she left the hospital in the spring of 1917. After unsuccessfully seeking work at the *Dallas Morning News,* she turned to the Crawfords for help. By then Kitty Crawford was home in Fort Worth but still too weak to work. So Porter was hired to take over Crawford's columns for the *Critic*. A story and photo appeared on September 15, 1917, introducing her to the readers.

Porter worked in Fort Worth for the *Critic* for several months, writing society notes and reviewing theater productions. She joined the Red Cross and quickly became its publicity chairman. She wrote articles promoting the work of the Red Cross and the Hospital Visiting Corps, which did work at the Camp Bowie Base Hospital.

She was living as well as working with the Crawfords and enjoyed getting to know their friends and the soldiers at Camp Bowie Base Camp. She attended dances at the Hotel Texas. She was having so much fun that she overdid things and became ill again. So she went home to her family in Beaumont.

Kitty Barry Crawford, however, was still not recovered. The decision was made to send her to Denver, where the climate was better for tuberculosis patients. While she was there, her old friend Jane Anderson visited her. Anderson liked Denver so much that she decided to settle there. She asked Crawford to share the lease with her, and Crawford agreed. So once again, Crawford and Anderson were roommates. Anderson's lover, a young Harvard grad, soon moved in as well.

The arrangement was uncomfortable for Crawford, so Anderson wrote to Porter, asking her to join them. Porter agreed immediately because she already was bored with being at home with her family. She also was eager to get to know Anderson. But things did not work out.

Photo of Katherine Anne Porter and Kitty Barry
Crawford, circa 1916. *Courtesy of Papers of
Katherine Anne Porter, Special Collections,
University of Maryland Libraries.*

Jane and her lover, Gilbert Seldes, patronized
Porter. Moreover, Anderson was acting errati-
cally, and it upset Crawford so much that she
finally left to spend two weeks at a hotel. Porter
remained at the house with Anderson and
Seldes. When the pair finally left, Crawford
returned, and she and Porter enjoyed a happy
couple of weeks with Crawford's little girl, four
years old at the time.

But Crawford and Anderson's influence on
Katherine Anne Porter was profound. Not only
had Crawford and her husband given Porter her
first newspaper job in Fort Worth but also
Crawford and Anderson imbued her with the

desire to be a journalist, to write stories, and to
travel. She soon got a job at the *Rocky Mountain
News.* She moved into a rooming house in
Denver when Crawford went into Agnes
Memorial Hospital in 1919.

When Crawford returned to Fort Worth,
Porter traveled with her to visit her own family
and then go on to New York, a place she had
dreamed about for years. They traveled in a
Pullman car that Garfield Crawford had reserved
so that his wife, their daughter Jane, a nurse, and
Porter could travel in comfort. Porter's admirers
filled the car with flowers. When the train pulled
out, Crawford watched them running down the
platform after it, waving handkerchiefs in
farewell. Once in Fort Worth, Porter said good-
bye to the Crawfords and went on to New York,
where, she wrote her sister, one day she would
"write as well as anyone in America."

The Crawfords would rescue Porter once
again, when she was accused of being a
Bolshevik in Mexico. She was out of money and
had nowhere to go. Crawford talked her husband
into sending her train fare, and Porter, thin and
tired, soon arrived in Fort Worth. She rested at
the Crawfords' home until she found an attic
workroom in the house next door where she
would work. She finally took a job with Garfield
Crawford's *Oil Journal* for $90 a month. She also
wrote an advertising column for the *Fort Worth
Star-Telegram* called "Let's Go Shopping with
Marie."

Crawford was busy raising money for a tuberculosis sanatorium in Fort Worth, and Porter
helped with that effort. She also appeared in
plays at the Little Theater. At the start of 1922,
however, she was ready to move on and hoped to
return to Mexico. Garfield Crawford refused to

pay her way to Mexico. He said he would buy her a ticket to New York. So she took the ticket and left.

While in Fort Worth, she had read *Century* and conceived the ambition to publish a story in that magazine. When she arrived in New York, she took one of her essays about Mexico to the editor, who bought it. That success fired her ambitions to write fiction. She wrote "Maria Concepción" and sold it to the *Century* for $600. She would go on to become one of the country's best-known female writers. (Read more about Porter's literary and theater career in the chapter "For the Price of a Good Cigar.")

Kitty Barry Crawford was very concerned with the struggle for woman's suffrage. The ratification of the Nineteenth Amendment on August 26, 1920, was deeply satisfying for her. She remained lifelong friends with Katherine Anne Porter. In her later years, Crawford worked as a freelance writer and was very involved in St. Alban's Episcopal Church in Arlington. She died in 1982, at the age of ninety-three.

Pauline Mears Naylor was born in 1896. She became interested in journalism in high school when she helped put out the first *Coyote* yearbook at Wichita Falls High School. At age sixteen she began working for the *Wichita Falls Daily,* covering everything from murder trials to oil news. She also began working for the Wichita Falls office of the *Fort Worth Star-Telegram* when she was a teenager and would spend the rest of her life connected to that newspaper in some fashion.

A young man named John Naylor was also working in Wichita Falls. They were married in San Antonio in 1918 when John was stationed there with the 358th Infantry Regiment. Even

Pauline Mears Naylor.
Courtesy of John Naylor, Jr.

though Germany would surrender in November of that year, John was sent to France, where he was gassed and shot before the war ended. While he was gone, Pauline returned to Wichita Falls and continued working for the *Star-Telegram.*

John was in the Army of Occupation in Germany and did not come home until late 1920. He went to work for the *Star-Telegram.* Sometime in 1922, they moved to Fort Worth. Pauline began part-time work for the *Star-Telegram* when her husband became oil editor. They had an apartment near downtown. They would walk to work to save bus fare and then buy something for dinner at the Turner Dingee Grocery Store on West Seventh Street on the way home.

The Naylors had four children, including twin girls. Naylor managed to raise the children, do volunteer work, and write for the *Star-Telegram.* The fact that her mother had come to live with them after Naylor's father died helped make her career possible. Mrs. Mears helped with the children and the house.

Naylor never hesitated about going back to work after her children were born. Her son John Jr. remembers being "parked" in the Sports Department while Pauline took care of business at the paper. He loved the sportswriters, and they were kind to the little boy.

John Naylor Sr. was soon tapped by Amon Carter to help him with oil investments. His office was separated from Mr. Carter's by the office of Katrine Deakins, Mr. Carter's personal secretary. Pauline Naylor and Deakins became close friends, because they both had to deal with volatile, powerful, intelligent men.

Naylor was also great friends with Mary

Sears, longtime society editor of the *Star-Telegram.* In 1936, Naylor was made club editor and wrote a clubwomen's column as well as feature stories and book reviews. Her interest in women's issues spanned her career. She knew that clubwomen were powers behind much of the reforms, social improvements, and cultural accomplishments of the city. In the late 1930s she began a multi-part series on the pioneer women who helped settle West Texas. In 1966 she wrote a historical piece on Katherine Anne Porter's Fort Worth years.

The Naylors lived in Fort Worth except for a brief stay in Miami from 1942 to 1944 while John was stationed there during World War II. He was in the Army Intelligence Corps, in charge of a highly classified "spy school."

Naylor was an elegant woman who would arrive in the office to type her column wearing an expensive suit with matching hat, gloves, and shoes. Her shoes would always be covered with the same fabric as her suit, a fact that fascinated the younger female reporters. She also often wore a fox stole draped around her shoulders, flinging it out of her way as she pounded on the Remington typewriters.

She had a typewriter at home too. She pounded it so hard that the copy desk editors would often hold up her copy to the light. It would look like lace, because all the "o's" were pushed through the paper, making hundreds of little holes.

Naylor did not suffer fools gladly. Once when a self-important young copy editor came in and asked rather rudely when her column would be done, she replied, "When I'm finished with it, young man." After he left, she turned to the rest of the staff in the Women's World Department and asked amiably, "When did we start hiring fools like that?"

Naylor never took her hat off to work. Her family reports that she would often have dinner started at home before she remembered to remove her hat. She enjoyed cooking, and was famous for her orange marmalade, which she gave as presents to the favored few.

Although she never attended college, and her husband had only attended college for a short time, they were very well read. Their house was filled with books, many of them fine first editions. Naylor was a member of the Jewel Charity Ball committee and the Fort Worth Woman's Club. She died in 1976, at the age of seventy-nine. Her granddaughter, June Naylor, works for the *Star-Telegram*.

Mary Elizabeth Sears was born in Fort Worth in 1902. When she was three years old, she contracted polio; however, much good would come from this affliction. Her parents taught her to swim in an effort to build up the leg affected by polio. On July 23, 1916, thirteen-year-old Sears went swimming in Fosdick's Lake, now called Oakland Lake. A sixteen-year-old girl named Faye Farrar was swimming there as well but ran into difficulties. She had disappeared underwater three times and could barely breathe when Sears swam to her and pulled her out.

When reporters and photographers showed up to take her picture and tell the story, Sears ran away and hid. Her mother sent them away, saying Mary had done only what she should have done under the circumstances, and it was not worth a story. But the Andrew Carnegie Hero Fund Commission heard the story and investigated. They eventually awarded Sears a bronze Carnegie medal and $500. More importantly,

they later increased that award to cover all her college expenses. When they asked her where she wanted to study, she picked Tufts University in a suburb of Boston. Her father's family was from Boston.

Sears studied English and graduated magna cum laude. After graduation she returned to Fort Worth and taught at a private school from 1924 to 1926. Then the newspapering bug bit her. She applied to James R. Record, associate editor of the *Star-Telegram,* who turned her down for lack of experience. But Sears was convinced there was a job for her in the news business, if only because there were so many misspelled names in the society columns. So she took a job writing about society for a giveaway paper called *The South Sider.* She interviewed people, put all her stories in a scrapbook, and sent it regularly to Record. Her tenacity finally persuaded him she was serious, and he told her very casually one Sunday to come down to work the next day.

The next day was Labor Day, 1928. Sears worked at the *Star-Telegram* for the rest of her career. When Bernice Foy, the society editor, died unexpectedly in 1932, Sears became head of the department.

"In those days, we did everything, and worked until everything got done," Sears said in a 1966 interview. Sears did movie and theater reviews and wrote book reviews, but her favorite beat was the Arlington Downs racetrack. At the track's Jockey Club, she interviewed celebrities such as Jack Dempsey, members of the Firestone family, and General Jimmy Doolittle. Once Sears pushed through guards to interview President Franklin D. Roosevelt. She told him that they had polio in common and ended up getting a great story.

When President Roosevelt's son, Elliott, and his wife moved to Fort Worth, Sears got to know them. But when the Elliott Roosevelts had a baby, the family put the lid on news coverage. The *Star-Telegram* heard that the baby had been born and dispatched Sears to get the story. Sears put on her hat and her best white gloves, went to the Roosevelt home, and sent in her engraved calling card. Elliott himself came out to confirm that, indeed, he had a baby daughter named Chandler.

In 1936 Sears wrote her impressions of the Max Schmeling and Joe Louis fight for the sports pages, a story that elicited a fan letter from Schmeling himself. In the early 1930s, Sears took on an additional career in the new medium of radio, with the *Star-Telegram's* two stations, WBAP and KGKO. Her show, one of the first interview talk shows ever, aired daily except Sunday. When Casa Mañana opened in 1936, she interviewed actor Everett Marshall; the "King of Jazz," Paul Whiteman; and a seventy-two-year-old woman who did handstands on a horse jogging around the stage.

On July 3, 1939, she married *Star-Telegram* staff artist Ronald A. Rhodes. Ronald died in 1963 at the age of fifty-eight. She began a column, "Chit-Chat," as a way to fill up space on her Sunday society pages. She wrote it every week for twenty years and never missed a Sunday paper. She was the third recipient of the Margaret Caskey Award for outstanding contributions to journalism, given by Theta Sigma Phi, now Women in Communications. She retired in 1966 and died in 1978 at the age of seventy-five.

Edith Alderman Deen was born in 1905 in Weatherford. She attended Stephen F. Austin State Teachers College and Texas Christian University before going to work for the *Fort Worth Press* in 1925 as a reporter. She made $15 a week.

She was woman's editor at the *Press* for almost three decades. She wrote a popular daily column called "From a Woman's Corner" that covered all manner of things involving women in Fort Worth. Many of her columns profiled women who were involved in social reform work, usually through a woman's club or in business.

She also wrote an eighteen-part series about women in the Bible that would later evolve into a best-selling book, *All the Women of the Bible,* published in 1955 by Harper & Row. It covered all 316 women of the Bible.

Her first husband, France Guedry, died after only two years of marriage. In 1944, Edgar Deen, an executive with Armour and Company, came to her office seeking publicity for a community teen project he was sponsoring. She married Deen in December of the next year. After her marriage, she moved her office to his North Fort Worth home and wrote her column from there for many years. She resigned from the *Press* in 1954 to devote herself to writing books. She also did a radio show from her study from 1949 to 1955.

Deen eventually wrote six books, all related to biblical subjects: *Great Women of the Christian Faith* in 1959; *Family Living in the Bible* in 1963; *The Bible's Legacy for Womanhood* in 1970; *All the Bible's Men of Hope* in 1974; and *Wisdom from Women of the Bible* in 1978. Her books were translated into many languages, and five of them were Christian Herald Family Bookshelf selections. Deen's books are still read and available in contemporary Fort Worth libraries.

By 1978, the books had sold more than two

million copies. When the City of Fort Worth declared Edith Deen Day on August 23, 1988, it was to mark the publication in paperback of her first book *All the Women of the Bible*. By then, the book was in its third edition and fortieth printing.

When she was in her fifties she entered Texas Woman's University to complete her degree in journalism. She then received her master's degree in 1960 from TWU. Her book *Family Living in the Bible* grew out of her thesis. Deen was a regent of TWU for twelve years. Both TWU and TCU gave her honorary doctor of letters degrees.

She served as first lady of Fort Worth when Edgar was mayor for three terms. Then, in 1965, at age sixty, she ran successfully for a seat on the city council herself, becoming the third woman elected to the council. She said the call asking her to run for council came just as she had been reading the story of prophets Deborah and Miriam. "I thought, 'Well, this may be it. Women must learn to serve in government. I'm not a militant suffragette, but a woman's voice is needed.'"

She won many awards for her writing, including being named a National Headliner, the top award of Theta Sigma Phi, now Women in Communications. She was appointed to the first Texas Commission on the Status of Women. She lectured nationwide, usually on the subject of women in the Bible.

After her husband died in 1967, Deen donated their 4,000-book library to the TCU Library and Archives. The collection included twenty-nine years of her daily column and personal correspondence with John F. Kennedy, Lady Bird and Lyndon Johnson, Hubert Humphrey, and Jim Wright. It also included a first edition of a biography of Susan B. Anthony,

Mabel Gouldy Utecht sitting at desk behind a typewriter. *Courtesy, Utecht Collection, Special Collections, The University of Texas at Arlington Libraries, Arlington, Texas.*

signed by the suffragist herself, as well as an autobiography of Amelia Earhart, signed by the aviator. Edith Deen died in January 3, 1994. (Read more about her, political career in the chapter "Braving the Smoke.")

Mabel Gouldy Utecht's father worked for the Santa Fe Railroad. He moved his family frequently before settling in Fort Worth. Perhaps it was that peripatetic childhood that made Utecht so fearless. She got used to dealing with new situations.

She got her first job at the *Fort Worth Star-Telegram* while still a student at North Side High School in the 1920s. She persuaded an editor to let her write a youth column. That determination stood her in good stead for next forty years of her journalism career. Not getting the story was simply not an option. After high school she became a general assignments reporter and then a political reporter. From there she moved to the federal courthouse beat, where she covered the integration of the Dallas public schools and several high-profile trials. In 1958 she got an exclusive interview with Kathryn Kelly, widow of gangster George "Machine Gun" Kelly. Kathryn Kelly was in court seeking to overturn a 1933 kidnapping conviction, and Utecht grabbed the opportunity.

Utecht often was the first woman on her various beats. She earned the respect of federal judges and attorneys who were at first skeptical of dealing with a woman. In Utecht's obituary, colleague Phil Record said, "She could hold her own against any male reporter in her day. She helped pave the way for other women."

Utecht loved the process of getting the news. Her sister Averill said that Utecht was "vigorous and she was very courageous. She didn't hesitate to go to the mat to get the news from people who might be difficult."

Utecht often told the story of covering President Harry Truman's celebrated "whistle-stop" tour in 1948. When his train stopped in Fort Worth, Utecht was sent to cover it. As Utecht tried to get close to the train, a Secret Service agent tried to elbow her out of the way.

"I was going to talk to the president of the United States; my city editor told me to talk to him and not to anyone else," Utecht would relate. Then, colleague Mack Williams recounted, she hit the Secret Service man on the head with her purse.

"She would do anything to get her assignment," Williams said.

Utecht left the *Star-Telegram* briefly when she married reporter Steve Stevenson and moved with him to New York, where she resumed her career. After his death in the 1940s, she returned to Fort Worth and to the *Star-Telegram*. Her second marriage to a Byron C. Utecht ended in divorce. Utecht was the first recipient of the Margaret Caskey Award for outstanding contributions to journalism. She died in March 1998, at the age of eighty-eight.

Claire Lunsford Eyrich was born December 16, 1912, in New Orleans. When she was a teenager, she won a writing contest sponsored by the *Times Picayune*. She majored in classical studies at Louisiana State University and wrote for the *Baton Rouge State-Times*. She and her husband, Norman G. Eyrich, had five children. They moved to Fort Worth in 1950. Just before Norman died in the early 1960s, Claire Eyrich went to work for the *Fort Worth Press*. A year later, she was hired by the *Star-Telegram*.

Eyrich never let other people's ideas about "woman's work" limit her. Although she worked in what was called Women's World Department, she wrote feature and travel stories and was probably best known for her reviews of mystery novels and her coverage of the fine arts and society.

Eyrich was a tiny woman, just under five feet tall even in the high heels she usually wore. But she had a brilliant mind, a wicked sense of humor, a dazzling smile, and an undaunted attitude about getting her story. She and society editor Cissy Stewart were a familiar sight at all the debutante and charity balls. It often seemed to neophyte reporters on the staff that, between the two of them, they knew everyone in Fort Worth. Anytime a reporter needed to check on any local history, he or she would go to Eyrich.

When the world-renowned Kimbell Art Museum was hiring its second director after the death of founding director Richard Fargo Brown, the museum refused to talk to the local press, preferring to announce its choice to all the media at a well-choreographed press conference. But *Star-Telegram* editors were determined to have the story first. So they turned to Eyrich, who made a few calls and quickly confirmed that the new director was Edmund "Ted" Pillsbury, director of Yale University's Center for British Art. The *Star-Telegram* got its scoop.

Eyrich was an intrepid travel writer. Jerry Flemmons, the *Star-Telegram's* travel editor, sent her off on exotic trips when she was well past retirement age. "And she was fearless," said June Naylor, a *Star-Telegram* contributor who worked with Eyrich in the travel section. "She was well beyond the age of most travelers when she'd eagerly go on assignments to the Amazon, Egypt, and the British Isles."

Eyrich was on a train trip in Canada when, through some mix up, she arrived literally at the end of line, Cissy Stewart remembered. "They told Claire she had to get off the train. She carried her luggage a mile or more into this tiny town, stayed at someone's home for the night and caught the train the next morning. It never entered her mind to complain."

Eyrich won numerous awards for her coverage of the fine arts and for her travel stories. She retired from the *Star-Telegram* in 1986 and moved to Austin. She continued to contribute travel stories and book reviews to the paper for years. In May 2003, at age ninety, Eyrich died sitting in her favorite chair, a new mystery opened on her lap.

Adelle Jackson Martin was not concerned that she had to wear a hat and gloves while working as a journalist. As an African-American woman in the 1950s, she was more concerned with getting her work done in spite of barriers erected by Jim Crow laws.

Martin was born in Mexia on April 4, 1920. When she married, she moved to Lubbock and attended Jones Business College. She and her husband had a son. After she and her husband separated, Martin and her son moved to Fort Worth. When she remarried in the 1940s, she moved to the Stop Six neighborhood and began looking for work. The Good Publishing Company of Fort Worth owned two "true story" magazines, one of which was called *The World's Messenger*. In 1949 she got a job there as a stenographer. *The World's Messenger* became *Negro Achievements*, which eventually became *Sepia*. Martin was a prime mover in this evolution. *Negro Achievement's* first publisher was a black man named Horace J. Blackwell. After he died in 1951, the magazine was on the verge of closing. Martin saved it by engineering a deal with a Jewish white man named George Levitan.

"I just heard that he had money and liked to gamble, so I persuaded him to come and take a look at the magazine."

Levitan bought the magazine and made arrangements for Martin and three other female staffers to take journalism classes at TCU. This was not easy, because blacks were not allowed there in the 1950s. Martin was made part of the team that designed Levitan's new magazine, which they called *Sepia.* Between 1949 and 1964, she served as managing editor, editor, and editorial director for the magazine.

When the University of North Texas integrated, Martin enrolled in journalism and writing classes. Her love of learning was lifelong. After she retired from *Sepia,* she earned an associate degree in criminal justice.

Sepia was in the same large format as *Ebony* and *Life* magazines, with an emphasis on photography. It featured positive stories on African Americans. In the 1950s a white-owned magazine edited by a black woman and published for a black readership was an almost certain formula for tension. It did not take long for conflicts to surface. Martin recalled a story about Pearl Bailey in which a white male writer wanted to mention that Bailey had had "nine or ten" husbands. Martin did not think it relevant to the story. The writer went over her head and appealed to the white publisher. The story ran with the references to Bailey's marriages. Such editorial decisions alienated blacks. More importantly to the publisher, it damaged *Sepia's* hope of overtaking *Ebony's* circulation.

"We could have, had it been black owned and operated," Martin said in an interview in 1996 for the Association of Women Journalists in Dallas/Fort Worth.

The magazine's circulation began to drop as episodes like the Bailey story increased distrust among black readers. Levitan turned to Martin to turn things around, promising her a cash bonus if she succeeded. "He gave me four

months. I did it in two. He gave me a Cadillac, not the cash bonus he had promised. I already had a Cadillac, I didn't want another one, but he insisted that was what I'd have," she said.

Levitan believed that if black people had too much money, they became too independent, she said. It was a common mindset. In that day of full-service gas stations, she encountered many white attendants who would refuse to put gas in a Cadillac driven by a black person. As managing editor of *Sepia,* Martin recruited talented writers and photographers, black and white, from around the nation. Once she took white photographer Al Panzera and two white reporters with her to do an interview with boxer Joe Lewis in the lobby of the Baker Hotel in Dallas. A hotel employee came over and told Martin she was not allowed in the lobby.

"I explained all these people were working for me. He said they'd have to leave too. We set up the interview in a black place," she said. Joe Lewis had a room at the Baker only because he was brought in through the back door, Martin told the AWJ.

Sepia is perhaps most famous for running the series of stories by John Howard Griffin that became the book and film, *Black Like Me.* Griffin had come to Martin in 1959 with his extraordinary idea of dyeing his skin black and traveling through the segregated South. The resulting book helped ignite public support for the growing civil rights movement.

Martin not only agreed to run the stories, she arranged meetings with the FBI, who were monitoring activities in the South, so they would know what was going on. She also sent Griffin money to finance his travel for the series. After the stories were published in 1960, "John couldn't live in Mansfield because of threats to his life, and I couldn't drive there," Martin said.

Martin left *Sepia* in 1964. In 1965, she began publishing monthly magazines, *The Brown Texan* (from 1963 to 1967) and *Minority Progress* (from 1972 to 1975). She died in February 2004, at age eighty-three.

When Japanese planes bombed Pearl Harbor on December 7, 1941, newsrooms across the United States emptied as male reporters and editors left, either to enlist or to cover the war. Just as was happening in other industries, almost overnight news jobs that had been closed to women were suddenly available. Women journalists made the most of the opportunity. They brought a fresh perspective to the news. Perhaps because they had felt the sting of stereotyping, they noted discrimination against others. That may be why these women did much of the first news coverage about segregation.

Madeline Crimmins Williams was born eight blocks from the Tarrant County Courthouse December 29, 1915. She always wanted to be a reporter. She and her sister-in-law Mary Helen Crimmins both went to work for the *Star-Telegram* during the war. When Williams was hired, she made $25 a week. When she left in 1951, she was earning $40 a week. She covered Chamber of Commerce and Rotary Club meetings, helped with the city hall beat, and even covered the opera.

She married courthouse reporter Mack Williams in 1947. They went to New Orleans for their honeymoon. But a hurricane hit, and they spent the rest of their honeymoon working. "Instead of roses for room service, we got four feet of water in the lobby. Everything smelled like dead fish," Williams said. And although they covered the storm together, the front-page story carried only Mack's byline.

"It was a man's world. You could say I was the leg woman," she said.

Later she was instrumental in changing the city's policy toward use of the city parks by African Americans. The always-outspoken Williams was assigned to write a feature story about black children celebrating Juneteenth in Forest Park. It was the one day of the year when blacks were allowed to use the city park's picnic grounds and swimming pool. Williams wrote an eye-opening piece about the segregation practices of Fort Worth in which she confronted the city attorney about the practice of barring blacks from parks for which they too paid taxes. Not long after her story ran, the city quietly opened the parks to everyone.

Her coverage of Fort Worth's 1949 Centennial celebration got her hooked on local history for the rest of her life. In 2002, she was honored by the Tarrant County Historical Commission.

She left the *Star-Telegram* to have a family but continued to freelance for the *Dallas Times Herald*. In 1968, she and her husband bought a small tabloid newspaper. They became co-editors and publishers of the *Fort Worth News Tribune*. Williams kept writing almost to the day she died, working for the *North Texas Catholic*, a diocesan newspaper, well into her eighties. She died in February 2003 at eighty-seven.

Grace Halsell came to work at the *Star-Telegram* in 1945 as that paper's first female police reporter. "As bad as war is, it gave women a lot of opportunities," she said of the seven years she spent on the Fort Worth paper. She covered accidents and fires and remembers going to

Grace Halsell as she was about to leave for France to cover the troops from Fort Worth. *Courtesy,* Fort Worth Star-Telegram *Collection, Special Collections Division, University of Texas at Arlington Libraries, Arlington, Texas.*

Dallas to cover an airplane crash. She did all this while wearing high heels.

"They knew they could always call me at three o'clock in the morning, and I would go."

Halsell began her journalism career at seventeen at the *Lubbock Avalanche-Journal.* She worked as copy girl at the *New York Times* before moving to Fort Worth in 1945. She told the Association of Women Journalists that after a stint covering police, she moved to city hall, then to features before becoming the amusement editor.

She wrote a daily column in which she recounted stories of trips to California and meet-

ings with glamorous movie stars like Clark Gable and Errol Flynn. Esther Williams once sent her a bathing suit. It was while she covered police, however, that she began to question why whites had more privileges than blacks.

At that time, blacks were not given courtesy titles in news reports, because the assumption was that they were not married. "Even at the *Avalanche-Journal,* no blacks could be married. We always said 'Tom Jones and Mary Jones' house burned down.' We assumed they weren't married."

When she was sent to Europe in 1951 to cover hometown servicemen, the differences in the way the races were treated became even more apparent to her. She never mentioned the race of the person in the story she wrote because she feared discrimination by an editor. She knew the stories on black soldiers would not get into the paper if the editor knew they were black.

"Maybe that was the first time I began to really rub shoulders and meet blacks and to see them in some official position," she said. She would pursue stories about race for the rest of her career.

She left the *Star-Telegram* to freelance in Europe and worked for newspapers around the world. She traveled extensively. In the mid-1960s, she worked as a staff writer for President Lyndon B. Johnson. Her experiences with racial discrimination continued when she had her skin darkened and lived as a black woman in Harlem and Mississippi. She wrote about this in her book *Soul Sister.*

She wrote thirteen books, including *In Their Shoes,* an autobiography detailing a white woman's journey living as a black, a Navajo, and Mexican illegal. She wrote extensively about

Grace Halsell is in the center of photo opening a box. *Left to right:* Pat Castillon, Pat's husband, George; E.D. Alexander and Peggy Spencer. The photo is from the *Star-Telegram Junior,* the in-house newspaper, and the caption says, "Abreast of Time – Gracie Halsell, comely city room adornment, flashes a gift from the tree which was as false as Santa's whiskers." *Courtesy,* Fort Worth Star-Telegram *Collection, Special Collections Division, University of Texas at Arlington Libraries, Arlington, Texas.*

Muslims and the Middle East, especially the Palestinians. Her last book explored Christian fundamentalists' end-of-the-world theology. It was published in 1999. She died in August 2000, at age seventy-seven.

Halsell's way as the *Star-Telegram's* police reporter had been paved by the *Fort Worth Press'* Mary Crutcher who also got her biggest break during World War II. Crutcher had known when she was a little girl that she wanted to work on a newspaper. In high school in Sweetwater, she worked for the *Sweetwater Record.* She worked for the *Denton Record Chronicle* while attending Texas State College for Women, now Texas Woman's University.

When she graduated in 1935, she got a job at the *Fort Worth Press.* She started writing obituaries, then minded the reference room and wrote a "little bit of everything," from church and school news to medical features.

One morning during the war she arrived at work to find a note in her newsroom mailbox. It said, "Report to the police station to work today." And with that, Crutcher became Fort Worth's first female police reporter. This small—only five foot two—woman gamely went to the police station to face some highly skeptical police officers. It did not take the officers long to learn that she was serious about her work and, more importantly, very good at it. By the time she left the beat, she had won the respect and even affection of the entire police force. They gave her a set of matched luggage as a going-away present with a card attached that said, "to the hard-nosed police reporter."

In 1989, retired Fort Worth police chief

Lawrence Wood Sr. told how Crutcher would pull up to a police blockade at a crime scene in a Yellow Cab. "You'd see her blonde head sticking out of the window. They would wave her on through," he said. "She kind of put up a tough front, but she was kindhearted."

The kindhearted part of that equation often escaped the young reporters who worked for her. In 1949, Crutcher was made assistant city editor of the *Press*. In 1970, she was made executive city editor. At one time she was one of only two female city editors on a daily paper in the state.

The *Press* was forever hovering on the edge of financial ruin. Things were run so tightly that reporters had to hand in the stub of an old pencil to get a new one. The *Fort Worth Press* Building was probably the only large building in downtown Fort Worth without central air-conditioning. But the young staff loved it. They were brash and feisty and lived to beat the bigger and much better financed *Star-Telegram*. Crutcher was responsible for much of that esprit de corps. She ran the newsroom like a combat general.

She struck fear into young, mostly male, reporters who worked for her. John Moseley, who worked the police beat, said she was "the only woman in the news business who ever made me cry." She chewed him out for bungling a story so thoroughly that, "there I was at 23, sitting in the newsroom at the police station with tears streaming down my face. Some detectives passed by, looked in and said, 'Mary must have gotten a piece of him.'" Moseley was called into the editor's office later that day, fully expecting to be fired. Instead, he was given a junket to New York as a reward for doing a good job. Crutcher had never mentioned the bungled story to anyone.

"If I ever became a newspaperman," said Moseley in 1989 when he was editor of the *Southwest Times Record* in Fort Smith, Arkansas, "Mary Crutcher made me one. She was a woman of courage, sensitivity, and fairness—she was a total professional. She was what newspapering was all about."

In 1960, Crutcher was the second recipient of the Margaret Caskey Award. She said the thing that scared her most about accepting the award was that the audience was going to be all women. "I've worked in an office full of men all my life, and I'd feel better about it if there would be men there," she said.

When the *Press* closed in 1975, editor Delbert Willis broke the news to the staff.

Then he said, "You folks go eat lunch and come back. The Scripps-Howard people will be here to talk to you."

Former staffers recalled Crutcher's retort: "Eat lunch, hell. Let's go drink lunch, then come back and meet the undertakers."

And with that, Crutcher led the parade to the Press Club for lunch and drinks.

After the *Press* folded, Crutcher and her friend Jean Wysatta started a little paper called *The Observer,* which lasted until the fall of 1978. Crutcher died March 8, 1989, and was buried in Sweetwater.

Martha Morris Hand Brown studied journalism at North Texas Agricultural College, now the University of Texas at Arlington, while working at the *Arlington Journal.* "When Pearl Harbor happened, she told her mother all the men journalists would be going into the military and that she was going to Washington to try her hand at getting a reporting job," her daughter Martha Hand II said in her mother's obituary.

A wedding shower for Martha Morris [Hand Brown], seated at the center of the photo holding two candlesticks. *Left to right* around her are Mary Sears, Milly Coleman, Claudia Clark, Mabel Gouldy Utecht, Mrs. James Record, and Ruth Riding Burns.
Courtesy, Fort Worth Star-Telegram *Collection, Special Collections Division, University of Texas at Arlington Libraries, Arlington, Texas.*

She joined thousands of young women—Brown was barely twenty—trying to get jobs in Washington. She got a job at the War Department, interviewing celebrities such as Clark Gable, who had enlisted.

Then she joined the Washington, D.C., bureau of the Gannett newspaper chain, where she got to know President Franklin D. Roosevelt. When Winston Churchill came to the United States, Brown asked FDR if she could "please"

have an interview with the prime minister. Her small-town manners paid off. She got her interview.

When the war ended, she studied journalism at Columbia University in New York and at the University of Texas at Austin. She worked for the Austin bureau of Hearst International News Service and was one of the first female editors in the Dallas bureau of the Associated Press. She met her husband, Ken Hand, when they both worked for the *Dallas Morning News*. After Ken's death, she married Jack E. Brown of Houston.

She worked for the *Star-Telegram* in the 1950s and in the 1970s. In her sixty-year reporting career, she covered just about everything except sports. Editors prized her because she was so versatile. She died March 18, 2006, at eighty-three.

It was a tragedy of war that got Catherine Gunn her job at the *Star-Telegram*. Her husband, Stanley, was a war correspondent for the paper. In 1944 he was killed by a bomb strike in the Pacific.

"It was absolutely one of the worst days at the *Star-Telegram*," said Janice Williams, who was a reporter at the time. "When the news came in that Stan had gotten killed, a dead hush fell over the newsroom. The first day was terrible. You did not even raise your eyes. You hid them in your work. No one said anything, it was so quiet. It was really bad, like losing part of the family. It was not a very big newsroom then. Everybody knew everybody and their families." And everybody knew Stanley's wife Catherine and their two children.

Within a year, Gunn was hired by the *Star-Telegram*. Shortly after that, she got polio, which left one leg permanently paralyzed. After her retirement, she suffered from post-polio syndrome. "I don't think polio did anything but slow her gait," said her longtime friend Mary Kanto. "It did not slow her living and capacity for having a zest for living."

Gunn worked on the city desk and covered the social services beat, but from 1950 until she retired in 1979, she devoted every October, November, and December to the Goodfellow Fund, the *Star-Telegram's* annual Christmas effort

to get clothing and gifts for needy children in Fort Worth. People called her Mrs. Santa Claus or Mrs. Goodfellow.

"The Goodfellows program—that was her Christmas," Mary Kanto said.

"She understood what poverty did to people," said friend and former co-worker Charlotte Guest. "She worked with them and talked with them. . . she understood intuitively the pain and could see the beauty."

Gunn died in June 1998 at age eighty-four.

Ruth Castillon was hired by the *Tyler Courier News* in 1941 when she graduated from the University of Texas at Austin. They paid her $17.50 a week to do society writing. After a few months, they offered her a news reporting job and she leaped at it.

She was assigned to cover the county courts. But when a major murder trial began, her editor took her off the story. Her editors made no bones about it. It was because she was a woman. "I argued with them, I told them, 'I can cover it as well as anyone,' but they said, 'no, we don't want you exposed to the ugliness of murder.'"

All this while, she wrote regularly to the *Star-Telegram*, seeking a job. But it was hard for anyone to get a job as the country emerged from the Great Depression.

In Tyler in 1942, Castillon met and married her husband. Almost immediately, he was sent to war with the U.S. Air Force. While he was gone, Castillon was determined to get a job at her hometown paper. "I went up the *Star-Telegram* dead serious this time, and as I walked across the floor of the city room, Mr. [James] Record said, 'We were looking for you. We have a job for you.'"

It was September 1942. Castillon became

The Home Breakers Union, left to right, Pat Scott [Castillon], Madeline Crimmins [Williams], Eleanor Wilson [Schott], Janice Conley, Rosalynn Grover, Milly Coleman, Rae Tright, Mary Helen McClendon [Crimmins], and Elizabeth Koons. *Courtesy,* Fort Worth Star-Telegram *Collection, Special Collections Division, University of Texas at Arlington Libraries, Arlington, Texas.*

the first woman to replace a man going off to war. She did everything from rewrite to reporting on the Chamber of Commerce, shortages caused by the war, and local servicemen who won honors in battle. "I would have died if they assigned me to the society pages. I was not interested in writing about parties and things like that."

Within weeks, Castillon was joined by several other young women in the newsroom as more and more of the men left for war. The editors were all much older men. "We wore them to distraction. If you can imagine professional people who were used to men, suddenly having young girls there doing men's work."

They wore dresses and high heels, hats and gloves, never pants, and were referred to as "James Record's Harem."

Castillon met her future sister-in-law, Pat Scott Castillon, in 1944. She remembers Pat Castillon as the auburn-haired beauty who came in as the serviceman's editor and ended up marrying Ruth's brother George.

When another young woman reporter came along that same year, Ruth and Pat tried to fix her up with a male colleague, only to discover he was married. So they jokingly dubbed themselves and their other female colleagues "the Home Breakers Union" or the HBU.

Pat Castillon did not have a degree in journalism. "I just wanted to do something exciting. I apologized because I didn't have a degree," she said. Managing Editor Record said that did not matter as long as she could communicate and write well. The next day she went to work interviewing the sisters, mothers, and wives of men who had gone to war and keeping Fort Worth up to date on transfers and awards the men won.

"We gals put out the paper, practically. I don't remember any of us feeling put upon. I think women have always had a pretty strong part at the *Star-Telegram*."

Pat Castillon worked there for seven years and then left to have a baby. After her husband died of cancer, she took a job as a teacher. Then, in 1959, an editor called to ask if she would like to be the newspaper's garden editor. "I told him, 'I don't know anything about gardening.' He said, 'That's OK. You can interview people.'"

So for almost twenty-five years, Pat Castillon worked part time, writing about gardening as well as writing features for other sections. She led trips to tour the gardens of Europe for many years. In 1981, she established the Treasure Tree Gift Shop in Fort Worth's Japanese Gardens. She married Spencer Baen and moved to Bryan in 1984. She died in October 2002 at seventy-nine.

Eleanor Wilson Schott was another member of the Home Breakers Union. She joined the *Star-Telegram* in 1943, having just graduated from the University of Texas at Austin. In 1996 she told the Association for Women Journalists, "I covered just about everything: the school run, the board meetings, Chamber of Commerce, the federal run." She also wrote an amusements column about movies, plays, and ballet. She and the other single young women on the staff worked

hard and partied hard. She remembered that they would have regular "meetings" of the HBU in one another's home where they shared experiences—and a few beers. They double-dated too. Many of these women kept in touch for the rest of their lives.

Schott was born in Fort Worth in 1923 and graduated from Arlington Heights High School. When she started at the *Star-Telegram*, she was paid $10 a week. It was while she was on the federal beat that she met her husband, Joseph Schott, the first unmarried agent in the Fort Worth FBI office. At the time of her death in 2007, they had been married for fifty-five years.

Schott was such a head-turning beauty that once, when she was part of the fashion press corps covering the shows in New York City, a designer drafted her into service as a runway model when a model failed to show. But she kept her biggest news scoop to herself for twenty years before revealing it in a *Fort Worth News Tribune* column—she had glimpsed a stark naked Bob Hope standing at attention while *Fort Worth Star-Telegram* publisher Amon Carter gravely placed a Shady Oaks Stetson on Hope's head.

"That [the hat presentation] was a serious ceremony for Mr. Carter," Schott said. One of Carter's many ways of promoting Fort Worth—the city Where the West Begins—was to present visiting celebrities and dignitaries with cowboy hats specially made for him, first by the Borsalina Company of Italy, and then, after Mussolini declared war on Ethiopia, by the American Stetson Company. He bought them through Washer Bros. in Fort Worth.

Hope had just returned from entertaining troops at the Berlin Airlift. Schott met Hope's

Eleanor Wilson [Schott] and Catherine Gunn getting ready to board a plane for the West Coast for ceremonies honoring war correspondents. L to R, Capt. Jack Dozier, pilot of the AT-7 transport plane; Miss Eleanor Wilson, who was to report the ceremonies; Mrs. Catherine Gunn, widow of Stanley Gunn, *Star-Telegram* war correspondent who was killed in the invasion at Leyte; and Staff Sgt. James C. McMillan, crew chief of the plane. *Courtesy*, Fort Worth Star-Telegram *Collection, Special Collections Division, University of Texas at Arlington Libraries, Arlington, Texas.*

plane at Meacham Field at 5:00 A.M. and turned in an article for the afternoon paper. But Hope was due in New Orleans the next day, so the *Times-Picayune* phoned the *Star-Telegram* to request that Schott file an update for their paper. So around noon, she walked across the street to the Fort Worth Club where Carter was throwing a luncheon for the star. Inside Hope's suite, the bedroom door was ajar. Schott walked past and saw all.

"He was standing at attention just stark naked," she recalled. "Bob Hope stood like he was dressed in full military regalia. I thought, 'My lord, if they see me!'" Monty Moncrief also saw and went and closed the door. Neither of them said anything about what they had seen. In those more modest times, she did not dare divulge what she had witnessed, especially because her powerful publisher was involved. When she finally did write about the incident twenty years later she did so in a column in the form of a letter to Hope: "I remember seeing you in your birthday suit."

One of Schott's most vivid memories was when soldiers from Weatherford were liberated from a Japanese POW camp. Most of the soldiers were from farm families who had no phones, so Schott and a photographer had to track down the families one by one. "We were the first ones to bring them the news that their sons were alive. I got the most satisfaction out of that," she said.

In Schott's obituary, Cissy Stewart Lale remembered one day when Schott wore a bright red dress and purple high heels to work only to be assigned to cover the funeral of a local dignitary. Schott knew she was not dressed appropriately, but her editor insisted. So Schott dug an

old plastic raincoat out of an office closet and went to the funeral. Even though her editors were convinced she would never get a decent story dressed so shabbily, she wrote "such a wonderful, wonderful" story that they awarded her the most coveted prize of all—a byline.

"They were only given for spectacular reporting," Lale said. "She was always an excellent reporter."

Schott continued working for the *Star-Telegram* when the war ended, covering fashion and writing an amusements column. In the 1970s and 1980s she worked for the *News Tribune* as an arts and entertainment columnist. She was always cheerfully ready to take on anything, an attitude that lasted all her life. She died January 5, 2007, just four days before her eighty-fourth birthday.

It was the Korean War that presented Jean Wysatta her big opportunities. Wysatta liked to be called a newspaperwoman, not a "journalist."

"When I first came into 'journalism'—that is, when a girl came in—she had to go into the women's area. By lying and cheating, I finally got into the newsroom," she said in a 1996 interview.

Wysatta graduated from the University of Texas at Austin in 1947. She got a job for $30 a week at the *San Angelo Standard-Times*.

"They were going to pay me $27.50, but I had a college degree," she laughed. She worked in the women's department there and then moved to the *Galveston News* in search of an editor who would let her do "hard" news. She had no luck there, so in 1950 she got a job at the *Houston Chronicle*. Again, she was put into the women's department, but she made friends in the city room. When the federal beat came open, she got it. "The boys were off to the Korean War

. . . so I did stories about POWs, casualties, obits," she said.

She and her husband moved to Fort Worth in 1956. Her husband soon lost his job, and Wysatta applied to the *Fort Worth Press* to help support the family. She did not get hired, but they did use her freelance material. Then a male reporter was called up for reserve duty, and she was hired to cover the medical and federal beats.

She was assigned to cover the visit of President and Mrs. Kennedy to Fort Worth in November 1963. "I went to the hotel to see the suite where they were to spend the night before going to Dallas. The decoration was terrible! You wouldn't buy the pictures on the wall at a garage sale! The view was of the bus station. I wrote a kind of tongue-in-cheek sidebar about the suite. This story comes out, and before the president arrived, the Carters and the Johnsons went up there and hung pictures from the museum, really high-class art. That was the kind of story I enjoyed, just a tiny part of history," she said.

Wysatta made no bones about the fact that she resented sitting next to men who made more than she did. The *Press* then made Wysatta woman's editor, and she enjoyed competing with Cissy Stewart of the *Star-Telegram*. "I made myself fashion editor because those were the only women who got to take trips," she said.

But after a while, she longed to return to the newsroom. Eventually someone quit, and she moved back to "hard" news. She became the first woman president of the Fort Worth Press Club in 1969.

After the *Press* folded, Wysatta and her mentor Mary Crutcher started a little paper called *The Observer*, which lasted until the fall of 1978. Then she did freelance writing and public rela-

tions work. Wysatta died in April 2002. She was seventy-six.

Latryl Layton Ohendalski credited Mary Crutcher, Edith Deen, and Jean Wysatta with making it possible for her to cross gender lines all the time when she was a young reporter at the *Fort Worth Press* in the 1950s.

In 1952 she became a front-page reporter for the paper. Within six months, she was made woman's editor, but she did not let that limit her. In New York on a fashion story, she found herself at the Waldorf Astoria the same night the all-male New York Economics Club hosted Soviet deputy premier Anastas Mikoyan, Russia's number two man.

With the help of the security people, Ohendalski hid out in the balcony and covered the event, the only woman in the room of 1,000 men. The next day the *Press'* page-one story bragged, "Our Reporter Only Gal at Mikoyan Feed."

On various fashion trips to New York, she covered a bus and cab strike and a jet crash at Idlewild. She would route herself home via Washington, where she would interview Texans such as First Lady Lady Bird Johnson and Speaker of the House Jim Wright. She freelanced for *McCalls* and the *New York Times*.

On November 22, 1963, she was up at dawn with nearly every other reporter in town to cover President Kennedy's every move. She had a breakfast interview with Jacqueline Kennedy and raced back to file it for the *Press'* afternoon edition. Then she found herself heading to Dallas' Parkland Hospital to wait on news of the mortally wounded president.

She met her husband, John, at the *Press*. She remained there until 1966 when her son was born. She went to work for the *Star-Telegram* in 1977, covering fine arts. She edited *Aura* magazine and freelanced for several newspapers. She died in June 2002 at age seventy-one.

Rosemary Gouldy was born in 1917 in a small town near Wichita Falls. In 1942 she married Ted Gouldy, who had been a galley boy at the *Fort Worth Record*. He later worked for the *Star-Telegram*. He became well known for his livestock report on WBAP radio as well as announcing the Fort Worth Stock Show rodeo over the radio.

In 1950, the Gouldys were part of a group that bought a company that published the *Weekly Livestock Reporter* and other publications. Three years later, Ted and Rosemary took control of the livestock publication when the partnership dissolved.

They quickly turned what had been a mom-and-pop operation into a regional publication with a circulation of 11,000 across Texas, Oklahoma, Arkansas, and Louisiana. As owner and publisher, Rosemary Gouldy was the "bookkeeping and financial brains behind the *Weekly Livestock Reporter* for the last fifty years," said Phil Stoll, editor and general manager of the paper in 2002. The paper gained influence as the cattle industry changed and new breeds were introduced from overseas. It became a "must read" for anyone connected with the cattle business. She retired after Ted died in 1993 but remained active in the publication. She died in December 2002, at age eighty-five.

Tony Page was born in Moscow, Idaho, in 1910. George Haddaway of Dallas, founder of *Flight* magazine, gave her her first job in aviation in 1940. Page's job was to travel the circulation

area three weeks out of the month. "Our circulation zoomed from direct sales in airports. In less than a year, she was sending in original news right out of aviation's grassroots. She learned early that people like to see their names in print, but most people just plain liked Tony," Haddaway said.

Page got her own pilot's license in 1941. After that she was aviation editor of *The Valley Times* in North Hollywood, California, and did freelance writing for other publications, including the *Cross Country News,* which had been founded in 1945 in Lubbock. In 1952, she returned to Texas, bought the *Cross Country News,* and moved it to Fort Worth. In Fort Worth she met Ruby Hickman, who became her closest friend. Hickman was an executive for Reed Pigman's American Flyers Airline, headquartered at Meacham Field. She is remembered by many as the Beatles "den mother" who accompanied them on their U.S. tour aboard an American Flyers plane.

In 1963, Page became the sixty-seventh woman in the "free world" to obtain a qualified helicopter rating. She was the fourth woman in Fort Worth to do so, joining Edna Gardner Whyte, Dr. Dora Dougherty, and Mrs. J. H. Orpen.

Page published the *Cross Country News* for more than thirty-five years. She was famous for her seemingly endless supply of slightly off-color jokes. She died in March 1988.

The pattern of wars and social justice movements creating opportunities for women in journalism continues. The Vietnam War and the women's movement opened doors in the late 1960s and 1970s for thousands of women to move into jobs that had been reserved for men, especially news management jobs. Both Iraq wars have seen more women serving as war correspondents than any previous American war.

The pioneers would be proud.

BIBLIOGRAPHIC ESSAY

The resources of the Fort Worth Public Library have been invaluable in writing this chapter. In the library's Genealogy and Local History Department, I used the vertical files, Tarrant County Historical Society records, city directories, and copies of *Fort Worth* magazine (a publication of the Chamber of Commerce) from 1930 to 1950. Much information came from the library's microfilmed copies of the *Fort Worth Star-Telegram*, as well as that newspaper's own online archives; and the *Dallas Morning News* Historical Archive (online). I also made use of the *Star-Telegram* archives at the Special Collections Division, University of Texas at Arlington Libraries.

Another invaluable source was a series of 1996 interviews with Adelle Jackson Martin, Jean Wysatta, Catherine Gunn, Eleanor Wilson Schott, Grace Halsell, Latryl Ohendalski, and Ruth and Pat Castillon by Jennifer Packer, Ann Thompson, Nichele Y. Hoskins, Anita Baker, Jennifer Mena, and Hollace Weiner, all members of the Dallas–Fort Worth chapter of the Association of Women Journalists. These interviews were done in preparation for a slide show [later video] for which I wrote the script and provided the narration at an AWJ banquet honoring these women. Additional information on Pauline

Naylor came from an interview I did with John Naylor Jr. and June Naylor on November 20, 2006. June Naylor also furnished a photo of Pauline. Bud Kennedy's column in the *Star-Telegram* of March 18, 1995, pointed me toward some wonderful information on Mary Sears.

I also drew on the archives of the Texas Press Women's Association [which became the Texas Press Women] from 1893 to 1925, the Texas Professional Communicators Records, Center for American History, University of Texas at Austin; and the *Handbook of Texas Online* for information on several of the women, including Ida M. Darden. Other sources of information on Ida M. Darden were Elna M. Green's article, "From Antisuffragism to Anti-Communism: The Conservative Career of Ida M. Darden," in *The Journal of Southern History* 65, no. 2 (May 1999), and the profile of Darden on the Texas State Library and Archive Commission website.

In addition to the above mentioned newspaper files, an important source of information on Kitty Barry Crawford and Katherine Anne Porter was Joan Givner's book, *Katherine Anne Porter, A Life* (University of Georgia Press, revised edition). Additional information came from Janis P. Stout's chapter on Katherine Anne Porter in *Texas Women Writers: A Tradition of Their Own*, edited by Sylvia Ann Grider and Lou Halsell Rodenberger [Texas A&M Press]; and Stout's "'Something of a Reputation as a Radical': Katherine Anne Porter's Shifting Politics" in *South Central Review* 10, no. 1 (spring 1993).

I also owe a huge debt of gratitude to Ruth Karbach for suggestions, guidance, and assistance in finding information on these women.

Contributors

PHYLLIS WONJOU ALLEN, a fourth-generation Texan, writes short stories and essays. Her short story, "The Shopping Trip," was published in *Kente Cloth—African American Voices in Texas* and won the Kente Cloth Short Fiction Award. She won a Katie Award from the Press Club of Dallas for Best Radio Commentary for a commentary presented on KERA 90.1 and the Best Short Fiction Award from Mary Hardin Baylor University for "Micayala's Gathering." Her essay, "Identity Crisis," was read on the NPR "This I Believe" series and will appear in a forthcoming book by that title. She has attended the Iowa Writers Summer Workshop for Short Fiction and the Hurston-Wright Workshop at Virginia Commonwealth University. She currently works for a telephone company but hopes to devote full time to writing in a few years.

Author JUDY ALTER writes fiction and nonfiction for adults and young adults, always with a special interest in women of the American West. She has received two Spur Awards from Western Writers of America and two Western Heritage (Wrangler) Awards from the National Cowboy Museum and Hall of Fame, along with the Owen Wister Award for Lifetime Achievement from Western Writers of America. She has been director of TCU Press since 1987 and is a regular columnist for the book page of the *Dallas Morning News*.

Corpus Christi native SANDRA GUERRA-CLINE has lived and worked in Fort Worth for twelve years. She is a features copy editor for the *Fort Worth Star-Telegram*, where she is an award-winning headline writer. She also contributes occasional feature stories on Latin-American culture to the *Star-Telegram*. Guerra-Cline is a graduate of the University of North Texas with a degree in journalism.

JAN L. JONES is a 1970 graduate of Abilene Christian University and holds an MS in drama from the University of North Texas. She taught English and theater in the Lake Worth

ISD for twenty years and English for another eleven years in the Crowley and Castleberry districts. She is the author of two books chronicling Fort Worth's theatrical history, *Billy Rose Presents Casa Mañana,* and *Renegades, Showmen, and Angels,* both published by TCU Press.

RUTH KARBACH thinks of herself as a time detective who finds Texas women with great stories. Her education in sociology and history, her social work career and her history museum background have all contributed to her passion about Fort Worth women and social change. The book of Fort Worth history has empty chapters about progressive women and their contributions, and Ruth hopes to fill some of those pages.

BRENDA TAYLOR MATTHEWS is associate professor of history at Texas Wesleyan University. She holds a Ph.D. from TCU and her work has appeared as chapters in several books. In 1998-1999 she was a Fulbright professor in Stuttgart, Germany, where she also presented several public lectures and workshops. She has won the Sam Taylor Fellowship for her proposal on research for *Historiography of Texas Immigration,* 2002, and *Our Ladies of Victory,* 2005. In 1995 she was named Wesleyan's Favorite Professor.

RUTH MCADAMS, whose Ph.D. is from TCU, has been teaching English for fifteen years at Tarrant County College, where her teaching duties include a Texas literature class in both on-campus and online formats. Chairing the department for the past four years has allowed her to start several programs close to her heart, such as a series of Evenings With Authors events with such names as our own Phyllis Allen, Randy Wayne White, and Lee Child. She has recently chaired a panel at the Texas State Historical Association on writing historical fiction, judged the TCU Press Texas Book Award, judged the Texas Distance Learning Association Hall of Fame Award, and was selected to judge the 2007 Texas Institute of Letters Book Award. Although she has presented dozens of papers and speeches at state and national conferences, her first publication is the 2006 afterword for Elmer Kelton's *The Smiling Country.*

SHERRIE S. MCLEROY is a graduate of Sweet Briar College. Her first career, from 1974 until 1988, was in museum administration; among other positions, she was first staff curator of the Galveston (Texas) Historical Foundation. Since then, she has been a writer and independent historical scholar and has written, co-authored, or contributed to fifteen books. Among them are *Red River Women* and *Grape Man of Texas: The Life of T. V. Munson,* which was named "Best Wine History Book in the World" for 2004 by the Gourmand World Cookbook Awards of Madrid, Spain. She contributed to *Forever Texas, A Book Lover's Guide to Texas, Quotable Texas Women,* and *The New Handbook of Texas.* From 2000 to 2002, she was a researcher, writer, and consultant on an historical exhibit of The Gladney Center.

SUSAN R. PETTY is Editor of TCU Press and has worked for museums and art galleries in Fort Worth and Dallas. As a Haakon Fellow, she did graduate work in art history at SMU, lectured at the Amon Carter on Thomas Eakins' painting, *The Swimming Hole,* and taught informal art history classes to various groups. While working at Harcourt Brace College Publishers, Petty was developmental editor of *Gardner's Art Through the Ages,* 10th and 11th editions, the first and also the best-selling art history textbook in the U.S. Petty has written feature articles for *Fort Worth, Texas* magazine and book reviews for the *Fort Worth Star-Telegram.* She occasionally hosts Community Cable Television's "Books in Review," and is often asked to speak to book clubs.

CAROL ROARK manages the Texas/Dallas History & Archives Division at the Dallas Public Library but remains a loyal Fort Worth citizen, despite her daily treks to the east. She holds a masters degree in American Studies from TCU and a Master of Library Science degree from UNT. Roark has written three books about Fort Worth and Tarrant County and edited the Tarrant County Historic Resources Survey volumes. Her primary research and writing interests are photographic and architectural history— particularly as they relate to Fort Worth— but she is willing to tackle almost anything once. Carol has lived in the historic Fairmount neighborhood for twenty-five years.

KATIE SHERROD is an independent writer, producer, and commentator based in Fort Worth, Texas. She has won several awards in newspaper, radio, and TV including the Dallas Press Club Award for her 2001 PBS documentary *Freedman's Cemetery Memorial: A Place of Healing,* narrated by Alfre Woodard and the Exceptional Media Merit Award from the National Women's Political Caucus. She was inducted into the Texas Women's Hall of Fame in 1987 for outstanding contributions in the field of communications, named one of Fort Worth's Outstanding Women in 1988 and Texas Woman of the Year in 1989.

CINDY C. SMOLOVIK is Senior Records Analyst for the National Archives and Records Administration-Southwest Region Records Management Program, where she assists federal agencies with the appraisal of permanent and temporary records and conducts training courses in federal record keeping practices. She was previously the Dallas City Archivist and an archivist for the Dallas Public Library and the Dallas Jewish Archives. She holds an M.A. in history from UTA and lives in Arlington with her husband and two children.

HOLLACE AVA WEINER is a Texas transplant born in Washington, D.C. A former writer with the *Fort Worth Star-Telegram,* she is the author of *Jewish Stars in Texas: Rabbis and Their Work* (Texas A&M University Press, 1999). She contributed to the anthology, *The Quiet Voices: Southern Rabbis and Black Civil Rights, 1880s to 1990s* (University of Alabama Press, 1997), and an excerpt from her rabbinical tales appears in *Literary Fort Worth* (Texas Christian University Press, 2002). A past-president of the Southern Jewish Historical Society, Weiner is archivist at Beth-El Congregation in Fort Worth and in 2002 wrote the synagogue's centennial history. She has won research fellowships from the American Jewish Archives and the Jewish Women's Archive.

JOYCE WILLIAMS likes to tell people about Fort Worth. She was history and special programs assistant at the Fort Worth Museum of Science and History for ten years, developing exhibits, public programs, and museum school programs. Currently she serves on the Heritage Trails Task Force, a community group working with the Fort Worth Chamber of Commerce, Downtown Fort Worth, Inc., and the Convention and Visitors Bureau to install historical markers in downtown.

Acknowledgments

THIS BOOK EXISTS BECAUSE MANY women and men helped us. The staffs of our excellent local university libraries were especially generous to us. Ann Hodges, Gary Spurr, Brenda McClurkin, Ruth Callahan, Blanca White, and Cathy Spitzenberger of the special collections department at the University of Texas at Arlington Library were of immense help. Martha Farmer, interlibrary loan librarian at Texas Wesleyan University's West Library; Dawn Letson and her staff, especially Ann Barton, at The Woman's Collection, Texas Woman's University Library; Melissa Speed, public services librarian, Tarrant County College, South Campus; and Mike Strom, TCU special collections, are owed a debt of gratitude.

Donna S. Kruse, manager; Betty Shankle, senior librarian/archivist; and Tom Kellam, senior librarian/archivist in the genealogy, history and archives departments of the Fort Worth Public Library; and Sammie Lee and Adrienne Jamieson in the genealogy department of the Dallas Public Library offered hours of skilled assistance. Geoffry P. Williams, university archivist/campus records officer at University at Albany, State University of New York, was generous with his assistance.

Organizations whose resources were helpful were the Fort Worth Young Woman's Christian Association; the Disciples of Christ Historical Society, Nashville, Tennessee; the Texas Board of Architectural Examiners; and the Jewish Women's Archive, Brookline, Massachusetts.

Individuals who gave much appreciated help are Douglas Jones, records manager, City of Fort Worth; Susan Pritchett, Tarrant County Archives; Ruth Anderson, Rock County Historical Society, Janesville, Wisconsin; Diana McDonald, Hedberg Public Library, Janesville, Wisconsin; Bob Addeman, office manager, Woman's Christian Temperance Union of Southern California, Los Angeles; Sister Martin Joseph Jones, archivist, Sisters of Saint Mary of Namur; C. Jane Dees and Renee M. Tucker, Fort Worth Museum of Science and History, and

Tricia Dixon, archivist, National Cowgirl Museum and Hall of Fame.

Individuals who assisted us in numerous and significant ways are Cissy Stewart Lale, retired *Fort Worth Star-Telegram* staff writer; Mary Rogers, *Fort Worth Star-Telegram* staff writer; Marsha Melton, *Fort Worth Star-Telegram* Library; Darla Matthews, Greenwood Cemetery; Karen Steele and Barbara Clark-Galupi, All Church Home; Dr. George Green, UTA department of history; Michelle Cyrus, Sorosis Club, Fort Worth; Midge Seaver, Harmony Club, Fort Worth; Brenda Hoffer, secretary of executive committee, Woman's Club of Fort Worth; Kathleen Shaw, former aide to Betty Andujar; and Pat Andrews, retired associate judge.

Family members and associates of women included in this book were very helpful, including Paula Barber and John Sproles, relatives of Alice Barber; Chuck Whitehead, Nell Whitehead Strong's adopted son; Greg Whitehead, Strong's grandson; Sherry Bando, Strong's granddaughter; Dr. Jack Terrell, Dr. Blanche Terrell's son; John Naylor, Jr., son of Pauline Mears Naylor, and Pauline's granddaughter, June Naylor.

Others are Fredrieka Ankele, Fort Worth; Dalton P. Hoffman Jr., Fort Worth; Dr. Walter Naff, Fort Worth; Mary Lyons, Fort Worth; John M. "Jack" Shelton, Amarillo; David Grebel, Arlington; Diane Lequar, Evanston, Illinois; Barbara Hotinski, Denton; Catherine Christensen, Irvine, California; Suzanne "Suzy" Smith Williams, Fort Worth; William W. Collins Jr., Fort Worth; Jane Cranz, Fort Worth; Edmund P. Cranz, Fort Worth; Ruth Poindexter, Fort Worth; Harry Max Hill, Fort Worth; Dr. Richard Selcer, historian and author, Fort Worth; Margaret Frazier, Harmony Club, Fort Worth; Kathryn Hawkes, Fort Worth; Sue Abrahamson, Fort Worth Federation of Women's Clubs; Jane Wittman, Greg Whitehead's secretary; Frank Kleinwechter of Benbrook; Sam Garcia and Esperanza Ayala, both of Fort Worth; and Roger Simon, legal writing professor at Texas Wesleyan University School of Law.

We thank you all.

❧

Index